W9-CMT-719

THREE EPISODES OF
MASSACHUSETTS HISTORY

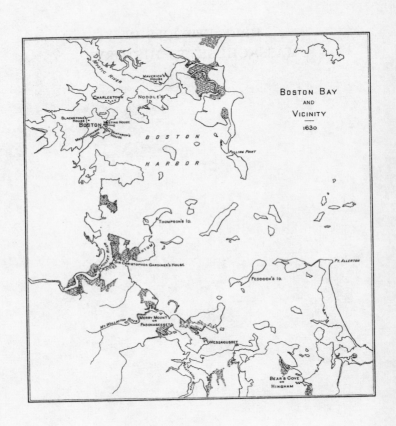

BOSTON BAY
AND
VICINITY
—
1630

THREE EPISODES OF
MASSACHUSETTS HISTORY

THE SETTLEMENT OF BOSTON BAY
THE ANTINOMIAN CONTROVERSY
A STUDY OF CHURCH AND TOWN GOVERNMENT

BY

CHARLES FRANCIS ADAMS

VOLUME I

REVISED

New York

RUSSELL & RUSSELL

1965

Copyright, 1892,
By CHARLES FRANCIS ADAMS.

REISSUED, 1965, BY RUSSELL & RUSSELL, INC.

L.C. CATALOG CARD NO: 65—18782

PRINTED IN THE UNITED STATES OF AMERICA

THE LIBRARY
SEABURY-WESTERN
THEOLOGICAL SEMINARY
EVANSTON, ILLINOIS

F67
.A31
V.1

PREFACE TO THE SIXTH IMPRESSION.

THE first of these "Three Episodes" is entitled "The Settlement of Boston Bay." This, to a certain extent, is a misnomer and deceptive, inasmuch as the settlement therein described was not the famous one of 1630, still commemorated on Boston's civic seal, but an anterior, and, so to speak, prehistoric settlement, of wholly different character. Of this settlement, unbroken from September, 1623, Weymouth — then known as Wessagusset — was the site; and from what is now Weymouth went forth the original occupants of the localities since known as Boston, East Boston, and Charlestown. This first settlement, moreover, was so obliterated by the more considerable migration of 1630, and the years immediately subsequent thereto, that in time the recollection of it passed away. It thus escaped the notice of historians even that the earliest attempt at the colonization of the shores of Boston Bay was feudal in character, originating with Sir Ferdinando Gorges, and representative, not of Puritanism and the Commonwealth, but of Church and State.

The connected history of this original, even if quite abortive, effort at colonization was first, so to speak,

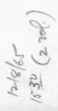
12/8/65
15.3º (2 vol.)

exhumed and pieced together in these volumes. As such, others, as well as the author, accounted it a veritable addition to Massachusetts annals, of some interest and not devoid of value. Attention was, however, first called to the consequences of the misnomer by the remark of a newspaper critic, who, after the manner of such, not apparently carrying his perusal beyond the table of contents, was deceived thereby. Assuming that the " settlement " in question was the familiar " Bostonia Condita, Æ. 1630," he thereupon innocently, and not unnaturally, went on to observe that the object of again recounting that story in this work was not at once apparent. Others, investigating in the same intuitive spirit, have doubtless drawn a like conclusion. The first of the " Three Episodes " has thus been summarily dismissed as a twice-told tale.

In so far as a statement in a preface can offset the effect of a misnomer, I take advantage, therefore, of a new impression to remove an idea altogether erroneous. The settlement of Boston Bay herein referred to and narrated was not that of 1630 of which Winthrop was the guide and prophet, but an anterior, and quite forgotten, settlement, effected in 1623, at Weymouth; a settlement promoted by Sir Ferdinando Gorges, and which, directly commissioned by Archbishop Laud, went forth under the immediate patronage of King James the First. This fact, and this fact only, justifies the narrative. For, as the twig is bent, the tree inclines. Had the Weymouth settlement taken root and flourished as did the later one of Boston, the course of

American development and history would have been quite other than it was. Of two germinal principles it was for a time a question which would survive, and bear fruit. In the event, the younger proved the fittest.

C. F. A.

LINCOLN, *July* 14, 1903.

PREFACE.

FIFTY years ago, the late Richard Frothingham undertook to write a history of Charlestown. The book was published in numbers, which appeared with sufficient regularity until the narrative reached the eventful 17th of June, 1775. The author then found himself irresistibly drawn from the smaller to the larger field, and the History of the Siege of Boston superseded the History of Charlestown, which remains to this day unfinished.

Eighteen years ago, the town of Weymouth had occasion to celebrate the two hundred and fiftieth anniversary of its settlement, and I was invited to deliver an historical address in commemoration of the event. In preparing it, my attention was first drawn to the early settlement of the region about Boston Bay ; the rest naturally followed, and step by step I found myself drawn into a study of the history of the town in which I lived.

My experience differed from Mr. Frothingham's in this respect : his narrative enlarged into an episode of general history after a century and a half of local history had been covered ; my narrative began with an episode of general history, — an episode involving not only much of that which is most interesting in the story of the settlement of Massachusetts, but also the concurrent course of events in England and Scotland.

When this part of the narrative was disposed of, it again immediately merged itself in another episode of general history, than which none connected with early New England is more interesting or characteristic, — more dramatic, more curious or more contested. As Sir Ferdinando Gorges and Thomas Morton passed off the little local stage, Mistress Anne Hutchinson and young Sir Henry Vane appeared upon it. And so they played their parts.

When they disappeared, it might naturally be supposed the slow, uneventful course of local narrative began. I did not find it so. On the contrary, the whole succession of events in the quiet Massachusetts town, — from the 16th of September, 1639, when a church was gathered, to the 11th of June, 1888, when the town voted to become a city, — the whole succession of these events, with no effort on my part, — indeed, I might almost say in spite of me, — seemed to lift itself up until it became sublimated and typical. It was the story, not of a town, but of a people.

Properly, therefore, and in a narrow sense, this book is a History of the Town of Quincy, in Massachusetts; in reality, it is what its title says, " Three Episodes of Massachusetts History."

CHARLES FRANCIS ADAMS.

Boston, *February* 1, 1892.

CONTENTS OF VOL. I.

THE SETTLEMENT OF BOSTON BAY.

I.

THE SETTLEMENT OF BOSTON BAY.

THE SETTLEMENT OF BOSTON BAY.

CHAPTER I.

"A NEW FOUND GOLGOTHA."

THROUGHOUT the years 1616 and 1617 the hand of death lay heavily on those then dwelling in the eastern portions of what is now the State of Massachusetts. The savages died, as a writer of that time phrased it, "like rotten sheep;" though what particular form in modern nomenclature the fatal sickness took has never been ascertained. Those who wrote about it shortly after called it "a plague," with which the inhabitants were "sore afflicted;" but in the seventeenth century the name "plague" was a convenient one, popularly used in connection with any fatal epidemic the nature and symptoms of which physicians did not understand.[1] There is no reason to suppose that the Massachusetts sickness bore any resemblance to the Black Death, which swept over Europe in the fourteenth century; or to the Sweating Sickness, which ravaged England in the fifteenth. Neither could it have been the plague of Florence and Lon-

[1] See Bradford, 102, 326; Johnson, *Wonder Working Providence*, 16; Young, *Chron. of Pilg.* 183, n.

don, which Boccaccio and Defoe have described ; for
that seems to have been a disease which, wherever
generated, was incident to the filth of mediæval cities,
and at home only in the midst of it.

It has been suggested that the epidemic of 1616–17
was a visitation of yellow fever.[1]   This conjecture is
based chiefly on the description of one of its symptoms,
given long afterwards by Indians, then old, but, at the
time of the sickness, young, who, speaking from distant recollection, said that "the bodies all over were
exceeding yellow, both before they died and afterwards."[2]   Yet that it was not the yellow fever is made
clear by two facts: its ravages were confined, as a rule,
to the aborigines, and did not extend to Europeans;
and, moreover, unlike most forms of plague, so called,
as well as yellow fever, it was not stayed by frost.
This appeared in the course of the winter 1616–17.
During that season a few Europeans were kept on the
coast of Maine.   The cold they found intense ; but,
though they "lay in the cabins with those people that
died, some more, some less mightily, not one of them
ever felt their heads to ache while they stayed there."[3]
And again, when in 1634 a similar mortality befell
the Indians of the Connecticut, a few Dutch from
New York, who had found their way into those parts
to trade, and were trying to pass the winter there,
almost starved "before they could get away for ice
and snow."[4]   Clearly, therefore, whatever the disease
may have been, it was not yellow fever.

Other authorities have, upon the whole, concluded
that it was an epidemic of small-pox.[5]   But this could

---

[1] Barry, i. 25.

[2] i. *Mass. Hist. Coll.* i. 148.

[3] iii. *Mass. Hist. Coll.* vi. 57.

[4] Bradford, 325.

[5] Dr. Holmes in the *Mass. Hist. So. Lowell Inst. Lectures,* 1869,

hardly have been the case. Small-pox was a disease with which all Englishmen of the seventeenth century had a terrible familiarity. Probably one face in four they laid their eyes on was seamed and pitted with pock-marks. They knew its every symptom. They were themselves liable to it. Yet Richard Vines and his companions, though they "lay in the Cabbins with those People that dyed," [1] neither had the disease themselves nor described it as small-pox. Thomas Dermer, also, a captain who sailed along the coast in 1619–20, and who must have recognized a pock-mark as soon as he saw it, spoke of the disease as "the plague;" though, wrote he, "we might perceive the sores of some that had escaped, who described the spots of such as usually die." [2] Nor is this all the evidence against the small-pox hypothesis. When the disease raged on the Connecticut, in 1634, it also made its appearance at Plymouth, sweeping away "many of the Indians from all the places near adjoining;" and now it attacked the Europeans also, so that Bradford described it as "an infectious fever, of which many fell very sick, and upwards of twenty persons died, men and women, besides children." [3] Among these was Deacon Samuel Fuller, the first New England physician, who had all his mature life been tending the sick. Dr. Fuller could hardly have seen the Indians dying of "an infectious fever," and then have died of it himself among his dying neighbors, and never have identified the malady as small-pox, if it had been small-pox. But in 1633–34 the

p. 261 ; Green, *Centennial Address before the Mass. Med. Society,* June 7, 1881, p. 12.

[1] Gorges, *Briefe Narration* (Prince Soc. ed.), chap. x.

[2] Purchas, iv. 1778.   [3] Bradford, 314.

small-pox did rage among the New England Indians,[1]
and Bradford, recognizing it at once, gives a fearfully
graphic account of their sufferings; and he adds,
"they fear [the small-pox] more than the plague."
This last would seem to be decisive. A man who
had seen both forms of disease, and who was thoroughly familiar with small-pox, distinguishes the Indian epidemic from it as an " infectious fever," and
as the less dreaded malady of the two. The great
Massachusetts pestilence of 1616–17 could, therefore,
hardly have been small-pox.

Whatever the epidemic was, it made clean work
within the limits of the narrow region to which its
ravages seem to have been confined. In fact, it practically swept out of existence that entire tribe of the
Algonquin race known as the Massachusetts, while
for the time it apparently left untouched their neighbors, the hostile Tarratines at the north, and the Narragansetts and ·Pequots to the south and west.

Before this final calamity fell upon them, all accounts concur in representing the Massachusetts as a
numerous people, and it is even said they were able
to muster in time of war as many as three thousand
fighting men.[2] This would indicate a total population
of at least five times that number, and was about the
supposed strength of the Pequots when, twenty years
later, they sustained a not wholly unequal struggle
with the combined colonies of Massachusetts, Plymouth and Connecticut. Captain John Smith, who in
1614 voyaged along the coast trading and exploring,

---

[1] It is a singular fact, noted by both Bradford (p. 327) and Winthrop (i. *120), that the English, who daily ministered to the savages
during this epidemic, did not contract the disease.

[2] I. *Mass. Hist. Coll.* i. 148.

saw something of the Massachusetts as they then were, and he describes them as a " goodly, strong and well-proportioned people," dwelling in a region which impressed itself upon him as " the paradise of all those parts ; for here are many isles all planted with corn, groves, mulberries, salvage gardens, and good harbors." He speaks of them, also, as " very kind, but in their fury no less valiant ; for, upon a quarrel we had with one of them, he only with three others crossed the harbor of Quonahassit [Cohasset] to certain rocks whereby we must pass, and there let fly their arrows for our shot, till we were out of danger."

There can be little doubt that, during this expedition, Smith entered, and to some extent explored, Boston Bay, especially its southern portions. His map, on which Quincy and Weymouth bays are very clearly indicated, is sufficient evidence of this. But if, as he says, he found the Massachusetts a " very kind " people, they certainly did not always so demean themselves. They were savages like the rest, and, as will presently appear, could upon occasion show themselves as treacherous as they were cruel ; though for that matter they, too, had their own wrongs to avenge. The traders along the coast were not only " stuberne fellows," but rough and lawless as well, and there had been repeated cases of kidnapping, one at least of which had been accompanied by unprovoked and wholesale killing.[1] If vessels from unknown shores had then visited the coast of England or of France, or were now to sail into the harbors of Massachusetts, and, on departing, carried off, never to be heard of again, such visitors as could be enticed on board, it is safe to say that those coming in other vessels of appar-

[1] Bradford, 97; Smith, *Gen. Hist.* 204.

ently similar character thereafter visiting those shores
would not be kindly received.   This was the exact case
of the savages of the New England coast; but history has recorded not much on their side of the story.
Saying little of their wrongs, it dwells at length on
their treachery, their cruelty, and their extermination.

Smith mentions a French trading-vessel which had
preceded him on the coast in 1614.   There are traces
among the early traditions of Boston Bay of two
other vessels of the same nationality ; one of which
was cast away upon Cape Cod, while the other came
into Boston harbor to trade, and did not again leave
it.   The dates of these two occurrences cannot be
fixed, but there seems reason to believe that both of
them happened somewhere between the time of
Smith's visit, in 1614, and the breaking out of the pestilence, two years later.

The mariners of the wrecked vessel, it would seem,
succeeded in saving not only their lives, but a considerable portion of their goods and stores, which they
endeavored to conceal on the sandy shores of Cape
Cod.   As soon as their presence became known the
savages began to gather, and finally set upon them,
killing all but a few, and compelling the survivors to
disclose the whereabouts of their property.   These
survivors were five in number, and their captors distributed them about in wretched captivity.   Sent
from one sachem to another to be made sport of, they
were fed with the food of dogs, while as hewers of
wood and drawers of water they experienced a fate
worse than that of slaves.   So Governor Bradford reported ;[1] whether the fate of these unfortunate French
sailors was worse than that of the "silly savages"

[1] Bradford, 98.

whom Captain Thomas Hunt, in 1614, kidnapped and sold at Malaga " for a little private gain for rials of eight," will never be known. But whether worse or not, the fate of the Frenchmen was bad enough ; and it can readily be believed that, first and last, as the ancient record expresses it, " they weept much." Of the five, two were at last redeemed from captivity by Captain Dermer as late as 1619 ; while another, more fortunate than the rest in respect to the chief into whose hands he fell, adapted himself to his new conditions, and even had a squaw bestowed upon him, by whom he left a child. Of yet another there has a tradition come down through two wholly disconnected sources [1] that he had saved a book, apparently a copy of the Bible, in which he often read ; and that finally he learned enough of their language to rebuke his tormentors, and to predict for them God's displeasure and the coming of a race which should destroy them.

Subsequently to the wreck on Cape Cod, the other of the two French vessels which have been referred to had found its way into the outer roads of Boston harbor, and cast anchor off Peddock's Island.[2] While she lay there, those on board of her apparently wholly unsuspicious of danger, the savages conceived the idea of her capture. Several years later one of those concerned in the affair, Pecksuot by name, exultingly recounted its details to some trembling, half-starved settlers, whose attention was doubtless not a little quickened by the well-grounded anticipation of a not dissimilar fate in near reserve for themselves at the hands of their informant. It is probable that the story lost nothing either in the telling or in its long-

[1] *N. E. Canaan*, B. I. ch. iii. (Prince Soc. ed. 131, 132, n.)
[2] *Ibid.* (Prince Soc. ed. 130, n.)

subsequent repetition; but there is a vivid picturesqueness about it.[1]

The plot was no less ingeniously devised than skilfully executed. Throwing a quantity of furs into several canoes, the savages paddled out to the anchored
vessel. As they approached, their aspect was, as
Smith expresses it, " very kind," and no weapons of
any sort, either bow or arrow, club or hatchet, were
anywhere visible; but, concealed under their robes
and belted about their loins, they carried their knives.
As they came alongside the trader they flung their
beaver skins upon its deck, and, in the usual way, proceeded to chaffer for their price; watching meanwhile, with savage cunning, until they might take
their victims wholly unaware. Then, at a given signal, the attack began, and they thrust their " knives
in the French mens Bellys." The surprise was complete. Most of the vessel's crew were butchered on
the spot; but the master, whose name has come down
to us as ffinch, less fortunate than the others in that
he was only wounded, crawled down into the vessel's
hold, whither his assailants did not dare to follow him.
There for a time he concealed himself. The savages
then cut the cable, and, the tide setting that way,
their prize soon drifted ashore, and " lay upon her
sid and slept ther." Presently the unfortunate master, whether overcome by persuasion or driven by hunger, wounds and despair, came up from his place of
refuge. He, too, was then despatched. Subsequently,
after the sachem had divided among his followers
everything easily movable, they destroyed the stranded
vessel, and " it mad a very great fier." A number of
years later, in 1631, an early settler in Dorchester,

[1] IV. *Mass. Hist. Coll.* iv. 480.

while digging in order to lay the foundations of a house, turned up some French coins, one of which bore the date of 1596.[1] They were embedded deep in the soil, and were in all probability part of the possessions of the unfortunate French mariners, which subsequently had served a purpose as the ornament of some Indian woman or the plaything of her child.

The tribe of the Massachusetts was thus in the full pride of savage manhood when under the very shadow of their doom. A " tawny " race of " tall and strong-limbed people," they were the possessors of " large corn-fields," and dwelt in the plantations which then covered the islands in Boston Bay. They felt their strength, and naturally enough exulted in it, meeting the suggestion of disaster with the boast that " they were so many, that God could not kill them." Two years later the pestilence came, and, as if by magic, " the country was in a manner left void of inhabitants." Hardly, it was afterwards estimated, did one in twenty escape ;[2] and though this probably was an exaggeration, yet an explorer who came upon the coast after the pestilence, comparing what he then saw with his recollections of a previous visit, wrote that as he passed along he found " some ancient plantations, not long since populous, now utterly void." [3] When, also, Samoset came into the settlement at Plymouth, he told those there to the same effect, that the place where they were was " called Patuxet, and that about four years ago all the inhabitants died of an extraordinary plague, and there [was] neither man, woman, nor child remaining."

No language of modern description could compare

---

[1] Winthrop, i. *59.   [2] Young, *Chron. of Pilg.* 258.
[3] Prince Soc. Pub. Gorges, i. 219 (n. 276).

in picturesque vigor with the simple words in which those who shortly after visited the scene described the all-pervading character of the mortality, or the completeness of the destruction it worked. It seems to have begun its ravages in 1616, and to have worn itself out, for want of fresh material rather than for any other cause, in 1617. Five years are not inconsiderable in the lapse of time, and the scars of distemper are, as a rule, rapidly effaced ; while, even if the shattered nerves of the survivors have in that interval failed to recover their tone, the dead at least, it might be supposed, would crumble into the soil. In the case of the Massachusetts Indians we know, from the evidence of Robert Cushman,[1] that five years later the spirit of the tribe was crushed, for, writing early in 1622 of its wasted condition, he said that " those that are left have their courage much abated, and their countenance is dejected, and they seem as a people affrighted." Neither had the lapse of those five years sufficed to obliterate even the physical reminders of death. The country was not only swept wellnigh clean of the living, and in some places absolutely clean, but it was full of bleaching bones. When in July, 1621, Governor Winslow made the first considerable excursion from Plymouth into the interior, penetrating as far as the northern limits of Rhode Island, he noted, as he crossed the Taunton River, that the land was very fertile, and had been for the most part under cultivation. " Thousands of men," he reported, " have lived there, which died in a great plague not long since ; and pity it was and is to see so many goodly fields, and so well seated, without men to dress and manure the same." They had perished so rap-

---

[1] Young, *Chron. of Pilg.* 183, 206, 258.

idly, and the terror among the living had been so
great, that they were not " able to burie one another ;
ther sculs and bones we found in many places lying
still above ground, where their houses and dwellings
had been ; a very sad spectackle to behould ; " [1] and
another writer speaks of the wigwams as lying " full
of dead corpses," while " howling and much lamenta-
tion was heard among the living, who, being possest
with great feare, oftimes left their dead unburied." [2]

The plague centre would seem to have been Boston
Bay.   Apparently there were not more than five hundred inhabitants, of whom some forty were fighting
men, left in all that region, and this handful of survivors cannot be said to have occupied the country in
any sense of the term.   The disease swept the islands
in the harbor wholly clear of inhabitants, and drove
the sachem Chickatabot from his plantation at Passonagessit, now Mt. Wollaston, overlooking Quincy
Bay.   The first white occupant of the abandoned
plantation thus described what he saw in the region
round about during the summer of 1622 : —

" They [had] died on heapes, as they lay in their houses ;
and the living, that were able to shift for themselves, would
runne away and let them dy, and let there Carkases ly above
the ground without buriall.   For in a place where many
inhabited, there hath been but one left a live to tell what
became of the rest ; the livinge being (as it seemes) not able
to bury the dead, they were left for Crowes, Kites and vermin to pray upon.   And the bones and skulls upon the severall places of their habitations made such a spectacle after
my comming into those partes, that, as I travailed in that
Forrest nere the Massachussets, it seemed to mee a new
found Golgatha." [3]

[1] Bradford, 102.   [2] II. Mass. Hist. Coll. ii. 66.
[3] New English Canaan, Book I. chap. iii (See notes in Prince Soc.
ed. 130–134.)

And in this way, as that eminent Christian divine and close student of the precepts of his Master, the Rev. Cotton Mather, charitably observed eighty years later, " the woods were almost cleared of those pernicious creatures, to make room for a better growth." [1]

[1] *Magnalia*, B. I. ch. ii. § 6.

CHAPTER II.

THE ARGONAUTS OF BOSTON BAY.

ON the afternoon of the $\frac{19\text{th}}{29\text{th}}$ of September, 1621, shortly before sunset, an open boat, or shallop as it was then called, entered Boston harbor, coming up along the shore from the direction of Plymouth. In it were thirteen men, ten Europeans and three savages, under the immediate command of Captain Miles Standish; and their purpose was to explore the country in and about Massachusetts Bay, as Boston harbor was then called, and to open a way to some intercourse with those inhabiting thereabout.[1] The party had left Plymouth with the ebb tide shortly before the previous midnight, expecting to reach their destination at a good hour in the morning: but the distance had proved greater than they supposed, and their progress slower; so that the nine leagues upon which they had calculated seemed to them more like twenty than the thirteen they really were. Once within the entrance of the harbor they steered directly for what looked to them like "the bottom of the bay," and came to anchor off Thomson's Island, passing the night on board the shallop. Either that evening or

---

[1] The account of this expedition is contained in Mourt's *Relation*, 57–60. This has been reprinted in II. *Mass. Hist. Coll.* ix. 57. Dr. Young included it in his *Chronicles of Plymouth* (pp. 224–229); and subsequently, in 1865, the *Relation*, very carefully annotated by Dr. H. M. Dexter, was made the first publication in the *Library of New England History*.

early the next morning, Standish, with others of the
party, landed on the island, and named it Trevore,
from William Trevore, one of their number.[1]

Having left Plymouth Tuesday night and passed
almost the whole of Wednesday in getting to their
destination, it was Thursday, the $\frac{20th}{30th}$, before Standish
and his companions were ready to extend their explorations to the mainland. Betimes that morning
they seem to have crossed the narrow channel which

[1] The course taken by Standish's party has given rise to much
question among the commentators. The words used by Mourt are,
"We came into the bottom of the bay." To one accustomed to sailing in Boston harbor and familiar with its entrances, this phrase,
used in connection with a boat coming up from Plymouth and making
the harbor by Point Allerton, can hardly bear a doubtful meaning.
The view from the channel off Point Allerton in the direction of
Thomson's Island is unbroken, while towards Boston it is obstructed
by a succession of islands. Any stranger so entering the harbor in a
small boat would naturally make for the open water near the mouth
of the Neponset, the apparent "bottom of the bay."

Moreover, Standish had Indian pilots and a distinct destination.
Unquestionably, also, he had Smith's chart of 1614. He was in search
of the principal sachem of the Massachusetts tribe. That tribe he
supposed lived near what Smith had called "the high mountain of
Massachuset," and set down as such on his map. Before the great
pestilence the sachem of the Massachusetts had dwelt at a place
called the Massachusetts Fields. (Young, *Chron. of Mass.* 305, 395)
His Indian pilots would naturally have directed Standish's course
towards where they knew these fields were, and in going there he had
Smith's "high mountain" directly before him. The Massachusetts
Fields lay just behind the Squantum headland, in what is now the
town of Quincy; and Thomson's Island is the nearest point to them,
not on the main shore.

In a deposition made long after, in relation to the ownership of
Thomson's Island, Standish stated that he visited this island in company with William Trevore the year he came into the country. (*N.
E. Hist. and Gen. Reg.* ix. 248.) It could only have been on this occasion: and apparently they must have landed on the island either
the evening of their arrival or early the next morning, as after
that the whole time of the explorers is accounted for in other directions.

separates Thomson's Island from the bold and picturesque promontory of Squantum, and, there landing,
found upon the beach a number of lobsters thrown in
a pile ready to be carried off. Off these they made
a breakfast. This done, Standish posted a couple of
men behind the cliff on the landward side to guard
the shallop, and then went inland looking for inhabitants, taking with him four others, with Squanto, one
of his three Indians, for a guide. The party had not
gone far when they met an Indian woman coming
for the lobsters they had eaten. Giving her something for them, they questioned her as to the whereabouts of her people. Though Chickatabot then, and
long afterwards, was the chief sachem on that side of
the Neponset, and is reputed to have lived on a little
cedar-covered hummock, still traditionally known as
the Sachem's Knoll, not far from where they were,
the woman seems to have belonged to the following of
a sagamore called Obbatinewat, who is mentioned in
the early records only in connection with Standish's
present visit. Accordingly it is not known where he
made his home, and at this time he may have been
lurking in the neighborhood of Savin Hill or Dorchester Heights. He certainly seems to have been
somewhere north of the Neponset; for, instead of
guiding the explorers to him, as she would have done
had he been south of that river, the woman pointed
out the place where he was, and then, taking Squanto
with her, left Standish and the others to return to the
shallop. She had apparently come across the bay to
the headland in a canoe. Retracing their steps to
where they had left their boat, Standish and the rest
made haste to follow her.

They found Obbatinewat at the place she had

pointed out, and, Squanto acting as interpreter, he described to them apparently how he belonged further to the north, but added that he was then living in such mortal terror of the Tarratines that he did not dare stay long in any fixed place. He further told them that the Squaw Sachem, by which title he seems to have designated the widow and successor of Nane-pashemet, the lately slain chief of the Massachusetts, was likewise hostile to him. Taking advantage of the hunted creature's terror, Standish explained to him how several sachems had already professed allegiance to King James, and promised that if he would do the same he should be protected against his enemies. Obbatinewat readily enough assented to this proposal, and then offered to guide the explorers to the place, on the other side by the bay, where the Squaw Sachem lived. Accordingly, taking him with them on the shallop, the party made their way among the islands, the great number of which they now with astonish-ment seemed first to realize, and entered the inner harbor. That afternoon they came to anchor, appar-ently on the Charlestown or Chelsea shore, near the mouth of the Mystic, and sent out their guides to look for savages. None were to be found; and again the party passed the night on their shallop, appar-ently not caring to run the risk of sleeping on the shore.

The next day they landed and pushed up into the country, in the direction, it would seem, of Medford and Winchester.[1] Presently, after marching about three miles, they came to an abandoned village; and, a mile further on, to the place where Nanepashemet

[1] The localities visited by the explorers from this point forward are very closely followed by Dexter in his notes to Mourt, pp. 127-9.

had lived, and where his house was still standing, a description of which they give. In a swamp, not far from this, they found the dead sachem's stronghold, being an Indian palisadoed fort, some forty or fifty feet in diameter, of the usual circular construction, with a single entrance by means of a bridge crossing the two ditches, the one within and the other without; and " in the midst of this palisado stood the frame of a house, wherein, being dead, he lay buried."

The explorers went but a mile beyond the stockade. They had then come to Nanepashemet's home, where he had been surprised by the Tarratines, about a year before as it is supposed, and killed. The house, if it can so be called, was another stockade, much like the one they had already seen, but standing on a hilltop. It had not been occupied since the sachem's death. Here the party stopped, and two of their guides were sent out to find the frightened Indians; for, as they marched along, it was evident the rumor of their approach had gone before, and the savages had fled to their hiding-places, leaving behind them only the poles of their hastily stripped wigwams, and, in one place, a pile of corn covered with a mat.

Presently their guides found some Indian women at a spot not far off, and thither the party went. The poor creatures had evidently taken refuge there, and in great alarm were trying to hide themselves, having brought with them such of their supplies as they could carry, for the unburied corn lay about in heaps. It was not without difficulty that their fears were quieted; but at last the friendly bearing of the strangers produced its effect, and the squaws took heart sufficiently to provide for them such food as they could. No males had yet been seen; but at length, after much sending and coaxing, a warrior was induced to show himself, " shaking and trembling for fear." He, too, was at last made to understand that the explorers meant him no harm, but wished rather to trade with him for his furs, and finally he gained confidence enough to promise to deal with them. They then asked him as to the whereabouts of the Squaw Sachem, but on this point seem to have got little satisfaction. They could learn nothing except that she was " far from thence."

The day being now spent, the party made ready to go back to their boat, and Squanto took the opportunity to urge upon them the propriety of plundering the Indian women of their furs and what little else they had ; " for, said he, they are a bad people, and have oft threatened you." To this proposal Standish and his companions made answer that, were they never so bad, " we would not wrong them, or give them any just occasion against us : for their words, we little weighed them ; but if they once attempted anything against us, then we would deale far worse then he desired." By this time the women had grown very friendly ; so friendly, in fact, that they accompanied the party the whole distance back to the shallop, where at last the spirit of trade proved so strong that they even " sold their coats from their backs, and tied boughs about them, but with great shamefacedness, for indeed they are more modest than some of our English women are." Then the explorers, " the wind coming fair, and having a light moon, set out at evening, and, through the goodness of God, came safely home before noon the day following."

The party were gone from Plymouth four days, from Tuesday midnight to Saturday noon, during what is now the end of September and early October.

They had also been most fortunate in their weather;
and on this point the slowness of the voyage up, and
the wind coming fair with a light moon on the
return, tell, in connection with the season, the whole
story. The record of a weather bureau would only
confirm it. They had first seen Boston harbor with
its islands and the region thereabout during the finest
season of the New England year, — the season of
clear, windless, autumn days, while the leaves, yet
scarlet and golden, are thick on the trees. Everything then conveys a sense of ripeness, with hardly a
suggestion of death, and the atmosphere, mild and yet
exhilarating, hangs like a veil over the landscape,
giving it a soft aspect, in strong contrast with the
sharp-cut brilliancy of the ordinary New England
day. It was during two of these rare days that
Standish and his companions rambled over the Squantum headland and the Medford hills, and along the
shores of the Mystic. In the distance they saw the
Blue Hills, hazy and shadowy against the sky, while
the swelling, forest-clad outline of the nearer landscape glowed with a dying verdure. It was not unnatural, therefore, that when they got home the Plymouth shore seemed to them tame and flat, and they
spoke in regretful terms of the broad harbor they had
just seen, and the beautiful region about it, and
wished " they had been ther seated."

It was now seven years since Smith's visit to that
region. He had been there at a different season of
the year, but had been impressed in the same way,
and had pronounced the vicinity of Boston Bay " the
paradise of all those parts." Otherwise no stronger
contrast could be imagined than between what he reported and what Standish saw; for, in place of the

" great troops " of " goodly, strong, and well-proportioned people," whom Smith found "very kind, but in
their fury no less valiant," Standish and his companions could only hunt up the skulking Obbatinewat,
who " durst not then remaine in any setled place,"
and the poor, cowering wretch who was coaxed in to
them, " shaking and trembling for feare." The islands, too, in the country of the Massachusetts, which
Smith saw planted with cornfields, groves, mulberries,
and salvage gardens, — these islands the Plymouth
explorers reported had been " cleared from end to end,
but the people were all dead or removed."

Many points in Boston harbor bear names of
Plymouth origin. Point Allerton, for instance, com-
memorates Isaac Allerton, who was for many years
deputy-governor under Bradford ; while the Brewsters,
opposite, were so called after the elder of the Plymouth church. While it is not known precisely when
these names were given, — whether by the explorers
of 1621, or by others at a later day, — Bradford says
that the Charles River was first identified on this occasion, " supposing that was it which Captaine Smith
in his mapp so named." The island Trevore soon
lost the designation given it by Standish, and has, since
1626, been known as Thomson's Island ; but the peninsula opposite has always retained its original name,
perpetuating the memory of the Indian interpreter
who guided the first party of Europeans that ever set
foot upon it. It has been suggested that it was then
and there called Squantum by Standish or Bradford
or Winslow, just as the name Trevore had been given
a few hours earlier ; but of this there is no evidence.
The name is a familiar one in the Indian dialect,
being that of a god ; by some said to be the good, as

opposed to the evil one, though the word itself would
seem to imply a god of wrath. It may therefore have
been the Indian name for the peninsula from time immemorial, just as Nahant was the name of the other
peninsula opposite to it, without the harbor; but it
is certain that Squantum has been known by that
name, or as Squanto, ever since the first European
lived near it, and that practically it does perpetuate
the memory of the Indian guide, and not that of the
Indian deity.[1]

That this should be so is, too, in every way fit and
proper. Squanto has not had his due place in New
England history given to him; for if human instruments are ever prepared by special providence for a
given work, he was assuredly so prepared for his.
Governor Bradford on behalf of the Pilgrims wrote
his best epitaph in these words: — " [He] was their
interpreter, and was a spetiall instrument sent by God
for their good beyond their expectation. He directed
them how to set their corne, wher to take fish and to
procure other comodities, and was also their pilott to
bring them to unknowne places for their profitt, and
never left them till he dyed."[2]

Squanto, in fact, was for a time perhaps the most

[1] A derivation of the name, as grotesque and far-fetched as it is
absurd, was at a later period found in the ubiquitous Lover's-leap le-
gend. An Indian woman was supposed to have put an end to herself
by springing from the bold crag which forms the peninsula's eastern extremity, and is still known as Squaw Rock. (See *Memorial
History of Boston,* i. 64.) Thence the name Squaw's Tumble, cor-
rupted into Squantum. Even John Adams, writing in 1762, speaks
of " the high, steep rock from whence the squaw threw herself who
gave the name to the place." *Works,* ii. 136. See, also, Drake, *Indians,* 106 ; Shurtleff, *Boston,* 505 ; Young, *Chron. of Pilg.* 191, n. ;
Young, *Chron. of Mass.* 257 ; III. *Mass. Hist. Coll.* viii. 176 ; *Wonder
Working Providence,* 16 ; Dexter, *Mourt,* 99, n. ; *N. E. Canaan,* 93.
[2] Bradford, 95.

essential factor to the prolonged existence of the
Plymouth colony, for it was he who showed the starving and discouraged settlers how to plant and tend
that maize, without their crop of which the famine of
the second winter would have finished those few who
survived the exposure of the first.   Not only, also, is
his name perpetuated by a promontory in Quincy
Bay, but the story of his life affords almost the best
introduction possible to an account of the settlement
of the region thereabout.   Full of the spirit of the
time, it tastes also of the soil.

CHAPTER III.

SQUANTO'S STORY.

SQUANTO, or Tisquantum, as he was indiscriminately called, was of the Pokánoket tribe, which had once occupied all the region between the Narragansetts and the Massachusetts, and had been sufficiently powerful to hold its own against both. The tradition ran that at one time it could muster three thousand warriors.[1] Squanto was a native of Patuxet, as Plymouth was called in the Indian dialect. It is not known when he was born; but in 1614, when Smith came to New England, he had in company with him one Captain Thomas Hunt, who, when Smith set out on his return voyage, remained behind to load his vessel with dried fish for the Spanish market. When ready to sail, this man apparently conceived the idea of supplementing his legitimate cargo by kidnapping a number of natives, with a view to selling them as slaves. This he proceeded to do, and, enticing a score or so of the Pokánokets on board his vessel, put to sea. Among them was Squanto.[2] Off Cape Cod he later kidnapped others of the Nauset tribe.

---

[1] 1. *Mass. Hist. Coll.* i. 148.

[2] The time and place of the kidnapping of Squanto have given the authorities a great deal of trouble. There are two distinct statements on the subject. Bradford (p. 95) says he was "carried away with divers others by one Hunt," and that he was "a native of this place" (Plymouth). Sir Ferdinando Gorges, on the other hand, says that Captain Weymouth happened to come into Plymouth in July, 1605, from

Hunt seems to have then gone to Malaga, where he
proceeded to dispose of his cargo, both dried fish and

his voyage to the Penobscot, "from whence he brought five of the
natives, three of whose names were Manida, Skettwarroes, and Tasquantum, whom I seized upon." (*Briefe Narration*, ch. ii., Prince
Soc. ed. ii. 8, n.) Accordingly Drake (*Book of Indians*, 71) says that
"it is impossible that Sir Ferdinando should have been mistaken"
in this matter; and Dr. Dexter (Mourt, 90, n.), after saying that
Squanto was clearly one of Weymouth's five captives, ventures the
supposition that he somehow got back from the kidnapping of 1605,
and was kidnapped again in 1614. (See, also, Bryant and Gay, *United
States*, i. 401; Young, *Chron. of Pilg.* 190, n.)

Nevertheless there can be no doubt that Gorges was mistaken in
his statement, and that the Patuxet savage was not kidnapped at
Pemaquid. In the first place, it is not supposable that a member of
the Pokánoket tribe would be passing the summer of 1605 in a visit
among his deadly enemies the Tarratines, whose language even was
not intelligible to him (III. *Mass. Hist. Coll.* vi. 59; Palfrey, i. 23, n.),
and be captured as one of a party of them in the way described by
Rosier (III. *Mass. Hist. Coll.* viii. 144). In the second place, Gorges
throughout is singularly careless in the references he makes to his
Indians. He mentions by name seven in all. He then, for instance,
in the *Brief Relation*, says he sent out two of them, Epenow and
Manawet, with Captain Hobson, in 1614 (II. *Mass. Hist. Coll.* ix. 5).
Afterwards, in the *Briefe Narration*, he says he sent out, not two, but
three, and gives their names as Epenow, Assacomet, and Wenape (III.
Mass. Hist. Coll. vi. 60); then, two pages further on (p. 62), he includes
Squanto among them. Again he speaks of Epenow as having been
taken with twenty-nine others, who were sold for slaves in Spain, —
very clearly referring to Hunt's proceeding in 1614 (ib. 58); and immediately afterwards (p. 60) he says he sent him out as a guide and
interpreter to an expedition some months earlier in the same year.
Finally, as respects Squanto, Gorges distinctly contradicts himself.
It is in the *Briefe Narration*, printed in 1658, and written at least as
late as 1637, that he names Tasquantum among the savages captured
by Weymouth. Meanwhile, in the *Brief Relation*, printed in 1622,
fifteen years nearer the event, he speaks of Tasquantum as "one of
those savages that formerly had been betrayed by the unworthy
Hunt." (II. *Mass. Hist. Coll.* ix. 7.)

Apparently the names of the five Weymouth savages were Manida,
Sketwarroes (III. *Mass. Hist. Coll.* vi. 50, 51), Assacomet, Wenape
(ib. 60), and Manawet (II. *Mass. Hist. Coll.* ix. 5). Epenow was a
Martha's Vineyard Indian, kidnapped earlier than 1614 by Captain

Indians; but before the latter were all sold, the proceeding came to the notice of the church, when the priests interfered, seizing upon the savages as heathen meet for conversion. Whether Squanto was one of those thus saved from Spanish servitude, or whether Hunt, finding him useful, kept him in his own hands, does not appear; but he is next heard of in England, where, towards the end of 1614 or the beginning of 1615, he was domesticated in the house of "the Worshipfull John Slany, of London, Merchant," dwelling in Cheapside, and one of the undertakers and treasurer of the Newfoundland plantation. By him Squanto next seems to have been sent out to Newfoundland, probably with Captain John Mason, who went there as governor, as he was called, though more properly as the resident business manager of the company. In 1615 Captain Dermer, an explorer in Gorges' interest, visited Newfoundland, and there found Squanto. Talking with him, he received the usual glowing account which exiled savages are wont to give of their native places, and conceived a strong desire to explore the region thus described. Accordingly he wrote to Gorges in relation to the matter, and, the next year, when he returned to prepare for his voyage, he took Squanto back to England with him.

Early in the season of 1619 Dermer, still accompanied by Squanto, sailed in one of Gorges' vessels

Edward Harlow (Smith, *Gen. Hist.* ii. 174), and picked up in London by one Captain Harley, who carried him to Gorges (III. *Mass. Hist. Coll.* vi. 58). Squanto alone was one of Hunt's victims, and Gorges first heard of him in Captain Mason's service in Newfoundland, through Captain Dermer, in 1618 (II. *Mass. Hist. Coll.* ix. 7). On this point see, also, the notes (146, 255, 293, 300) in Baxter, *Sir Ferdinando Gorges*, in the Prince Society Publications.

bound for the Maine fishing stations. Leaving this
vessel at Monhegan, they set out on the 19th of May,
in an open five-ton pinnace, and coasted along the
shore to Plymouth. But it was now nearly five years
since the kidnapping of Squanto, and in the mean time
the great plague of 1616–17 had ravaged all those
parts; so they found the place void of inhabitants.
They were all dead. Leaving Plymouth, Dermer
next touched at Cape Cod, where he redeemed from
captivity one of the French crew shipwrecked there
three years before, and then on the $\frac{12\text{th}}{22\text{d}}$ of June he
reached a large island south of that cape. Turning
back, he then returned to Monhegan, arriving at that
place on the $\frac{20\text{th}}{30\text{th}}$ of the same month.

After refitting, and sending home an account of
what he had seen, Dermer now started for Virginia,
still in his pinnace. While off Cape Ann he came
very near being wrecked; and at Cape Cod he fell
into the hands of the Indians, and barely escaped
with his life, being saved by Squanto, who, as Dermer
wrote, "entreated hard for me." Squanto seems now
to have left him, but apparently only for a short time,
while Dermer himself, having continual trouble with
the natives, went on to Martha's Vineyard. Here he
fell in with Epenow, another of Gorges' Indians, who,
a number of years before, had been kidnapped and
taken to England by Captain Edward Harlow. Unlike Squanto, Epenow seems to have been an ingrained
savage, crafty and cruel. Being a captive in London,
he had in the summer of 1614 effected his deliverance
in a very clever way; for, exciting the cupidity of
Gorges and Captain Harley by wonderful stories of
the hidden wealth of his native place, he had induced
them to fit out a vessel on which he went as inter-

preter and guide. He was to lay open to them the
mines of Martha's Vineyard. They were not without
suspicions of the wily fellow, and he was kept under
close watch, being clad " with long garments, fitly to
be laid hold on if occasion should require." Nevertheless, when they reached Martha's Vineyard, and his
friends in their canoes were lying about the vessel, he
suddenly slipped overboard and made his escape, " although he was taken hold of by one of the company ;
yet, being a strong and heavy man, could not be
stayed." A combat ensued, in which the Europeans
do not seem to have had the advantage. " And thus,"
wrote Gorges, " were all my hopes of that particular
made void and frustrate, and they returned without
doing more."

When, therefore, Dermer came to Martha's Vineyard in 1619, and there met him, Epenow had been
for five years in the enjoyment of his recovered liberty ; but on this occasion he apparently treated Dermer well, giving him, as Dermer himself says, " very
good satisfaction in everything almost I could desire."
Continuing his voyage, the explorer seems to have
passed through Long Island Sound and Hell Gate,
where he was nearly wrecked, and at last reached
Jamestown. There he passed the winter.

The next season, having in the mean time put a deck
to his pinnace, Captain Dermer again sailed for Cape
Cod. Squanto was now certainly with him. Landing on Martha's Vineyard, he once more, according to
Gorges, encountered Epenow, who now showed the
other side of his character. The statement of Gorges
is not to be implicitly accepted ; but whether Epenow
had any connection with the affair or not, Dermer's
party was certainly attacked by the Indians, and all

of them killed, excepting one man who had been left
in the boat, and Dermer himself, who was grievously
wounded. In fact, Gorges says, he received fourteen
wounds; while, according to Bradford, the savages
would have " cut off his head upon the cuddy of his
boat, had not the man rescued him with a sword.'
Notwithstanding his hurts he made shift to get to Virginia, where, to the great discouragement of Gorges,
he subsequently died.[1]

The conflict between Dermer and the Indians, which
resulted so disastrously for the former, must have
taken place in the summer of 1620, and only a very
few months before the arrival of the Mayflower at
Cape Cod. Bradford says that at the time Squanto
was with Dermer, but it does not appear when he separated from him. It may have been then; or he may
have gone back to Virginia with Dermer, and, after
the death of the latter, found his way to his own country in some trading vessel. In any event, having thus
had no little experience as a voyager along that coast,
he was living in the winter of 1620–1 with the remnants of the Pokánokets within the territory of Mas-
sasoit; and on Thursday, the $\frac{22d}{1st}$ of $\frac{March}{April}$, a very fair,
warm day, at about one o'clock in the afternoon, he
walked into the Plymouth settlement in company with
Samoset.

It has already been mentioned[2] that during the five
years of Squanto's absence the pestilence had literally
exterminated his tribe. Scarce any had been left
alive, and he was the only surviving native of Patuxet.
It is probable, therefore, that he now actually felt
more at home among the settlers than among his fellows, and certainly he never afterwards showed the

[1] *Brief Relation,* 19, Prince Soc. ed. i. 219, n.   [2] *Supra,* 26.

slightest disposition to return and cast in his lot with
the latter. When he came into the settlement it was
as a sort of herald to announce the coming of Massasoit with his train of sixty men; but the next day,
when the rest went away, he remained, and to good
purpose; for the Plymouth people had none too much
to eat then, and it probably was in consequence of
this painfully apparent fact that "Squanto went at
noone to fish for Eeles. At night he came home
with as many as he could well lift in one hand, which
our people were glad of. They were fat and sweet.
He trod them out with his feete, and so caught them
with his hands, without any other instrument."

Squanto died towards the close of November, 1622,
and his connection with the Plymouth settlement
extended, therefore, over a period of only twenty
months; but those months covered the crucial period
for Plymouth, and during them his services were in
constant requisition. Early in April, about four
weeks after Squanto made his appearance, the Mayflower sailed for home, and Bradford then goes on to
describe how —

"Afterwards they (as many as were able) began to plant
ther corn, in which servise Squanto stood them in great
stead, showing them both the maner how to set it, and after
how to dress and tend it. Also he tould them, excepte they
gott fish and set with it (in these old grounds), it would
come to nothing; and he showed them that in the midle
of Aprill they should have store enough come up the
brooke, by which they begane to build, and taught them how
to take it, and wher to get other provissions necessary for
them; all which they found true by triall and experience.
Some English seed they sew, as wheat and pease, but it
came not to good."

No sooner was it possible to dispense a little with Squanto's services as a planter than they were called into requisition as an interpreter for, "haveing in some sorte ordered their bussines at home," the magistrates bethought themselves of Massasoit's visit to them in March, and determined to send a return embassy to him with suitable presents. Stephen Hopkins and Edward Winslow were made choice of for this service, and on Monday, $\frac{2d}{12th}$ July they set out under Squanto's guidance, bearing with them as propitiatory gifts "a Horse-man's coat of red Cotton, and laced with a slight lace," and a "copper Chayne." Massasoit's home was on the Narragansett Bay, a distance of some forty miles from Plymouth by the road they took, but Squanto, telling the ambassadors what they should do in each exigency as it arose, pressed them on so energetically that the journey was finished betimes on the second day. Then, his work as guide being done, he acted as interpreter and master of ceremonies.

"Having delivered our foresayd Message and Presents, and having put the Coat on his backe, and the Chayne about his necke, [Massasoit] was not a little proud to behold himselfe, and his men also to see their King so bravely attyred."

This took place on a Wednesday. The next day Massasoit entertained his guests, and was very earnest with them to stay longer, —

"But wee desired to keepe the Sabboth at home : and feared we should either be light-headed for want of sleepe, for what with bad lodging, the Savages barbarous singing (for they use to sing themselves asleepe), lice and fleas within doores, and Muskeetoes without, wee could hardly sleepe all the time of our being there ; we much fearing, that if wee should stay any longer, we should not be able to recover home for want of strength. So that on the Fryday morning [July $\frac{6th}{16th}$] before Sun-rising we took our leave and departed."

Bradford adds that the ambassadors " came both weary and hungrie home," having " found but short commons." Squanto they had left behind, for Massasoit had retained him for the time being, to send from place to place in search of beaver skins ; so, having served as a planter, a guide and an interpreter, he was now doing active duty as a commercial agent.

A few weeks after the return of Winslow and Hopkins, in the early part of August, a boy named John Billington, the son of one of the settlers, lost himself in the woods and wandered off in a southerly direction until he came to an Indian village, at what is now Sandwich, some twenty miles from Plymouth. He was thence taken to Eastham, and, his whereabouts having been discovered by the magistrates through the aid of Massasoit, it was determined to send a party to recover him. As usual, Squanto accompanied the party as its guide and interpreter, — Tokamahamon, another Indian, also going along, — and the next morning they landed at Barnstable. Here an incident occurred which throws a strong gleam of light on the kidnapping proceedings of Weymouth, Hunt and the rest along that coast, showing as it did the harsh afflictions heaped on the doomed and plague-stricken race. It can be told only in the words of the historian of the expedition : —

" One thing was very grievous unto us at this place ; There was an old woman, whom we judged to be no lesse than an hundred yeeres old, which came to see us because shee never saw English, yet could not behold us without

breaking forth into great passion, weeping and crying ex-
cessively. We demaunding the reason of it, they told us,
she had three sons, who when master Hunt was in these
parts went aboord his Ship to trade with him, and he carried them Captives into Spaine, (for Tisquantum at that
time was carried away also,) by which meanes shee was deprived of the comfort of her children in her old age. . . .
So we gave her some small trifles, which somewhat ap-
peased her."

From Barnstable the party moved along the shore
to Eastham, and there, remaining on board their boat
as a precaution against any possible hostilities on the
part of the savages, who swarmed in great numbers
about it, they sent Squanto on shore to negotiate for
the return of the lost boy. This he did successfully.

"After Sun-set, Aspinet came with a great traine, and
brought the boy with him, one bearing him through the
water: hee had not lesse then an hundred with him, the
halfe whereof came to the Shallop side unarmed with him,
the other stood aloofe with their bow and arrowes. There
he delivered us the boy, behung with beades, and made
peace with us, wee bestowing a knife on him, and likewise
on another that first entertained the Boy and brought him
thither. So they departed from us."

During this expedition alarming rumors had reached
the ears of those engaged in it of an attack on the
friendly Massasoit by the powerful tribe of Narragansetts, who, unreduced in numbers by the great plague
of 1617, occupied the country to the west. It appeared that among Massasoit's sachems was one called
Corbitant. This chief, more jealous if not more far-
seeing than the rest, did not fancy the neighborhood
of the Plymouth colony, and consequently was now
allying himself with the Narragansetts. Corbitant

seems to have appreciated at their true importance the services Squanto was rendering the Europeans; for he declared that if Squanto " were dead, the English had lost their tongue," and, to use the language in Mourt, he spoke " disdainfully of us, storming at the Peace between Nauset, Cummaquid and us, and at Tisquantum the worker of it." Accordingly, with savage directness, Corbitant sought the first occasion to destroy Squanto. He did not have long to wait.

At about this time another Indian, Hobamack by name, had cast in his fortunes with the Europeans. Though unacquainted with the English tongue, Hobamack proved an important acquisition to the settlement, for among the savages he was a warrior of known prowess. Later he professed Christianity, and received an allotment of land in Plymouth; neither, more fortunate than Squanto in this respect, has his fidelity to his new friends ever been called in question, for " though he was much tempted by enticements, scoffs, and scorns from the Indians, yet could he never be gotten from the English, nor from seeking after their God, but died amongst them, leaving some good hopes in their hearts that he went to rest."

Shortly after the return of the Eastham expedition Squanto and Hobamack were despatched among the Indians to ascertain the facts about the rumored attack on Massasoit. Corbitant, learning of their presence, surprised them at an Indian settlement some fourteen miles west of Plymouth, in what is now Middleborough, and at once proceeded to pick a quarrel with them, presently drawing his knife; upon which Hobamack fled, leaving his companion behind, and made his way in great terror to Plymouth, where he appeared, " all sweating," and spread the news of

Squanto's danger. A meeting of the settlers was at
once held, and energetic action decided upon. It was
resolved to send Standish with a strong party of fourteen men to make a night surprise, with instructions,
if they found that Squanto had indeed been killed,
"to cut off Corbitant's head." Meanwhile they were
also to seize another sachem, of doubtful friendliness,
and hold him as a hostage until definite word could
be obtained as to the safety of Massasoit. The party
set out on the $\frac{14th}{24th}$ of August, and succeeded the next
night in surprising the village, though they failed to
secure Corbitant, who, it appeared, after threatening
Squanto, had gone away with his followers without in-
juring him. In the panic of the surprise some of the
Indians made an attempt to escape, and were badly
wounded. The next morning, after making loud
proclamation of the vengeance they would ·inflict on
Corbitant if he did not desist from his acts of hostility, or if Massasoit was injured, Standish and his
party returned to Plymouth, bringing with them the
wounded of the previous night and the rescued Indian.

A month later took place that expedition to Boston
Bay which has already been described, when the peninsula of Squantum was visited and perhaps so named.
This closed the season ; and, being now well recovered in health and strength, the little colony, reaping
the natural fruits of their own prudent energy, or, as
Bradford more piously phrased it, finding that the
Lord was with them in all their ways, began to gather
in their small harvest and to make ready their dwellings against the winter. Thanks chiefly to Squanto,
during all that summer there had been no want felt.
And now, when autumn came, there came with it
great flocks of water-fowl and of wild turkeys, nor did

they want of venison or meal or Indian corn; "which made many afterwards write so largly of their plenty hear to their freinds in England, which were not fained, but true reports."

In November the ship Fortune arrived, bringing its welcome addition to the numbers of the colony; and, being immediately loaded, was despatched on her return voyage a fortnight later. Part of her return cargo, and apparently the most valuable part of it, was two hogsheads of beaver and other skins; and for these also the settlers were indebted to their Indian friend, for, as Bradford writes, there was not "any amongst them that ever saw a beaver skin until they came hear and were informed by Squanto."

Some time in December, not long after the sailing of the Fortune, an Indian messenger appeared in the settlement in company with the friendly Tokamaha-mon, and inquired for Squanto. It was a messenger from Canonicus, chief of the Narragansetts. On being informed that Squanto was not then at home, the messenger seemed to be rather relieved than other-wise, and, leaving for him a bundle of new arrows encased in a rattlesnake's skin, prepared to return at once, but was detained until the next morning, the settlers hoping to learn something further. Failing in that, they then dismissed him, with a threatening message to his chief, and he took himself off in a vio-lent storm without tasting food, thankful apparently to escape with a whole skin. Presently Squanto got back, and, the arrows being shown him, he was called upon to interpret their significance. This he did, say-ing that they and the rattlesnake's skin, sent in that manner, imported enmity; that, in fact, it was a chal-lenge. Thereupon the arrows were taken from the

skin, and the famous return challenge of powder and
shot sent back in it to Canonicus, to that chieftain's
infinite alarm.

Nothing further calculated to excite fears of any
immediate danger happened at that time, but subsequently, so far as Squanto was concerned, these events
assumed another meaning in the minds of the settlers.
The winter wore slowly away. The little settlement
was always in readiness against attack, but there was
comparative plenty in the land, and, with a sufficiency
of food, there was little sickness. That this plenty
was largely due to the active intervention of him who
had "directed them how to set their corne, wher to
take fish, and to procure other comodities," and in
whose death a year later "they had a great loss," the
governor of the colony is witness. Yet Bradford's
testimony has not prevented modern authorities from
reaching the conclusion that all this time "Squanto
was in the interest of Corbitant, and lived among the
English as a spy."[1] This startling conclusion seems
to be based entirely on certain occurrences which befell during the six months between the first visit of
the Plymouth people to Boston Bay in September,
1621, and their second visit in the succeeding April.
While those occurrences, as will be seen, do not justify
the inference in regard to Squanto which has been
drawn from them, they do afford a notable illustration of the innate childishness of the Indian character, and of the shrewd cunning with which the Plymouth elders played upon it.

Naturally enough, as their earliest friend and interpreter, Squanto plumed himself greatly on his importance to the English settlement, and regarded with

[1] Drake, *Book of Indians*, 103.

no friendly eyes the growing estimate in which Hobamack was there held. Squanto was, in fact, jealous of
Hobamack ; and his jealousy was reciprocated. But
Massasoit was a personage of far more consequence to
the Plymouth people than Squanto even ; and Hobamack stood in much closer relations to Massasoit than
Squanto. His rival, therefore, shone with a borrowed
light most painful to Squanto. Consequently he seems
to have set to work, much as an intriguing boy might
do at school, to undermine both Hobamack and Massasoit, so as to leave himself supreme in the eyes of
his brother savages as the white man's Indian. His
plot was a perfectly transparent one, and a good occasion for its development presented itself at the time
of the April expedition of 1622, to Boston Bay.

Hobamack had already intimated to the magistrates
his suspicion of the Massachusetts Indians, repeating
rumors as to some alliance between them and the
Narragansetts, and hinting that suspicious whisper-
ings were going on between Squanto and his friends
outside. In this way he seems by degrees to have
conjured up a conspiracy, with Squanto for the prime
mover in it, the purpose of which was to get Standish
and his party, during the expedition to the Massachusetts, away from their boat to some Indian village,
under a pretence of trading, and to fall upon them
there. There is no evidence that any such conspiracy
ever existed except in the jealous brain of Hobamack ;
and indeed the story of the subsequent settlement
of Boston Bay shows very clearly that at this time
it could not have existed. Nevertheless, naturally
enough, considering the remote and oppressive solitude of the Plymouth settlement, the nervousness
proved contagious, and even the magistrates took the

alarm so that a meeting of notables was held and the
situation fully discussed. At this meeting Standish's
counsels seem to have prevailed, and a bold, even an
outwardly defiant, course was decided upon. The expedition to Boston Bay was not to be abandoned or
even postponed; on the contrary, it was to be sent off
at once, and both Squanto and Hobamack were to go
with it as guides. Accordingly, early in April, Standish set sail, taking with him ten men and the two
Indians.

Then at last Squanto's plot, the result of his whis-
perings and his mysterious comings and goings, revealed itself. Scarcely had the departing boat
rounded the Gurnet, shaping its course to the northward, than an Indian of Squanto's family, panting
for breath and with the blood trickling from a fresh
wound on his face, came running in from the woods.
Meeting some of the settlers who chanced to be outside of the village, and looking back as if he expected
to see the pursuers close at his heels, he called upon
them to get within the defences. He was immediately taken to Governor Bradford, and made out to say
that not only the dreaded Corbitant but their supposed friend Massasoit were both close at hand, in
league with a body of Narragansetts to attack the
place in Standish's absence. Immediately the gates
were closed, every one repaired to his post, and three
guns were fired as a signal for the expedition, if still
within hearing, to return. Fortunately, the breeze
having died away, Standish's party had found themselves becalmed just beyond the Gurnet, and had
there come to anchor. As soon as they heard the
alarm, therefore, they took to their oars and rowed
back to the town, arming themselves and making
ready for the fight.

Presently they landed, and the wounded Indian was confronted with Hobamack. Then the truth began to leak out. Squanto had not calculated on the dying away of the wind before he and Hobamack were fairly off for the Massachusetts, and he had hoped apparently to embroil the settlers and the savages before matters could be explained, thus kindling " such a flame as would not easily be quenched." If this was his plan, the return of Hobamack effectually spoiled it ; for no sooner did the latter hear the pretended fugitive's story than he stoutly insisted that it was false, declaring that, if any such conspiracy as that alleged really were on foot, he could not but have known it. Accordingly, as no hostile savages made their appearance, the alarm gradually subsided, and Hobamack's squaw was sent out to make her way to Massasoit's village and ascertain what was going on. Arriving there, she not only found everything perfectly quiet, but, apparently without in any way extenuating Squanto's conduct, she told the sachem of what had taken place at Plymouth, and thereby excited his extreme indignation. Squanto's shallow scheme thus recoiled on himself. His object was, and is, apparent enough. He had gone about to breed suspicion and fear between the colonists and Massasoit. He wanted no rivals near the Plymouth throne. His conduct was not that of a spy ; indeed, it showed clearly enough that he was acting in collusion neither with Corbitant nor with Massasoit. He was simply a very shallow intriguer who had got up an alarm, the utter groundlessness of which even he should have seen could not long be concealed. Naturally he was the chief sufferer from it ; for, not only did it shake the confidence of the settlers in him, but through it he incurred the dangerous enmity of Massasoit ; and this, as by degrees the advantage he had taken of the credulity of his less sophisticated fellows came to light, just failed of costing Squanto his life.

He had " sought his owne ends, and plaid his owne game, by putting the Indeans in fear, and drawing gifts from them to enrich himselfe ; making them beleeve he could stur up warr against whom he would, and make peece for whom he would. Yea, he made them beleeve they kept the plague buried in the ground, and could send it amongs whom they would, which did much terifie the Indeans, and made them depend more on him, and seeke more to him than to Massasoyte."

But in the matter of worldly cunning the God-fearing elders of Plymouth, with all their simplicity, were far more than a match for any savage ; so when, a little later on, it came to the question of surrendering Squanto to Massasoit under the provisions of their treaty with the latter, they contrived to evade the obligation. At the same time they sedulously stimulated the jealousy between their two Indian guides, Squanto cleaving to Bradford for protection against Massasoit, while Hobamack attached himself to Standish, so that " the governor seemed to countenance the one, and the captain the other, by which they had better intelligence, and made them both more diligent."

The alarm into which Plymouth had been thrown resulted, therefore, in nothing except the loss to Squanto of much of the prestige he prized so highly, for Governor Bradford reproved him sharply, and all the neighboring Indians were cautioned against giving any credence to him. Nevertheless he was altogether too useful a person to be lightly cast off. He could not yet be spared ; and so, when a few weeks later the expedition again set out for the Massachusetts, he went with it. On its return after a successful but somewhat tempestuous voyage, Massasoit himself was found to be at Plymouth, having come there to explain away the suspicions against himself, and at the same time to take vengeance on Squanto. Governor Bradford did his best to pacify his savage ally, but was only very moderately successful in his efforts; for, though Massasoit went away himself, he no sooner got home than he sent back a messenger asking that Squanto might be put to death. When this request was not complied with, the persistent savage seems to have again sent the messenger back to Plymouth, this time in company with others on a sort of formal embassy, demanding the delivery to them of Squanto in conformity with the articles of the treaty entered into between the Plymouth people and himself a year before. Things now assumed a very serious look for Squanto. The question of his delivery apparently rested with Governor Bradford, who seems not only to have felt the weight of the treaty obligations, but to have hesitated greatly at the danger of incurring the enmity of Massasoit as the price of saving to the settlement even so useful an instrument as its single interpreter. The Indian messengers would not be put off; they said that the sachem had sent them there with his own knife to kill Squanto, and they were enjoined to bring back his head and hands as evidence of his death. Seeing that the governor hesitated, they offered a great number of beaver skins to obtain his consent. These he declined; but none the less Bradford seems to have made up his mind that Squanto could not be saved, and he even took steps preparatory to abandoning him to his fate. Squanto

meanwhile seems to have demeaned himself in true
Indian fashion.   Being sent for, he made no effort to
fly or hide, but came out, and, before the assembled
community and his savage pursuers, boldly accused
Hobamack of being the worker of his overthrow ; and
then yielded himself to the magistrates to be delivered up or not, as they should decide.

They decided to give him up; but, just as he was
about to be surrendered into the hands of his execu-
tioners, to the utter amazement of every one a strange
boat was seen in the distance coming out from behind
the Gurnet, and slowly making its way across the harbor's mouth.   A miracle could hardly have been more
opportune for Squanto, or excited greater surprise
among those who were deliberating over his fate ; for
it was now nearly eighteen months that the little community had been gazing in their deep isolation to seaward, and once only during that time had their eyes
been gladdened by the gleam of an unfamiliar sail.
So the sudden appearance of a mere boat in the offing
at just this time naturally excited unbounded surprise
and hardly less alarm; it seemed as if it must have
some hidden connection with Massasoit's demand, and
a rumor crept about the excited and anxious throng
that the boat contained Frenchmen from the Narragansett Bay, allies of the hostile savages; and Governor Bradford told the emissaries that he must be
sure what its presence might signify before the prisoner could be delivered to them.   Fortunately for
Squanto, they had by this time grown impatient ; perhaps, also, the appearance of the strange sail may
have excited apprehensions in their minds as well ; in
any event, " being mad with rage, and impatient at
delay, they departed in great heat."

Squanto's escape was a narrow one, and due to the merest chance; for, as will presently be seen, the strange boat contained merely some pioneers of the party destined a few months later to attempt the first abortive settlement on the shores of Boston Bay, and its appearance had no connection with anything then going on at Plymouth. It was none the less most opportune, and Massasoit does not seem to have again attempted to molest Squanto in Plymouth; and Squanto took good care that he should have no opportunity to lay hands on him outside of the settlement. None the less, Squanto's time was approaching. The events which have been described took place in May, 1622. In July following, the party arrived which has just been referred to as attempting the first settlement on Boston Bay, and established itself there in the early autumn; but, as will presently be seen, the improvidence of those composing it soon brought them to the verge of starvation. Nor were the Plymouth people, owing to the shortness of their own harvest, in position to supply the wants of others. Under these circumstances, towards the close of 1622, a joint expedition in search of supplies was agreed upon, which Squanto undertook to pilot round Cape Cod to the as yet unvisited south coast. According to his own account, he had twice before rounded the cape, once with Dermer, and again, as he asserted, with a French party of which there is no record. He now seems to have piloted the expedition safely as far as the shoals off Orleans, when the angry look of the ocean in front terrified the master, and he hurriedly put into Chatham harbor, — Squanto, who had been there three years before with Dermer, giving some slight direction. Here the voyage ended. Squanto was still confident that he could take the vessel across the shoals; and in this he had the support of the natives, who said that large vessels had gone through. It was accordingly determined to make one more attempt. But it was not to be. Squanto was the staff and the stay of the expedition, — its pilot, its interpreter, its mediator. Without him it was impossible to proceed further, " because the master's sufficiency was much doubted, and the season very tempestuous, and not fit to go upon discovery, having no guide to direct." And now, in the simple language of Bradford, —

" In this place Squanto fell sick of an Indean feavor, bleeding much at the nose (which the Indeans take for a simptome of death), and within a few days dyed ther ; desiring the Governor to pray for him, that he might goe to the Englishmen's God in heaven, and bequeathed sundrie of his things to sundry of his English freinds, as remembrances of his love ; of whom they had a great loss."

CHAPTER IV.

WESTON'S "RUDE FELLOWS."

THOSE in the boat, the sudden appearance of which off the entrance to Plymouth harbor had saved Squanto's life, were the forerunners of a larger party sent out by one Thomas Weston, "a merchant of London," to establish a plantation, or trading post, on the shores of Boston Bay. Thomas Weston was well known to the Plymouth people, for he had been one of the active promoters of the commercial enterprise which had led to their coming to New England, though his connection with it, being of the pure money-making kind, was, as the result showed, to the advantage of no one. He seems to have been a man of a type not uncommon in the days of Elizabeth and James I., — English adventurers, half traders and half explorers, who probably required the inducement only to ripen into something closely resembling a freebooter. His head was full of schemes for deriving great and sudden gain from the settlement of the North American coast, in regard to the possibilities of which he shared to the full all the sanguine faith of Raleigh, Gorges and Smith. Though he does not seem to have ever himself visited the country prior to his coming in the year 1623, there can be little doubt that he was familiar with the published accounts of it; and in all probability he had been concerned in fishing and trading ventures to the Banks of Newfoundland and

the neighboring coasts. He may have prospered in
them. At all events, in 1620 he was possessed of
some means, and was eager to try his fortune in those
parts in a more systematic way, and, for that time,
on a considerable scale.

He is first mentioned in the early chronicles of the
Plymouth colony in connection with the proposed
transfer of a portion of the Rev. John Robinson's lit
tle congregation from their place of refuge in Holland
to some point in North America. Weston was then
(1619–20) the treasurer, as well as the agent and moving spirit, of the company calling itself the Merchant
Adventurers of London. As such, and in its behalf,
he was looking about for the material with which to
effect a permanent settlement for trading purposes
somewhere within the Virginia patent. He was not
without personal knowledge of Robinson's people,
having had dealings with certain of them in previous years; and, though he could hardly have had
any deep sympathy either with their religious views
or their social aspirations, he had in some way befriended them. Being now refugees in Holland, they
were considering a scheme of settling under the Dutch
jurisdiction at New Amsterdam, as New York was
then called, when Weston, coming over to Leyden from
London for the purpose, dissuaded them, making, on
the part of the Merchant Adventurers, liberal promises of aid in both ships and money as inducements for
them to coöperate with him and his associates. Subsequently the negotiation was transferred to London;
but it did not move smoothly, and it required Mr.
Treasurer Weston's utmost efforts to save the project
from complete abandonment. His associates among
the Merchant Adventurers evidently had no confi-

dence in it, and, under one pretence or another, withdrew their support. He was himself, in his utter discouragement and disgust, repeatedly on the point of doing the same; and if he had, there can be little doubt that the Plymouth settlement would not have been effected when and where it was. Thus, whether what is now one of its most striking pages was to be altogether omitted from the history of America, depended through long weeks of the spring and summer of 1620 on the wavering action of a London trader and speculator, — vulgar, obscure and mercenary.

But at last, seeing the extent to which both himself and the Leyden exiles were involved, Weston, in the words of Governor Bradford, " gathered up himself a litle more," and in conjunction with Robert Cushman, the agent of the exiles in London, took the decisive step of chartering the Mayflower. It was already the middle of June, and six weeks more of " going up and downe, and wrangling and expostulating," were to try the patience of all before the Speedwell, on what is now the first day of August (1620), was got under weigh at Delft-Haven to join the Mayflower at Southampton, where the final details of the joint contract between the parties to the enterprise were to be agreed upon. A paper had been drawn up at an early stage of the negotiation, in which the amounts to be contributed and the rights reserved on each side had been set down ; but Weston and his associates were disposed to take every advantage they could of the necessities of the Leyden people. Step by step their demands became unconscionable, and Cushman, acting under a conviction that his so doing was absolutely necessary to secure their further coöperation, assumed the responsibility of altering the preliminary

agreement in several important respects. Though
Carver was in England at the time with Cushman, the
changes thus assented to by the latter do not seem
to have come to his knowledge, or been communicated
to the others, until the whole outward bound party
reached Southampton; then they refused point-blank
to approve the agreement as altered. Weston, thereupon deeply incensed, returned to London, after
plainly notifying the emigrants that they need look
for no further assistance from those whom he represented, but must now " stand on their owne leggs."
He was as good as his word ; and this, their first difficulty with Thomas Weston, cost the Pilgrims dear;
for, being in sad want of funds and wholly unable to
wait, they were compelled, in order to go on with their
voyage, to sell a part of their storès, finally setting
out with scarcely " any butter, no oyle, not a sole to
mend a shoe, nor every man a sword to his side,
wanting many muskets, much armoure, &c."

At last, though not until after what is now the
middle of September, the Mayflower got finally well
under weigh. Weston seems then to have waited in
the firm belief that the lapse of a few weeks would
witness her return, freighted with the products of the
New World ; but it was eight long months before she
brought back anything from Plymouth, and then
nothing more substantial than tidings. Those whom
she carried out, struggling through the long winter
against disease, due to want and aggravated by exposure, — seeing in the vast, dark wilderness which surrounded and crushed them not even the face of a savage, — had naturally found little opportunity to trade.
This, Weston in no way realized ; and accordingly by
the next vessel, the Fortune, which set sail in July,

a few weeks after the return of the Mayflower, he did
not fail to send out a long letter in which he again
recounted his grounds of complaint. Especially did
he dwell on the return of the Mayflower empty, —
the last, and in his eyes the most inexcusable, shortcoming of the Pilgrims.

"That you sent," he wrote, "no lading in the ship is
wonderfull, and worthily distasted. I know your weaknes
was the cause of it, and I beleeve more weaknes of judgmente then weaknes of hands. A quarter of the time you
spente in discoursing, arguing and consulting would have
done much more. . . . And consider that the life of the
bussines depends on the lading of this ship, which, if you
doe to any good purpose, that I may be freed from the
great sums I have disbursed for the former, and must doe
for the later, I promise you I will never quit the bussines,
though all the other adventurers should."

The vulgar adventurer addressed this harsh rebuke
to the gentle and high-minded Carver; but, when he
wrote it, Carver had been already three months dead.
Bradford had succeeded him as governor, and as such
he returned to Weston's missive a pathetic and digni-
fied reply : —

"At great charges in this adventure, I confess you have
beene, and many losses may sustaine ; but the loss of his
[Carver] and many other honest and industrious mens lives
cannot be vallewed at any prise. Of the one, ther may be
hope of recovery, but the other no recompence can make
good. But I will not insiste in generalls, but come more
perticulerly to the things themselves. You greatly blame
us for keping the ship so long in the countrie, and then to
send her away emptie. She lay five weks at Cap-Codd,
whilst with many a weary step (after a long journey) and
the indurance of many a hard brunte, we sought out in the
foule winter a place of habitation. Then we went in so

tedious a time to make provission to sheelter us and our
goods, aboute which labour many of our armes and leggs can
tell us to this day we were not necligent.   But it pleased
God to vissite us then, with death dayly, and with so generall
a disease, that the living were scarce able to burie the dead;
and the well not in any measure sufficiente to tend the sick.
And now to be so greatly blamed, for not fraighting the
ship, doth indeed goe near us, and much discourage us.
But you say you know we will pretend weaknes; and doe
you think we had not cause?   Yes, you tell us you beleeve
it, but it was more weaknes of judgmente, then of hands.
Our weaknes herin is great we confess, therefore we will
bear this check patiently amongst the rest, till God send us
wiser men.   But they which tould you we spent so much
time in discoursing and consulting, &c., their harts can tell
their toungs, they lye."

At the close of the letter to which this was the
reply, Weston had called upon the settlers to assent
to the agreement, about the terms of which there had
been so much dispute at Southampton.   Cushman,
who had come over in the Fortune and seems always
to have acted with Weston, urged them to comply,
and he was supported by letters from those at Leyden: so at last, in the hope of getting further aid in
their present sore need, Bradford and the rest yielded
the points at issue.   They signed their names to the
amended agreement, and sent it out by the Fortune,
which was despatched on her return voyage upon the
13th of December; nor, in their eager desire to conciliate their London partners, did they fail to find a
return cargo for her.   She went back loaded with
clapboards, besides two hogsheads filled with the skins
of the beaver and otter.   But so far as Weston was
concerned, both the signing of the agreement and the
strenuous effort to load the vessel resulted in nothing;

for, in spite of his strong assurances of continued aid,
" he was the first and only man that forsook them,
and that before he so much as heard of the return of
this ship or knew what was done."

It was the middle of February, 1621–2, before the
Fortune reached England, and Weston had then already severed his connection with the Merchant Adventurers. The cause of his so doing is neither clear
nor of moment, though there would seem to have been
trouble in the organization, and a probably not un-
founded distrust of Treasurer Weston. He, too, was
evidently alarmed at the extent to which he had personally become involved in the Plymouth enterprise,
and was not indisposed to secure himself from loss,
— if need be, at the cost of his partners. His idea
seems to have been to send out a private expedition
of his own, with a view to reaping the benefit, on his
individual account, of whatever those of Plymouth
had acquired in the way either of experience or of
profit. Accordingly, as early as January, 1621–2,
he and one other of the Adventurers, a Mr. Beau-
champ by name, purchased a small vessel, called the
Sparrow, and fitted her out for a fishing and trading
voyage ; designing her to be the forerunner of a more
considerable expedition which they proposed to send
out a few weeks later. The company on board the
Sparrow included a few men who were engaged to
leave the vessel on her arrival at the fishing stations
on the coast of Maine, and thence to find their way
by boat to Plymouth, looking up as they went along
some convenient place in which to fix a settlement.

The Sparrow arrived at the Damariscove Islands
early in May, and the party destined for Plymouth
prepared to finish their voyage in an open boat.[1] The

---

[1] iv. *Mass. Hist. Coll.* iv. 478.

reckless want of foresight which characterized all
Weston's undertakings then became manifest, for
none of the men composing this party knew anything
of the coast they were to skirt along, nor had any
pilot been provided. Not only were they expected to
find their own way to Plymouth, but it had been taken
for granted that they would there be supplied with
whatever they might need until the arrival of the main
expedition. The master of the Sparrow not being able
to procure any pilot, his mate, who seems to have been
a dare-devil English sailor, volunteered, and under his
guidance the pioneers set out. They touched at the
Isles of Shoals, and then at Cape Ann. Thence they
struck across to Massachusetts, or Boston, Bay, where
they passed some four or five days exploring. They
now selected for the proposed plantation a site on the
south side of the bay, as in that vicinity they found
the fewest natives ; and then, becoming gradually op-
pressed by the vastness of the surrounding solitude,
which day by day seemed to bring home to them a
more realizing sense of the smallness of their own
number, the party determined to go on to Plymouth.
From lack of acquaintance with the coast the harbor's mouth was missed ; but, as the boat was crossing
from the Gurnet to Manomet, it was sighted in the
offing, and guns were fired as a signal. Hearing
them, the adventurers changed their course and stood
in. They had arrived just in time to be the acciden-
tal means of saving Squanto's life, in the way already
described.

The sense of relief at Plymouth was naturally great
when it became known that the sudden apparition of
the strange boat had no connection with any Indian
troubles. Those who came in it, too, brought letters

and tidings from home, thus breaking a silence of
nearly a year; so, destitute though the newcomers
were, they were cordially welcomed by the scarcely less
destitute settlers. But the letters, long looked for,
were found, when read, to contain cold comfort, — so
cold, indeed, that the magistrates kept it to themselves.
They brought tidings of dissension among the Merchant Adventurers, and made it plain that little further assistance was to be looked for from that source.
There was also a vagueness, a "shufling" as Bradford
expressed it, in the tone of these letters, suggestive
of something underhand; while Weston's scheme for
securing to himself, by means of another and rival
settlement, the fruits of their own patient endurance,
was but thinly veiled under professions of friendliness
and mutual assistance.

Nevertheless, for the time being there was but one
thing to do. It was out of the question to bid the
newcomers be gone; so they were kindly received,
and still further reduced the short commons then prevailing at Plymouth. Indeed, the immediate necessities were at this time so pressing that it was decided a
party under Edward Winslow should accompany the
Sparrow's shallop on its return to the Damariscove
fishing stations, and endeavor there to procure some
supplies. Nor was this mission wholly unsuccessful.
The fishing vessels were, it was true, not over-well
provided themselves; but the story of want and patient endurance, now told, so moved the not over-ac-
tive sympathies of the rough mariners that they vied
with each other in sending the settlers, without price,
everything they could possibly spare; and the provision thus obtained sufficed, when doled out under the
careful husbanding of the magistrates, to keep the

settlement alive until after the harvest. Besides saving Squanto's life, therefore, the arrival of Weston's
shallop had served still another useful end. It was a
revelation, as it were, to the Plymouth people of a
new and before apparently undreamed-of means of
communication with mankind. The Damariscove stations were only some forty leagues from Plymouth,
and each season they were resorted to by as many as
thirty sail. The forlorn Pilgrims now for the first
time learned their way thither. Subsequently they
not only opened through this channel a tolerably regular intercourse with their friends in London and
Leyden, but at a somewhat later day they established
a permanent station of their own on the Kennebec,
where Augusta now is, and there for years carried on
a profitable trade.

Meanwhile, in London, his associates in the Merchant Adventurers had got rid of Weston by buying
out his interest in the company, and he was busy fitting out his own expedition; though, as usual, with
more energy than judgment. He bought two vessels,
the Charity, of one hundred tons, and the Swan, of
thirty. His plan was to have the Charity make voy-
ages to and fro across the Atlantic; she was to carry
men and supplies out, bringing back fish, furs and the
other products of his New England El Dorado. The
smaller vessel meanwhile was to remain at his proposed settlement, to enable his agents there the better
to trade along the coast. So far his scheme was well
devised; but, when it came to organizing it, he showed
both lack of discretion and complete ignorance of the
conditions essential to success. Himself an ingrained
adventurer, eager for gain and over-confident in all
things, he was out of all patience with the discoursing,

arguing and consulting of the Plymouth people. He
cared nothing for religious freedom in the present,
or an empire's future growth. What he wanted was
trade; and he wanted it now. He was convinced, accordingly, that the Leyden expedition had been made
up of unsuitable material, and organized on a wrong
plan. Not only had it been encumbered with women
and children, but its material outlook had been subor-
dinated to religious considerations. In his own enterprise he proposed to have no repetition of these mis-
takes. No families, no women and children, were to
be sent out; only able-bodied men. These, too, were
to be under the immediate direction of his own agents,
who were to have a constant eye to trade, and trade
alone.

As he did not propose to go out himself until another year, he put the expedition under the charge of
his brother Andrew, and his brother-in-law, one Richard Greene. Of Greene nothing is known. Andrew
Weston is described[1] as a headstrong, hot-tempered
young fellow, very prejudiced, on his brother's account, against both the Plymouth people and the
Merchant Adventurers. Clearly he was without experience, and in no way fitted for the work in hand.

Having thus provided a head for his enterprise,
Weston next went to work on its bone and sinew.
Apparently he proceeded much after the fashion of a
recruiting-officer, or some ship-agent picking up a
large crew, for he seems to have sent out into the
streets and alleys of London, and engaged all the
able-bodied men who, having nothing else to do, offered themselves. He himself referred to his company as being largely made up of "rude fellows,"

[1] Bradford, 120.

whose profaneness might scandalize their outward
voyage ; while Thomas Morton, who probably accompanied the party, described them as "stout knaves"
and "men made choice of at all adventures," or, in
other words, as a gang of vagabonds collected at hap-
hazard.[1]   Meanwhile the London correspondents of
the Plymouth people took care to advise them of the
impending visitation.

As it was Weston's plan to trade exclusively on his
own account, it was obviously his interest to cultivate
friendly relations with the colonists, for if possible he
wanted to prevent their looking upon his enterprise
as in any way antagonistic to their own.   Accordingly
he seems to have tried to prevent any letters or information reaching those at Plymouth by his vessels ;
but, in this, he was overreached by two of his former
associates in the company of Merchant Adventurers,
Edward Pickering and William Greene, who, getting
hold of one of his men, induced him to take charge
of a letter from them to Bradford, warning the latter
of Weston's probable design, and of the low and
mercenary character of his people.   For the purpose
of more surely concealing this missive, its bearer was
directed to buy a pair of shoes, and sew it in between
the soles.   In some way Weston got wind of the
thing and intercepted the letter, which he did not
hesitate to open and read,[2] and there found himself
described as one whom his former associates in the

---

[1] *N. E. Canaan,* 106, 117.

[2] It will not do to regard the opening of this letter as additional
evidence of Weston's low and unscrupulous character.   That method
of gaining information seems in the seventeenth century to have been
regarded as perfectly justifiable.   On certain noteworthy occasions
neither Bradford nor Governor Winthrop hesitated to have recourse
to it.   (See Bradford, 173, and Winthrop, i. *57.)

Merchant Adventurers' Company were glad to be rid
of, — " being a man that thought himselfe above the
generall, and not expresing so much the fear of God
as was meete," — while his brother Andrew was set
down as " a heady yong man, and violente." His
purpose, it was further explained, was to get anything
which might be in readiness for shipment at Plymouth
into his vessels, and to appropriate it to his own use.
Though he opened this letter, Weston neither suppressed nor destroyed it. On the contrary, contenting himself with an indignant denial of the impu-
tations on his purpose and good faith, he forwarded
letter and commentary together to those to whom the
first was addressed. One other letter was also smug-
gled over at the same time. It was from Robert
Cushman to Governor Bradford, though it had the
appearance of being written by a wife in England to
her husband at Plymouth, and found its way to its
destination without being intercepted. It confirmed
the warning intimations of Pickering and Greene. In
this letter, too, Weston's former ally, not to say tool,
in his hagglings with the Plymouth people, evinced a
shrewd, trading instinct altogether in advance of anything of the sort which Weston was disposed to con-
cede to his old associates. Said he: — " If they [Wes-
ton's people] offerr to buy anything of you, let it be
shuch as you can spare, and let them give the worth
of it. If they borrow anything of you, let them leave
a good pawne." On the back of the same letter was
a postscript from another friendly hand, in which the
estimate held by Weston and Morton of those composing their company was further confirmed; the writer
describing them as "so base in condition (for the most
parte) as in all apearance not fitt for an honest mans
company."

The fact of Weston's forwarding the letter from
Pickering and Greene after it once came into his
hands is strong evidence that he never had any such
knavish plan as they imputed to him. It would rather
seem to have been his purpose from the beginning to
establish a plantation and private trading-post somewhere in what was then known as the Massachusetts
Bay; and he certainly had a patent covering a grant
of territory there, obtained probably, though it is not
extant and nothing is now known regarding it, from
the Council for New England. Bradford says that
Weston's attention had been drawn to Boston Bay
through letters from Plymouth in which Standish's
September explorations there had been described. He
had also undoubtedly heard of it from William Trevore. This man, it will be remembered, was among
Standish's companions in the expedition of 1621. He
had come out in the Mayflower, not as one of the
Plymouth company, but under an engagement to stay
in the country a year; and, his year ending in November, 1621, he returned to England on the Fortune,
reaching London some time in February, 1621–2.
The Sparrow, carrying Weston's advanced party, had
sailed a month before, and the Charity and Swan, with
his main company, followed about two months later.
In all probability, therefore, Weston's patent was taken
out in March in consequence of information obtained
from Trevore, who at about the same time also described the places he had visited to David Thomson,
an agent of the Council for New England, likewise
then turning over in his mind a plan of emigration.[1]
There can, accordingly, be little doubt that Weston's
expedition was destined to Boston Bay; and it may

[1] *Proc. Mass. Hist. Soc.* May, 1876, 361, 373.

even have been something more than chance which,
during the month of May, carried to those parts the
advance party from the Sparrow, though they undoubtedly had left England before any news of Standish's explorations could have reached there.

The Charity and the Swan left London in company
about the middle of April, 1622, and reached Plymouth towards the end of June, or during the early
days of July. Andrew Weston was apparently in
charge of the larger ship ; and there is reason to suppose that he took with him Thomas Morton, already
mentioned, a sport-loving lawyer of Clifford's Inn, as
well as a born adventurer and humorist. The Charity was bound for Virginia as well as Plymouth;
and, stopping at the latter place only long enough to
land her portion of the threescore " lusty " men
who made up the body of Weston's company, she proceeded on her voyage. Whether Andrew Weston
went in her does not appear ; but Richard Greene remained at Plymouth, and speedily started off in the
Swan to Boston Bay for the purpose of there arrang-
ing for the reception of the others, while Morton, who
had also remained, apparently accompanied him.[1]
The great body of their followers they left at Plymouth, where they soon began to show themselves for
what they were, — a helpless, improvident, and unruly crew. A number of them were sick and required
to be nursed, — a new burden imposed upon the already overworked women, — while the rest developed

[1] Morton's statement is as follows: " In the Moneth of Iune,
Anno Salutis 1622, it was my chaunce to arrive in the parts of New
England with 30. Servants, and provision of all sorts fit for a plan-
tation : and whiles our howses were building, I did indeavour to take
a survey of the Country." (*New English Canaan,* 59; see, also,
Prince Soc. ed. 6.)

a decided disinclination for labor, combined (for it
was now July) with a marked appreciation of Indian
corn, which they found, though green and unprofit-
able, very "eatable and pleasant to taste;" not that
those who planted the corn were negligent in watching it, or that the magistrates were slow in meting out
punishment to the transgressors, but, "though many
were well whipt for a few ears of corne, yet hunger
made others to venture." Under these circumstances,
what with sickness and fasting and flogging, there
was nothing to occasion surprise in the fact that
neither planter nor pilgrim thereafter recalled the
memory of that summer at Plymouth with gratifica-
tion. The latter looked anxiously forward to the day
when God in his providence would disburden them of
the former; while the former requited with a language
rather of reviling than of gratitude the stern, unsym-
pathetic care expended upon them.

At length, apparently some time in August, the
Swan reappeared from Boston Bay. Greene and his
party had, it would seem, been received in the most
friendly way by the Indians, who, few in numbers and
cowed in spirit, gladly welcomed those whom they
hoped would prove their protectors against still powerful neighbors; for their dealings with the Plymouth
people had removed from the minds of the Massachusetts all fears of the whites, and they were sincerely
anxious to have a permanent settlement near them;
indeed, they had already begged Standish to establish
one. Weston's agents therefore, so far as a location
was concerned, had but to choose.[1] Exchanging presents with Aberdecest, the local sachem, they finally
chose for their place of settlement a site known by the

[1] Young, *Chron. of Pilg.* 298; IV. *Mass. Hist. Coll.* iv. 481

Indians as Wessagusset, near the mouth of a little
stream called the Monatiquot, which empties into one
of the southern estuaries of Boston Bay.[1] While the
fewness of the Indians in the immediate vicinity was
undoubtedly a consideration, the choice of this spot
was probably due quite as much to the fact that it lay
south of all the principal streams separating the Massachusetts from the Plymouth territory, thus making
intercourse by land between the settlements comparatively easy. The site of the new plantation having
been fixed upon and the necessary preparations made,
prompt measures were taken for the transfer thither
of all those of the company who were well enough to
be moved ; for a number of them had still to be left
behind under the care of that Samuel Fuller already
mentioned, who, from the time of the first landing to
1634, was the surgeon and physician at Plymouth,
and, as such, was "a great help and comforte unto
them ; as in his facultie, so otherwise, being a deacon
of the church, a man godly and forward to doe good."
Dr. Fuller's treatment seems in the present case to
have proved successful ; for, later in the season, the
invalids joined their companions at Wessagusset. The
Charity had meanwhile returned from Virginia ; and
now Weston's enterprise might be looked upon as
fairly started.

But scarcely were the newcomers seated in the place
they had chosen than ominous rumors began to reach
Plymouth, the poor Massachusetts complaining bitterly of them, alleging abusive treatment and theft.
It was not in the power of the Plymouth magistrates

[1] The site of Weston's settlement was found indicated on Winthrop's map of 1634, discovered in London by Henry F. Waters. It
was immediately north of the glacial ridge known as Hunt's Hill on
the south side of the Weymouth Fore-river. *Proc. Mass. Hist. Soc.*
Series II. vii. 24–30.

to do more in the premises than offer anxious remonstrances; and these, it hardly needs to be said, were
of little avail. Thus matters went on until early in
October. The Charity then returned to England,
Andrew Weston and Thomas Morton, it would seem,
going in her, while Richard Greene was left in charge
of the plantation. He was, it is said, fairly provided
with supplies; but he does not seem to have been
competent, and his followers were wasteful. Accordingly while the Charity was still almost within sound-
ings, and before the winter's ice had begun to make,
there was scarcity at Wessagusset. Realizing at last
the situation, and his own lack of capacity to deal
with it, Greene wrote to Bradford proposing a joint
expedition in search of food, — he furnishing the
vessel, while the Plymouth people were to provide
commodities for barter. A written agreement was
entered into on this basis, and by the middle of October everything was in readiness for a voyage to the
south side of Cape Cod. But the expedition seemed
fated. At first Greene, who had gone down to Plymouth on the Swan, fell suddenly ill there and died.
He was succeeded in command at Wessagusset by a
man named John Saunders, who was apparently even
more incompetent than his predecessor. Still, realizing the pressure of growing want, Saunders' first act
in authority seems to have been the writing of another
letter to Plymouth urging the immediate prosecution
of the voyage. So, as soon as might be after burying
Greene, the Swan was started off, Standish going in
command and Squanto acting as pilot. This was the
expedition referred to at the close of the preceding
chapter, — that in the course of which Squanto died.
It did not start until after the month of November

had begun, according to the present calendar, and the
season was late for a passage round Cape Cod. The
Swan therefore encountered easterly winds and heavy
weather, and was forced to put back. Again the
party started; and again it was compelled to return.
The combined exposure, fatigue and anxiety seem to
have proved too much even for Standish, who now
broke down under an attack of fever and gave up the
command, Bradford taking his place. The outlook
was bad. Though it was yet not the close of November, — though the winter was wholly before them, —
the want was hardly less severe at Plymouth than at
Wessagusset. Indeed, it is probable that the scarcity
was greatest at Plymouth; but in that patient, frugal
and well-ordered community everything was eked out
to the utmost, while at Wessagusset little thought was
bestowed on the morrow. But frugality and patience
could only mitigate the growing need, and the Plymouth people required no urging from without to be-
stir themselves; so once more the expedition started,
but only to give those composing it a rough experience of the " dangerous shoulds and roring breakers "
which two years before had frightened the captain of
the Mayflower into Provincetown, and which have
since made what is called the back side of Cape Cod
a terror to mariners. At last they found themselves
off Monomoy Point, on Pollock's Rip, and were in no
little danger of foundering; but the wind and tide
apparently favored them, and the master of the Swan,
thoroughly frightened, was glad enough to find himself safe in Chatham harbor. Here a party landed,
and Bradford, through the medium of Squanto, endeavored to establish friendly relations with the Indians. These were few in number, and at first very

shy ; but when at last they were persuaded the strangers only wished to trade, they overcame their fear
sufficiently to give them some venison and other food,
and in the course of a day or two their bartering in-
stincts were sufficiently worked upon to induce them
to part with eight hogsheads of corn and beans from
their scanty store. Encouraged by this success, the
party determined to attempt once more the southern
passage, but Squanto's illness and sudden death,
which have already been described, put an end to the
project by depriving the party at once of its pilot and
its interpreter ; so, the wind setting in the right quarter, they rounded Cape Cod again and laid their
course directly for Boston Bay. Here they got nothing. Not only did they find the savages suffering
from a new outbreak of the pestilence, but the poor
creatures were bitter in their complaints of the Wessagusset people. They were not only dying daily, but
they were daily robbed. Nor was this all. Weston's
outspoken contempt for the trading capacity of Plymouth people to the contrary notwithstanding, it was
apparent that the ignorance of his own representatives
had spoiled the market. They gave as much for a
quart of corn as had before sufficed to buy a beaver
skin.

Leaving Boston Bay, the expedition now went to
the inside of Cape Cod, to see if anything could be
picked up along the shores of what are now the towns
of Eastham, Yarmouth and Barnstable. The stormy
weather continued, and the Swan was at one time in
no little danger of being cast away ; indeed, the shallop which the Plymouth people had brought along, to
carry what was bought from the shore to the vessel,
was swept off, and so damaged that, when found al-

most buried in the sand, it was no longer serviceable. As there was no carpenter in the party, it became necessary to leave both corn and boat in charge of the natives until at some other time they could return and fetch them away. The partners now separated. Inasmuch as some twenty-eight or thirty hogsheads of corn and beans had been secured, the expedition could not, in view of the rough weather which had been encountered, be considered otherwise than successful. It would seem, nevertheless, that either the discomfort on board the Swan must have been very great, or the company little congenial; for, rather than go back in her, Governor Bradford and his party, sending word to those on board to meet them at Plymouth, set out on foot for a fifty-mile midwinter tramp home. They presently arrived there safe, though weary and footsore, and, three days later, the Swan made her appearance. An equal division was made of the food the expedition had secured, and the Wessagusset party returned to their plantation; but in January another joint expedition started for Eastham, Standish, who had meanwhile recovered, being now in command. Besides being stormy, it was bitterly cold, and the suffering from exposure was aggravated by insufficiency of food; but the shallop lost in November was recovered, and a portion of the supplies then collected was secured. Another division was made, and once more the Swan returned to her moorings in the Weymouth fore-river.

Affairs at Wessagusset now rapidly went from bad to worse. From the beginning to the end, those living there merely demeaned themselves after the manner of their kind. Upon their first arrival, seeing the weakness of the plague-stricken savages and conscious

of their own strength, they had been arrogant and
abusive. It was said that they meddled with the
Indian women; what was far worse in the savages'
eyes, they had certainly stolen their corn. As the winter increased in its severity, so did the scarcity, and
at last gaunt famine stared the settlers in the face.
Meanwhile their bearing towards the savages had
passed from one extreme to the other. Day by day
their arrogance and self-confidence vanished, until,
ceasing by degrees to be careless purchasers, they appeared as naturally as possible in the more congenial
character of cunning thieves. Stricken, and but the
shadows of their former selves though they were, the
Massachusetts Indians soon realized what this change
meant, and their demeanor altered accordingly. From
cowering before the whites they began to despise them
and domineer over them.

Alarmed at the threatening aspect of affairs, Saunders towards the middle of February renewed his efforts to purchase food. The Indians refused to sell,
saying — no doubt truly enough — they had none to
spare. Then he determined to take by force what he
could get in no other way, and began to prepare for
the hostilities sure to ensue. The plantation at Wessagusset, like that at Plymouth, seems to have consisted of a few rude log buildings surrounded by a
pale, or stockade, in which were several entrances protected by gates. This stockade was now strengthened
and perfected, and all the entrances save one secured.
But, before resorting to open violence, Saunders had
sufficient good sense to let the Plymouth people know
what he intended. They had at least to be put upon
their guard. Accordingly he sent a letter to Governor Bradford informing him of the severe straits

they were in at Wessagusset, and of what they proposed to do. Restitution at some future time of whatever might now be taken was, of course, promised.

Such an unprovoked outrage as that now suggested could not fail to complicate very dangerously the relations between the Plymouth people and the natives. Seriously alarmed, Governor Bradford at once called the elders into council, and among them they drew up an answer to Saunders' communication, but addressed to his company as a whole, which they all signed. In it they labored in characteristic fashion to divert those to whom they were writing from the course proposed. They gravely pointed out that this course was not only in contravention of the laws of God and of nature, but that it was calculated to bring to nought King James' policy, both as respects the enlargement of his dominions and " the propagation of the knowledge and law of God, and the glad tidings of salvation " among the heathen. Leaving high considerations of state and religion, they then came to particulars. The attention of those at Wessagusset was called to the fact that their case was no worse, if so bad, as that of Plymouth, where they had but little corn left, and were compelled to sustain life on groundnuts, clams and mussels ; " all which they [at Wessagusset] had in great abundance, — yea, oysters also, which we [at Plymouth] wanted." Therefore, it was argued, the plea of necessity could not be maintained. But, finally, those who put their names to the paper came to the real point in the case, and flatly informed their neighbors that, in case recourse was had to violence, those guilty of the violence would have to take care of themselves, and need look for no support from Plymouth ; and, moreover, if they escaped the savages

they would not escape the gallows as soon as some
special agent of the crown should come over to inves-
tigate the proceeding. In addition to this general
and public reply, Bradford by the same messenger
wrote privately to Saunders, warning him that he, as
the recognized head of the company, would be held to
a personal accountability, no matter who else might
escape; and so, in a friendly way, advised him to desist in time.

These energetic remonstrances had the desired effect, and, abandoning all idea of force, Saunders now
determined to start at once for the fishing stations at
Monhegan, there to procure food. Before doing so
he first went to Plymouth ; and the utterly destitute
condition of his party was made plain by the fact that
the supplies on hand did not suffice to victual a crew
for the Swan on a short voyage of some forty leagues
to the coast of Maine. Leaving her, therefore, at
Wessagusset, Saunders set out, though the winter
could not yet be said to be over, in an open shallop,
Governor Bradford letting him have a small supply
of corn. Considering the season, the coast and the
frail craft in which he went, the attempt was a perilous one, and whether he ever reached his destination
does not appear, for his name is not again mentioned.
Certainly he never returned to Wessagusset. Perhaps, finding himself unable to obtain supplies at the
fishing stations, he had stayed there awaiting the arrival of the fleet, rightly thinking it worse than useless for him to go back empty-handed.

CHAPTER V.

THE WESSAGUSSET HANGING.

A few days after Saunders left for Monhegan, Standish set out on another of his winter excursions in search of food, going to Manomet, in what is now Sandwich. During the expedition of the previous November, Governor Bradford had bought some corn at this place, but, owing to the loss of the shallop, had been unable to ship it. He had accordingly left it in charge of the savages; and this corn Standish now meant to bring away. Leaving some two or three men in charge of his shallop, and taking with him as many more, he landed and went some distance inland to the habitation of Canacum, the local sachem. He had not been there long before he noticed that he was much less hospitably treated than Bradford had been, and presently a couple of Massachusetts Indians made their appearance, — one of whom, Wituwamat by name, the Plymouth men well knew. A significant interview between him and Canacum then took place in Standish's presence.

Talking violently and incoherently in his Indian dialect, Wituwamat drew a knife, which hung about his neck, from its sheath, and presented it to his host. He spoke, as it subsequently appeared, of the outrages perpetrated on the natives at Wessagusset, and of a conspiracy which had been formed to destroy the settlement there. The object of his visit now was to induce the Cape Cod Indians to join in it, and he was urging Canacum to take advantage of the occasion, which so unexpectedly offered, to cut off Standish and his party. The knife about his neck was one which he had obtained from Weston's people.[1]

It is, of course, impossible to form any estimate of the military capacity of Miles Standish, for it was never his fortune to have the conduct of any considerable affair. His field of operations and the forces under his control were always small, and it may well be that he would have proved unequal to anything larger. Nevertheless, both on this and on other occasions presently to be described, he showed himself something more than merely a born fighter; for he rose to an equality with difficult and dangerous situations, and he did it through the easy, because instinctive, exercise of one of the most important attributes of all great commanders, — a correct insight into the methods and characteristics of the men immediately opposed to him. He knew what the occasion called for when the occasion presented itself. He did not need time to think the thing out; nor, seeing what the occasion called for, did he hesitate. He acted as quickly as he thought. With him it was not a word and a blow, it was a glance and a blow: but the eye was true and the blow well directed and hard; for, in advance of delivering it, he had measured his opponent correctly.

Before he came to New England the Plymouth captain had never seen a savage: but, once he came in contact with a savage, his instinct told him, and told him correctly, how a savage should be dealt with; and he seems never to have made a mistake. In the

[1] Young, *Chron. of Pilg.* 310–12.

presence of savages he always bore himself boldly.
He seems to have been gifted by nature with a quick
ear as well as eye, for he was already more familiar
than any one else at Plymouth with the Indian speech;
but now he could make nothing of Wituwamat's fierce
harangue. It sounded to him like gibberish; but gibberish or not, he saw that harm was intended. It
was his custom always to treat the Indians he met in
friendly fashion, but he suffered no liberties to be
taken, and above all never evinced the slightest sign
of fear. If they stole from him, he compelled immediate restitution; if they insulted him, he fiercely resented it. The neglect with which he was now treated
by Canacum was in strong contrast to the consideration which the sachem showed towards Wituwamat.
It was an Indian insult. Accordingly, expressing
himself in angry and defiant fashion, Standish made
ready to return to his boat. Nothing further seems
to have taken place at the moment, and the Indian
women were induced by some trifling reward to carry
the corn down to the shore. There the party had to
wait until morning, and the night which followed was
probably as anxious a night as Standish ever passed.
The air bit shrewdly and it was very cold. Against
Wituwamat in particular he was, as the sequel showed,
meditating dire vengeance, and the wrath he was nursing may to a degree have counteracted the effects of
the piercing wind from which he in vain sought shelter; but the events of the afternoon had alarmed him,
and he wanted to get back to Plymouth with the least
possible delay. The immediate situation, also, was
by no means free from danger. A mere handful of
men, far from home on an exposed coast in the dead
of winter, they were surrounded by savages bent on

their destruction. Nor were they alone. Among the
others gathered at Canacum's lodge was a Paomet,
or Cape Cod, Indian, whom they had seen before, but
the oppressive friendliness of whose carriage now was
extremely suspicious. Not only had he insisted on
coming down to the shore with them, but he had voluntarily even carried some of the corn, an ignominious act for a male Indian. Neither, after so doing,
had he returned to Canacum's lodge in company with
the women; but, making a pretext of the cold, he remained with the Plymouth party, crouching before
their fire. Under the circumstances it is not matter
for wonder, therefore, that Standish rested not at all
that night, " but either walked or turned himself to
and fro at the fire; " nor that, when the waking savage asked him why he did not sleep, he answered him
that — " He knew not well, but had no desire at all to
rest." But the watches even of that long winter night
slowly wore themselves away without further cause for
alarm; and, the next day, the wind coming fair, the
party got safely back to Plymouth.

Meanwhile, during Standish's absence, tidings had
come of the dangerous sickness of Massasoit. Winslow was at once despatched to visit him, with the Indian Hobamack as a guide, and arrived only just in
time to save his life. The unfortunate man was lying
in his habitation, blind and almost unconscious, while
six or eight women were violently chafing his arms,
legs and thighs to keep heat in him, and a crowd of
men, engaged in their incantations, were, as Winslow
described it, " making such a hellish noise as it dis-
tempered us that were well, and therefore unlike to
ease him that was sick." With the aid of a little
sensible treatment, nature got the better of the dis-

order; but Massasoit, naturally attributing his recovery to the skill of his visitors, could not sufficiently express his gratitude. The sense of it was still fresh when, on the morning of the fourth day of his visit, Winslow prepared to set out on his way back to Plymouth. Seeing him about to depart, Massasoit then took aside Hobamack, who was one of his own men, and told him of a conspiracy which had been formed to destroy the Wessagusset settlement. All the tribes of southeastern Massachusetts, he said, had been induced to join in it, and he had himself been earnestly solicited to do so during the earlier days of his sickness. Among others concerned in this plot, he named the people of Paomet and Manomet. In true Indian style he now urged decisive action, advising the Plymouth people " to kill the men of Massachusetts who were the authors of this intended mischief." All this Hobamack, as he was bid, repeated to Winslow on the way back; so that, when the latter reached home and there met the party just returned from Manomet, the presence of the two Massachusetts men at Canacum's lodge was accounted for. The full significance of the treatment Standish had received became apparent.

There could no longer be any doubt of the existence of a widespread Indian conspiracy. As yet it was directed only against the Wessagusset settlement; but it needed neither Wituwamat's defiant action nor Massasoit's warning to awaken the Plymouth people to the fact that their own fate was involved in the fate of their neighbors. Should the warwhoop ring in triumph over the smoking ruins of Wessagusset, the woods back of Plymouth would not long be quiet. To appreciate the effect of this sudden revelation of danger upon the minds and nerves of the settlers, it must be remembered that the Virginia massacre had occurred exactly one year before, and that all its harrowing details, freshly brought by the Charity and other vessels on their return from the scene of it, must have been uppermost in the mind of every one within the Plymouth stockade, and the constant theme of discussion. They knew whatever history now tells of the incidents of that dread 22d of March, 1622, when at one and the same instant a merciless blow, which had been planned with impenetrable secrecy, fell upon an unsuspecting people.[1] They knew how indiscriminate the murder had been, how neither age nor sex had been spared, what atrocities had been committed on the quick and the dead. The Virginia community at the time it sustained this blow was a large one compared to what their own was now. The very dead in the massacre exceeded the whole number of the Plymouth settlers by nearly threefold; and yet, up to the hour of the Virginia attack, the savages had cunningly borne the aspect of friendliness.

So great and abiding had been the alarm caused at Plymouth by the knowledge of these things that, with the famine of the past winter and forebodings for the next never absent from their minds, the people there during that summer of want and weakness had devoted half their time and strength to building a fort of refuge. But, even when their fort was completed, they remained at most but a pitiful handful, — not sevenscore, all told, — a speck, as it were, of civilized life between the sea on the one side and that impenetrable forest, within which lurked the savage, on the other. It was true the pestilence had left but few

[1] Bancroft, i. 142 (ed. 1876).

Indians in their immediate vicinity; but not far away were the Narragansetts, an unscathed and warlike tribe, whose missive of "arrows lapped in a rattlesnake's skin" had already come to them as a challenge, and in regard to whose movements and intentions rumor was constantly busy.

There is something appalling in the consciousness of utter isolation. The settlers at Plymouth were but men and women, and their children were with them, and it was impossible they should not exaggerate rather than diminish the danger. Fortunately they were a stolid, unimaginative race; and, even though directly from the busy life and complete security of Holland, the neighborhood of the forest seems to have soon become a thing customary and little alarming to them. Simple, straightforward and self-reliant, to them sufficient unto the day were the labors and dangers thereof. Above all else, perhaps, they were held up by that strength of endurance — that staying power, if so it may be called — which is always found associated with any deep religious feeling bred of independent thought. The grateful Massasoit, moreover, had now done for them what another of his race had done for Jamestown; and, with the experience of Jamestown fresh in mind, to be forewarned at Plymouth was to be forearmed.

By this time it was the end of March, and the day for the annual election of magistrates was at hand. When it came about, Governor Bradford made known the situation in open court, and it was there anxiously debated. Finally, without reaching any decision in public meeting, the matter was left in the hands of three men, Bradford the governor, Isaac Allerton the assistant, and Miles Standish; and these three were

authorized to call into their councils whomsoever else
they saw fit, and to do whatever the common safety
might seem to require. They decided on immediate
and decisive action. Having so decided, they dismissed all scruples from their minds and determined
to deal with the savages after a savage's own fashion.
Plot was to be met with plot.

The plan of campaign was a simple one. Standish
was to go at once to Wessagusset, taking with him as
many men as he thought sufficient to enable him to
hold his own against all the Massachusetts. When
there, pretending that he was come, as he had repeatedly come before, to trade, he was first to make known
his purpose to the settlers, and then, acting in concert
with them, was to entrap the conspirators and kill
them. The last words of his instructions showed
clearly enough that they were framed by himself, and
that, as revengeful as he was choleric, he retained a
fresh recollection of the scene in the lodge of the sachem of Manomet. He was enjoined to forbear his
blow, if possible, " till such time as he could make
sure [of] Wituwamat, that bloody and bold villain before spoken of; whose head he had order to bring
with him, that he might be a warning and terror to
all of that disposition."

While these events were taking place at Plymouth,
there was at Wessagusset a complete and wretched
unconsciousness of impending disaster. Under the
pressure of suffering, all pretence even at order and
discipline would seem to have been abandoned after
Saunders left for Monhegan. Those composing the
company no longer lived together within the stockade;
but, hunger overcoming the sense of fear, they had
divided themselves, and were scattered about near the

Indian villages, in which, for a handful of food, they
performed the most menial of services, degrading
themselves into mere hewers of wood and drawers of
water. Some had already bartered away their clothes
and their blankets ; and soon, of course, insufficient
food and exposure brought on disease. Gradually
many of them became so weakened that they could
hardly continue the search for something wherewith
life might be sustained. What in the way of nourish-
ment they could have found at that season it is not
easy to make out, for the winter had been a severe
one, and the ground, full of frost, was covered with
snow and ice. It is said they lived mainly on nuts
and shell-fish, and that one miserable wretch, while
digging for the latter, got caught in the mud, and, not
having strength to extricate himself, was drowned by
the rising tide. Yet, judging by the mortality among
them, their sufferings, as compared with those of the
Mayflower's people during the winter of their arrival,
would not seem to have been great. At Plymouth,
out of more than one hundred persons who composed
the entire company in December, 1620, scarce fifty
remained alive in April, 1621. At Wessagusset, during the winter of 1622–3, ten only out of sixty are
reported to have died. It is true that in the one case
there were many women and children, while in the
other all were able-bodied men ; yet, under the circumstances, the proportion of one to six cannot be
looked upon as an excessive or, indeed, even as a
large mortality. Considering who they were, and
what they had to go through, it is, perhaps, rather
matter for surprise that all of them did not die.

   The bearing of the savages had meanwhile become
such as was naturally to be expected. " Rude fel-

lows " at best, Weston's people were never calculated
to command respect, and it was some time since they
had ceased to inspire fear. Now they were objects of
mere hatred and contempt. They counted the greater
number, but the savages were the masters. As masters, too, these latter did not confine themselves to
threats and insults. On the contrary, " many times
as they lay thus scattered abroad, and had set on a pot
with ground-nuts or shell-fish, when it was ready the
Indians would come and eat it up. And when night
came, whereas some of them had a sorry blanket, or
such like, to lap themselves in, the Indians would take
it and let the other lie all night in the cold." If
treatment of this kind was resented, the savages
threatened the settlers, or flung dust in their faces, or
even struck at them with their knives.

The natives, moreover, on their side, had good
grounds of complaint. Wretchedly poor, even for
New England Indians, they had nothing but a few furs,
and hardly food wherewith to sustain life. Yet they
had been outraged, and they were still robbed. They
had complained to the Plymouth people, but their
wrongs were unredressed. Under these circumstances
the Indians showed in their conduct a self-restraint
and respect for persons which, had the position been
reversed, would assuredly have been looked for in
vain among Europeans. When pilferers were caught
in the very act of stealing the hidden seed-corn, instead of inflicting punishment themselves on the spot,
the Massachusetts brought the wrong-doers to the
plantation, and delivered them up to be dealt with by
their own people. But whippings and confinement
could not hold in restraint thieves who were starving.
Again the hidden stores were broken into, and again

with angry threats the malefactor was brought back to the block-house. Thoroughly frightened now, the settlers told the savages to take their prisoner and to deal with him as they saw fit. This they refused to do, insisting that the settlers should punish their own thieves. His companions thereupon took the culprit out, and, in full sight of those he had robbed, hanged him before their stockade.

This was that famous Wessagusset hanging, which passed into literature as a jest, and then, received back into history as a traditional fact, was long used as a gibe and reproach against New England. It happened in this wise : — Thomas Morton, who, as it has already been surmised,[1] came out with young Weston in the Charity in June and returned to England in her with him in October, published, some fifteen years later, an account of his experiences in New England. Though he did not, it would appear, care to dwell upon his connection with Weston's abortive enterprise, for the obvious reason that he was then, as will presently be seen,[2] a hanger-on of those with whom the very name of Weston was a scandal, he could hardly fail at times incidentally to refer to it. Of this particular episode of the hanging he gave the following characteristic account : —

" One amongst the rest, an able bodied man that ranged the woodes to see what it would afford, lighted by accident on an Indian barne, and from thence did take a capp full of corne; the salvage owner of it, finding by the foote some English had bin there, came to the Plantation and made complaint after this manner.

" The cheife Commander of the Company one this occasion called a Parliament of all his people, but those that

[1] *Supra,* 59.   [2] *Infra,* 163, n., 268, 277.

were sicke and ill at ease. And wisely now they must consult upon this huge complaint, that a privy knife or stringe of beades would well enough have qualified, and Edward Iohnson was a spetiall judge of this businesse ; the fact was there in repetition ; construction made that it was fellony, and by the Lawes of England punished with death, and this in execution must be put for an example, and likewise to appease the Salvage ; when straight wayes one arose, mooved as it were with some compassion, and said hee could not well gaine say the former sentence, yet hee had conceaved within the compasse of his braine an Embrion, that was of spetiall consequence to be delivered and cherished ; hee said that it would most aptly serve to pacifie the Salvages complaint, and save the life of one that might, (if neede should be,) stand them in some good steede, being younge and stronge, fit for resistance against an enemy, which might come unexpected for any thinge they knew. The Oration made was liked of every one, and hee intreated to proceede to shew the meanes how this may be performed : sayes hee, you all agree that one must die, and one shall die ; this younge mans cloathes we will take of, and put upon one that is old and impotent, a sickly person that cannot escape death, such is the disease one him confirmed that die hee must ; put the younge mans cloathes on this man, and let the sick person be hanged in the others steede : Amen sayes one, and so sayes many more.

"And this had like to have prooved their finall sentence, and, being there confirmed by Act of Parliament to after ages for a precedent. But that one, with a ravenus voyce, begunne to croake and bellow for revenge, and put by that conclusive motion, alledging such deceipts might be a meanes hereafter to exasperate the mindes of the complaininge Salvages, and that by his death the Salvages should see their zeale to Iustice ; and therefore hee should die : this was concluded : yet neverthelesse a scruple did represent itself unto their mindes, which was, — how they should

doe to get the mans good wil? This was indeede a spetiall obstacle: for without that, they all agreed, it would be
dangerous for any man to attempt the execution of it, lest
mischiefe should befall them every man; hee was a person
that in his wrath did seeme to be a second Sampson, able to
beate out their branes with the jawbone of an Asse: therefore they called the man, and by perswation got him fast
bound in jest; and then hanged him up hard by in good
earnest, who with a weapon, and at liberty, would have put
all those wise judges of this Parliament to a pittifull *non
plus* (as it hath beene credibly reported), and made the
cheife Iudge of them all buckell to him." [1]

Thirty years after the publication of the "New English Canaan," when its author had long been dead and
the book itself was forgotten, Butler's famous satire
of "Hudibras" appeared. In speaking of this work
Hallam has remarked, in his "Literary History of Europe," that the inexhaustible wit of the author "is supplied from every source of reading and observation.
But these sources are often so unknown to the reader
that the wit loses its effect through the obscurity of
its allusions." [2] The truth of this criticism was strik-
ingly illustrated in the present instance. Either the
author of "Hudibras" had at some time in the
course of his reading come across the "New English
Canaan," or he had met Thomas Morton and heard
him tell the story, which, as a highly utilitarian suggestion of vicarious atonement, appealed to Butler's
sense of humor and thereafter lingered in his memory.
Moreover, while in 1664 the Puritans of New England were fair game, whatever Samuel Butler found
was his; and so, making, as a thing of course, those

[1] *N. E. Canaan*, B. III. ch. iv.
[2] *Lit. Hist. of Europe*, Part IV. ch. v. § 23.

improvements of fact which literary exigencies demanded, the incident, as finally transmuted by his
wit, appeared in the following form in what long continued to be one of the most popular and generally
read of English books: —

> " Our Brethren of New-England use
> Choice malefactors to excuse,
> And hang the Guiltless in their stead,
> Of whom the Churches have less need;
> As lately 't happened: In a town
> There liv'd a Cobler, and but one,
> That out of Doctrine could cut Use,
> And mend men's lives as well as shoes.
> This precious Brother having slain,
> In times of peace, an Indian,
> (Not out of malice, but mere zeal,
> Because he was an Infidel),
> The mighty Tottipottymoy
> Sent to our Elders an envoy,
> Complaining sorely of the breach
> Of league held forth by Brother Patch,
> Against the articles in force
> Between both churches, his and ours,
> For which he craved the Saints to render
> Into his hands, or hang th' offender;
> But they maturely having weigh'd
> They had no more but him o' th' trade,
> (A man that served them in a double
> Capacity, to teach and cobble),
> Resolv'd to spare him; yet to do
> The Indian Hoghan Moghan too
> Impartial justice, in his stead did
> Hang an old Weaver that was bed-rid."

But the real humor of the thing was yet to come.
The actual hanging took place in 1623. When,
nearly half a century later, its memory was thus ac-
cidentally revived, the Cavalier reaction was at its
height; and everything which tended to make the
Puritans and Puritanism either odious or contemptible was eagerly laid hold of. They had become the

target for ribald jesting, — the standing butt of the
day. The New England provinces also, and Massachusetts in particular, were known chiefly as the place
of refuge of the chosen people ; — there alone did they
retain a secure ascendency. Morton's absurd fiction,
as improved and embellished by Butler, was accordingly not only laughed over as a good jest forever,
but, gradually passing into a tradition, it seems at
last [1] to have even assumed its place as one of those
historical incidents, vaguely but currently accepted as
facts, which periodically reappear in spite of every
effort to put an end to them. Such were, and are,
the famous Blue Laws of Connecticut ; [2] and, again,
that limitation which prevented lords of the manor in
feudal times from killing more than two serfs, after
the hunt, for foot-warming purposes ; [3] or, finally (a
yet more familiar example in later history), that dramatic sinking of the Vengeur, which not even Carlyle's exposure has sufficed to exorcise. [4]

[1] *N. E. Canaan*, Prince Society Publications, 96, 251, n.
[2] Trumbull, *Blue Laws True and False*, 44.
[3] Carlyle, *French Revolution*, B. I. ch. 2 ; New York *Nation* (No.
338), December 21, 1871, p. 400.   " *Was it ' Serf ' or ' Cerf ' ?* "
[4] Verne, *Twenty Thousand Leagues under the Sea*, P. II. ch. 20.

CHAPTER VI.

THE SMOKING FLAX BLOOD-QUENCHED.

IT has already been mentioned that the winter of 1622-3 was one of at least the average New England severity. Beginning with a succession of storms in November, the harbors had been filled with ice until early March, while the snow still lay upon the ground in April.[1] In all its leading features, the wintry scene at Wessagusset must then have been what it now is. The rolling hills into which the country is broken stood out against each other and the sky, offering to the view stretches of dazzling snow against which black masses of the leafless forest were sharply outlined. Groves and clumps of savin fringed the shore and crested the hills to the south and west; while northward lay the island-studded bay, an expanse of snow and ice, broken here and there by patches of water, which, according as the sky was obscured or clear, showed inky blackness or a cold steel-blue. Immediately in front of the plantation, the swift flow and ebb of the tide must, for long weeks, have now lifted the ice until it was high upon the marshes, and then let it fall until it rested on the flats, or lay piled in huge, broken cakes in the inlets or upon the beach. The solitude and the silence were intense; for at that season both the forest and the air were devoid of animal life, unless now and again the stillness was

[1] Young, *Chron. of Pilg.* 302, 308; IV. *Mass. Hist. Coll.* iv. 482-3.

broken by the howl of a wolf, or a flock of carrion-crows were seen to wing their clumsy way in search of food.

Neither, in the case of Weston's settlement, was the presence of ice and snow merely a cause of tedium and discouragement; for, while the latter lay among the trees, making it very difficult to search for nuts and roots, the former so covered the salt marshes and beach that it must for considerable periods have been quite impossible to get at the shell-fish. While the Wessagusset people were thus cut off from their two principal sources of supply, their stock of powder had also run low; nor, mere sixteenth century London vagabonds, were they familiar with the haunts and habits of game. So there was little left for them to do through the long winter months but to hang, hungry and shivering, about the fires in their log-huts, the mud-sealed walls of which offered but a poor protection against the outer cold. And so, with the ice-bound river before them and the snow-clad wilderness behind, they awaited, with what patience men both freezing and starving could, the slow approach of spring.

The settlers mingled freely with the Indians, hanging about their villages by day and sleeping in their huts at night, thus affording them every possible advantage in case of sudden attack; but, when the feelings of hostility which had slowly been excited at length ripened into a plot, it was not only cunningly devised, but also well concealed. The utter destruction of the settlement was proposed; and to assure this it was necessary for the savages to seize, at one and the same moment, not only the stockade and the block-house within it, but also the Swan, which lay at her moorings in the river. There would then be no place of refuge for the scattered settlers, and they could be destroyed in detail and at leisure. In furtherance of their design the Indians, it would seem, gradually edged up towards the stockade, moving their wigwams nearer and nearer to it. At the same time they were busy constructing canoes, in which latter work they were aided by some of their intended victims.[1] By this time one at least of the settlers had become thoroughly alarmed.[2] This was Phinehas Pratt, who, coming over in the Swallow, had been among the six who afterwards in May reached Plymouth in the shallop. He was now bent on making his escape from Wessagusset. The journey he proposed for himself was both difficult and dangerous. The distance was not great, — hardly, indeed, more than twenty-five miles, — but the way was through so complete a wilderness that a few years later this region became known throughout the province as the Ragged Plain, it was such a "strange labyrinth of unbeaten bushy wayes in the wooddy wildernes."[3] It had apparently been completely depopulated by the plague of 1617; and since then the underbrush had not been burned away, the frequent watercourses stopping such fires as were set. Accordingly it was now become a tangled undergrowth of bushes and brambles growing over an upland country, interspersed with swamps and cut by running streams.

Pratt may possibly have made the same journey before, though this is not probable; and now, as will be seen, he almost immediately lost his way. He had

---

[1] Young, *Chron. of Pilg.* 342.
[2] iv. *Mass. Hist. Coll.* iv. 482.
[3] Wood, *Prospect*, 13, 61.

neither a guide nor a compass. It was the end of
March, it is true, and the rigor of the winter was
broken; but great belts of snow were still lying on
the north sides of the hills and in the hollows, and he
was not only insufficiently clad, but weak from want
of food. The sense of danger overcoming all fear, he
made up a small pack and got ready to set out. His
first object was to steal away unobserved by the
savages. Taking a hoe in his hand, therefore, as if he
were going out in search of nuts or to dig for clams,
he very early on the morning of what is now the
first of April left the stockade, and made his way
directly towards some wigwams standing not far off
and close to the edge of a swamp. When near
enough to see any movement which might be going
on, he made a pretence of digging, which he kept up
until he had satisfied himself that no one was stirring;
then, slipping into the thicket, he hurried off towards
the south. Running and walking by turns, he made
all the progress he could during the morning, but was
often obliged to go out of his way to avoid the snow;
though at some points he could not go around, and so
was obliged to cross it, — to his great alarm, for his
footprints were almost sure to reveal his course. He
seems soon to have lost his way; and this probably
saved his life, for when his absence became known to
the savages, and they sent one of their number after
him, he escaped simply from the fact that his pursuer
followed the direct trail. Until about noon the sky
appears to have been sufficiently clear to enable him
to make out in a general way the direction he was to
take, but, as is apt to be the case in the early New
England April, the clouds gathered as the day wore on,
until at length the sun became so obscured that the

fugitive wholly lost his way, and for a time wandered aimlessly about. Later in the day it cleared again, and the glow of the setting sun both gave his bearings to the frightened wanderer, and restored to him a degree of hope and heart. Going on once more, he soon came to the North River, which he found deep and full of rocks. There was no help for it; he had to ford the icy stream, which he only succeeded in doing with much difficulty. Getting at last to its southern bank, he found it too dark to go further. His condition was indeed pitiable. Weak and wet, cold and hungry, — worn out with his long day's tramp, — he had but a handful of parched corn to eat, and his fear of pursuit was so great that he did not dare to light a fire. He at last came to a deep hollow in the woods, in which many fallen trees had lodged; and here he ventured to kindle a feeble blaze, before which he passed the night listening to the wolves as they howled in the forest about him. Fortunately the sky became clear, and he was able to make out the pole star, thus assuring himself of the direction he was to take.

The next morning he attempted to go on, but, whether from being too foot-sore and weary, or because of the cloudiness of the sky, he soon found himself unable to do so, and returned to his resting-place of the previous night. The third day of his journey broke clear, and once more he started on his way; but it was not until about three o'clock in the afternoon that, emerging suddenly from the forest, he found himself, to his great joy, on the outskirts of Plymouth. He had made his way by bearing to the south and east, skirting the marshes, and had come out at some point in what is now Duxbury. His escape was a narrow one, for the next day his pursuers were lurking in the neighboring woods. Having assured themselves that their quarry had eluded them, they then turned aside and pursued their way southward, apparently in‑ tending to notify their confederates of what had hap‑ pened.

Pratt had reached Plymouth on the third of April, or March 24th as it then was, the day after the annual election. The course to be pursued in crushing out the conspiracy had already been decided on, and the whole available force of the settlement placed at the disposal of Standish, who was well acquainted with the field in which he was to operate. His plan was to stamp the danger out at once; he did not propose to simply scare the conspirators into a temporary aspect of friendliness. Above all, it would appear, he was bent on killing Wituwamat; for Wituwamat had affronted him in presence of savages, and Stan‑ dish meant by making an example of him to restore his own prestige in Indian eyes. Cost what it might, that prestige he proposed to maintain. Accordingly Standish now preferred to incur additional risk rather than do anything likely to excite suspicion, and so prevent the complete carrying out of his plan. He knew that the Massachusetts were scattered, and at most did not number more than thirty or forty fight‑ ing men; but they had been in the custom of seeing the Plymouth leader come on his trading expeditions with a few companions only, and if he now appeared with a large armed force they might be put on their guard, and the prime movers in the conspiracy at least would be careful not to trust themselves within his grasp. So he chose but eight men to go with him, and when Pratt arrived the preparations were all com‑

pleted and the party ready to set out. The news brought by the refugee was simply confirmatory of what the Plymouth people already knew, though the account he gave of the condition of affairs at Wessagusset revealed the imminence of the danger. The necessity for instant action was clearer than ever. Whatever was to be done must plainly be done at once. The weather was wet and threatening, — in fact a dreary easterly storm, such as is not unusual in a New England spring, would seem to have prevailed. Regardless of this, on Monday (then the 25th of March, but now the 4th of April) Standish ordered his party on board their shallop and got under weigh for Wessagusset. The force consisted of ten men in all, including in the number Standish himself and the Indian Hobamack. Pratt was too weak from the effects of his journey to accompany them.

As they sailed with a fair as well as a strong wind, the party must have reached Weymouth River on the afternoon of the same day on which they left Plymouth. They soon made out the Swan lying quietly at her moorings, and went alongside of her, but found no one on board; nor was any one in sight on the beach. Alarmed apparently at this absence of all movement, and for the moment afraid that the blow they came to avert had already fallen, instead of at once landing at the stockade they fired a musket to attract the notice of any one on the shore near by. In answer to their signal a few stragglers, among whom was the master of the Swan, soon showed themselves, abandoning for the moment their anxious search for nuts. In reply to Standish's inquiry, how they dared leave the vessel so unprotected, they explained to him that they did not consider any precautions necessary, — that they had no fear of the Indians, and indeed lived with them, suffering them to come and go in the settlement with perfect freedom. Learning further that those whom Saunders had left in charge upon his departure were at the plantation, Standish landed and went thither. Finding them, he forth-with proceeded to explain the purpose of his coming. Thoroughly alarmed at what he told them, Weston's people at once became obedient, promising to do as Standish should bid, and thereupon, assuming general command, he went to work maturing the details of his counter-plot. Enjoining strict quiet and secrecy he sent out messengers to call in the stragglers, who amounted to a third part of the company, and at the same time gave notice that any one who left the stock-ade without permission would be put to death. Then out of his own slender supplies, taken from the little reserve kept for seed at Plymouth, the new com-mander rationed the entire place, causing a pint of corn a day to be served out to each man.

As the stormy weather still continued, the work of getting in the stragglers proved a somewhat long one, and an Indian meanwhile came into the plantation with some furs, ostensibly to trade, but in reality it was supposed to see what was going on. He reported Standish's arrival to the other Indians, who seem to have suspected the purpose of his coming, but failed to realize with how formidable an opponent they had now to reckon ; and, moreover, it would appear that the demoralized conduct of Weston's party had in-spired the savages with a feeling of contempt for Euro-peans generally, which had been strengthened by the apparent impunity with which Wituwamat had in-sulted Standish in Canacum's lodge. Accordingly,

when others of them presently came into the stockade,
they did not hesitate to indulge in threats and insulting gestures, even flourishing their knives in the faces
of the whites. Wituwamat himself, little aware of
the decree which had gone out against him, was among
those who thus tempted fate. Indeed, he seems to
have reënacted with variations that Manomet performance which was soon to cost him his head; for,
dauntingly drawing his knife, which he carried slung
about his neck, he held it up before Standish's eyes,
and bade him take note of the face of a woman carved
on the handle. Then he added that at home he had
yet another knife on which was the face of a man; by
and by the two should marry. With those knives, he
boasted, he had already killed both English and
Frenchmen; and presently the knife he held in his
hand should see and act, but it should not speak.
Pecksuot, another brave of great size and strength,
a companion of Wituwamat, was also there; and, not
to be outdone in bravado, he taunted Standish, in true
Indian style, on the smallness of his stature, and compared it with his own; for, though not a sachem, he
boasted himself a warrior of courage and repute.

The next day (our 6th of April as it would seem),
Pecksuot and Wituwamat, accompanied by two other
savages, one of them a younger brother of the latter,
again came into the stockade, and were permitted to
enter the principal block-house. Standish was there
with some four or five of his own company. His hope
had been to get a larger number of the savages together before he fell upon them, but he had begun to
doubt whether he could succeed in so doing. And
now the two most dangerous of them were fairly within
his grasp, and he seems suddenly to have resolved to

seize the occasion. To each his work was assigned,
and a signal had been agreed upon. Watching his
chance to take his man unawares, with a stealth which
exceeded that of the savages, Standish, suddenly giving the signal, sprang upon Pecksuot. He was the
largest and most formidable of them all. Instantly
the door was flung to and made fast. The struggle had begun. It was a short fierce death-grapple.
Standish had snatched the knife at Pecksuot's neck
from its sheath and driven it into him. The others
had fallen upon Wituwamat and his companions.
Though taken wholly by surprise and at a fearful disadvantage, the savages neither cried out, nor tried to
fly, nor asked for quarter. Catching at their weapons
and vainly resisting, they struggled to the last. It
was incredible, Winslow afterwards wrote, how many
wounds the two warriors received before they died.
Three out of the four were despatched on the spot;
while the other one, Wituwamat's brother, and scarcely
it would seem more than a boy, was overpowered and
bound fast.

It remained to complete the work thus bloodily
begun. A messenger was hurried off to a party at
another point, bidding them at once despatch any
Indian men in their power. They killed two. His
boy prisoner Standish hung out of hand, killing also
one more Indian found elsewhere. There were a few
women in the camp. These Standish made prisoners, placing them under the charge of some of the
Wessagusset people; but they were subsequently released without any further harm being done them.
Another Indian, through "the negligence," as it is
expressed, of the man who should have murdered him,
escaped and spread the alarm, thus preventing the full

accomplishment of Standish's purpose, which seems to have been the indiscriminate killing of all the males of the tribe.

Having thus disposed of those within his reach, Standish the next day took with him a party, some half dozen in number, and went out, under the guid ance of Hobamack, in search of the sachem Aber- decest and the main body of his people. Word of the massacre had reached the sachem's village during the previous night, and all the men, taking their weapons, had left it. Standish had not gone far before he discovered them, apparently making their way in the direction of Wessagusset. Both parties, getting sight of each other at about the same time, hurried to secure the advantage of a rising ground near by. Standish got there first, and the Indians, seeking at once the protection of the trees, let fly their arrows. The skirmish was hardly worthy of the name. The savages had lost their leading warriors the day before, and when Hobamack, uttering his war-cry and casting aside his garment of furs, ran upon them tomahawk in hand, they turned and fled in terror to a swamp near by, in the mire and under- growth of which they found a hiding-place. One only of them seems to have been injured, his arm having been shattered by a ball from Standish's musket. It was not easy to get at the panic-stricken creatures, and neither taunts nor challenges could induce them to show themselves ; nor, indeed, is it surprising that the poor wretches were reluctant to come out and be killed. Their further pursuit was therefore aban- doned, and the party returned to the stockade.[1]

[1] These are the incidents described by Longfellow in the Seventh Part of his poem, *The Courtship of Miles Standish.* In using his ma-

Though the object of the expedition was now accomplished, before Standish returned with his own company to Plymouth the course to be pursued by Weston's people had to be decided upon. They could remain where they were ; if they did not wish to

terials it cannot be too much regretted that Mr. Longfellow did not see fit to adhere more closely to the facts as they stand recorded. It certainly does not appear that for poetical effect he has improved upon them. His poem is a New England classic. Probably at least nine people out of ten, who know of these incidents at all, know of them through it. This also will continue to be the case. Nothing certainly can be more Homeric and picturesque than Pratt's struggle through the wilderness, — than Standish's voyage in his open boat to Wessagusset, along the bleak surf-beaten shore, in the stormy eastern weather, — than the fierce hand to knife death-grapple in the rude log-house within the Wessagusset stockade. The whole is, in the originals, full of life, simplicity and vigor, needing only to be turned into verse. But in place of the voyage we have in Longfellow's poem a march through the woods, which never took place and contains in it nothing characteristic, — an interview before an Indian encampment " pitched on the edge of a meadow, between the sea and the forest," at which the knife scene is enacted, instead of in the rude block-house, — and finally, the killing takes place amid a discharge of firearms, and " there on the flowers of the meadow the warriors " are made to lie ; whereas in fact they died far more vigorously, as well as poetically, on the blood-soaked floor of the log-house in which they were surprised, " not making any fearful noise, but catching at their weapons and striving to the last." And as for " flowers," it was early in April and there was still snow on the ground.

Reading *The Courtship of Miles Standish*, and looking at the paintings upon the walls of the Memorial Hall at Plymouth and of the Capitol at Washington, it is impossible for any one at all imbued with the real spirit of the early colonial period not to entertain a hope that the time may come when a school of historical poets and painters shall arise who will deal truthfully and vigorously with these scenes, studying the localities and the authorities carefully and in a realistic spirit, instead of evolving at once facts, dress, features and scenery from an inner and where not a weak at least a grotesque consciousness. In our early New England scenes the real facts are good enough, strong enough and picturesque enough for any one, be he historian, poet or painter. They certainly have not yet been, nor are they likely soon to be, improved upon.

do that, they might either follow Saunders to the
eastward, or, accepting an offer made by Bradford
through Standish, return with the latter to Plymouth.
As to the last proposition, it would seem that even the
hardships of the recent winter had failed to obliterate
from the memory of those "profane fellows" the
severe justice, the long prayers and the short commons
of the preceding summer. They evinced small inclination to return to Plymouth. As to remaining where
they were, Standish contemptuously assured them that
he would not fear to do so with a smaller force than
theirs; but they were not Standishes, and felt no call
to the heroic. Moreover, they were thoroughly out of
conceit with the wilderness, and especially with a
New England wilderness in winter. All their hopes
and anticipations at coming had been disappointed, and
they were tired of looking for Weston's appearance
and the supplies that were to come with him. Doubtless, too, they were terrified at the murderous deeds in
which they had just taken part; and, weak and few
as they knew the Indians to be, they were afraid of
them. They dreaded the day of savage reckoning
which might come after their energetic ally should be
gone. In short, the single desire with most of them
was to get away from the hateful place, and that as
directly and quickly as possible; but in doing so they
not unnaturally wished to go where there was a chance
of finding something to eat. The majority therefore
determined to follow Saunders, — hoping either to
meet Weston at the fishing stations, or, if they failed
in that, to at least work their way back to England.
Following his instructions, Standish then proceeded to
supply the Swan as well as he could for her short
voyage; and so scant was his store, that when he had

done this, he scarcely had food enough left for his own
party until they could get back to Plymouth. The
Swan and the Plymouth shallop set sail from Wessagusset in company ; but when they came to the harbor's mouth they stood away on different courses, the
former going off to the north and east, while the latter
followed the familiar trend of the shore to the south.
Standish had obeyed to the letter the stern instructions which he had himself inspired at his setting
forth ; for, safely stowed away in his boat, a ghastly
freight, he bore back with him the gory head of
Wituwamat, " that bloody and bold villain before
spoken of."

Such was the ignominious end of the first attempt
at European settlement on the shores of Boston Bay.
When he heard of it at Plymouth the sedate Bradford
gave evidence that though he was a Pilgrim and a
Separatist he was also a human being, for he sent a
grim chuckle of exultation after Thomas Weston's
vanishing and vagabond crew. " This was the end
of these that sometime bosted of their strength," he
wrote, " and what they would doe and bring to pass, in
comparison of the people hear ; . . . and said at their
first arrivall, when they saw the wants hear, that they
would take another course, and not to fall into such a
condition as this simple people were come too. But
a mans way is not in his owne power ; God can make
the weake to stand ; let him also that standeth take
heed least he fall." Weston's attempt at a plantation
certainly had fallen, for there remained of it at
Wessagusset nothing but some deserted block-houses.
A few stragglers, three probably in all, including one
man who had thrown his lot in with the savages,
abandoning civilized life and taking unto himself a

squaw, were left behind when the others went away. They had disregarded the summons to come in, and after the massacre could not be reached ; but the Plymouth people subsequently did what they could to save them. The savage who had followed Pratt, and, instead of stopping at Plymouth, gone on further south, had, on his return, come into the settlement and at once been secured. In manacles and under strict guard, he was confined in the new fort, that being the first day that ever any watch was there kept. When Standish safely returned, and Wituwamat's head was perched in triumph on the roof of the captive's prison, he " looked piteously " at it, and, being asked whether he recognized it, answered " Yea." Doubtless he expected his own head would soon keep it company. But Governor Bradford, rightly concluding that enough in the way of severity had now been done, ordered the prisoner's release, sending through him a message to the sachem Aberdecest to the effect that he must at once deliver up in safety the three captive settlers, and see that no damage was done to the buildings at Wessagusset. The buildings remained undisturbed ; but, before Bradford's message reached Aberdecest, the captives had already been despatched. The messenger thereupon did not dare return to Plymouth ; and, indeed, such was the terror felt among the Massachusetts lest the revenge they took on these men should be visited on their own heads, that for a time no one among them dared show himself. A woman at last came in bringing a very humble message. She said that Aberdecest would fain be at peace with Plymouth, and that in obedience to their commands he would have sent the captives had they not been already dead when those commands reached him. It would seem, also, that their killing was not unaccompanied by that ingenious refinement of torture which ever made death preferable to Indian captivity; for afterwards, speaking of their fate, one of the savages said, — "When we killed your men they cried and made ill-favored faces."[1]

Some months later the news of the Wessagusset affair reached Leyden, and by it the beloved pastor of the Plymouth church was sorely moved. He wrote an earnest letter to his people in which he took the side of the natives, and expressed himself in a way which shows at once the high moral tone both of him who wrote the letter and of those to whom it was written. It contained all that could now, in the ripe philanthropy of two centuries and a half later, be said in condemnation of what had been done.

"Concerning the killing of those poor Indians, of which we heard at first by report, and since by more certain relation, oh! how happy a thing had it been, if you had converted some before you had killed any; besides, where blood is once begun to be shed, it is seldom staunched of a long time after. You will say they deserved it. I grant it; but upon what provocations and invitements by those heathenish Christians? Besides, you, being no magistrates over them, were to consider, not what they deserved, but what you were of necessity constrained to inflict. Necessity of this, especially of killing so many, (and many more, it seems, they would, if they could,) I see not. Methinks one or two principals should have been full enough, according to that approved rule, The punishment to the few, and the fear to many. Upon this occasion let me be bold to exhort you seriously to consider of the disposition of your Captain, whom I love, and am persuaded the Lord in great mercy and for much good hath sent you him, if you use him aright.

[1] IV. *Mass. Hist. Coll.* iv. 486; Young, *Chron. of Pilg.* 344.

He is a man humble and meek amongst you, and towards
all in ordinary course.   But now if this be merely from an
human spirit, there is cause to fear that by occasion, especially of provocation, there may be wanting that tenderness
of the life of man (made after God's image) which is meet.
It is also a thing more glorious in men's eyes, than pleasing
in God's, or convenient for Christians, to be a terror to
poor, barbarous people; and indeed I am afraid lest, by
these occasions, others should be drawn to affect a kind of
ruffling course in the world.   I doubt not but you will take
in good part these things which I write, and as there is
cause make use of them."

That the Wessagusset killing amounted to a massacre, and a cold blooded one, — that it failed to include
all the male Indians thereabouts simply because they
could not be so entrapped that they might all be
slaughtered at once, — that, so far as it went, it was a
butchery, — all this admits of no doubt.   The savages
were the first occupants of the soil; they had sustained many and grievous wrongs at the hands of
those newcomers whom they had welcomed; there
was for them in this world no redress.   Had the situation been reversed, and the Indians, after similar
fashion, set upon the Europeans in a moment of unsuspecting intercourse, no language would have been
found strong enough to describe in the page of history
their craft, their stealth and their cruelty.   In this,
as in everything, the European has had the last word.
He tells the tale.   Under these circumstances, while
it is impossible to deny, it is contemptible, as is so
often done, to go about to palliate.   Yet, admitting
everything which in harshest language modern philanthropy could assert, there is still no reasonable
doubt that, in the practical working of human events,

the course approved in advance by the Plymouth magistrates, and ruthlessly put in execution by Standish, was in this case the most merciful, the wisest and, consequently, the most justifiable course. The essential fact was, and is, that the settlers were surrounded by Indians and had to deal with them ; and Indians were not Europeans. They could be dealt with successfully, either in the way of kindness or severity, only by dealing with them as what they were,— partially developed, savage, human beings. Now it has already been observed that Standish understood the Indian character, and correctly measured the savage as an antagonist. He understood the Indian, too, through no process of reasoning, for it may well be questioned whether reasoning was exactly Miles Standish's strong point. It was with him evidently a matter of intuition. In other words, he had the same natural faculty for dealing with Indians which some men have for dealing with horses, and others with dogs ; and this natural faculty caused him at the outset to realize that truth which Parkman says the French, — both soldiers and priests, — though more successful than any other Europeans in dealing with the savages, learned only slowly and through bitter experience, — the truth, namely, that " in the case of hostile Indians no good can come of attempts to conciliate, unless respect is first imposed by a sufficient castigation." [1]

That the Indians in this case, however made so, were hostile, that a widespread conspiracy existed, and that their plague-stricken condition alone prevented the ill-ordered proceedings at Wessagusset from ending in a general and on the part of the savages most justifiable Indian war, can admit of no

[1] *Old Régime*, 183.

doubt. If the Massachusetts were weak, the Narragansetts and the Pequots were strong. The movement, once successfully started, might well set the whole immeasurable wilderness in commotion. The course of true wisdom, therefore, was to extinguish the spark, and to extinguish it completely, — not to wait to fight the flame. Least of all was the time meet for making proselytes. Stung by the wrongs they had endured, and despising those at whose hands they had suffered, the savages were in a frame of mind little receptive of gospel truths. They were thinking rather of scalps and the war-path than of conversion. Chastisement had to precede conciliation; and consequently, in the perilous case in which those composing it at Plymouth then were, John Robinson's flock stood more in need of Miles Standish, however fierce and unreasoning, than of himself, however forbearing and saintly.

It is far nobler to preach and to convert than to strike; but there are times when a blow is necessary, and then it is well if one blow sufficeth. Standish struck the savages at Wessagusset in the way they best understood. Stealth, it is to be remembered, is to the Indian what strategy is to the European. It is his method of conducting war. In 1623 he saw nothing in it that was cowardly, nothing that was brutal; and he sees nothing now. On the contrary he dealt in concealments, in conspiracies, in deceits and in surprises. To take your enemy unawares, and kill him, was in his eyes the great warrior's part. To attack him openly was in his eyes folly; to have mercy on him when vanquished was weakness. Standish therefore merely beat them, and he beat them terribly, with their own weapons. He showed himself more stealthy, more deceitful, more ferocious and more daring than he among them whom, in all these regards, they most admired. With his own hand he had killed their strongest and fiercest warrior, who was also the most cunning of them all, their master in treacheries; and he had killed him with the knife snatched from the warrior's own neck. Hence the Indian's fear of Standish now knew no bounds. Those implicated in the conspiracy against Wessagusset were at once conscience and panic stricken. Aberdecest in his terror forsook his habitation and removed daily from place to place. Canacum, remembering the scene in his wigwam, hid himself in the swamp, and there died of privation and exposure. Yet another sachem, hoping to ingratiate himself with the avenger, sent a canoe laden with peace - offerings to Plymouth. Near the mouth of the harbor it was cast away, and three of his emissaries were drowned. Thomas Morton wrote that such a terror was Standish, after this event, " that the savages durst never make to a head against them any more ; " [1] while the historian of Plymouth said that " this sudden and unexpected execution, together with the just judgment of God upon their guilty consciences, hath so terrified and amazed [the savages] as in like manner they forsook their houses, running to and fro like men distracted, living in swamps and other desert places, and so brought manifold diseases on themselves, whereof very many are dead." [2]

Thus at the cost of seven lives, ruthlessly, treacherously taken, immediate Indian hostilities were averted, and the inevitable life and death struggle with the aborigines was deferred for half a century, when it had to result in the swift destruction of the inferior race. That it should also have resulted in consigning

[1] *N. E. Canaan*, 108.   [2] Young, *Chron. of Pilg.* 344–5.

to hopeless West Indian slavery the infant grandchild
of that Massasoit whose friendly caution now saved
Plymouth, must remain a blot on New England history in comparison with which the Wessagusset killing
was an act of mercy. He, at least, might have been
saved and converted, that he might have become to a
Massachusetts progeny what Pocahontas is to one of
Virginia. For a New-Englander to trace a descent
from Massasoit would indeed be matter of family
pride.[1]

Meanwhile the Wessagusset killing was Standish's
last combat with the Indians, for from that time forward, as long as he lived, there was peace between
them and the Plymouth colony. At Wessagusset
also a few straggling settlers a little later lived for
years buried deep in the solitude, and the savages
did not molest them. In fact, so far as the dying
tribe of the Massachusetts was concerned, the fierce
blow struck in those early days of April, 1623, was a
final one. They could not rally from it. Out of less
than twoscore warriors seven had been taken off.
Massacre thus completed the work of pestilence. It
may have been necessary, — almost certainly it was
best; but, thinking of the terrible wasting which the
broken-spirited tribe had so recently undergone at the
hand of Providence, it must be admitted that, on this
occasion at least, the Plymouth Fathers broke the
bruised reed and quenched the smoking flax.

[1] See the volume entitled *Indian History, Biography and Genealogy:
Pertaining to the good Sachem Massasoit*, prepared by Gen. E. W. Pearce
and published at North Abington, Mass., in 1878, by Mrs. Zerviah
Gould Mitchell. Mrs. Mitchell, who claimed to be a descendant in
the seventh generation from Massasoit, was in 1888 still living at Bet-
ty's Neck on the Indian reservation in Middleborough, Mass. She
had children. The family is Indian.

CHAPTER VII.

SIR FERDINANDO GORGES AND THE COUNCIL FOR NEW ENGLAND.

"THE pale and houses at Wessagusset," which Bradford cautioned the savages not to destroy, were destined to remain unoccupied a few months only; for Weston's company departed early in April, 1623, and by the middle of September following the place was taken possession of by others. Captain Robert Gorges, the individual at the head of those composing the new enterprise, was a very different person from Thomas Weston, and yet in his way quite as little calculated to grapple successfully with the hard problem of New England colonization. Weston was a merchant adventurer, a man of the city and a trader; Gorges was a gentleman adventurer, a man of the court and a soldier. The object of the former had been the establishment of a plantation and trading-post. The dream of the latter was to find a species of palatinate for himself, a little principality of his own, in the New World.

Robert Gorges was the younger of the two sons of that Sir Ferdinando already mentioned in connection with Squanto's European experience. Like Raleigh and Smith, only in less degree, the elder Gorges remains one of the picturesque characters in the settlement of English-speaking America. He stands out among the rest with the face and bearing of a cava-

lier. Though his name had a Spanish sound, there
was no Spanish blood in the Gorges veins; on the
contrary, himself a typical Englishman of the Elizabethan period, Sir Ferdinando came of old West
Country stock, of pure English descent, being connected with the Russells and the Raleighs. Of his
early life scarce anything is known, even the date of
his birth, which took place somewhere between 1566
and 1569, being uncertain. For some reason it seems
not to have been recorded.[1] When quite young, Sir
Ferdinando devoted himself to that half naval, half
military career so common among the men of that
time, and followed it steadily for more than half a
century. The first mention made of him is as a captain in the force sent to the relief of Sluys, when that
place was besieged by the Duke of Parma in the
spring of 1587. The next year he was a prisoner of
war at Lisle. In 1589 he was engaged in the siege
of Paris, and, it is said, was borne wounded from the
breach by Henry of Navarre himself. Two years afterwards he is heard of again as one of the officers of
the contingent sent over by Elizabeth under the command of the Earl of Essex to assist the Huguenots,
and with that force he took an active part in the siege
of Rouen.[2] A few years later he was made military
governor of Plymouth, and when, in 1597, the Ferrol
expedition was sent out against Spain, Gorges was
appointed one of the counsellors of Essex, who was
in chief command, with the rank of sergeant-major.
He sailed in command of the Dreadnaught; but
when, shortly after setting out, the unlucky fleet was

---

[1] Baxter, *Memoir of Gorges* (Prince Society Publications), 3.
[2] Devereux, *Earls of Essex*, i. 271; Markham, *The Fighting Veres*;
IV. *Mass. Hist. Coll.* vii. 342.

dispersed by a gale, he returned with the others to
port. The expedition refitted and again set sail, but
this time ill-health compelled Gorges to remain behind, and he did not rejoin it. Recognized as one of
Essex's officers, he seems to have been warmly attached to that unfortunate nobleman; and, indeed, at
a little later day, it was in connection with Essex's
mad attempt at an insurrection that the name of Sir
Ferdinando finds its only mention in English history,
— a mention which he himself would gladly have foregone. The incident, as will presently be seen, had a
remote but not unimportant bearing on the subsequent
course of events in the settlement of Massachusetts.
In that settlement the two opposing forces in church
and state, which then divided England, were again
confronted; there, too, Cavalier was opposed to Puritan, and on the Cavalier side Gorges was the central,
it might almost be said the only leading figure. Essex was the popular Puritan hero, and Gorges' connection with him affected the whole subsequent life and
political standing of the latter. It becomes in this
way a part of American history.

Hot-headed, generous, attractive and shallow, Robert
Devereux, the second Earl of Essex, was the favorite
of Queen Elizabeth's later years. She demeaned herself towards him, after her wont. First she raised
him, when hardly more than a boy, to high commands
for which he was not fitted; then she rebuked his
petulance by soundly boxing his ears in presence of
her counsellors; finally she signed his death warrant,
and, having done so, ever afterwards mourned for him.
When, after his disastrous Irish failure in 1600, Essex
returned in hot haste to court, Gorges was military
governor of Plymouth. Failing to obtain the redress

he demanded at the Queen's hands, the Earl a year later summoned all his friends to London. To Gorges among others, though there had been no communication between them for two years previous, he wrote a letter full of complaints of the treatment he had received. Gorges responded in person ; and, coming up to London, took part in the treasonable conferences held at Essex-house during the first week of February, 1601. When finally, on Sunday the 8th, apparently more because he knew not what else to do than with any definite plan, Essex sallied out into the Strand on foot at the head of his band of friends and retainers and made his bootless insurrectionary rush into the city, Gorges was at his side. After the hopelessness of exciting even a tumult became apparent, the Earl tried to make his way back to Essex-house, in which he had left Popham the Chief Justice and Egerton the Lord Keeper (sent in the morning by the Queen to command him to desist from his purposes) locked up and under guard ; but the return was not so easy as the going forth. At Ludgate the now panic-stricken and fast dwindling party found their path obstructed by a chain drawn across the street, and guarded by a company of soldiers. A parley took place, followed by a futile effort to force the way. Gorges then bethought himself of a plan by which the Earl might possibly yet be extricated from his desperate position. The utter failure of the movement from Essex-house was not yet known at court, where the tumult occasioned by it in the city had probably caused alarm if not panic. It was, therefore, barely possible that some terms might be obtained, could the friends of Essex but communicate with the court at once, before the alarm subsided.

The charge subsequently made against Gorges was that, in doing what he now did, he acted solely on his own responsibility, and with a view to his own safety. He, on the contrary, always asserted that before leaving Essex he told the Earl of his scheme, and was authorized to do something in that way if he could. This seems wholly probable. It is to be remembered that everything was in confusion. Something had to be done, and that immediately. There was no time for discussion. Essex himself was so bewildered and agitated that the sweat flowed from him like water, and he was capable neither of receiving counsel nor of giving orders. Under these circumstances, in the midst of the flight from Ludgate, Gorges, it would seem, hurriedly proposed something to his bewildered leader. The latter did not well understand what it was, but it seemed to hold out a chance ; so he assented to it, as he would have assented to anything else. Gorges then slipped away, and succeeded in getting back to Essex-house.

His idea was to release Popham, the Chief Justice, with whom his personal relations were close, and go with him at once to Westminster, there to make, through his intervention, such terms as might be possible for the Earl. Unfortunately Chief Justice Popham was a sturdy Englishman whose nerves were not easily disturbed. He had been improving his hours of confinement with his eye at a keyhole,[1] taking

---

[1] Popham presided as Chief Justice at the trial of some of the conspirators. In the course of the proceedings as reported in the case of Sir Christopher Blunt (*State Trials*, ed. 1766, vii. 52), appears the following : — " The Lord-Chief-Justice hereupon asked Sir Christopher Blunt, why they stood at the great chamber-door, with muskets charged and matches in their hands ; which, through the key-hole, the Lord-Chief-Justice said, he discerned."

observations of those of the conspirators having him
in charge ; and now, though quite willing to leave
Essex-house, he wholly refused to do so unless the
Lord Keeper, the companion of his mission, left it
with him. Gorges had to act on his own responsibility and instantly, for moments were precious. Doing
so, he ordered the release of the Lord Keeper likewise,
and, hurrying the two into a boat at the riverside,
started for Westminster. As they went he put the
best face he could on the situation. He represented
the tumult in the city as formidable, and tried to im-
press on Chief Justice and Lord Keeper the necessity
of something being done at once to appease it. His
scheme was, perhaps, as feasible as any which could
then have been devised, had there but been time in
which to carry it out ; for, in reality, the alarm all
day at court had been much greater and more general
than he could have supposed. The Queen alone had
maintained her composure. But before Gorges reached
the council chamber the panic had already begun to
subside, for tidings were fast coming in of Essex's
complete failure and the growing difficulties of his
position. It was known that the Earl's capture had
become a question of merely a few hours. Her fallen
favorite's *insurrectio unius diei*, as Elizabeth contemptuously called it, never achieved the proportions
of a good-sized city riot.

Essex meanwhile, after his repulse from the chain
at Ludgate, turned back into the city, and, getting
down to the riverside, succeeded at last in making his
way back to Essex-house by water ; but only to find
himself there surrounded, with both the Chief Justice
and the Lord Keeper released and gone. In his utter
desperation he and those about him seem to have sup-

posed that some use as hostages might now have been
made of those two high officials; but it is not easy
to see what this use could have been. There was
nothing for the Earl and his followers to do except to
surrender themselves. This both they and those who
held them surrounded knew perfectly well. It would
have been a distinct aggravation of their offence if,
when they surrendered, the two highest officials of
the law had been found still prisoners in their hands.
As a matter of fact, therefore, the release by Gorges
of Egerton and Popham in no way made worse a
situation which was already hopeless. As it grew towards night the unfortunate Earl gave himself up,
having continued to the very end a pitiable spectacle
of hesitating irresolution.

Ten days later the trial took place. Of the guilt
of Essex there could be no doubt; but the evidence
chiefly relied upon against him was contained in the
written examinations of certain of his associates,
prominent among whom was Gorges. It was in connection with Gorges also that the most striking and
painful incident of the proceedings occurred, — the
incident which impressed itself most vividly on the
memories of all present. Up to the point at which
Gorges' examination was produced, no witnesses had
been called or oral evidence given. But when the
counsel for the crown read from this paper the statement that, as a result of the February conferences at
Essex-house, the decision as to the course to be pursued had been left wholly with the Earl, who had
thereupon on Saturday evening " resolved the next
day to put in practice the moving of his friends in
the city," — when this statement was read Essex was
greatly moved. He at once demanded that the wit-

ness should be produced, in order that he might interrogate him face to face. Gorges was at the time a prisoner in the Gate house. He was sent for and brought into Westminster Hall, where the Lords were sitting as a court for the trial of a peer; and there, after he had repeated his statement, adding further "that he advised the Earl, at his return out of the city to his house, to go and submit himself to her Majesty," the following painful colloquy ensued : —

Essex. Good Sir Ferdinando, I pray thee speak openly whatsoever thou dost remember; with all my heart I desire thee to speak freely; I see thou desirest to live, and if it please her Majesty to be merciful unto you, I shall be glad and will pray for it; yet I pray thee, speak like a man.

Sir F. Gorges. All that I can remember I have delivered in my Examination, and further I cannot say.

Essex. Sir Ferdinando, I wish you might speak anything that might do yourself good; but remember your reputation, and that you are a gentleman; I pray you answer me, did you advise me to leave my enterprise?

Sir F. Gorge. My Lord, I think I did.

Essex. Nay, it is no time to answer now upon thinking; these are not things to be forgotten; did you indeed so counsel me?

Sir F. Gorge. I did.

Essex. My Lords, look upon Sir Ferdinando, and see if he looks like himself. All the world shall see, by my death and his life, whose testimony is the truest.[1]

Even this meagre abstract of what passed shows that it was the most striking episode of the whole trial. Essex had before been wrangling fiercely with Coke; and later there was a bitter passage between him and

[1] Jardine, *Criminal Trials*, i. 334.

Bacon, a passage which history has not forgotten.[1]
But Coke and Bacon were lawyers and counsel for the
crown; with Gorges it was different. In Gorges, Essex was confronted with his own familiar friend, the
confidant of his schemes, now turned state's evidence
against him. Those present at the trial reported that
Sir Ferdinando was in appearance pale and discom-
posed; and, indeed, this is still apparent in his replies;
while, on the other hand, the mingled pathos, haughti-
ness and despair of Essex ring through his questions.
The "remember that you are a gentleman," following
hard on the "I see thou desirest to live," and ending in the passionate cry, "look upon Sir Ferdinando,"
all combined to make up a scene which Englishmen of
that day never forgot.

All else in Gorges' connection with Essex's mad
folly and unhappy fate admits of extenuation or excuse. That trial scene does not. It is final and
fatal. Gorges never got over it, and it cannot now
be explained away. His answers to the other charges
which were, subsequently to the Earl's death, made
against him, are clear and satisfactory. It was alleged
that early on the morning of the fatal Sunday he had
met Sir Walter Raleigh in a boat on the Thames, and
had betrayed to him Essex's design; but Gorges answered very truly, that the meeting took place before
witnesses, and with the Earl's knowledge and consent, while Raleigh was already fully informed as to
all that was going on, and indeed had sought the interview, in consequence of this knowledge, for the
express purpose of warning his kinsman, Sir Ferdinando, to look after his own safety while he yet could.

[1] Macaulay, *Essays, Lord Bacon;* Campbell, *Lives of Lord Chancellors,* ch. liii.

So as to the release of the imprisoned Chief Justice and Lord Keeper, the supposed hostages. Gorges well replied to the charge of treachery in this matter, that he acted with such consent of the Earl as the hurry and tumult of the situation permitted, and that at least, in what he did, he meant for the best. But when at last it came to the scene in Westminster Hall, with Essex and Gorges face to face, it was not possible to extenuate. It was plain that his imprisonment and the fear of a traitor's death had so wrought upon Gorges' mind that he could not resist the temptation to save, if he could, his own head by giving evidence which bore hard on his chief.

His shortcoming stopped there, and his attitude then and afterwards, when compared with the ignoble bearing of Bacon in the same memorable proceedings, almost commands respect. Gorges failed to remember that he was a gentleman; perhaps, even, he was a cowardly apostate, — but an eager one he was not. What he did, he at least did to save his life. Unlike Bacon, he did not seem to feel a joy in the work of pressing down his falling patron; nor later did he seek to insure his own safety by traducing the memory of his friend. On the contrary, while freshly smarting under the stigma of treachery with which the Earl had forever branded him, — while yet a prisoner in the Gate house, trembling for his head, — he wrote of Essex, and took his own appeal to the verdict of posterity, in words so manly, direct and pathetic that they seem rather to belong to the nineteenth century than to the sixteeenth. Certainly Gorges never wrote so well again.

"Like will to like, and every man will keep company with such as he is himself; he was of the same profession that I was, and of a free and noble spirit. But I must say no more, for he is gone, and I am here; I loved him alive, and cannot hate him being dead; he had some imperfections — so have all men; he had many virtues — so have few; and for those his virtues I loved him; and when time, which is the trial of all truths, hath run his course, it shall appear that I am wronged in the opinion of this idle age. In the mean time, I presume this that I have said is sufficient to satisfy the wise and discreet: for the rest, whatever I can do is but labor lost, and, therefore, I propose not to trouble you nor myself at this time any further." [1]

The appeal was taken in vain. The popularity of Essex with his countrymen is one of the inexplicable things in English history. His biographer confesses himself unable to account for it; [2] yet in 1626, a quarter of a century after the Earl's death, the Duke of Buckingham, exulting in the glory he felt sure was to come to him from the Isle of Rhé expedition, could think of no stronger way of expressing his hopes than by boasting that " before midsummer he should be more honored and beloved by the commons than ever was the Earl of Essex." [3] By the Puritans especially Essex was wellnigh adored; he was looked upon not only as their patron and protector, but as one of themselves. So strong, indeed, was the hold he had on the hearts and memories of this most tenacious and vindictive of all types of men, that it was still plainly to be seen forty years later, when they and the King came to blows. The secretary of the Long Parliament, in writing its history,[4] mentions the popularity

---

[1] *Sir Ferdinando Gorges*, ii. 117, 118, Prince Society Publications.

[2] Devereux, *Earls of Essex*, ii. 192.

[3] Disraeli, *Curiosities of Literature* (ed. 1863), iii. 458.   See, also, Birch, *Memoirs of the Reign of Queen Elizabeth*, B. XII.

[4] May, *Hist. of Long Parl.* 162.

of the father as a principal reason for the appointment to chief military command of his son, — another
Earl of Essex, without the assistance of whose great
name Clarendon does not scruple to say it would have
" been utterly impossible for the two houses of Parliament to have raised an army then." [1]

It was this darling of the people, this protector of
the Puritans, that Sir Ferdinando Gorges was thought
to have betrayed. When a vague general impression
of this kind in regard to any individual takes possession of the public mind, it is almost impossible to dis-
lodge it. If this is true even now, when counter evidence can be spread before the eyes of every one, it
was much more true in 1601. So far as the people
and the Puritans were concerned, Gorges might as
well have spared himself the trouble of his disavow-
als. He never again found any favor in their eyes.
On the contrary, as will presently be seen,[2] twenty
years later, at the very moment when the enterprise
which was the dream of his life seemed nearest to success, Gorges found himself confronted and thwarted
by a Puritan House of Commons, acting under the
strong lead of the most vindictive man of that vindictive time, — a man who must have remembered
him chiefly in connection with the dramatic scene in
Westminster Hall, at the crisis of the trial of the two
Earls.

Queen Elizabeth survived Essex a little over three
years. With her death the cloud of royal displeasure, which had cast a dark shadow of uncertainty on
the lives of all the Earl's associates, disappeared, and
when in March, 1603, James ascended the throne they
found themselves once more at liberty and even in fa-

---

[1] *Rebellion*, B. V. § 33.　　　　[2] *Infra*, 126–9.

vor. Gorges, who had been released from prison in January, 1601, was now reappointed to his old government at Plymouth. He was there, rusting away in the dull routine of arsenal life, as a man of active mind needs must, when in 1605 Weymouth returned from his voyage to the coast of Maine. The deep interest which his explorations and reports of the country excited in the mind of the governor of Plymouth have already been alluded to.[1] Possessing much of his kinsman Raleigh's love of adventure and craving for the unknown, Sir Ferdinando then went systematically to work informing himself in every possible way of that new country beyond the seas, to occupy which became thereafter the labor as well as the dream of his long life. In season and out of season he was instant upon it. Nothing sufficed to draw away his mind from it. He had, too, a long life still before him; for in 1605 he could not yet have reached his fortieth birthday, and he survived his misadventure with Essex through nearly half a century.

The Penobscot savages brought over by Weymouth remained three years under Gorges' protection. They had then become more or less familiar with his language, and had enlightened him so far as they could as to the region of which they were natives. He believed their fanciful stories; and gradually his mind became absorbed in plans for preëmpting, as it were, all modern New England. Sir John Popham was still Chief Justice, and Gorges' relations with him would seem to have been of the most intimate character; for he interested Sir John in his schemes, and the Chief Justice was a man of substance. In the spring of 1606 two royal patents were obtained,[2]

---

[1] *Supra,* 24-5.   [2] Baxter, *Gorges,* ii. 12.

through Popham's influence, incorporating the First
and Second Colonies, as they were designated, or the
London and Plymouth Companies, as they were subsequently called, from the places at which their meetings were customarily held.   Though not named among
the patentees of either, Popham and Gorges attached
themselves to the latter, or Plymouth Company, the
grant to which covered all the territory along the coast,
and for fifty miles inward, between the mouth of the
Potomac and the northern extremity of what is now
the island of Cape Breton.   During the same spring
of 1606 preliminary exploring parties were sent out,
one by Gorges and another by Popham.   The first of
these resulted disastrously, for the vessel was captured
by the Spanish, and the release of its company was at
last obtained only with great difficulty and through
Popham's influence at court.   The other, or Popham
expedition, was more fortunate ; and the favorable
reports brought back by it so encouraged the adventurers that early in the summer of 1607 they sent out
and established on the coast of Maine what has since
been known as the Popham Colony.   The experiment
was pretentious and short-lived.   A single winter at
the mouth of the Kennebec sufficed ; and before the
autumn of 1608 was ended, the President being dead,
the Admiral, the Commander of the Forces, the Master of the Ordnance, and all the other high-titled
functionaries of the little trading-post, made haste
back to England.

In the mean time Popham had died, and Gorges
was thus deprived of his influence and wealth.   The
loss was the heavier because his own means had been
much reduced by the failure of 1606.   As he himself
expressed it of another, his " hopes were frozen to

death . . . and [he] was necessitated to sit down with
the loss he had undergone." His associates now all
fell away from him ; nevertheless for the next twelve
years Gorges continued his explorations and ventures,
— sometimes alone, sometimes in partnership with
others. Purchasing a vessel, he became himself a private trader, sending it out to the Banks and coast for
fish and furs, a good market for which was always to
be found. He even kept a party of men permanently
established through several seasons among the Penobscot savages. The business apparently was not un-
profitable, but the scale upon which he was compelled
to conduct it was small and lacking in system ; or, as
Gorges expressed it, "what I got one way I spent another, so that I began to grow weary of that business,
as not for my turn till better times." In 1614, in partnership with Shakespeare's patron and his own old
confederate in the Essex treason, the Earl of Southampton, he sent out under Captain Hobson the expedition to hunt for gold mines in Martha's Vineyard,
under the guidance of Epenow.[1] He naturally secured no fruits from this venture, except a convincing
experience that the Indian was as cunning as the information to be obtained from him was unreliable.
A year later another expedition was sent out, this
time under the command of Captain John Smith ; but
again ill-fortune waited on Sir Ferdinando. What
between stress of weather, which dismasted one vessel,
and the French, who captured the other, the enterprise was a total failure.

Thus things went on until 1620, the profits made in
fishing and trading being eaten up in futile attempts
at colonization. But all the while Gorges was acquir-

[1] *Supra*, 26–7.

ing information and experience. In these respects he
was indefatigable. He got together all the journals,
letters and charts he could lay his hands on, and carefully studied them. He took possession of each new
savage he heard of in England, and rejoiced greatly
when accident again threw in his way one whom he
formerly had, and then for a time lost sight of. The
stock of information he laid in from all these sources
must, from a purely trading point of view, have been
sufficiently reliable, for most of it was derived from
actual experience at the trading stations and on the
fishing grounds; but when, through the reports of his
Indian captives, he sought to learn something of the
interior of the land, the result was ludicrously deceptive. The Lake Irocoise, as Champlain was called,
then became less than an hundred miles from the sea,
and in it were four islands full of pleasant woods and
meadows, the home of the deer, the elk, the beaver
and the martin. The waters of the lake were alive
with the choicest species of fish; and on its shores, it
was hinted, were mines of gold and precious stones.
All the surrounding region was made accessible by
great rivers, flowing gently through a pleasant country, in which broad plains and fertile valleys were
studded with noble trees.[1] The singular feature about
the ideal was that it came so near to the reality, and
yet was so very different from it. The lake, the
rivers, the valleys, the trees, the fish and the game,
even the mines, were there; only it so chanced that
when taken all together, and with winter thrown in,
instead of making up that inviting Laconia which his
savages described and Gorges imagined, they resulted
in repellent New England. The picture was true

[1] Belknap, *Am. Biog.* i. 376–7.

enough so far as it went; merely the shadows had not been put in.

However deceptive it may have been, this brilliant vision dwelt in Gorges' mind, the result of years of patient toil and experience and inquiry; and in 1620 he seems to have thought the time had at last come for another effort on a larger scale. He accordingly gathered himself up for it. The thing first to be done was to secure a new royal patent. The Plymouth Company was not in the right hands. It did not represent enough capital, or enterprise, or power. Its charter was, moreover, defective in several important respects. Territorially, it covered the seacoast and fifty miles only into the interior; and the company had never made any regulation to secure to itself the exclusive right of fishing in the adjacent waters. In other words, inasmuch as it had secured the exclusive enjoyment of only what was valueless, as a monopoly it was not a success.

His old associates of the Essex faction being now in high favor at court, Gorges had no great difficulty in securing a fresh charter such as he desired. In those days a domain across the Atlantic, larger than a first-class European kingdom, was as carelessly assigned away to some body of petitioning adventurers as, under similar views of title, — could they but be imagined, — a like territory in the centre of Africa might now be granted to a company proposing to construct a railroad across the desert of Sahara. Neither in his new attempt did Gorges mean to find himself without such assistance as high rank and court influence could bring him. He caused, therefore, the names of many of the most prominent characters in the kingdom to be associated with his own in his new

patent.[1] There were forty of them in all, and the list
reads like an abstract from the Peerage. First among
" our right trusty and well beloved cousins and coun-
cillors " came the Duke of Lenox, " Lord Steward of
our Household," followed by " our High Admiral,"
Buckingham, Pembroke, the " Lord Chamberlain of
our Household," Hamilton, Arundel, Bath, Southampton, Salisbury, Warwick, Haddington and Zouch,
" Lord Warden of our Cincque Ports," — a duke,
two marquises, six earls, a viscount, three barons and
nineteen knights, besides the Dean of Exeter.

All of these, and a few more who claimed no title
higher than the modest one of Esquire, were incorporated under the name and style of " the Council established at Plymouth, in the county of Devon, for the
planting, ruling, ordering and governing of New-England, in America." The grant to them covered all
the territory, from sea to sea, between the 40th and
48th degrees of latitude, — in other words, the whole
vast belt between a line on the south carried through
from Philadelphia to the Pacific, and a parallel line
from Chaleur Bay at the north and east, across Canada and Lake Superior, and thence, a single degree
only south of the present northwestern boundary of
the United States, from the Lake of the Woods to
Puget's Sound. It practically included the whole of
what are now known as the Northern States of the
Union, as well as the best portion of Canada and the
Pacific States. At the time, nothing of course was
known of the interior, for Drake's adventurous voyage, during which he wintered in San Francisco Bay
and followed the coast as far up as the 48th parallel
in search of a northwestern passage, had occurred but

[1] Hazard, i. 103–18.

forty-two years before. This unknown domain was
now, on the third day of November in the year of
grace 1620, turned over by James Stuart — so far as
it could be turned over — to the governor of the
arsenal at Plymouth, as a private domain, to be parcelled out between himself and some thirty-nine other
persons whom he chose to associate with him. The
truly singular feature in the whole episode is that
this bit of parchment, so ignorantly and so carelessly
signed, proved thereafter to be the Great Charter of
New England ; and to this day that parchment is the
foundation of territorial bounds and real-estate holdings in three states of the Union and in several of the
British provinces.

As regards exclusive privileges, the deficiencies of
the old charter were effectually cured, and the patentees at least had no grounds now for complaint. The
new charter carried with it complete jurisdiction, civil,
martial and maritime, criminal and ecclesiastical,
" not only within the precincts of the said Collony,
but also upon the Seas in going and coming to and
from the said Collony." It further gave the patentees full power and authority to encounter, resist and
repel, take and surprise " by Force of Arms, as well
by Sea as by Land," all persons with " their Ships,
Goods and other Furniture, trafficking in any Harbour, Creeke, or Place, within the limits " granted.
The vessels of those concerned in this trafficking, together with their cargoes and apparel, were liable to
forfeiture, half to the crown and half to the company.
It does not need to be pointed out that, if enforced,
this grant excluded the fishermen on the Grand Banks
from the necessary use of the shore. Not only could
they no longer trade along the coast for furs, but,

unless specially licensed, they could not use its harbors and inlets for such necessary purposes of their calling as stations for refreshment, the curing of their fish, or the hauling or mending of their nets. Everything thereafter was to be done under a permit, and that permit was to be paid for. Never was there, as Lord Coke vigorously put it, a more audacious attempt at "a monopoly of the wind and sun."

Such exclusive privileges as these could not even in those times be expected to pass unchallenged, and exception to them was in the first place taken by the old South Virginia Company. Those interested in that company found themselves deprived of the right to fish in the North Atlantic. They at once lodged their complaint before the King in Council; and a long contest ensued, during which the significance of Gorges' selection of patentees became apparent. Buckingham was King James' "Steenie," — the unscrupulous, all-powerful favorite; Lenox, Clarendon tells us, was "used to discourse with his Majesty in his bed-chamber rather than at the council-board;" Pembroke "was the most universally loved and esteemed of any man of that age;" Hamilton "more out-faced the law, in bold projects and pressures upon the people, than any other man durst have presumed to do;" Arundel "was never suspected to love anybody, nor to have the least propensity to justice, charity or compassion," but, next to the officers of state, in his own right and quality he preceded the rest of the Council; Salisbury, "born and bred in court," and descended from "a father and grandfather, wise men and great ministers, whose wisdom and virtues died with them, and their children inherited only their titles. . . . No man so great a tyrant in his country,

or was less swayed by any motives of justice or honor."
These and men like these made up the list of patentees of the Council for New England; and they were
not only potent at court, but themselves members of
the Privy Council. The consciences of those about
King James were far from nice. In sitting on the
complaint of the Virginia Company, Buckingham,
Salisbury and the rest were sitting in their own case;
and before them Gorges had no difficulty in holding
his ground. His grant was triumphantly sustained.
But the other party did not propose to remain quiet
under this defeat; and, in the hour of his success,
Gorges received an ominous assurance that, his victory before the Lords of the Privy Council notwithstanding, he should hear more of the matter in the
next parliament.

On the day when the charter of the Plymouth Company bore date, the voyage of the Mayflower was
nearly two months old, and exactly eight days later
her anchor was dropped in Provincetown harbor.
The soil on which the weary Pilgrims were about to
land had thus, since their departure from Southampton, become the private property of a knot of hangers-
on about Whitehall. Still, there was no danger that
a resting-place would be denied them. On the contrary, their opportune arrival was a great piece of
good luck for Gorges, and so regarded by him. For
years he had in vain been trying to induce settlers to
go to the New England coast, and now at last these
people had gone there of their own accord. A prospect therefore unexpectedly opened itself to those interested in the new company of having some occupants for their domain other than wild animals and
wild men. Accordingly, a few months later, a patent
was very readily issued to the Plymouth partners.

But it was not until the next summer that Gorges knew of the settlement at Plymouth. In the interim his hands were full of work at home; for at last, after nearly twenty years of dragging, political events in England began to move more rapidly. On the 30th of January, 1621, that new parliament met, with the advent of which the patentees of the Council for New England had been threatened at the close of the contest before the Privy Council. It was the third parliament of King James, the second having been dissolved nearly seven years before, and the leaders of his Majesty's opposition in it lodged temporarily in the Tower. It was to prove, also, a very famous parliament in history; for not only did it impeach Bacon, but it was instant in the presentation of grievances, and with it began that movement which twenty-eight years later, as old Auchinleck is said to have expressed it to Dr. Johnson, "gart kings ken that they had a lith in their neck."

The Puritan movement, now more than half a century old, had, since the death of Essex, acquired a greatly increased momentum, and in this parliament its representatives crowded the benches of the Commons. The one thing they probably knew of the representative man of the Council for New England was Essex's despairing cry, — "My Lords, look upon Sir Ferdinando, and see if he looks like himself." But this was not for Gorges all, nor even the worst. While the parliament of 1621 might well be known as the Grievances Parliament, it might even better be known as Sir Edmund Coke's Parliament. The attorney-general, who at the trial of twenty years before had so ferociously pressed law and evidence against Essex, had since then risen to be Chief Justice of the

King's Bench; and, five years before the parliament met, he had been ignominiously dismissed from that high position by royal command. The natural vindictiveness of Coke's temper had been thoroughly roused by undeserved disgrace. Indeed, he now mainly lived to revenge it. He had been returned to the new parliament; and the high office he had formerly held, as well as his known hostility to the court, pointed him out as a leader of the opposition. Hitherto he had professed high-church principles ; he now placed himself at the head of the Puritans. Twenty years before, as attorney-general of the crown, he had browbeaten Essex when struggling for his life. Always good at browbeating, he was now to have an opportunity to obliterate from the minds of his followers the recollection of what he had then done in that line, as attorney-general, by showing them what he could still do in it as Speaker of the Commons. But, instead of Essex, that man was to stand before him whom the Puritans looked upon as having been to Essex what Judas was to Christ.

Parliament met on the 30th of January. Those interested in the South Virginia Company were as good as their word ; and Gorges found himself at an early day summoned to the bar of the Commons, sitting as a committee of the whole on grievances. Sir Edmund Coke scowled from the Speaker's chair. A long hearing ensued, — first before the whole House, and then before a special committee, — in which, both alone and with the aid of counsel, Gorges did the best he could in defence of his charter. While his lawyers confined themselves to the legal points involved, he vigorously pressed general considerations on the committee. He claimed the territory granted by right of

discovery and exploration, — by occupancy even. He
urged the systematic enlargement of England's domain, together with the propagation of the gospel, —
both, he claimed, " matters of the highest consequence,
and far exceeding a simple and disorderly course of
fishing," the interruption of which was now complained of. Then he proceeded to show, —

" That the mischiefe already sustained by those disorderly
Persons, are inhumane and intollerable ; for, first, in their
manners and behaviour they are worse than the very Savages, impudently and openly lying with their Women, teaching their Men to drinke drunke, to sweare and blaspheme
the name of *GOD*, and in their drunken humour to fall together by the eares, thereby giving them occasion to seek
revenge ; besides, they couzen and abuse the Savages in
trading and trafficking, selling them Salt covered with Butter instead of so much Butter, and the like couzenages and
deceits, both to bring the Planters and all our Nation into
contempt and disgrace, thereby to give the easier passage
to those People that dealt more righteously with them ; that
they sell unto the Savages Musquets, Fowling-Pieces, Powder, Shot, Swords, Arrow-Heads, and other Armes, wherewith the Savages slew many of those Fisher-Men, and are
grown so able and so apt, as they become most dangerous
to the Planters." [1]

That Gorges pleaded his cause with knowledge is
wholly probable ; and he says himself that in his
delivery he " did express more passion than ordinary."
It was wholly in vain. Apart from all question of
monopoly, it may well be doubted whether any cause
identified with and championed by Sir Ferdinando
Gorges would have stood a chance with that parliament. As it was, when at last Coke reported a list

[1] *Briefe Narration*, B. I. ch. xx.

of public grievances on behalf of the Commons, as
Gorges expressed it, " that of the patent of New-England was the first."

Fortunately for the patentees, James soon came to
an open issue with the Commons. The King wanted
subsidies; they, reforms. Parliament paid small heed
to words from the throne when it met; for though, to
use James' own expression, he often piped to them,
the members would not dance. The King doubtless
would willingly enough have sacrificed Gorges and
his patent, a mere pawn in the game, if by so doing
he could have gained a point; and, indeed, it would
inevitably have come to this, had not the pretensions
of Coke, backed by the Commons, become so high.
But at last, wearying, as he himself put it, with having his " words sent back as wind spit into my own
face," the King in June caused parliament to ad-
journ; and, when it again met in November, it was
only to be dissolved in January. Nothing had been
done in the matter of the Council for New England,
and Gorges breathed more freely. Nevertheless, as
he subsequently found and bitterly confessed, the
public declaration which had been made of the Commons' " dislike of the cause shook off all my adventurers for plantation, and made many of the patentees
to quit their interest, so that in all likelihood I must
fall under the weight of so heavy a burden." He did
fall. Though he struggled on for a time, not realizing it, Gorges' project had received a death-blow.
The Puritan Parliament had looked on Sir Ferdinando, and Essex was avenged.

CHAPTER VIII.

"MONS PARTURIENS."

PARLIAMENT had been dissolved in January, and during the same month Weston sent out his advanced party in the Sparrow. In the course of the next month the Fortune, having both Cushman and the sailor William Trevore on board, reached London. Weston was then busy preparing his larger expedition, which sailed two months later, and it must have been during the six weeks which followed that he took out his patent.[1]

[1] *Mass. Hist. Soc. Lowell Inst. Lectures* (1869), 147, 154. As nothing is known of Weston's patent except that it was taken out (*supra*, 58), there is no means of fixing upon the territory covered by it. There can be no doubt that Trevore was lavish of his information, and that the story of what he saw lost nothing in the telling. He talked freely to Weston (Bradford, 122), and described Boston Bay to Thomson (*N. E. Hist. and Geneal. Reg.* ix. 248), and undoubtedly to Thomson's superior in office, Gorges. Yet, though Weston's party established itself at Wessagusset, it does not follow that his patent covered that region, or that it was based on information as to localities derived from Trevore. On the contrary, the site of his plantation was fixed, as Pratt asserts (IV. *Mass. Hist. Coll.* iv. 478; *supra*, 52), by the small advance party which had sailed the month preceding Trevore's return to London. That this party should by chance have selected that very site on the whole coast which Weston's patent, based on Trevore's talk, subsequently covered, is to the last degree improbable. It would seem far more likely that Weston, from the reports of Smith and the captains of his own fishing vessels, already had some knowledge of Boston Bay; that the advance party was directed to go there; and that when a little later he applied for a patent, in the light of such local information as he could obtain from Trevore, he

Gorges at this time was no less busy than Weston. His hopes revived with the dissolution of the parliament, and he was actively at work organizing. The record of the business meetings of the Council for New England begins in May, 1622, the month succeeding that in which Weston's larger expedition set sail, and, significantly enough, the very first entry relates to a complaint against Weston, and a petition to the Privy Council for the forfeiture of his ship to the company's use. Nothing apparently came of either complaint or petition. Though the meetings of the Council were now frequent, the attendance was not large, more than six or seven rarely being present. Gorges and Dr. Barnaby Gooch, the treasurer, were nearly always there; but the titled patentees scarce ever showed themselves, though the Duke of Lenox and the Earls of Arundel, Pembroke and Warwick did so now and then. The company apparently never had any office or regular place of meeting, but the patentees were called together at Whitehall, or at its treasurer's rooms, or elsewhere as might prove convenient. It is doubtful whether it ever had even a chest for its books, though at its third meeting on July 12, 1622, an order was passed for procuring one. Its treasury would rarely seem to have been otherwise than empty.

Complaints as to the disorderly doings of the fish-

arranged to have it cover the region on the south side of the bay. If this was the case, it may fairly be surmised that the Robert Gorges patent, issued a few months later, covered adjoining territory. In that case the peninsula of Boston, and the townships of Dorchester and Quincy as well as Weymouth, may have been included in the Weston patent. Cushman surmised (Bradford, 122) that it covered a region south of Cape Cod. He evidently knew nothing about it; and not only the course of Weston's advanced party, but his whole plan of action, makes this improbable. Fortunately the question is one of little interest, and apparently of no historical significance.

ermen and traders on the North Atlantic coast, upon
which Gorges in his argument before the committee
laid so much stress, continued to come in, and it was
necessary to do something in relation to them.   Probably also the active members of the Council thought
the present a favorable time to begin to raise a reve-
nue from their exclusive privileges.   The work of po-
licing the coast of half a continent was expensive ; and
if it had to be done, it seemed but right that those
who frequented the coast should pay for it.   Accordingly, at a meeting of the Council on the 5th of July,
four members being present, steps were taken to procure the issuing of a royal proclamation against all
unlicensed trading, and other infringements of the
rights of the patentees.   On the 6th of the following
November the desired proclamation was published.   It
was a document sweeping in its terms.   It forbade all
persons without the license of the Council, which was
merely another name for Sir Ferdinando Gorges'
permit, from either trading with the natives or visiting the coast of North America between Delaware
Bay and the Gulf of St. Lawrence.   The penalty was
forfeiture of vessel and cargo.   In anticipation of this
Order in Council, the company had, at its meeting on
the 28th of October, considered what would be a fair
charge for a license, and " it was thought fitt to demand from [the fishermen] five fishes out of every
hundred."   Two weeks later at another meeting, the
proclamation having in the mean time appeared, an
order was passed providing that it, and the regulations
of the Council for New England in pursuance thereof,
should be posted " uppon the mayne Mast of every
Shipp to bee obedient hereunto." [1]

[1] The Proclamation of November 6, 1622, is in Hazard, i. 151. The

The plan for the better enforcement of these regulations which naturally suggested itself was to send out some person clothed with authority to represent the Council on the spot, and Gorges doubtless intended at the proper time to fill this position himself; but that time had not yet come. He was the mainstay of the enterprise, and his presence in England now was indispensable to it; but he had two sons, and it naturally occurred to him that here was an excellent opening for one of them. Of these two sons, the second, Robert by name, had adopted his father's calling. Young and anxious to see service, Robert Gorges, it would seem, did not share in Sir Ferdinando's disgust at seeing the "free spirits" of the time willing "servilely to be hired as slaughterers in the quarrels of strangers," and accordingly he had sought experience and pay in the Venetian service. He now came back to England, probably recalled by his father, and

records of the Council for New England are in the *Proceedings of the American Antiquarian Society* for April, 1867, and October, 1875. Smith, in his *True Travels*, says (p. 47) that the charge for licenses to fish were fixed by the Council "for every thirty tons of shipping to pay them five pounds; besides, upon great penalties, neither to trade with natives, cut down wood for their stages, without giving satisfaction . . . ; with many such other pretences for to make this country plant itself, by its own wealth." He implies also that this policy was sufficiently enforced to cripple trade. There is nothing in the records of the Council showing that any such regular tariff as five pounds for each thirty tons was ever established; it is not, however, at all improbable that this was about the rate ordinarily attempted to be charged. Some Barnstable merchants had sent out three vessels, aggregating two hundred and twenty-five tons, in ignorance of the proclamation. They paid forty pounds in composition for licenses. (*Records*, Feb. 4, 1622.) A license was granted to another Barnstable owner, for one vessel, for which he paid £6 13s. 4d. (Ib. May 5, 1623.) These sums, however, would seem to have been exacted only while the just issued proclamation was fresh in men's minds. It was soon disregarded.

turned his thoughts towards America. The prospect was certainly alluring. He was young, adventurous and unoccupied. He was offered a position of consequence and authority. The performance of his duties would carry him to a world across the sea, — a world full of adventure and novelty. His father knew more of it than any other Englishman except Captain John Smith; and to his father it was a region of surpassing natural attraction, though in winter perhaps a little "over cold." Smith, who had been there, was to the full as enthusiastic as Sir Ferdinando, who knew of it only by report. Six years before, Smith had published his "Description of New England," and now, as young Robert Gorges turned its pages over, he came across such passages as these : —

"And surely by reason of those sandy clits, and clits of rocks, both which we saw so planted with gardens and cornfields, and so well inhabited with a goodly, strong and well-proportioned people, besides the greatness of the timber growing on them, the greatness of the fish, and the moderate temper of the air, who can but approve this a most excellent place, both for health and fertility? And of all the four parts of the world that I have yet seen, not inhabited, could I have but means to transport a colony, I would rather live here than anywhere. And if it did not maintain itself, were we but once indifferently well fitted, let us starve. . . .

"Here nature and liberty affords us that freely, which in England we want, or it costeth us dearly. What pleasure can be more than being tired with any occasion ashore, in planting vines, fruits, or herbs, in contriving their own grounds to the pleasure of their own minds, . . . to recreate themselves before their own doors in their own boats upon the sea, where man, woman and child, with a small hook and line, by angling, may take divers sorts of excellent fish

at their pleasures? . . . And what sport doth yield a more
pleasing content, and less hurt and charge, than angling
with a hook, and crossing the sweet air from isle to isle,
over the silent streams of a calm sea? . . .

" For gentlemen, what exercise should more delight them
than ranging daily these unknown parts, using fowling and
fishing for hunting and hawking? . . . For hunting, also,
— the woods, lakes and rivers afford not only chase sufficient for any that delights in that kind of toil or pleasure,
but such beasts to hunt, that besides the delicacies of their
bodies for food, their skins are so rich as they will recom-
pense thy daily labor with a captain's pay." [1]

To a country thus described by him who had most
experience of it, young Captain Robert Gorges was
importuned to go in chief command, and the owner of
a principality. It would not have been in human
nature to reject the offer.

It was no part of the plan of either the elder or the
younger Gorges, that the latter should go out to his
new government unattended. On the contrary he was
to go in some state, as befitted the Lieutenant of the
Council for New England. He was also to take a
body of settlers with him, who were to serve as the
pioneers of that larger body with which Sir Ferdinando
hoped himself to follow in the succeeding year. But
to get ready and equip the pioneer party required
both time and money; and, while money could only
with difficulty be raised, the disorders on the coast
called for immediate action. A temporary arrangement was accordingly made, and at a meeting of the
Council on November 8, 1622, a commission was
granted to Captain Francis West to go to New England as " Admirall for that Coast during this Voyage."

[1] *Generall Historie*, 209, 219.

Captain Thomas Squibb, or Squeb, as the name is
spelled in the more familiar records, was appointed
his assistant. West's commission bore date the last
day of November.

Of this voyage of Captain Francis West little is
known, except that he made his appearance at Plymouth towards the latter part of June of the next year;
but where he had been or what he had been doing in
the intermediate time does not appear. That "the
Admirall for that Coast" had but indifferent success in his efforts to restrain interlopers, and enforce
the regulations of the Council would appear from
Bradford's remark that " he [the Admirall] could
doe no good of them, for they were to stronge for
him, and he found the fisher men to be stuberne fellows."

Exactly a month after the execution of West's commission a patent for land was issued to Robert Gorges.[1]
The territory covered by it lay on the northeast side
of Boston Bay, having a sea-front of ten straight
miles, and included all islands within a league of the
shore. It extended thirty miles into the interior.
This grant, subsequently pronounced void by the lawyers as being " loose and uncertain," [2] covered apparently the whole territory between Nahant and the
mouth of the Charles, including Lynn and the most
populous portions of what is now Middlesex County
as far west as Concord and Sudbury. There can be
little doubt it was located on information received
from Trevore, and was intended to include the pleasant
region through which he had rambled in company
with Standish a little more than a year previous.[3]

---

[1] III. *Mass. Hist. Coll.* vi. 75.   [2] Hutchinson, i. 6.
[3] Knowing how indefatigable Sir Ferdinando Gorges was in collect·

His destination and private domain being thus fixed,
Robert Gorges set to work getting together those who
were to compose his company. Such difficulties as he
had to encounter were due wholly to the want of
means, but these were very considerable. Sir Ferdinando's private resources, never great, had already
been taxed to the uttermost. The Council for New
England was rich in titles and influential at court;
but, when it came to levying assessments, the dukes
and marquesses and earls, whose names sounded so
well in the patent, could not be induced to respond to
the amount of a poor hundred pounds apiece. In fact
they were not there themselves to supply money.
They were there to make sure of the favor of the
Privy Council, and to act as stool-pigeons; and in the
latter capacity they served their turn as poorly as in
the former they served it well. The city had been
tried, but to no purpose. The London men of capital
were Puritans, and as such had neither fondness for
Sir Ferdinando Gorges nor confidence in his projects.
A scheme for raising £100,000 in that quarter had
been discussed at the first meeting of the company,
but at its second meeting it was "respited in regard
of the Difficulty of findeing security." A ship for
the company's use was building at Whiteby, in York-
shire. It was probably the vessel in which subsequently Robert Gorges went out; but the greatest difficulty was now found in raising the funds necessary
to finish and equip her, and she lay for several months

ing information in regard to New England from every conceivable
source, it is unreasonable to suppose that he had not questioned
Trevore closely in regard to the whole region explored in the September excursion of 1621 (*supra*, 16–18), and was not fully informed as to
its advantages, and the mistake the Plymouth people had made in
not settling there.

idle at Whiteby, receiving "great prejudice" and at "heavy charge." At last, in June 1623, it was found necessary to mortgage her to such of the patentees as were willing to advance the money needed to complete her equipment.

Notwithstanding these discouragements, Robert Gorges, all through the winter and spring of 1623, went on actively with his preparations. At last things seemed to be in a promising state of forwardness, and Sir Ferdinando then seems to have resolved on a great effort, — a final *coup de théâtre*, as it were.[1] The ground on which the majority of the patentees excused themselves from paying in the £110, which had been fixed as the contribution of each, was that they had nothing to show for their money. Something more tangible than the mere receipt of a treasurer was asked for. The number of adventurers, moreover, was not full. The charter required forty, and there were but a few over a score. Under these circumstances, as the season of 1623 suitable for the despatch of an expedition slipped away, a reorganization was determined upon. It was resolved to give new life to the enterprise, — life sufficient at least to send the Lieutenant of the Council out to his government with a certain prestige. Accordingly, on Sunday the 29th of June, a meeting of the Council was called at Greenwich. The object of the meeting was to allot the territory, covered by the patent, in severalty among the patentees. Each was to have his domain marked out upon the map so that he could see what it was, with his own name written against it. Gorges evidently spared no effort to make the occasion impressive, and King James himself was induced to be

[1] *Proc. Am. Ant. Soc.* Oct. 1875, 96.

present. Of the patentees eleven attended, and the arrangement was that twenty lots of two shares each were to be drawn, — those who drew these double shares parting with one of them to some other person, so that the full number of forty might be secured. Of the eleven members present ten drew for themselves, and ten other lots were drawn for absent members. The King drew for Buckingham. Copies of the map on which this drawing was recorded are still extant. Smith says [1] it was one of his maps, — the same which, in 1616, he had submitted to Prince Charles, — but this statement, like many others made by the famous " President of Virginia and Admiral of New England," has failed to bear examination. The map in reality made use of on this historic occasion was one essentially different from Smith's, prepared by Sir William Alexander and first published in the following year, 1624.[2] Upon this map, or " plot," were now written down, just within the coastline from the St. Croix to Buzzard's Bay, the names of the new proprietors, — twenty in number. The Earl of Arundel drew the easternmost allotment, and next to him came Sir Ferdinando. Mt. Desert fell to Sir Robert Mansell, and Casco Bay to the Earl of Holderness. Buckingham drew the region about Portsmouth ; and the Earl of Warwick, Cape Ann. The site of Boston and all its neighboring cities and towns was assigned to Lord Gorges, while the country bordering on Buzzard's Bay went to Dr. Gooch.

And in this way, on a Sunday afternoon in June of

[1] *True Travels*, ch. xxiii. 47 ; *Advertisements*, ch. x. 22.

[2] Deane, *Proc. Am. Ant. Soc.* Oct. 1875 ; *Sir William Alexander* (Prince Soc. Pub.), 123, 196, 216 ; Winsor, *Nar. and Crit. Hist. of Am.* iii. 305, 341.

the year 1623, at Greenwich near London, was New
England parcelled out among twenty persons; of
whom, as Captain John Smith remarked, "never one
of them had been there," while half of them did not
deem the thing of sufficient importance to be present
at the parcelling.

CHAPTER IX.

THE "RIDICULUS MUS."

THE meeting of the Council for New England at Greenwich, in the presence of King James himself, was the send-off, so to speak, of Robert Gorges and his company; for a month later, or in the early days of August, 1623, they set sail and reached their destination in Boston Bay about the middle of September. Captain Gorges was commissioned by the Council "as their Lieutenant, to regulate the state of their affairs," [1] but for the rest the official style of his new attempt showed that Sir Ferdinando had not been unmindful of the experience of the past. As respects the number of accompanying officials, their titles and dignity, the fiasco of 1607 at Fort St. George was not reënacted. For his assistance in his new government Robert Gorges was simply provided with a council, consisting of Captain Francis West (the admiral of the company then upon the coast), Christopher West (also then engaged in a voyage to New England, an account of which he subsequently wrote), and the Governor of Plymouth, *ex officio*. He was further authorized to add others to these in his discretion.

So far as jurisdiction was concerned, the powers, civil and criminal, entrusted to young Gorges were of

---

[1] Bradford (p. 149) speaks of him as having "a commission from the Counsell of New England, to be generall Governor of the cuntrie."

the amplest description, for he was authorized to arrest, imprison and punish, even capitally. Nor was this all; he was clothed with ecclesiastical as well as civil authority. Sir Ferdinando was a professor of high-church principles, and the Council for New England had no sympathy with Puritans. In all its plans a special prominence had been given to the propagation of the gospel, and the present was distinctly to be a Church settlement in the Massachusetts Bay, as contrasted with the Separatist settlement already effected at Plymouth. Robert Gorges accordingly took with him at least two ordained clergymen, one of whom, William Morell, bore an ecclesiastical commission conferring on him general powers of visitation and superintendency over the churches of New England.[1] As there was but one church — that at Plymouth — then in New England, the significance of this commission was apparent. Not impossibly, though it is a mere surmise unsustained by evidence, the Rev. William Blackstone, the ordained companion of Morell, may originally have been designed to take charge, under the power of superintendency just referred to, of the Plymouth pulpit, while Morell himself was to minister at the Bay.

The mere suggestion of such a commission as Morell was armed with, could not but have revived in the minds of any and all of Robinson's flock terrifying memories of Scrooby and of Archbishop Bancroft. Not without cause might they, in their fear, have asked themselves if the earth did indeed contain no wilderness so remote that an Established Church could not follow them into it to persecute. But fortunately force, or at least a semblance of force, is essential to all active persecution; and, as respected force, the

[1] Bradford, 154.

representative of the Church was in this case but indifferently supplied. Moreover, notwithstanding the apprehension that a knowledge of their presence and authority would have excited, neither Morell nor Blackstone seem to have been men of a persecuting turn of mind, though this could not have become apparent until later; nor even though they might have been liberally inclined, did it necessarily follow that their civil superior, Sir Ferdinando Gorges, was so likewise: and Sir Ferdinando under the new order of things always loomed up as the possible governor-general in a near future.

When it left England, therefore, in the midsummer of 1623, the Robert Gorges company represented something more than a possible realization at last of Sir Ferdinando's life dream, — something more even than the dignity and authority of the Council for New England. Patronized by King James and commissioned by his Primate, it also represented, however feebly, the seventeenth century church and state of England. Insignificant as respects numbers in itself, it went out in the full belief that it was a mere forerunner of a much more considerable movement; for the elder Gorges proposed himself to follow the next year, bringing with him " so great a number well fitted for such purpose " as would " quickly make this to exceed all other Plantations." [1]   Robert Gorges' own following, moreover, though small, seems to have been composed of good material, fairly well selected for the work in hand. There were families in it as well as single men, — mechanics, farmers and traders, as well as gentlemen and divines.[2]

---

[1] *Sir William Alexander* (Prince Society Publications), 196.

[2] It hardly admits of question that a record of this expedition, and

Before the party reached their destination the days were becoming short and the nights chill; for, the month of September being well advanced, the season of growth was wholly over, while the forest glowed with the mellow tints of autumn. It only remained to prepare as rapidly as possible for the winter now close at hand. Instead, therefore, of at once seeking a place of settlement within the limits of his own grant on the northeastern side of the bay, Gorges seems to have been glad to take advantage of the immediate protection offered by Weston's deserted buildings, which had now been vacant about six months. At Wessagusset, accordingly, his party landed, and there a portion of them permanently remained. The continuous occupancy by Europeans of the region about Boston Bay dates from the latter days of September, 1623.

Notifying the authorities at Plymouth by letter of his arrival, the new "generall Governor of the cuntrie" almost immediately started for the coast of Maine. He did not even await the appearance of Bradford at Wessagusset, in prompt response to his missive. As the vessel Gorges came in was bound

the subsequent settlement effected by it, was kept by Blackstone. Such a record Winthrop alludes to in his History (i. *43; and, see also, *Proceedings of Mass. Hist. Soc.* 1878, p. 197); and when Blackstone died in 1675, at Cumberland, R. I., there was included in the inventory of his library the item of "10 paper books." (ii. *Mass. Hist. Coll.* x. 172.) These paper books were lost in the general destruction of Blackstone's movables, the year after his death, at the outbreak of King Philip's War. They probably contained the record referred to by Winthrop. In addition to Morell and Blackstone, Robert Gorges was accompanied, according to his father, by certain " of his kinsmen of his own name, with many other private friends" (iii. *Mass. Hist. Coll.* vi. 70); while Phinehas Pratt remembered him as coming "with six gentlemen attending him, and divers men to do his labor and other men with their families." (iv. *Mass. Hist. Coll.* iv. 486.)

to Virginia, he probably wished, in view of the late-
ness of the season, to delay her in her voyage as little
as possible; and yet he wanted at once to hunt up
Weston, against whom the anger of his father and of
the Council for New England was hot. The cause
of complaint does not seem to have arisen out of the
disorders of the Wessagusset plantation so much as
from some irregular proceedings of Weston's nearer
home. Exactly what these were cannot now be ascertained; but England was then at war with the
Emperor, and the usual strict regulation had been
made against the export of munitions. A favorite
method of evading this regulation was to send the
munitions out of the country under pretence that they
were for use in the colonies, and then to change their
destination. Against this practice several of the orders of the Council for New England were directed.
It would seem that Weston had obtained from the
Council a license for the export of a considerable
amount of ordnance and munitions, under pretence
that he required them for arming his vessels and fortifications in America. He had then disposed of them
on the Continent.[1] Naturally the English authorities
were very indignant over this proceeding, and Sir
Ferdinando Gorges had been sharply censured on account of it, — received "a shrowd check," as his son
expressed it to Governor Bradford.[2] It would even
appear that warrants were out against Weston, and
that, while his settlement was struggling to its end in
New England, the former treasurer of the Merchant
Adventurers of London was himself in hiding at home.
Eluding the officers, Weston disguised himself as a

---

[1] *Records of Council*, May 31 and Feb. 18, 1622.
[2] Bradford, 150.

blacksmith, and came over in one of the early fishing
vessels of 1623 to join his company. Reaching the
stations in Maine some time in March, he learned of
the severe strait in which those at Wessagusset then
were, and, indeed, he very probably may have there
met Saunders, who must have got to the stations
direct from Wessagusset, if he got to them at all,
about the same time as Weston. If such was the case,
the doleful winter's tale of his plantation must then
have become known to him, though the Swan, with
the main body of his company, had not yet arrived at
Monhegan. Evidently hoping to reach Wessagusset
in time to prevent further disaster, Weston set out in
a shallop accompanied by one or two men, — very possibly taking Saunders back in the same boat in which
he had come. But Weston was now not so fortunate
as Pratt and his companions had been the previous
year; for, while feeling his way along the coast, the
adventurer was overtaken by a gale and cast away
near the mouth of the Merrimack. He succeeded in
struggling ashore only to fall into the hands of the
savages, who stripped him of everything he had, even
to the clothes on his back. Making his escape from
them, Weston at last, though more than half naked,
found his way to Piscataqua, where he chanced upon
David Thomson with his little party, who must have
just landed from the Jonathan, and were then busy
getting themselves some shelter.[1] Thomson had appeared before the Privy Council less than a year
before, on behalf of the Council for New England, to
urge a complaint against Weston, and consequently
knew him well ; nevertheless, now taking pity on his
former opponent, Thomson supplied him with clothes

[1] *Proceedings of Mass. Hist. Soc.* May, 1876, pp. 362-3.

and other necessaries sufficient to enable him at last
to find his way to Plymouth. The sudden appearance in such a plight of the man whom, only three
years before, they had looked upon as a patron, and
who in fact had settled their destinies, excited no little
astonishment in the minds of the Pilgrims. As usual,
too, they indulged in some moralizing on the " strang
alteration ther was in him to such as had seen and
known him in his former florishing condition ; so un-
certaine are the mutable things of this unstable world !
And yet men set their harts upon them, though they
dayly see the vanity thereof."

His present low estate evidently made Weston feel
only more keenly the different positions he and his
present hosts had once occupied towards each other ;
but, curbing his tongue, he now asked them to lend
him some beaver skins, the only merchantable commodity they had. He assured them that he had a ship
coming over ladened with supplies, and that when it
arrived they should be repaid. Great as were their own
necessities, the Governor and the assistants finally let
their former patron have one hundred skins, though
they had to do it in an underhand way ; for they seem
actually to have feared that the giving away, as it
were, at such a time as that, of the only thing they had
of value might " make a mutinie among the people,
seeing ther was no other means to procure them foode
which they so much wanted, and cloaths allso." Getting his beaver skins, Weston returned to the fishing
stations, where, at last, he found the Swan. His
company had already scattered, but, gathering a few
of them together, and bartering his skins for supplies, he next seems to have embarked as a trader on
the coast. In this capacity he found his way into

Plymouth harbor shortly after the arrival of Robert
Gorges at Wessagusset.

But the Lieutenant of the Council had meanwhile
started for the coast of Maine in search of Weston
himself. Before he had gone far Gorges was overtaken by a storm, and, realizing that he was on his
way to unknown waters without a pilot, he put about
and ran into Plymouth. He was still lying there
when the man he was in search of also made his
appearance. Organizing at once a species of council,
the new Governor of New England summoned the
late Treasurer of the Merchant Adventurers before it.
There were two grounds of complaint against the latter ; one related to the disorderly doings at his Wessagusset plantation, and the other to the illicit-arms
transaction in England. The first charge was easily
met, for Weston had not been at Wessagusset at the
time of the misdoings in question, and, indeed, had
been the greatest sufferer by them ; but, when it came
to the second charge, he had no satisfactory defence to
offer. Nevertheless, through the intervention of Bradford young Gorges seems to have been mollified, and
the whole proceeding would have amounted to nothing,
had not Weston, when he saw how satisfactorily things
were going, thought proper to indulge in various pro-
voking sarcasms. This led to an explosion on the
part of Gorges, who seems to have been an indiscreet,
hot-headed youth ; and he now angrily declared that
he would either curb Weston there, or, if he could
not, he would send him under arrest back to England.
The last alternative seems to have frightened Weston
thoroughly, who took an early opportunity to sound
Bradford as to whether the proceedings against him
really meant anything, or whether he was correct in

supposing that they were all taking parts in a farce, — a harmless reproduction, in fact, at Plymouth, of the famous scene in the island of Barataria, with Robert Gorges enacting the part of Sancho Panza.[1] Neither Bradford nor his assistant Allerton were men much given to jesting on serious subjects; and accordingly, to his very considerable dismay, Weston was assured that, if Gorges, as Lieutenant of the Council, decided to send him back a prisoner to England, they had no power to hinder the so doing. They further very plainly told Weston that his unruly tongue was fast getting him into serious trouble. The prisoner's demeanor thereupon underwent a marked change. From being defiant he became humble, and supplicated Bradford's good offices in his own behalf. For some reason which does not appear, — it may have been a sense of gratitude for services formerly rendered, or it may have been an unwillingness to have events take such a course as would lead to any exercise of authority at Plymouth by a representative of the Council for New England, or it may, and not improbably was, from the conscientious desire to serve as peacemakers, — for some reason the Plymouth magistrates seem in this case to have been anxious to prevent matters from going to extremes. Bradford, therefore, again interceded. This time he had more trouble, but at last he so far mollified Gorges that Weston was discharged on his simple promise to appear whenever he might be sent for.

Altogether Robert Gorges passed about two weeks

---

[1] It is not very probable that Weston had ever heard of Don Quixote. The second part of that work had, however, appeared in 1615, eight years before the events here recorded, and Thomas Morton at least was already familiar with it. See *N. E. Canaan*, 128, 142.

at Plymouth, and when he returned to Wessagusset
it was by land, his ship being left at Plymouth to
be made ready to continue her voyage to Virginia.
Later, the presence there of this and Weston's vessel
nearly caused the destruction of the settlement; for, as
the seamen of the two were making merry ashore on
Guy Fawkes' day, the weather being quite cold, they
succeeded in setting the house they were in on fire.
The flames spread rapidly, and for a time the common
storehouse was in danger. This was saved, and the
great Plymouth fire of November 5, 1623, was at last
got under control, after it had destroyed three or four
buildings, together with everything in them : but, had
the common storehouse gone, the settlement must have
been abandoned; for the winter was close at hand,
and, under the circumstances, the disaster would have
entailed famine. Even as it was, several families,
losing everything they possessed, were compelled to
go back to England in Gorges' vessel. Since then
there have been many great conflagrations in Massachusetts, and untold destruction of wealth thereby, —
notably one conflagration in Boston two hundred and
forty-nine years later, almost to a day; but not one
of these compared, in the extent of proportional loss
and alarm occasioned by it, with that Plymouth fire
of 1623, which was due to the "rude company" which
belonged to those two ships of Gorges and Weston.

Shortly after the fire the Gorges vessel sailed for
Virginia; but the Swan was destined to pass a second winter at Wessagusset, and, indeed, had at this
time been seized by order of Robert Gorges, and was
in charge of one of his officers. While it may have
been that, upon reflection, the Lieutenant of the Council was not wholly satisfied with the result of his

arraignment of Weston, it is possible, also, that when he returned to Wessagusset and found himself there buried in the solitude of an autumnal wilderness, the possession, even for a season, of Weston's vessel, occurred to him as desirable. In any event, he hardly got back to his company before he issued a warrant for the arrest of Weston and the seizure of the Swan, and sent one Captain Hanson, as he was called, to Plymouth with it. Bradford still did his best to shield Weston, taking exception to the form of the warrant and refusing to allow its service. An intimation was at the same time given to Weston that he had better be gone. But Weston was now apparently at the end of his resources; for he had a numerous and unruly crew on the Swan, whose wages were in arrears, his supplies were nearly exhausted, and the winter was on him. He seems to have concluded therefore that, upon the whole, for him to be arrested and have his vessel seized was as good a solution of the sea of troubles in which he found himself submerged, as was likely to offer. So when, shortly after, a new warrant came from Wessagusset, with written instructions for its immediate service, no further objection was made, and both vessel and prisoner were removed to Boston Bay.

This exercise of authority on the part of Gorges seems to have resulted exactly as Bradford anticipated. There were no provisions on board the Swan, and the crew were clamorous for their wages. Even if he did not pay them their wages, Gorges, retaining the vessel, had to feed them. He seems to have made no attempt to send Weston to England.

Thus, as the winter wore itself away, its utter dreariness to Gorges and his personal companions can easily be imagined. They had come to enjoy the pleasures of the wilderness. Locked up in a desert of ice and snow, — inhabiting a log hut on the edge of a salt marsh, with a howling, unexplored forest behind and round about them, — well might they, with the mercury at zero, ask themselves where was that "moderate temper of the air," where "those silent streams of a calm sea," which Smith had pictured ? — Young men accustomed to the soft winter climate of Devon were exposed to the blasts of Greenland. Where, too, was the "fowling and fishing"? — The waters were covered with ice, and the woods were impassable with snow. And so Robert Gorges got through the long winter as best he could, probably cursing John Smith for a liar, and heartily wishing himself back in the Venetian service, or even the dreary tedium of Plymouth. Towards spring he went to the eastward fishing stations in the Swan, taking Weston along, apparently as his pilot. On his way the returning Lieutenant stopped at Thomson's Piscataqua plantation, and there met Christopher Levett, who was associated with Gorges as one of his Council, and had only arrived from England a few weeks before. From Levett, and from the fishing vessels which were then reaching the stations, Captain Gorges received letters from his father, and tidings of events as late as the beginning of the year. The news was all bad. Nothing had come of Sir Ferdinando's efforts; the patentees would not respond to the calls for money; his resources were exhausted; his friends had withdrawn themselves; a new parliament was impending; and, altogether, as the elder Gorges afterwards wrote, "these crosses did draw upon us such a disheartened weakness as there only remained [of the Council for New England] a

carcass in a manner breathless." Under these circumstances Sir Ferdinando advised his son to return
home "till better occasion should offer itself unto
him."

When he received these tidings it did not take
Robert Gorges long to decide upon his course. Possibly his health was already failing, for he is said to
have died not long after he got back to England; but,
whether failing in health or not, he was thoroughly
disgusted with his experience in the wilderness, — and
not without reason. Besides the hardships incident
to the climate, and the cruel disenchantment on that
score which he had undergone, the representative of
the Council for New England had found his official
position one of little consideration and no encourage-
ment. His single attempt to exercise any authority
had resulted only in the miserable wrangle with Weston; and, as for the interlopers he had come to restrain, whether fishermen or traders, it was plain that
they were "to stronge" for him, as they had been
before for "Admirall" West, and so he was fain to
leave such "stuberne fellows" severely alone. It was
small matter of surprise, therefore, that, as Bradford
contemptuously expressed it, young Gorges did not
find "the state of things hear to answer his quallitie
and condition," and that he returned to England
"having scarcly saluted the cuntrie in his Gover-
mente." He took with him a portion of his company,
probably his personal friends and relations, but the
rest he seems to have left under the charge of the
Rev. Mr. Morell. Had Robert Gorges sailed on his
homeward voyage directly from Wessagusset, it is
very possible the settlement there would have then
been finally abandoned; but as he apparently went

back by way of the Maine fishing stations, the bulk
of those composing it remained behind and only dispersed by degrees. Later some returned to England,
while others went on to Virginia. A few were content to abide at Wessagusset, and for another year the
Rev. William Morell continued there with them.

But little more remains to be said of Robert Gorges
or Thomas Weston. Before they parted, a settlement
considerably to the advantage of the latter seems
to have been effected between them. Not only was
Weston released from arrest, but his vessel was restored to him, and compensation made in kind for
whatever loss he had sustained. He thereupon once
more reappeared at Plymouth, and thence went to
Virginia. Subsequently he seems for a time to have
been engaged in trading along the coast, but for how
long, and whether to good purpose or otherwise, does
not appear. The only further mention found of him
in Bradford is in connection with the mutinous spirit
of discontent in the crew of the pinnace called the
Little James, which at about this time was sent out
for the service of the Plymouth Colony. Weston was
suspected of having given them bad advice. He at
last drifted back to England, where long afterwards,
in the spring or summer of 1645, about the time of
the battle of Naseby, he died at Bristol, a victim of
the plague.[1]

Robert Gorges had died long before. The two thus
vanish. Both were men of the most ordinary type, —
the one by nature a coarse English huckster, the other
an ambitious and apparently brainless boy : but in
history they must each of them always continue to be
mentioned as inseparably connected with very consid-

[1] Bradford, 153, n.; Clarendon, *Hist. of the Rebellion*, ix. §§ 16, 43.

erable events. Gorges was at the head of the first permanent settlement on the shores of Boston Bay. Though as a settlement it resulted in so little that it wholly failed to influence the course of subsequent events, and has been deemed worthy of but scant notice in history, yet it was a distinct and organized attempt replete with possibilities. The key-point to the eastern coast of Massachusetts was then waiting for a first occupant. Had the resources and business capacity of the elder Gorges been at all equal to his activity and persistence; had he been able to control, of ready money, a few thousand pounds more; had his son been a man of a little stronger will or more robust body, — Endicott, Winthrop and Saltonstall would, seven years later, have found the place in which they then sat down so effectually closed against their movement that they must necessarily have been forced to go elsewhere.

It is scarcely profitable to waste conjecture over what might have been, had the events of the past been other than they were: but, as will presently be seen, it was years before the Gorges claim ceased to be a cause of anxiety to the later Puritan settlers. At one time it threatened them with dangers which it seemed impossible to escape, — dangers which made doubtful the peace and even the permanence of the colony; yet in the end it came to nothing. Time and the course of larger events disposed of it. In half a century more, nothing remained of the work of Gorges, or of the Council for New England, but some parchment titles which were extinguished after infinite litigation and at considerable cost.

It was not so with Thomas Weston. His work remained. He was just that blind instrument of fate which Gorges failed to be, and so blundered unconsciously into a small part in a great drama. He performed it wretchedly ; but the part was none the less his, it was essential to the development of the drama, and it must always remain an indisputable historical fact that the individual coöperation of Thomas Weston was at one period indispensable to events which compose the second page in the history of a continent. The mark of the adventurer — vulgar, mercenary, broken-down though he was — will forever continue indelibly fixed on that page. He was one of those who, without ever knowing it, become necessary instruments in the hands of fate for the immediate working out of great events.

The number of those whom Robert Gorges left behind in Weston's plantation is at most merely a matter of antiquarian interest, nor is it probable it will ever be known. They were certainly few. Bradford mentions the fact that they received some assistance from Plymouth to enable them to overcome the hardships always incident to new settlements ; but otherwise, for the year immediately succeeding the departure of Gorges, there is no record of them. In the spring of 1625, Morell also returned to England, having passed the intervening twelve months among his own people at Wessagusset, though he took ship from Plymouth. It was then he first informed the authorities there of the ecclesiastical commission which he held ; for, during his sojourn in Massachusetts he seems to have passed his time in a quiet, unobtrusive way, attending to his own duties and troubling no one, while a priest of another description would almost assuredly have proved a mischief-maker. Being a good classical scholar, as well as a man of observing

mind and gentle tastes, he whiled away the tedium
of Wessagusset by composing a Latin poem, which,
together with a rough metrical translation of it, he
published after his return to England.[1] Unfortunately
he indulged himself only in poetic generalities, and
made no attempt to describe what he himself saw, or
the events of which he was a part, and accordingly
what he wrote has comparatively little either of permanent value or of interest.   Yet one thing is apparent from it.   A spring and summer at Wessagusset
had effaced, from his mind at least, the first impres-
sions made by a New England winter.   He was,
indeed, as much charmed by the natural beauties of
the region about Boston Bay as he was disgusted with
the aborigines who inhabited it.   He speaks in terms
as glowing as Captain John Smith's of "her sweet
ayre, rich soile, blest seas," where, as he renders his
more melodious Latin,

> " The fruitfull and well watered earth doth glad
> All hearts, when Flora 's with her spangles clad,
> And yeelds an hundred fold for one,
> To feede the bee and to invite the drone.
> . . . .
> All ore that maine the vernant trees abound,
> Where cedar, cypres, spruce, and beech are found.
> Ash, oake, and wal-nut, pines, and junipere ;
> The hasel, palme, and hundred more are there.
> Ther 's grasse and hearbs contenting man and beast,
> On which both deare, and beares, and wolves do feast.
> . . . .
> The ayre and earth if good, are blessings rare,
> But when with these the waters blessed are,
> The place is compleat ; here each pleasant spring
> Is like those fountains where the muses sing.
> The easie channels gliding to the east,
> Unlesse oreflowed then post to be releast,

[1] Both poem and translation are reprinted in I. *Mass. Hist. Coll.* i.
125.

> The ponds and places where the waters stay,
> Content the fowler with all pleasant prey.
> Thus ayre and earth and water give content,
> And highly honor this rich continent." [1]

But when he came to dealing with the noble red man, Morell is free in his expressions of disgust : —

> " They 're wondrous cruell, strangely base and vile,
> Quickly displeased, and hardly reconcild.
> .   .   .   .
> Themselves they warme, their ungirt limbes they rest
> In straw, and houses, like to sties."

With the Indian women he was far more favorably impressed, and gives a pretty picture of their " baskets wrought with art and lyne," and the straw hangings in which they wove

> " Rare stories, princes, people, kingdomes, towers,
> In curious finger-worke, or parchment flowers."

In regard to the settlement of which he was a part,

[1] The greater felicity of the Latin version, which has a remote ring of the Georgics, may be inferred from the following specimens : —

> " Est locus occiduo procul hinc spaciosus in orbe,
> Plurima regna tenens, populisque incognitus ipsis.
> Felix frugiferis sulcis, simul æquore felix :
> Prædis perdives variis, et flumine dives,
> Axe satis calidus, rigidoque a frigore tutus.
> .   .   .   .
> Prospera tranquillus contingit littora portus,
> Altus, apertus, ubi valeant se condere naves,
> Invitis ventis, securæ rupe et arena.
> Æquora multiplices præbent tranquilla marinas
> Temporibus solitis prædas retentibus hamis :
> Halices, fagros, scombros, cancrosque locustas,
> Ostrea curvatis conchis, conchasque trigones,
> Cete, etiam rhombos, sargos, cum squatina asellos.
> His naves vastas onerat piscator honestus :
> His mercator opes cumulat venerabilis almas,
> His pius ampla satis faciat sibi lucra colonos."

one thing only can be inferred from Morell's pamphlet. Before he left, it had become apparent to those composing the little community that a great mistake had been made in placing them at Wessagusset. In the preface to his poem Morell accordingly speaks, with something like feeling, of the hard lot of men who are " landed upon an unknown shore, peradventure weake in number and naturall powers, for want of boats and carriages ; " being for this reason compelled, with a whole empty continent behind them, " to stay where they are first landed, having no means to remove themselves or their goods, be the place never so fruitlesse, or inconvenient for planting, building houses, boats, or stages, or the harbors never so unfit for fishing, fowling, or moving their boats."

The settlers at Wessagusset were, in fact, repeating on a smaller scale the experience of those at Plymouth. They had chanced to put themselves in a wrong location. Through trade alone, in the absence of any comprehensive scheme of colonization, could they hope to obtain those supplies from abroad absolutely essential to their continued existence ; but for trading purposes neither Plymouth nor Wessagusset were favorably placed. The furs, which were the only product of the country, came from the interior. The single means of communication with the interior was by the rivers ; the canoe was the only conveyance. Wessagusset, it is true, was at the mouth of the little Monatiquot ; but the Monatiquot was hardly more than a brook, and certainly could not have been navigable for five miles, even by a birch-bark canoe. Meanwhile the Neponset, the Charles and the Mystic all flowed into Boston Bay, and each of them afforded considerable access to the interior. Into them the brooks, the ponds and the swamps, which were the haunt of the beaver, the otter and the mink, emptied or drained.

Neither was Wessagusset more advantageously situated as respects the ocean. A large fleet, numbering not less than fifty sail, then traded annually along the coast, and Boston Bay was so well known as a place of resort that the appearance of vessels there had long since ceased to excite surprise among the Indians; but Wessagusset was accessible to these vessels only by a narrow and devious river-channel, winding among shoals and tidal flats. Ships visiting the bay could, indeed, rarely have attempted to follow the channel, but, lying at the anchorage below, must have communicated with the settlers by boat. From the outset, probably, Hull was used as a meeting-point.

There is, accordingly, some reason to suppose that, about the time Morell returned to England, those whom he left behind at Wessagusset began to do on a small scale what the Plymouth people shortly after did on a much larger scale.[1] These latter, having no facilities for trade at home, first sent out expeditions from time to time to Boston Bay, and then established a permanent trading station at Hull. Later they reached out further, and established a similar station on the Kennebec; and finally, in 1633, they attempted one even on the Connecticut. From these came what little prosperity they had, for their soil at home yielded them at best but a scant subsistence. In the same way, in 1625, those whom Morell had left at Wessagusset began to reach out to the more favored points in Boston Bay. Blackstone moved across to the north shore, and finally established himself, where

[1] *Mem. Hist. of Boston,* i. 78.

five years later Winthrop found him, on the western
slope of the peninsula of Shawmut, opposite the
mouth of the Charles.   Thomas Walford, an English
blacksmith, who probably came as a mechanic with
Robert Gorges, presently went over, taking with him
his wife, and built himself an " English palisadoed
and thatched house," near the mouth of the Mystic,
at Mishawum, as what is now Charlestown was called.
Finally, Samuel Maverick, being then a young man of
22,[1] came over in 1624,[2] bringing with him his wife,
Amias,[3] and built at Winnisimmet, or Chelsea, a
house which thirty-five years later was still standing,
" the Antientist house in the Massachusetts Government."   The following year he fortified this house
" with a Pillizado and fflankers, and gunnes both
belowe and above in them, which awed the Indians
who at that time had a mind to Cutt off the English.
They once faced it, but, receiveing a repulse, never
attempted it more."   This stronghold of Maverick's
probably served also as the common trading station.
William Jeffreys, John Bursley and some few others
remained at Wessagusset.   In this way the little colony by degrees distributed itself about the shores of
the bay, Maverick and Walford only being within the
limits of the Robert Gorges grant.[4]   They were all
that was left of the expedition which when it departed
from England in August, 1623, supposed itself to be
the mere advance guard of a great system of colonization which was to establish the party of Church and
King on the soil of the New World.

[1] Savage, *Gen. Dict.*
[2] *Proc. Mass. Hist. Soc.* Series II. i. 236, 372 ; iv. *Mass. Hist. Coll.*
vii. 318.
[3] Sumner, *East Boston*, 161.
[4] Young, *Chron. of Mass.* 51, n.

CHAPTER X.

"THOMAS MORTON OF CLIFFORD'S INN, GENT."

AT or about the time Morell left Wessagusset to follow Robert Gorges back to England, a Captain Wollaston sailed into Boston Bay in command of a vessel which there completed its voyage. On board of it was a little company of adventurers, consisting of three or four men of some substance, having with them thirty or forty servants, as they were called, or persons who had sold their time for a period of years. Those in control of the expedition, of whom Wollaston was chief, seem to have had no object in view except immediate gain, which they, like Weston, thought to secure by establishing a plantation, trading-post and fishing station on the shores of Massachusetts Bay. Of Captain Wollaston himself almost nothing at all, not even his Christian name, is known. A veritable bird of passage, he flitted out from an English obscurity, rested for a brief space upon a hillock on the shore of Boston Bay, giving to it his name as a memorial forever, and then forthwith disappeared into the oblivion from which he came. Among the Plymouth people, Bradford says, he bore the reputation of being "a man of pretie parts," and of "some eminencie;" and beyond this nothing is now known of him.[1]

[1] See Introduction to the *N. E. Canaan*, Prince Soc. ed. 1-2.

With one exception, that exception being Thomas Morton of Clifford's Inn, Gent., as he was pleased to describe himself, even less is known of Wollaston's companions.   Of Thomas Morton it will remain to speak more at large presently, but it needs only here be said it was probably from Morton that Wollaston and his companions derived such knowledge as they had of the region in which they proposed to sit down. Otherwise they were as ignorant of it as Weston or Robert Gorges ; or more probably they, like Gorges, misknew it, so to speak, through deceptive descriptions from the imaginative pen of Captain John Smith. But, as compared with Thomas Morton, Smith was tame and matter-of-fact in his enthusiasm over New England.

Morton, it has already been seen,[1] was probably a companion of young Andrew Weston when the latter came over to New England on his brother's ship, the Charity, in June, 1622.   The Charity, it will be remembered, after disembarking the Wessagusset company, went on to Virginia, whence she presently came back to Massachusetts, and, towards the end of September or early in October, sailed on her return voyage to England.   Morton landed with Green and the rest, and apparently remained with them at Wessagusset during the summer, returning with Andrew Weston to England in the early autumn.[2]   If such

---

[1] *Supra,* 59.

[2] Morton, in his book, never refers to himself as having been in Weston's company, or as having had any connection with him.   Under the circumstances this silence on his part is not difficult to account for.   At the time he wrote the *New English Canaan,* Morton was a dependent on Gorges and the Council for New England.   Weston's expedition had left a very bad reputation behind it, and a peculiarly disagreeable association in Gorges' mind.   Morton, therefore, had every inducement to ignore his own connection with it.   None the less,

was indeed his experience, it is little cause for surprise that he was enamoured with New England, for he saw it under its most agreeable aspect. With a keen love of nature, he found himself for a whole season rambling in a virgin wilderness. Passionately fond of sport, the bay was alive with fish, and the forest with bird and beast, — and all for him. There was no suggestion of winter. It was indeed in every aspect what Smith had described, — fresh, primeval, tree-covered New England. He had come to it also while it shone with the freshness of June; and, roaming through its unoccupied forest wilderness during the months of July and August, he had gone away just as the full ripeness of the summer was mellowing into rich autumnal tints. Accordingly it had seemed to him an earthly paradise, nor could he find language glowing enough in which to do justice to it : —

"And when I had more seriously considered of the beauty of the place, with all her fair endowments, I did not think that in all the known world it could be paralleled; for so many goodly groves of trees, dainty, fine,

his own statement is curiously precise, and is consistent only with the theory of his visit of 1623, set forth in the text: "In the Moneth of Iune, Anno Salutis, 1622, It was my chaunce to arrive in the parts of New England with 30 Servants, and provision of all sorts fit for a plantation: And whiles our howses were building, I did indeavour to take a survey of the Country." The Charity was the only vessel which came to New England in June, 1622. Weston's was the only party. At Wessagusset only did such a party build any houses. While those houses were building, Morton rambled about the country. The Charity returned to England "in the end of September or beginning of October." No mention is made of Morton in the subsequent winter experiences at Wessagusset. Had he remained there. some mention could hardly fail to have been made of him. Consequently it would seem that he must have gone back in the Charity. See Savage's note to Winthrop, i. *34; Young, *Chron. of Pilg.* 334, n.; Introductory matter to Prince Soc. ed. of *New English Canaan, passim.*

round, rising hillocks, delicate, fair, large plains, sweet
crystal fountains, and clear running streams, that twine in
fine meanders through the meades, making so sweet a mur-
muring noise to hear as would even lull the senses with delight asleep; so pleasantly do they glide upon the pebble
stones, jetting most jocundly where they do meet, and, hand
in hand, run down to Neptune's Court to pay the yearly
tribute which they owe to him as sovereign Lord of all the
springs.   Contained within the volume of the land [are]
fowls in abundance, fish in multitudes, and [I] discovered,
besides, millions of turtle-doves on the green boughs, which
sat pecking of the full, ripe, pleasant grapes that were supported by the lusty trees, whose fruitful load did cause the
arms to bend; while, here and there dispersed, you might
see [also] lilies of the Daphnean tree, which made the land
to me seem Paradise; for in mine eye 't was Nature's mas-
ter-piece, — her chiefest magazine of all, where lives her
store.   If this land be not rich, then is the whole world
poor!"

Going back to England, he was eager to return to
America: for not only was he fascinated with the
country as a sportsman and lover of nature, but he
confidently believed that a most profitable trade with
the savages might be opened; and, in the absence of all
evidence bearing directly on the origin and movements of the Wollaston company, it may fairly be inferred that he who thus described this paradise of
"lilies of the Daphnean tree," guided that company
to a destination in Boston Bay, naturally directing his
own and his companions' course to those places which
he so vividly recalled.   Wessagusset the newcomers
found still occupied by the remnants of Gorges' company, who had now been there nearly two years.
Necessarily, therefore, they had to look elsewhere for
an abiding-place.   A couple of miles or so north

of Wessagusset, on the other side of the Monatoquit
and within the limits of what is now the city of
Quincy, was a place called by the Indians Passonagessit.   The two localities were separated from each
other not only by the river, which at its mouth widens
out into a spacious tidal estuary, but by the numerous
salt-water creeks and basins which here indent the
shore, and into which drained the tangled and then
impassable swamps.   At Passonagessit the newcomers
established themselves, and the place has ever since
been known as Mt. Wollaston.   For the purposes of
the adventurers, Passonagessit was in many respects
a better location than Wessagusset.   They had come
to trade.   However it may have been with the others,
in Morton's mind at least the plantation was, in all
probability, a mere incident to the more profitable
dealing in furs ; and consequently a prominent position on the shore, in plain view of the entrance to the
bay, would be with him an important consideration.
This was found at Passonagessit.   It was a spacious
upland, rising gently from the beach, and, an eighth
of a mile or so from it, swelling into a hill.   No considerable stream connected it with the interior, but it
lay at the mouth of a creek which emptied into a
quiet tidal bay formed by two promontories a couple
of miles apart.   Beyond lay the islands of Boston
Harbor, in apparently connected succession, among
which the ship channel threaded its devious way.
But Passonagessit, as those who now occupied it
doubtless soon found out, labored under one serious
disadvantage.   There was no deep water near it, and,
except at the flood of the tide, it could be approached
only in boats.   Nevertheless, among and behind the
neighboring islands there were good and ample an-

chorage grounds, and, so far as planting was concerned, the spot they had chosen, lying as it did close
to " the Massachusetts fields," had some years before
been cleared of trees by the sachem Chickatabot, who
had there made his place of dwelling until the time
of the great pestilence, when he had abandoned it.
At Passonagessit he had buried his mother.

The adventurers built their house nearly on the
centre of the summit of the hill, where it slopes gently
away from the water to the west and south, and from
it they commanded a wide view in all directions.   On
the side towards the bay every entrance to the harbor
was in plain sight, so that no vessel could enter without its presence being instantly known.   On the other
side, at the distance of a mile or so, the land towards
the interior began to rise into round, swelling heights,
beyond which lay the heavily wooded range referred to
by Smith as "the high mountaine of Massachusit," and
named on his map the Chevyot Hills.   To the north,
across the marshes and a shallow tidal bay, was
Squantum, where Standish had first landed ; and still
further, on the other side of the Neponset, Mattapan.
The hills of Shawmut — on the western side of the
larger of which Blackstone was even then building the
first house of future Boston — could be seen still
further to the north, and deep in the recesses of the
harbor, though not more than four or five miles away.
Wessagusset lay to the south, and, except for the
woods which covered the uplands, within easy view.
Between it and Mt. Wollaston were the river, the
tidal basin, and the marshes intersected by creek.   All
the region in the immediate vicinity of the shore was
interspersed with swamps, full of vermin and impassable except when solid with frost, but through and

among which ran gravel ridges, affording to those acquainted with them easy means of passage. Except
where comparatively small patches of land had been
cleared for Indian cultivation, the country was covered by a dense forest growth.

A season must have passed away while the party
were engaged in building their houses and laying out
a plantation. The winter followed. One winter on
that bleak shore seems to have sufficed for Captain
Wollaston, as it had sufficed for Robert Gorges, and
in the course of it he came to the conclusion that
for him there was little profit and no satisfaction to
be got out of New England. Accordingly, early in
1626, he determined to go elsewhere ; and, taking with
him a number of the articled servants, he set sail for
Virginia, leaving one of his associates, Rasdall by
name, in charge of the plantation. If he did not find
in Virginia a place of settlement to his liking, Captain Wollaston there found at least a ready market for
his servants ; and it is said he soon sold the time of
those he took with him on terms satisfactory to himself. He then sent back directions to Rasdall to turn
the government of the plantation over to another of
the associates, named Fitcher, and himself to come at
once to Virginia, bringing with him another detachment of the servants. These, also, Wollaston disposed
of. But now the presence of Thomas Morton began
to make itself felt at Mt. Wollaston. His associates
apparently intended to break up the enterprise and
abandon the plantation. Such a course in no way
commended itself to him. He liked the country, and
he seems to have felt satisfied that a longer stay in it
would be not only to his taste, but could be made extremely profitable.

Of this man's earlier life, before he came to America, nothing whatever is now known. He had certainly received a classical education of some sort ; for, though he could not write English, he yet throughout all the odd jumble of his composition shows, amid an elaborate display of that pedantry then so much in vogue, some familiarity with the more common Latin writers. In his letter to the Countess of Lincoln, Governor Dudley speaks of him as " a proud insolent man," who had been " an attorney in the West countries while he lived in England ; " and he further intimates that Morton had been there implicated in some foul crimes, on account of which warrants were out against him.   Nathaniel Morton, in his " Memorial,' pieces out this indictment by intimating that the crime thus referred to was the killing of a partner concerned with Thomas Morton in his first New England venture ; and Thomas Wiggin, of Piscataqua, corroborates Nathaniel Morton to some extent by stating, on the authority of Thomas Morton's " wife's sonne and others," that he had fled to New England " upon a foule suspition of murther." [1] But in accepting charges made against Thomas Morton by the magistrates of Plymouth or Massachusetts, or by those sympathizing with them, it is necessary to make allowances and exercise much caution, for in their eyes he was not only a profane man, a scoffer and a wine-bibber, but he was also a thorn in their sides.   Moreover, he was a spy, and in league with their enemies. They had treated him with Puritan severity, and he in turn answered with intrigue and reviling. They accordingly believed anything that was said against him, and did

---

[1] See introductory matter to the Prince Soc. ed. of *N. E. Canaan*, *passim*.

not hesitate to record rumors as facts. Yet, so far as
the stories of his heinous crimes in England were concerned, it is very clear that, though twice they sent
him back a prisoner to answer for them, no proceedings were ever taken against him, nor could he even
be kept in confinement.[1]

[1] A disposition has been recently evinced, by certain writers of
Church of England proclivities, to adopt Morton's cause and take up
the cudgels on his behalf as against the New England sectarians.
Morton was a born Bohemian and reckless libertine, without either
morals or religion, and he probably cared no more for the Church of
England than he did for that of Rome. The *New English Canaan*
speaks both for itself and its author. From beginning to end, it is saturated with revelry and scoffing. But in his quarrel with his Puritan neighbors Morton found himself thrown into close alliance with
Gorges and Laud. His only chance of getting either revenge or justice lay through them. Accordingly he posed to them, as well as he
knew how, as a Church of England martyr. The part was not a very
congenial one, and he made an odd piece of work with it; but still he
did masquerade as a devotee, after a fashion. His method of putting
the matter is by no means one of the least characteristic passages of
his most amusing book. He had been describing with immense gusto
the revelries, drunkenness and debauchery at Mt. Wollaston, — how a
barrel of excellent beer and "a case of bottles" had been provided
for all comers, and "the good liquor" had been "filled out;" how
the "lasses in beaver coats" had been "welcome to us night and
day;" how "he that played Proteus (with the helpe of Priapus) put
their noses out of joynt as the Proverbe is," — he had just been describing these scenes, when, on the next page, his tone changes. The
people at Plymouth, he goes on to say, planned to subvert his plantation, "and the rather, because mine host was a man that indeavoured
to advance the dignity of the Church of England; which they (on
the contrary part) would laboure to vilifie, with uncivile termes: enveying against the sacred booke of common prayer, and mine host
that used it in a laudable manner amongst his family, as a practise of
piety."

This comical allusion to the Church of England and the " sacred
booke of common prayer" was enough. The amusing old debauchee
and tippler became a devout martyr at once, or at least as nearly the
semblance of one as he could make himself. Such references to him
as the following are then found: "It still remains for Massachusetts
to do justice to Morton, who had his faults, though he was not the

That Morton had been married would appear from
the letter of Wiggin which has just been referred to.
He says of himself, also, that he was "bred in so
genious a way" that in England he had the common
use of hawks in fowling, so that he was unquestionably an accomplished sportsman after the fashion of
that day. Whatever the experiences of his earlier life
may have been (and the chances are that they were
sufficiently varied), Bradford says that, when he came
to America, Morton was a "kind of petie-fogger of
Furnevell's Inne," while ten years later, when he published the "New English Canaan," he describes himself in its title-page as "of Clifford's Inn, Gent." It
is, therefore, fairly to be inferred that he was more
or less a lawyer. That he was not wholly without

man his enemies, and notably Bradford, declared him to be." (Preface to White's *Memoirs of the Protestant Episcopal Church,* p. xxii. n.)
"The text-books used [at the Merry-Mount school of atheism] were
the Bible and Common Prayer," and "it is undeniable that Morton
became an object of aversion largely for the reason that he used this
Prayer Book." (*Mag. of Am. History,* viii. 83.) "Boston, however,
was resolved, and accordingly they invented the charge of cruelty
against the Indians, as well as insinuations respecting [Morton's]
treatment of their women, whom, in reality, he had sought to instruct
in the principles of religion." (Ib. 89.) Again the same author, in
a paper on William Blackstone, in *The Churchman* of September 25,
1880, says: "The first mention of Blackstone is that of June 9, 1628,
when he was assessed twelve shillings towards the expense of arresting Morton of Merry-Mount, though there is nothing to prove that he
paid the tax or sympathized with the proceeding." This statement is
incorrect. There is certainly evidence to prove that Blackstone both
paid the tax and sympathized in the proceeding, though the sufficiency of that evidence may be questioned. Bradford mentions Blackstone by name as one of those subscribing to the letter to the Council
for New England, sent to England with Morton, and also as one of
those contributing to the charge of the arrest (I. *Mass. Hist. Coll.*
iii. 63). No evidence could be more direct. See, also, the ingenious
version of the whole episode of Merry-Mount given by Oliver in his
Puritan Commonwealth (pp. 37–39).

means is evident from the fact that he owned an interest in the Wollaston venture; though here again Bradford takes pains to say that the share he represented (" of his owne or other mens ") was small, and that he himself had but little respect amongst the adventurers, and was slighted by even the meanest servants. But whether he had means of his own or not, and with whatever lack of consideration he may have been treated by his companions, there can be no doubt that Morton was a man of convivial temper and a humorist. That his moral character was decidedly loose is apparent from his own statements, and such religious views as he had must have been mixed in character; yet, withal, he was a close observer, and his strange, incoherent, rambling book contains one of the best descriptions of Indian life, traits and habits, and of the trees, products and animal life of New England, which has come down to us. The man had, in fact, an innate love of nature, and an Englishman's passion for field sports. What, except love of adventure, ever originally brought him to New England, is not likely to be known; but, when once he got there, he was never able to take himself off, nor could others drive him away. At home he was probably a disreputable London lawyer, not unfamiliar with the Alsatian life which Scott has depicted in his " Fortunes of Nigel." As such he was fonder of the tavern than of chambers, and felt much more himself when ranging the fields with hawk or hound than when rummaging law books; for he seems really to have been an adept in the mysteries of falconry, and probably Thomas Morton is the only man who ever flew bird at quarry in Massachusetts. Indeed, he grows warm and almost lucid as, in his description of the country,

he tells of its falcons and goshawks and lannerets, —
of hood, bells and lures; and describes how, on his
first coming, he caught a lanneret which he " reclaimed,
trained and made flying in a fortnight, the same
being a passinger at Michuelmas." This man — born
a sportsman, bred a lawyer, ingrained a humorist and
an adventurer — by some odd freak of destiny was
flung up as a waif in the wilderness on the shores of
Boston Bay. For him his lines had then fallen in
pleasant places; nor was it strange he liked the life,
being robust of frame, eager in the chase and fond of
nature. He was of those whom the harsh, variable
New England climate, with its brilliant skies, its bra-
cing atmosphere, its rasping ocean winds and its extremes of heat and cold, does not kill, — and such it
exhilarates. So, not even a succession of winters
passed on the bleak summit of his seaside hill ever
made Thomas Morton swerve from his belief that
New England was " Natures Master-peece," without
a parallel in all the world. He was of one mind with
the Rev. Francis Higginson of Salem when he wrote,
" A sup of New Englands Aire is better than a
whole draught of old Englands Ale."

CHAPTER XI.

THE MAY-POLE OF MERRY-MOUNT.

It would seem most probable that Rasdall, with the second detachment of servants, had followed Wollaston to Virginia some time during the summer of 1626. The company had then been at Passonagessit over a year; and, as supplies were running short, the general spirit of the settlement was far from being one of contentment. Morton did not fail to take advantage of this condition of affairs,[1] gradually instilling into the minds of those few of the servants who still remained unsold a suspicion, for which doubtless there were very sufficient grounds, that it would be their turn next to go to Virginia. He then suggested that, if they would make him the head of the little settlement, they could all dwell together as equals, protecting one another, and deriving profit from planting and from trade. Exclusive of Fitcher, who was now in charge, there were but seven left at the plantation. All of

[1] It is a noticeable feature in the *New English Canaan* that Morton never once mentions Wollaston's name, or makes any reference to the facts connected with the change in the control at Mt. Wollaston described by Bradford. Yet Bradford must have derived his knowledge of these facts from Fitcher, or from those neighbors of Fitcher's among whom he was forced " to seeke bread to eate, till he could get passages for England." Morton subsequently also, at two different periods, passed a considerable time at Plymouth, where undoubtedly the proceedings at Merry-Mount were common town-talk. His silence, therefore, on the earlier incidents connected with his life in New England is extremely suggestive of an unwillingness to talk about them.

these Morton won over to his views, and at last a
species of mutiny broke out, as the result of which
Captain Wollaston's deputy was fairly put out-of-doors,
and compelled to seek food and shelter at Wessagusset.   Then began at Mt. Wollaston a singular episode
in connection with New England history, — an episode,
the bizarre effect of which it is not easy to describe.

Morton had come to New England with two very
distinct ends in view, — the one, enjoyment, the other,
profit; and he was equally reckless in his methods of
obtaining each.   It will be necessary later on to refer
to his methods as a trader, in regard to which he pre-
serves in his book a discreet silence; but his pleasures,
and the enjoyment he found in that free country life,
— these he dilates upon with a free hand and running
pen.   He delighted in wandering, fowling-piece in
hand, over all the neighboring hills, or sailing in his
boat on the bay.   With the Indians, he was evidently
the most popular of Englishmen; for not only did they
act as his huntsmen and guides, but they participated
in his revels, — and not the men only, but the women
also.   Indeed, one of the principal allegations subsequently made against Morton referred to the very
anomalous relations existing between himself and the
neighboring squaws.   Finally his taste for boisterous
enjoyment culminated in a proceeding which scandalized the coast.

The winter of 1626–7 at last wore itself away.
As the spring advanced towards the first of May,
great preparations were on foot at Mt. Wollaston,
though to the dwellers there the place was no longer
known either by that name or as Passonagessit.   It
was Ma-re Mount now; and in the name of Ma-re
Mount, too, lay thinly concealed a play upon words of

some significance,—for, whereas Merry-Mount would,
in its avowed gracelessness, have been well calculated
to stir the pious indignation of the Plymouth Separatists, and to be held up against the neighboring plantation as proof sufficient of the evil practices there in
vogue, Ma-re Mount, if the name were so pronounced
and spelled, was simply an appropriate as well as a
highly characteristic display of Latinity.   Having decided upon the name, it only remained to confirm it
by suitable ceremonies as a memorial; and, when it
came to doing this, it hardly needs to be said that
Morton was a stout friend of the rough, open-air
amusements which still cause the England of those
days to be referred to in ours with the pleasant prefix
of "merrie."   So, now, on May-day, a pole was to be
reared at Ma-re Mount, with revelry, games and re-
joicings after the English wont.

Of what actually took place at Mt. Wollaston, on
this May-day of 1627, we know through the account
left us by Morton,—himself "mine host" of the occasion, or Lord of Misrule,—and, whether it be
strictly accurate in all respects or not, that account
lacks neither minuteness nor picturesque effect.   Ab-
stinence, except in Puritan circles, was not a virtue of
the time.   On the contrary, the reign of James I. was
a period of "heavy-headed revel, east and west," during which drunkenness, whether in man or woman,
was looked upon as hardly worse than an amiable
weakness.   Morton was no reformer.   A barrel of
strong beer and a liberal supply of bottles containing
yet stronger fluids were, therefore, part of the good
cheer made ready for all comers on the festal day.
The May-pole was the stem of a pine-tree, eighty feet
in length, wreathed with garlands and made gay with

ribbons, while, near its top, were nailed the spreading antlers of a buck. When at last the holiday came, this pole was dragged, amid the noise of drums and the discharge of firearms, to the summit of the mount, and there firmly planted; the savages, who had flocked in to see the white man's revels, lending a willing hand in the work. After the fashion of the period, Morton was fond of scribbling verses, in which it is not easy now to detect poetry or rhythm or sense; so for this occasion he had what he called a poem in readiness, a copy of which was affixed to the pole.[1] Of it the author wrote that although it had reference to then current events, yet it " being Enigmattically composed pusselled the Seperatists most pittifully to expound it." Time certainly has failed to cast any new light

[1] THE POEM.

Rise Œdipeus, and if thou canst unfould,
What meanes Caribdis underneath the mould,
When Scilla sollitary on the ground,
(Sitting in forme of Niobe) was found;
Till Amphitrites Darling did acquaint,
Grim Neptune with the Tenor of her plaint,
And causd him send forth Triton with the sound,
Of Trumpet lowd, at which the Seas were found,
So full of Protean formes, that the bold shore,
Presenteth Scilla a new parramore,
So stronge as Sampson and so patient,
As Job himselfe, directed thus, by fate,
To comfort Scilla so unfortunate.
I doe professe by Cupids beautious mother,
Heres Scogans choise for Scilla, and none other;
Though Scilla's sick with greife because no signe,
Can there be found of vertue masculine.
Esculapius come, I know right well,
His laboure 's lost when you may ring her Knell,
The fatall sisters doome none can withstand,
Nor Cithareas powre, who poynts to land,
With proclamation that the first of May,
At Ma-re Mount shall be kept hollyday.

upon its meaning.   Bradford says that these " rimes "
affixed to this " idle or idoll May-pole " tended " to
the detraction and scandall of some persons ; " but
who those persons were he fails to specify, and Morton denied the charge.   In any event, with the exception of the two last lines, in which the first of May is
proclaimed a holiday at Ma-re Mount, this earliest of
all American efforts at lyric verse is a hodge-podge of
pedantry, which the author's own commentary fails to
make intelligible.

Nevertheless, such as it was, " the poem " was
ready ; and no sooner did the May-pole stand erect
than the scrawl was fastened to it, and then the revels
and the merriment began.   Joining hands, the whole
company circled in rude dance round about the ant-
lered and garlanded pine, making the shore ring with
their shouts and laughter.   They had also a song [1] of

[1] THE SONGE.

> Drinke and be merry, merry, merry boyes ;
> Let all your delight be in the Hymens ioyes ;
> Iô to Hymen, now the day is come,
> About the merry Maypole take a Roome.
>> Make greene garlons, bring bottles out
>> And fill sweet Nectar, freely about.
>> Vncover thy head and feare no harme,
>> For hers good liquor to keepe it warme.
> Then drinke and be merry, &c.
> Iô to Hymen, &c.
>> Nectar is a thing assign'd,
>> By the Deities owne minde,
>> To cure the hart opprest with greife,
>> And of good liquors is the chiefe.
> Then drinke, &c.
> Iô to Hymen, &c.
>> Give to the Mellancolly man
>> A cup or two of 't now and than ;
>> This physick will soone revive his bloud,
>> And make him be of a merrier moode.

a highly Bacchanalian character, another of Morton's productions; and this he says was sung by one of the company, who also acted as a Ganymede, filling out the good liquor to his companions as they at intervals struck into the chorus.   These verses Bradford apparently looked upon as " tending to lasciviousness ; " but, though rather less unintelligible, they were hardly more harmonious or better worth preserving than " the poem," except that one line, that in which reference is made to "lasses in beaver coats," has some significance as throwing a gleam of light on the make-up of the motley crew which gambolled about the May-pole.

Allowing for the difference between the old and new styles, May-day, in the year 1627, fell upon what is now the eleventh of the month.   It is, therefore, more probable than it otherwise would be that the occasion at Merry-Mount resembled in some respects the sweet English anniversary, the observance of which it was thus sought to transplant ; but, whether the Massachusetts May-day of 1627 resembled the ideal English May-day or not, the episode which has given it a place in history now breaks in upon the leaden gloom of the early New England annals like a single fitful gleam of sickly sunlight, giving the chill surroundings a transient glow of warmth, of cheerfulness, of human sympathy.   Before that May-day at

> Then drinke, &c.
> Iô to Hymen, &c.
> > Give to the Nymphe thats free from scorne
> > No Irish stuff nor Scotch over worne.
> > Lasses in beaver coats come away,
> > Yee shall be welcome to us night and day.
> To drinke and be merry &c.
> Iô to Hymen, &c.

Mt. Wollaston, there is a record of but one single attempt to introduce into New England those games and sports which were peculiar to certain anniversaries of the mother land. The result of that attempt was not propitious. The incident is familiar, but it will always bear repetition. It occurred at Plymouth, in December 1621.

The first year in the life of the little settlement was then just drawing to its close. A few weeks before, a small vessel had arrived in which were thirty-five immigrants, most of whom, as Bradford expresses it, " were lusty yonge men, and many of them wild enough, who litle considered whither or aboute what they wente." They were not Puritans, and much less were they Separatists; but, when landed, they were in due time disposed of among the several families. Presently came Christmas-day, the day in all the year from time immemorial associated in the English mind with thoughts of home and kindliness and goodwill to men, — a day set apart for games, feasting and jollity. On this Christmas morning at Plymouth the Governor arose, and, as was the custom on other days, called the men together to go out to work. Most of the newcomers, liking not the innovation, excused themselves on the ground of conscientious scruples against labor on that day. The Governor, in a passage " rather of mirth than of waight," which carries with it still the echoes of a grim chuckle, thus goes on to tell in his own language of the ready wit with which he discomfited the revellers. They had alleged conscientious scruples : —

" So the Governor tould them that if they made it mater of conscience, he would spare them till they were better informed. So he led-away the rest and left them ;

but when they came home at noone from their worke, he found them in the streete at play, openly; some pitching the barr, and some at stoole-ball, and shuch like sports. So he went to them, and tooke away their implements, and tould them that was against his conscience, that they should play and others worke. If they made the keeping of it mater of devotion, let them kepe their houses, but ther should be no gameing or revelling in the streets. Since which time nothing hath been attempted that way, at least openly." [1]

Thus early the psalm drowned the stave in New England. The sudden breaking in of Morton's rollicking chorus on that solemn silence seems, therefore, like a thing arranged. There is much fitness in it, also, for it sounds like a protest of human nature at the attempted suppression of its joyous and more attractive half. When the faint echoes of that chorus reached Plymouth, language in which adequately to express their reprehension of such doings wholly failed the people there. Neither were their feelings quite so inexplicable or so wholly without reason as might now at first appear, for May-day was, in the reigns of Elizabeth and James, by no means the innocent, joyous welcoming of spring which tradition represents it. That was essentially a gross and immoral, as well as an intemperate period. Christmas was at least a Christian festival. May-day was not. It was of distinctly Pagan origin, whether traced back to the Druids or to the Romans. It represented all that was

[1] One of the formal " objections against the laws of New England," submitted to the Lords of the Council for Trade and Plantation in 1677 as a part of the proceedings instigated by Randolph, was in these words: " Whosoever shall observe such a day as X^tmas by forbearing labor, feasting, &c., shall forfeit 5ˢ." v. *Mass. Hist. Coll.* i. 502.

left of the worship of Flora ;[1] and in the last half of
the sixteenth century there was a great deal of that
worship left.   As Philip Stubs, writing in 1585, says,
" of fourtie, threescore, or an hundred maides going
to the wood [a-Maying] there have scarcely the third
part of them returned home againe as they went."
This then was what May-day represented, not only to
Bradford and his people, but to Morton and his crew.
It was a day of incontinence.

Incongruous and laughable, the situation had its
dramatic features also.   It was not a vulgar modern
instance of the frontier dance-hall under the eaves of
a conventicle.   There was a certain distance and
grandeur and dignity about it, — a majesty of solitude, a futurity of empire.   On the one hand, the
sombre religious settlement; on the other, the noisy
trading-post, — two germs of civilized life in that
immeasurable wilderness, unbroken, save at Merry-
Mount and Plymouth, from the Penobscot to the
Hudson.   Yet that wilderness, though immeasurable
to them, was not large enough for both.   Merry-
Mount was roaring out its chorus in open defiance of
Plymouth, and Plymouth was so scandalized at the
doings at Merry-Mount that, when he heard of them,
Governor Bradford thus expressed himself : —

" They allso set up a May-pole, drinking and dancing
aboute it many days togeather, inviting the Indean women,
for their consorts, dancing and frisking togither, (like so
many fairies, or furies rather,) and worse practises.   As if
they had anew revived and celebrated the feasts of the Roman Goddes Flora, or the beasly practieses of the madd
Bacchinalians."

[1] Mather, *Testimony against Prophane and Superstitious Customs,
Preface.*

CHAPTER XII.

NANTASKET AND THOMSON'S ISLAND.

BETWEEN the year 1625, when Wollaston landed his company, and 1627, when Morton set up his May-pole, two new settlements, if such they deserve to be called, had been effected on Boston Bay. One of these was at Nantasket, or Hull; the other at Thomson's Island and Squantum.

It would seem that a sort of outlying trading-post, "something like an habitation," was established at Nantasket as early as 1622, the season following Miles Standish's first visit, and in consequence of it; though in all probability it was nothing more than one of those shore stations which, located at various points on the coast, especially in Maine, were occupied during certain seasons of each year by the fishermen and traders. It has also been stated [1] that in this year three men, named Thomas and John Gray and Walter Knight, purchased Nantasket of Chickatabot, and there settled themselves. The next addition to their number, if these persons did indeed sit down at Hull at this time, came in a very questionable and far from heroic or triumphant way.

The episode of John Lyford and John Oldham, the next dwellers, though only temporary, at Hull, is one of the most characteristic and entertaining in the early history of Plymouth. Both had come over early,

---

[1] Drake, *Boston*, 41.

— Oldham in the Anne, which arrived in July, 1623, a couple of months before the coming of Robert Gorges, and Lyford in the spring of 1624, some nine months later. Neither of them belonged to the general body, as it was called, of the Plymouth associates. Oldham came on his own account, it being agreed that individual holdings should be assigned to him and others, and that they should be subject merely to the general government; while Lyford, who was an Episcopalian clergyman, was sent over, apparently, at the instance of a portion of the London adventurers. Oldham was a strong-willed man of violent temper, restless, adventurous and eager of gain, — " a mad Jack in his mood," as Morton called him. Lyford was commended by those who sent him out as "an honest plaine man, though none of the most eminente and rare," but he proved to be a disreputable, broken-down clergyman, of loose morals and no self-respect. Before Lyford's arrival, Oldham had already begun to cause trouble, spreading discontent among those in the general body, and sending back to England very discouraging accounts of the condition of things. Bradford describes Lyford's landing as follows : —

" When this man first came a shore, he saluted them with that reverence and humilitie as is seldome to be seen, and indeed made them ashamed, he so bowed and cringed unto them, and would have kissed their hands if they would have suffered him ; yea, he wept and shed many tears, blessing God that had brought him to see their faces ; and admiring the things they had done in their wants, &c., as if he had been made all of love. . . . After some short time he desired to joyne himselfe a member to the church hear, and was accordingly received. He made a large confession of his faith, and an acknowledgemente of his former disorderly walking, and his being intangled with many corruptions, which had been a burthen to his conscience, and blessed God for this opportunitie of freedom and libertie to injoye the ordinancies of God in puritie among his people, with many. more such like expressions."

Poor creature as he was, Lyford seems to have been received at Plymouth with great consideration, and consulted by the magistrates on the more important matters of public concernment. Thus all went on smoothly for a while ; but, presently, began indications of trouble, which, of course, assumed the form of faction. All the perverse and discontented elements of the little community centred about Oldham and Lyford, and it was at Plymouth as it might have been in a boys' school. But the story of what ensued can only be told in Bradford's own words : —

" At lenght when the ship was ready to goe, it was observed Liford was long in writing, and sente many letters, and could not forbear to communicate to his intimats such things as made them laugh in their sleeves, and thought he had done ther errand sufficiently. The Governor and some other of his freinds knowing how things stood in England, and what hurt these things might doe, tooke a shalop and wente out with the ship a league or two to sea, and caled for all Lifords and Oldums letters. Mr. William Peirce being master of the ship, (and knew well their evill dealing both in England and here,) afforded him all the assistance he could. He found above twenty of Lyfords letters, many of them larg, and full of slanders, and false accusations, tending not only to their prejudice, but to their ruine and utter subversion. Most of the letters they let pas, only tooke copys of them, but some of the most materiall they sent true copyes of them, and kept the originalls, least he should deney them, and that they might produce his owne hand against him. . . . This ship went out towards evening, and in the night the Governor returned. They were somwaht blanke at it, but after some weeks, when they heard nothing, they then were as briske as ever, thinking nothing had been knowne, but all was gone currente, and that the Governor went but to dispatch his owne letters. The reason why the Governor and rest concealed these things the longer, was to let things ripen, that they might the better discover their intents and see who were their adherents. And the rather because amongst the rest they found a letter of one of their confederats, in which was writen that Mr. Oldame and Mr. Lyford intended a reformation in church and commone wealth ; and, as soone as the ship was gone, they intended to joyne togeather, and have the sacrements, &c.

"For Oldame, few of his letters were found, (for he was so bad a scribe as his hand was scarce legible,) yet he was as deepe in the mischeefe as the other. And thinking they were now strong enough, they begane to pick quarells at every thing. Oldame being called to watch (according to order) refused to come, fell out with the Capten, caled him raskell, and beggerly raskell, and resisted him, drew his knife at him ; though he offered him no wrong, nor gave him no ille termes, but with all fairnes required him to doe his duty. The Governor hearing the tumulte, sent to quiet it, but he ramped more like a furious beast then a man, and cald them all treatours, and rebells, and other such foule language as I am ashamed to remember ; but after he was clapt up a while, he came to him selfe, and with some slight punishmente was let goe upon his behaviour for further censure.

"But to cutt things shorte, at length it grew to this esseue, that Lyford with his complicies, without ever speaking one word either to the Governor, Church, or Elder, withdrewe them selves and set up a publick meeting aparte, on the Lord's Day ; with sundry such insolente cariages too long here to relate, begining now publikly to acte what privatly they had been long plotting."

This brought matters to a crisis, and a General Court, which was but another name for a Plymouth town-meeting, was summoned, before which Lyford and Oldham were arraigned on general charges of conspiracy, civil and spiritual, with intent to disturb the peace. Lyford of course met these charges with a sweeping denial of their truth: —

" Then his letters were prodused and some of them read, at which he was struck mute. But Oldam begane to rage furiously, because they had intercepted and opened his letters, threatening them in very high language, and in a most audacious and mutinous maner stood up and caled upon the people, saying, My maisters, wher is your harts? now shew your courage, you have oft complained to me so and so ; now is the time, if you will doe any thing, I will stand by you, &c. "

The appeal fell on deaf ears. Whether his sympathizers were, indeed, " strucken with the injustice of the thing," as Bradford says, or whether they wisely realized that they were in a small minority, matters but little ; but when called upon by Lyford, at a later stage of the proceedings, they one and all denied him. Even Billington, the confirmed reprobate of the settlement, who at a later day committed a murder and was hanged for so doing on the first gallows ever erected in Massachusetts, — even this man, when appealed to, protested against being supposed to have anything to do with the faction of the accused.

" Then they delte with him aboute his dissembling with them aboute the church, and that he professed to concur with them in all things, and what a large confession he made at his admittance, and that he held not him selfe a minister till he had a new calling, &c. And yet now he contested against them, and drew a company aparte, and sequestred

him selfe; and would goe minister the sacrements (by his
Episcopall caling) without ever speaking a word unto them,
either as magistrats or bretheren. In conclusion, he was
fully convicted, and burst out into tears, and 'confest he
feared he was a reprobate, his sinns were so great that he
doubted God would not pardon them, he was unsavorie
salte, &c.; and that he had so wronged them as he could
never make them amends, confessing all he had write against
them was false and nought, both for matter and manner.'
And all this he did with as much fullnes as words and tears
could express."

In fact, while Oldham was something of a man,
Lyford was a canting, hypocritical priest. He was
also, as afterwards appeared, a wolf in sheep's clothing. Both of them were ordered to leave Plymouth :
but, while Oldham was to go at once, Lyford had permission to remain six months ; and he did not fail to
take advantage of the opportunity thus afforded him
to give the government of the little community such
further trouble as he could.

The trial before the General Court would seem to
have taken place at midsummer. In August a vessel
was despatched to England, and by her Lyford sent
another letter " in great secrecie, but the party in-
trusted with it gave it the Governor." This letter
being " brefer than the former " the Governor inserted
in his history. It is signed " John Lyford, Exille : "
but for the rest, though it finished the writer's chances
of making his peace at Plymouth, it now reads like
a sufficiently moderate statement of discontent. Nevertheless the *odium theologicum* had now been excited, and, through all the following months, not only
the little community in New England, but the company of adventurers in London, was torn by dis-

sension. Unfortunately for Lyford, the controversy
brought to light facts of a very unpleasant nature
affecting his moral character, — facts which Bradford
took a grim satisfaction in spreading upon his pages
with cruel particularity. The preacher's domestic relations do not seem to have been happy or exemplary.
Nevertheless he and his family remained at Plymouth
through the winter.

About the 20th of March of the next year Oldham
suddenly reappeared, in company with some others.
It had been part of his sentence that he should not
return without leave first obtained, but in his angry,
self-willed way he paid no regard to this.

"And not only so, but suffered his unruly passions to
rune beyond the limits of all reason and modestie ; in so
much that some strangers which came with him were
ashamed of his outrage, and rebuked him ; but all reprofes
were but as oyle to the fire, and made the flame of his col-
ler greater. He caled them all to nought, in this his mad
furie, and a hundred rebells and traytors, and I know not
what. But in conclusion they committed him till he was
tamer."

The finale of this whole episode is told even better
in the words of Thomas Morton than in those of Governor Bradford. It includes, furthermore, all that
needs to be said of Lyford, as well as his companion
in persecution and exile. The angry and abusive Oldham, it will be remembered, had been "clapt up a
while," and then, with an injunction to "goe and
mende his manners," he was again dismissed into
exile, as Morton says, —

"After a solemne invention in this manner: A lane of
Musketiers was made, and hee compelled in scorne to passe
along betweene, and to receave a bob upon the bumme by

every musketier, and then aboard a shallop, and so convayed to Wessaguscus shoare, and staid at Massachussets, to whom Iohn Layford and some few more did resort, where Master Layford freely executed his office and preached every Lords day, and yet maintained his wife and children foure or five, upon his industry there, with the blessing of God and the plenty of the Land, without the helpe of his auditory, in an honest and laudable manner, till hee was wearied and made to leave the Country."

This happened at about the time of Wollaston's arrival; and, not improbably during the same season, Blackstone and others of the Wessagusset settlement moved across to the north side of Boston Bay. The exiles from Plymouth found Nantasket to be but an "uncoth place," as Bradford subsequently termed it, and a year later a portion of them, Lyford being of the number, were easily induced by the Dorchester company to move over to Cape Ann, and there sat down, with others sent over for the purpose, where the town of Gloucester now stands, then a place, as the historian Hubbard enigmatically describes it, "more convenient for those that belong to the tribe of Zebulun than for those that chose to dwell in the tents of Issachar." [1] Lyford was to minister spiritually to the new settlement; but it proved a short-lived affair, and subsequently he made his way with his family to more congenial Virginia, where presently he died. Oldham meanwhile, with some others, stayed at Nantasket, preferring to trade on his own account, independent of all companies; though later he found his

[1] "Zebulun shall dwell at the haven of the sea; and he shall be for an haven of ships; and his border shall be unto Zidon. Issachar is a strong ass couching down between two burdens: and he saw that rest was good, and the land that it was pleasant." Genesis xlix. 13-15.

way back to Plymouth, where he will presently be met
with again. In the mean time the settlement at Nantasket, such as it was, had become apparently permanent.[1]

Of David Thomson, the first occupant of Squantum
and the "Farm-school island," not much, but sufficient, is known. Morton speaks of him as a Scottish
gentleman, both a traveller and a scholar, who had
been quite observant of the habits of the Indians.[2]
Before coming to America he had been in some way
connected with Gorges, if not indeed a dependent upon
him ; for his name repeatedly appears in the records of
the Council for New England, to which he apparently
served as an agent or messenger, representing it in
matters before the Privy Council. A patent covering
a considerable grant of land was issued to him by the
Council in November, 1622 ; and it has already been
mentioned that in the February preceding he had
learned something of the country from the sailor,
William Trevore, whose name Standish says he gave
to the island upon which Thomson subsequently settled, and where he died. There is, indeed, some
reason for believing that Thomson, availing himself
of the information thus obtained from Trevore, either
at this time or a little later on, secured from the Council for New England an additional patent covering
Squantum and the adjacent islands.[3] However this
may have been, Thomson seems to have come over to
New England early in 1623, bringing with him his
wife, and a number of articled servants. He was as-
sisted in his enterprise, which was of much the same

---

[1] *Mem. Hist. of Boston,* 79.
[2] *New English Canaan* (Prince Soc. ed.), 128, n.
[3] *Supra,* 58 ; Bradford, 208, n.

general character as Wollaston's, by some Plymouth
merchants, and, according to Samuel Maverick,[1] he
established himself on a point of land at the entrance
to Piscataqua River, now known as Little Harbor,
where he " built a Strong and Large House, enclosed
it with a large and High Palizado and mounted Gunns,
and being stored extraordinarily with shot and Ammunition was a Terror to the Indians, who at that
time were insulting over the poor weake and impover-
ished Planters of Plymouth." It must have been very
shortly after Thomson's party landed at the mouth
of the Piscataqua, that Thomas Weston, wrecked,
tumbled ashore and stripped by the savages to his
shirt, found his way to them ; while, a little later on,
in the spring of 1624, their plantation was visited by
Levett and Robert Gorges.[2] Apparently not fancy-
ing the region about the mouth of the Piscataqua,
Thomson, two years later, in 1626, moved down to
Boston Bay, and there established himself on the island
which has ever since been known by his name. There
he lived until his death, which occurred not later than
1628. Johnson, in his "Wonder-Working Providence," asserted that Thomson, probably in 1627, had
aided Samuel Maverick in building a small fort on
Noddle's Island, now East Boston, " placing therein
four murtherers to protect him from the Indians," but
other records show that this common place of refuge,
and probable storehouse and trading-post, was built
as early as 1625 and was at Winnisimmet, or Chelsea,
and not on Noddle's Island. David Thomson accordingly could not have aided in its construction.[3]

---

[1] *Proc. Mass. Hist. Soc.* Series II. i. 234.

[2] *Supra*, 152; Winsor, *Nar. and Crit. Hist. of Am.* iii. 326, 366.

[3] *Proc. Mass. Hist. Soc.* Series II. i. 366–73.

When Thomson died, he left a widow and infant son, and to this son the General Court of Massachusetts at a later day confirmed the title to Thomson's Island.[1]

Mt. Wollaston lay just midway between Wessagusset and Thomson's Island, and a mile or so in a straight line from each, all three places being on the same side of the bay and quite accessible to each other. Nantasket and the settlements on the north shore were, on the contrary, across the bay, and could at that time be easily reached by the others only by water. Of the number of those dwelling in the several plantations, except in the case of Merry-Mount, we have no knowledge. At Merry-Mount there were seven, all men. At Wessagusset and at Hull both, there were probably several families. Thomson, Maverick and Walford were married, and each had one or more children. How many servants they and the others had, we have no means of knowing, but at the outside there may have been, in 1627, somewhere in the neighborhood of fifty human beings, of all ages and both sexes, dwelling in seven separate communities, on the shores of Boston Bay.[2]

[1] *Infra*, 342.

[2] The different authorities for the above dates, statements, etc., will be found cited in the paper in *Proc. Mass. Hist. Soc.* June, 1878, 194–206, and in *Mem. Hist. of Boston*, i. 63–86.

CHAPTER XIII.

MORTON'S ARREST.

HAD " mine host of Ma-re Mount," as Morton loved best to style himself, been content with the sports of the field, or with making observations on the habits of the Indians and the products of the country, he might probably have lived his life out at Passonagessit. Certainly such neighbors as he had in 1627 at the quiet Plymouth settlement forty miles away would have been unlikely to disturb him, and the straggling planters more immediately about the bay would have had neither the disposition nor the power to do so. He might even have erected a new May-pole with every recurring spring, and danced about it with his followers, white and red, to his heart's content ; and his scandalized compatriots would at most only have remonstrated with him over his ungodly courses. But these were only Morton's amusements ; and, while he was in America for amusement, he was there also for business. He was fully alive to the large profits which were to be made out of the fur trade, and in carrying on that trade he was restrained by no scruples. The furs, of course, came from the interior and from the Indians ; and in his dealings with the Indians Morton adopted a policy natural to him, but which imperilled the very existence of the infant settlements along the coast. The two things the savages most coveted were spirits and guns, — fire-water and firearms. Beads and knives and hatchets and colored cloth were very well at first, but these soon lost their attraction. Guns and rum never did. For them they would at any time give whatever they possessed. The trade in firearms had been strictly forbidden by King James' proclamation issued at the instance of the Council for New England in 1622, shortly after the granting of the great patent.[1] The companion trade in spirits, less dangerous to the whites but more destructive to the savages, though scandalous, was not under the ban of law; but Morton cared little either for law or scandal, and the savages flocked to him as to their natural ally. They hung about his plantation and acted as his guides; and he probably treated them well; for they certainly participated in his revels, though he emphatically denied that he was in the custom of selling them spirits. They were also his huntsmen, and, though the charge was vehemently urged against him, he nowhere denies that he put guns into their hands and instructed them in the use of firearms. They proved apt pupils. Thoroughly familiar with the haunts and habits of every description of game, they were swift of foot and quick of sight, and, learning how to use their new weapons, the Indians soon realized what effective arms they were, and naturally became eager to possess them.

There had for years been a petty trade in firearms carried on by the traders and fishermen as they trucked along the coast, but it had never taken any regular shape, nor, indeed, assumed formidable proportions. It would seem, also, to have been confined to the coast of Maine; for in the whole record of the Plymouth settlement, from the time of the first

[1] *Supra,* 132.

skirmish with the Cape Cod savages in December, 1620, to the Wessagusset killing, no gun was ever found in an Indian's hand. The bow and the knife were his only weapons, and he stood in mortal terror of gunpowder. It now seemed as if Morton was about to reduce this dangerous trade to a regular system. In cheap exchange for his surplus weapons, there poured into the store room at Merry-Mount a profusion of furs of the bear and the otter, the marten and the beaver, together with those choicer deer skins which the savages valued at three or four beaver skins, and the robes of the black wolf, one of which was looked upon as the equal of forty beavers, and as being a gift worthy of the acceptance of a prince.

The profit of the traffic in furs was as large then as it was nearly two centuries later, when upon it the foundations of the Astor fortune were securely laid, and for a time trade at Merry-Mount was brisk. Indeed, Morton says that in the course of five years one of his servants was thought to have accumulated, through his dealings in beaver skins, no less than a thousand pounds; and in those days a thousand pounds was the equivalent of more than ten thousand now. This was doubtless an exaggeration; yet it is evident that at ten shillings a pound in England, — which Morton names as the current price, while Bradford says that he never knew it less than fourteen, — beaver skins, which cost almost nothing in America, afforded a margin of profit sufficiently large to excite the cupidity of any one. It certainly excited Morton's; so he gave the Indians all the firearms he could spare, in unequal exchange for their furs, and then took steps to replenish his stock from England against the next season's trade, for, according to Bradford,

he sent out for "above a score" of weapons. Thus
Merry-Mount "beganne to come forward," as Morton
himself expressed it, and its reputation, such as it
was, spread far up and down the coast. The masters
of the trading vessels were also a lawless set, and
naturally they preferred to deal with men of their
own kind, while the fleet was a considerable and rapidly growing one, numbering already over fifty sail,[1]
more and more of which probably every season looked
into Boston Bay for barter and refreshment. Things,
indeed, went prosperously with the remnant of the
vanished Wollaston's party, and those of them who had
put their trust in Morton's promises doubtless felt for
a time that their faith was justified by the event.
They looked forward to a life of pleasant license, combined with an ever-increasing profit; and the money
they easily made was recklessly spent.

As might naturally have been expected, Morton's
neighbors watched his proceedings with a disfavor
which soon quickened and deepened into alarm. At
first they were merely scandalized at his antics, and
disposed to complain because his people, like Weston's before him, by their reckless way of dealing, demoralized trade. The savages were getting a more
correct idea of the value of their wares. Nothing
now had any attraction in their eyes except firearms
and ammunition; but, in the strong language of Governor Bradford, "they became madd, as it were, after
[these], and would not stick to give any prise they
could attaine too for them." But the injury done
in a trading point of view, great as this was, became insignificant when compared with those other
consequences to which the presence on the coast of

[1] Young, *Chron. of Mass.* 5, n.

such a place as Merry-Mount must inevitably lead.
Here was a vast country without any pretence of a
police. It was the yearly resort of a most lawless
class, caring only for immediate gain. Once let such
a gathering place as Morton's become established,
and it would indeed become a nest of unclean birds.
Desperate characters, runaway servants, criminals
who did not dare to go back to civilization, would
flock to it and there find a refuge, until, as Bradford
pointed out, the outnumbered settlers would " stand
in more fear of their lives and goods from this wicked
and debauched crew than from the savages themselves."

The danger was indeed imminent. It mattered little
whether Morton realized what he was doing and fore-
saw its consequences, or failed to realize it and fore-
saw nothing. The infant settlements had quite as
much to dread now from the gathering scum of civilization as they ever had to dread from anything except
sickness, fire and famine. They were to run the
gauntlet of all dangers. Moreover, unlike the adventurers at Mt. Wollaston, those composing these settlements had come to New England to stay. They
had brought with them their wives and children, and
were living at best in feeble communities, on the verge
of an unknown wilderness far removed from human
protection. Comparatively speaking, the Plymouth
people were organized and numerous, for they counted
as many as two hundred, dwelling together in some
twoscore houses within a stockade half a mile in cir-
cumference. The others were but straggling plantations composed of solitary families, as in the cases of
Maverick, Walford and Thomson, or even of single
individuals, as in Blackstone's case, with perhaps a

servant or two.   How great the sense of common danger was, is apparent from the fact that from Portsmouth to Boston it brought all together; and when
Governor Bradford came to recording these events in
his history, he gave vent to an outburst of indignation and alarm which is in curious contrast with the
usual moderation of his language : —

" O the horiblnes of this vilanie ! how many both Dutch
and English have been latly slaine by those Indeans, thus
furnished ; and no remedie provided, nay, the evill more
increased, and the blood of their brethren sould for gaine,
as is to be feared ; and in what danger all these colonies
are in is too well known.   Oh ! that princes and parlements
would take some timly order to prevente this mischeefe, and
at length to suppress it, by some exemplerie punishmente
upon some of these gaine thirstie murderers, (for they deserve no better title,) before their collonies in these parts be
over throwne by these barbarous savages, thus armed with
their owne weapons, by these evill instruments, and traytors
to their neigbors and cuntrie."

Elsewhere, too, he declared that at a later day the
savages were better supplied with firearms and ammunition than the Europeans themselves, and that somehow they were provided with powder and shot when
the English were unable to get them, — a fact which
has often since been noted in the annals of Indian
warfare.   Indeed, Bradford's language, just quoted,
is but the commencement of a long refrain — a lamen-
tation and an ancient tale of wrong — which has gone
up from the frontier for two centuries and a half.   It
is as clearly heard through the reports of the War
Department of the last half of the nineteenth century
as through the pages of the annalist of the first half
of the seventeenth.

Morton's neighbors had now become thoroughly
alarmed, for Indians with guns in their hands were
prowling through the woods. It was currently believed that along the entire coast there were no less
than sixty weapons in their possession, and a single
trader was reported to have sold them during the
season of 1627 as many as twenty, with an hundred
weight of powder. The savages were as yet in pursuit only of game and furs, but to men living in such
absolute solitude as those early planters, even the poor
survivors of the Massachusetts tribe were a cause for
apprehension; while behind the impenetrable veil of
the forest were the dreaded Narragansetts. Rumors of
what they were intending were always in the air. The
Indian may be cowed, but he does not change his nature, and it was now five years since Wituwamat's
ghastly head had been perched on the top of the
Plymouth block-house. The lesson taught at Wessagusset might be forgotten; the wrong inflicted there
might yet be avenged.

The situation grew daily more precarious, and the
instinct of self-preservation told the planters plainly
enough that such a condition of affairs could not long
continue; either illicit trade must be checked, or the
straggling settlers must leave the country. But the
course to be pursued to remedy the evil was not
equally clear, for, if it came to a trial of strength, the
master of Merry - Mount, even without his Indian
allies, was more than a match for all the settlers about
Boston Bay combined. His retainers as yet were few;
but the place was young, and as its existence became
known it would increase both in numbers and in ill-
repute, so that before long it might be beyond the
power even of the Plymouth colony to abate the grow-

ing nuisance. Under these circumstances their fears compelled the heads of the various plantations to arrange a meeting at which they might take counsel for the common safety. This meeting seems to have taken place in the early spring of 1628, the Hiltons from Dover, and Conant, Balch and Palfrey from Salem, as well as those seated about Boston Bay, either participating in it, or joining in the action decided upon. It was determined to ask the comparatively powerful Plymouth settlement to take the matter in hand, and letters setting forth the facts in the case, and the sense of common danger, were accordingly written and taken to Plymouth. After full consideration the magistrates there made up their minds to do as they were desired, and so a joint communication was drawn up and forwarded to Morton by a messenger, through whom he was asked to return his reply. This document, Bradford says, was friendly and neighborly in tone; but in it Morton was admonished to forbear his evil practices. The result of the interview which followed would seem to have been anything but satisfactory to the remonstrants, for Morton undertook to carry things with a high hand; indeed, he sent back word to the Plymouth magistrates that they were meddling in matters which did not concern them, that they had no jurisdiction over him or his plantation, and that he proposed to trade with the Indians in any way he saw fit. With this reply, which probably was not unlooked for, the discomfited messenger returned home.

The course now pursued by the Plymouth people was highly characteristic and strictly Scriptural: —

"They sente to him a second time, and bad him be better advised, and more temperate in his termes, for the countrie

could not beare the injure he did ; it was against their
comone saftie, and against the king's proclamation. He
answered in high terms as before, and that the king's proclamation was no law ; demanding what penaltie was upon
it. It was answered, more then he could bear, his majesties
displeasure. But insolently he persisted, and said the king
was dead and his displeasure with him, and many the like
things ; and threatened withall that if any came to molest
him, let them looke to themselves, for he would prepare for
them."

This downright defiance, also, the master of Merry-
Mount seems to have emphasized by a liberal use of
expletives ("oaths and other contumelies"), which
were probably far more frequently heard in the neighborhood of his May-pole than under the shadow of
the Plymouth meeting-house.

However it may have been with the morality of the
transactions complained of, Morton, in the position he
took, showed himself better versed than his admon-
ishers in the law of England. On the first point
made by him he was clearly right. The proclamation
of 1622 was not law. That had been settled fifteen
years before by the Court of King's Bench, under the
lead of Chief Justice Coke ; and now, to enforce King
James' proclamation of 1622 against Morton, the
Plymouth magistrates must have had recourse to King
Charles' Star Chamber, — the last tribunal on earth
for them, of all men, to appeal to, though there an
illegal penalty, for the violation of a proclamation
which was not law, could in certain cases at that time
have been exacted. As regards his second point, that
the King's proclamation died with him, though Hume
in his history asserts that this difference between statutes and proclamations did exist, — the former being

perpetual, and the latter expiring with the sovereign
who emitted them, — yet Lord Campbell says that he
was unable to find a trace of such a distinction anywhere in the books.[1] On this point, therefore, the
law of Thomas Morton was probably as bad as that
of David Hume.

But, whether Morton's views as to the legality of
King James' proclamation were sound or otherwise,
was not then to be debated. The question with the
neighboring settlers was one of self-preservation, and
the Plymouth magistrates had now gone too far to
hesitate about going further. If they did hesitate,
there was plainly an end to all order in New England,
for, conscious that he had browbeaten them, Morton's
insolence would in future have known no bounds.
They decided, therefore, to send Miles Standish to
Boston Bay with a sufficient force to insure Morton's
summary arrest.

This conclusion was reached probably in May,
1628. Acting, it would seem, on information obtained
from Morton's neighbors and in conjunction with
them, Standish, towards the end of the month, set out
for Boston Bay, taking eight men with him. He
found Morton at Wessagusset, to which place he was
in the habit of resorting, as he himself expressed it,
"to have the benefit of company," though, on the
present occasion, it would seem more than probable
he had been beguiled there under some pretence, in
order to make surer his arrest. In any event, there
Standish found and secured him. As soon as Morton
realized that he was trapped, his whole tone and demeanor seem to have undergone a surprising change,

---

[1] Campbell, *Chief Justices*, i. 273–5 (London, 1849); *New English
Canaan* (Prince Soc. ed.), 26–7.

and from being profane and defiant he became suddenly virtuous and astonished, innocently inquiring as to the reason of his being subjected to such violence. In reply he was reminded of the criminal acts to which his attention had twice been called; whereupon he at once, with sublime impudence, wished to know who was the author of the charges against him. His custodians declining to give him the desired information, Morton stood upon his rights as an Englishman, and, peremptorily refusing to answer the charges, demanded that he should forthwith be set at liberty. Naturally Standish did not take this view of the case, and prepared to remove the prisoner early the next morning to Plymouth, while measures were taken to secure him over night. To this end six men were, as Morton asserts, put on guard over him, — one of them, the better to prevent any chance of escape, lying on the bed by his side. According to the prisoner's account of what followed, his captors, thoroughly elated with the successful execution of their plan, indulged during the evening in some grim festivities with their Wessagusset hosts, festivities in which Morton, notwithstanding his general disposition that way, felt no heart to participate. The sleep of those specially entrusted with the safe-keeping of the prisoner was in consequence of the soundest; so that presently the wakeful Morton contrived to slip quietly off the bed, and succeeded in passing two doors without being detected; but, as he went out, the last or outer door shut so violently as to awaken his guard. What is then supposed to have ensued can be adequately described only in " mine host's " own language : —

"The word which was given with an alarme, was, — ô. he 's gon ! — he 's gon ! — what shell wee doe, he 's gon ! —

the rest (halfe a sleepe) start up in a maze, and, like rames, ran theire heads one at another full butt in the darke, Their grand leader, Captaine Shrimp, tooke on most furiously, and tore his clothes for anger to see the empty nest and their bird gone. The rest were eager to have torne theire haire from theire heads; but it was so short, that it would give them no hold."

Morton was once more at liberty. It was in the dead of night and a storm was gathering, so he immediately vanished in the darkness. It was useless to try to follow him. In a direct line he was but a mile or two away from Mt. Wollaston, but the Monatoquit ran between him and it. He had no means of crossing the river, and was, therefore, compelled to take the longer way about, following the streamlet up until he came to a fording-place, which increased the distance he had to go to about eight miles. But, knowing the country well, he easily found his way, being, moreover, aided in so doing by the bursting of a thunder-storm, the incessant lightning of which revealed to him the path. He hurried along, resolved on forcible resistance.

As soon as he reached his house he set actively to work making preparations for defence. There was, indeed, no time to be lost. Standish and his party would, with the early day, be in search of him; and they had but to cross the Monatoquit, or round a headland in the bay, and a short walk across the open upland would bring them to his door. At this time Morton's company consisted, all told, of seven men, but five of these were then away from home, — probably inland looking for furs. This was fortunate for Standish, though it would seem more than likely that he was well aware of the fact, and had timed his

coming accordingly. The available force at Merry-
Mount was thus reduced to three, — Morton and two
others. Nothing daunted by this disparity of numbers, these three got ready such guns as they had on
hand, four in all, with an ample supply of powder
and ball. Having then made fast the doors, they proceeded to defy the enemy over their cups.

They had not long to wait, for a friendly savage
soon made his appearance with tidings that the pursuers had left Wessagusset and were close at hand.
Soon they came in sight, and, in contemptuous disregard of any preparations which might have been made
to resist them, walked defiantly up to the door of the
fortified house, — or, as Morton described it, " they
came within danger like a flock of wild geese; [or]
as if they had been tailed one to another, as colts to
be sold at a fair." None the less this display of cool-
ness evidently had its effect, for, of the garrison of
three, one was frightened, while another had, in his
efforts to keep up his courage, become hopelessly and
helplessly drunk. Morton's means of defence were,
therefore, now reduced to his own unaided strength;
but still he did his best to keep up appearances, and
met Standish's call to surrender with a scoffing defiance, until the latter proceeded to break in the door;
whereupon Morton sallied bravely out, musket in
hand, followed hard by his single staggering retainer,
and even made as if he would fire on the Plymouth
captain. The struggle that ensued was brief and
ludicrous, for, pushing aside the carbine, Standish
seized Morton, who, as his weapon was subsequently
found to be charged half-way to the muzzle, was
himself probably the worse for the healths which he
says he had just drunk with his two followers " in

good *rosa solis*," and consequently little capable of
resistance. While this was going on, Morton's reeling comrade completed his master's overthrow by
running "his owne nose upon the pointe of a sword
that one held before him as he entred the house;"
but even he sustained no great injury, as Bradford
goes on to say that "he lost but a litle of his hott
blood." The result of "this outragious riot," as Morton termed it, was that the master of Ma-re Mount
again became a prisoner, and this time with small
prospect of escape.

Morton was at once removed to Plymouth, where a
council was held to decide on the disposition to be
made of him. According to the prisoner's own account, a part of the magistrates were in favor of executing him out of hand, and so making an end of
the matter. They were not disposed, by sending him
to England to answer for his misdemeanors, to run
the risk of having him there make trouble for them.
Standish, Morton asserts, was of this mind, and, indeed,
was so enraged at the suggestion of more moderate
treatment that he threatened to kill the prisoner with
his own hand sooner than have him sent away; but the
milder counsels of the others prevailed. It was early
June, and no vessel was then expected to sail from
Plymouth; so, either because it was not convenient
to keep their prisoner among them there, or because
an outward-bound vessel was more likely to be found
at the fishing stations, the prisoner was taken to the
Isles of Shoals, from whence, a month later, a chance
was found of sending him to England. He went in
charge of John Oldham, who a year or two before
had made his peace with Plymouth, and since been
at "libertie to goe and come, and converse with them

at his pleasure," and who now was commissioned to
represent the associated planters in this matter. Oldham was sent at the common charge, and supplied
with two letters; one to the Council for New England, signed by some of the principal men of each
plantation, the other from the Plymouth magistrates
to Sir Ferdinando Gorges. These letters were dated
the 9th of June, and in them Morton's offences were
clearly set forth, — especially the traffic in firearms,
and his maintaining a house which was a receptacle
of loose persons "living without all fear of God or
common honesty; some of them abusing the Indian
women most filthily, as it is notorious."

CHAPTER XIV.

BOSTON FOUNDED.

EIGHTEEN months passed away before Thomas Morton made his way back again to Merry-Mount, and he then found such few of his followers as still remained about the place sobered and discouraged. Ma-re Mount had in the intervening time become Mount Dagon, and the May-pole was level with the ground. Between the early summer of 1628 and the autumn of 1629 certain events had taken place on the shores of Massachusetts Bay, small in themselves but big with remote results.

On the 6th of September, just three months after Miles Standish's energetic abatement of the Merry-Mount nuisance, and probably about the time that Oldham, having Morton in charge, reached England, John Endicott landed at Salem. The patent under which he claimed a title to the soil had been issued by the Council for New England, and bore date March 19, 1628, covering a large portion of the territory adjacent to Boston Bay; and the party he brought with him to occupy the grant was the advance guard of a migration. The whole coast from St. Croix to Buzzard's Bay, covered by the great patent of 1620, had, it will be remembered, been divided in severalty at the royal Greenwich drawing of Sunday the 29th of June, five years before; and the particular portion of it now again granted away had fallen to the lots of the Earl of Warwick, Lord Gorges and others. But, as the Greenwich drawing was merely one of Gorges' schemes for infusing new life into his project, and putting some money into the treasury of the Council, when it failed to accomplish those ends it was quietly dropped from memory. No further mention of it was made, and, except in the case of Lord Sheffield, nothing seems ever to have been done to confirm the grants which it was intended should result from the drawing; and, as no patents were ever issued, there were none to surrender. The scheme, like so many others of Sir Ferdinando before and after, had come to nothing.

Meanwhile the request for a grant to Endicott and his associates now reached Gorges through an influential channel, — " the thrice-honored Lord of Warwick." Sir Ferdinando was at Plymouth when the Earl's missive came to him ; but he readily assented to the request contained in it, and, apparently without further formalities, a patent was issued under the seal of the Council. It may have been owing to the fact that this patent was issued at the request of the Earl of Warwick that it was made to cover the region against which the name of that nobleman was inscribed on Alexander's map, after the Greenwich drawing, for the patent under which Endicott claimed covered generally the territory between the Merrimack and the Charles rivers, though its precise bounds could not possibly be fixed. They extended " from the Atlantick and Westerne Sea and Ocean on the East Parte, to the South Sea on the Weste Parte," and covered everything within the space of three English miles to the northward of the Merrimack, and to the southward of the Charles, " or of any or everie parte " of either of those streams ; also everything lying within

the space of three miles to the southward of the south-
ernmost part of Massachusetts, meaning Boston, Bay.
Whatever, therefore, might be excluded from it, it was
clear that the whole region in which Wessagusset,
Mount Wollaston, Thomson's Island and Shawmut
were situated, was included in it.

Morton's establishment was thus brought clearly
within the jurisdiction of Endicott. The existence
and character of the Wollaston trading-post must have
been known in England, and it is not at all improbable
that its prompt suppression had been there decided
upon ; but, whether this was so or not, John Endicott, that typical Puritan magistrate, must certainly
have learned, as soon as he landed at Naumkeag, of
the decisive action taken by the Plymouth people
three months before. That action doubtless, also,
commended itself to him, though probably he regretted that more condign punishment had not been
meted out to the evil-doer ; nor did he delay taking
such steps as were still in his power to make good
this shortcoming. Accompanied by a small party he
crossed the bay, and, making his appearance among
Morton's terrified followers, he hewed down the May-
pole, rebuked them sternly for their profaneness, and
" admonished them to looke ther should be better
walking. So they now, or others, changed the name
of their place againe, and called it Mounte-Dagon,"
after that sea-idol of the Philistines, at whose memorable feast at Gaza

" The morning trumpets festival proclaim'd
Through each high street."

After this visit of Endicott's no mention whatever is
found of those settled about Boston Harbor until the
next summer, though, in the mean time, events were

taking place in England calculated to hasten forward
the long delayed occupation of those parts. John
Oldham, having Thomas Morton in his custody, had
landed at Plymouth during the later summer or early
autumn of 1628, having passed the outward-bound
Endicott in mid-ocean. As Oldham bore letters to
Gorges, there can be no question that, landing at
Plymouth, he there met Sir Ferdinando at once; and
it is also probable that Oldham, who was an enterprising man, had come out to England with some scheme
of his own for obtaining a patent from the Council for
New England, and establishing a trading connection.
Robert Gorges was then dead, and the title to his
grant on the northeast side of Massachusetts Bay had
passed to his brother John.[1] So the result of Oldham's
interviews with Sir Ferdinando and John Gorges was
that the latter conveyed to him the whole district between the Charles and the Saugus rivers, for a distance, into the interior, of five miles on the former and
three on the latter. This deed not improbably may
have borne the same date, January 10, 1629, as a similar deed of a yet larger tract, out of the same grant,
which John Gorges executed to Sir William Brereton.
The lands thus conveyed were distinctly within the
limits covered by the grant of the Council to Endicott and his associates. Sir Ferdinando subsequently
claimed that the later grant was made with a distinct
reservation on his part of all rights conveyed to his
son Robert under the earlier one, nor does there seem
to be any reason to doubt that such was the intention; but the business of the Council for New England was always transacted in a careless, slipshod way.
Grants were made, equal in extent to half-a-dozen

[1] *Mass. Hist. Soc. Lowell Institute Lectures* (1869), 154.

English counties, and patents, of which no copies seem to have been kept, issued for them.[1] To these grants, accordingly, no great attention was paid. Nevertheless, the formal conveyance to John Oldham by John Gorges of a very considerable tract, in the heart of the Massachusetts Bay concession, at once raised a serious question of title.

The ideas and projects of those associated with Endicott had now become much enlarged. Less active-minded and scheming than Gorges, they represented what he did not, — some property, and a large number of men and women bound together by a strong common feeling, and ready to leave their country, not as adventurers temporarily absenting themselves, but never to come back to it. The leaders of this movement had gone on from step to step, their vision widening as they went. They, as well as the Council for New England, had friends at court; and now, seeing how doubtful a title they held under the grant of the Council, — confronted already by claimants under earlier grants, — they went directly to the throne. A royal confirmation of their patent was solicited, and, through the intervention of Lord Dorchester, obtained. On the 4th of March, 1629, King Charles' charter of the colony of Massachusetts Bay passed the seals.

This whole proceeding could not but have been extremely offensive to Gorges. Apart from any question affecting his son's title to territory now in dispute, the granting of the charter by the crown seemed to cast a doubt on the validity of the grant by the Council for New England, if it did not supersede its

---

[1] For a list of the grants made, or alleged to have been made, by the Council, see Palfrey, i. 397; and Dr. Haven's history of these grants already referred to, in *Mass. Hist. Soc. Lowell Inst. Lectures.*

authority. It must besides have mortified the Governor of Plymouth greatly to find himself outgeneralled at court, for there, at least, he had been accustomed to make things take the shape he wanted. In any case, from that time forward, however he might dissemble and by speech or letter pretend to seek its welfare, the infant colony had to count Sir Ferdinando as its most persistent and, the result soon showed, its most dangerous enemy, — an enemy in whose cunning hands king, primate and attorney-general in turn became puppets. Fortunately for Massachusetts, while Gorges was poor, King Charles was needy.

Oldham, probably now acting in collusion with Gorges, entered into active negotiations with the representatives of the Massachusetts company, and endeavored to secure a position of trust and confidence in their service. Cradock and his associates were at first disposed to listen to him; but, whether Oldham himself believed in what he said or not, — though, judging by the character of the man, it is altogether probable he did, — he decidedly overshot his mark. He promised too much. He was not now dealing with the sanguine, speculative Gorges, but with a company of slow, hard-headed men of affairs; and a promise of a threefold return on their venture, in as many years, only shook faith in the maker of such a promise. All that Oldham asked was that the management of the new company's trade in furs should be left in his hands: were this but done he wanted no pay for himself, if only he might have the surplus made over a profit of three hundred per cent. in the three years; and he who held out these glowing hopes was not only an experienced American planter, as the first settlers were called, but he had a title hardly less good

than the company's own to a considerable portion of
its grant. Governor Cradock and his assistants seem,
therefore, to have been so really anxious to reach an
understanding with Oldham that continual meetings
took place, and the matter was under discussion all
through the spring months of 1629. Taking his stand
apparently on the grant from John Gorges, Oldham
tried to compel the company either to entrust to him
the exclusive management of its trading affairs, or else
to leave him at complete liberty to trade as he saw fit
within the limits conveyed to him by Gorges, — and
this, not only on his own account, but in company with
any one else he chose. In fact, Oldham asserted his
practical independence of the Massachusetts company.
By degrees, as the defects of temper and judgment,
which Oldham had already manifested at Plymouth,
showed themselves again, Cradock, Venn and the rest
got to know the kind of man with whom they had to
deal. Enterprising as a trader, and by temperament
daring, John Oldham belonged to a type still common
enough among the English and in New England, — a
type in which the characteristic good qualities of the
race are spoiled by being developed in excess. A
human bull-dog, or, as Morton well described him, " a
mad Jack in his mood," he was obstinate, factious and
violent. Once he had made up his mind, nothing
could change him ; he must either have his way or
fight. The fact that the majority, as during the Lyford troubles at Plymouth, were all the other way,
only served to make him more headstrong, and, if need
be, more outrageous. Standing on what he considered
his rights, he recognized on the other side force only,
— nor that, even, until his every effort at resistance
had been put down. So now, in dealing with a com-

mittee of the Massachusetts company, Oldham showed himself wholly impracticable. Nothing could be done with him. The trade in beaver skins was the most immediately valuable privilege which the company possessed, and it proposed to retain that trade in its own hands; indeed, the profits to be derived from it had already been set aside as a fund, out of which the common defence and public worship were to be provided for.[1] Oldham's proposition was, therefore, out of the question.

Still it was not until April that all hopes of reaching an understanding were abandoned. Then, when committee after committee had tried its hand and failed to make the smallest progress, the matter was at last referred to counsel, and the company was advised to treat the Robert Gorges grant as void in law, on the ground that it was not sufficiently definite; and in pursuance of this advice, it was decided to have nothing more to say to Oldham, leaving him to take his own course. But the great value of possession in all disputes about title was as well understood then as now, and so Cradock, under instructions, forthwith wrote out to Endicott, informing him of the course that had been decided on, and that Oldham was himself at that very time trying to fit out a vessel in which he proposed to go over and take independent possession of his claim. Endicott was then instructed, as the deputy of the company on the spot, to deal summarily with the interlopers if they made their appearance; but, above all, he was enjoined to send at once a strong party of forty or fifty persons to effect an actual occupation of the disputed territory.

These instructions bore date the 17th of April,

[1] Young, *Chron. of Mass.* 148.

1629.   Three vessels were then lying in the Thames, loading with emigrants and their stores destined for New England.   As soon as the instructions were ready, one of these, the George, was hurried away in advance of the rest, having " special and urgent cause of hastening her passage."   Before negotiations were openly broken off, and Oldham given to understand that the company would have nothing more to do with him, the George had been already a month on her way.   Oldham had been outwitted, and, for the time at least, he was powerless.

The George reached Salem on the 20th of June, and Endicott acted promptly.   Some of those who came over at this time had emigrated at their own expense, and among these were three brothers named Sprague, the sons, it is said, of a Dorsetshire fuller. Instead of settling at Salem, the Spragues and a few others, acting as it may be supposed with something more than the " joint consent and approbation " of Endicott, started off through the woods and made their way towards the region which five months before had been conveyed by John Gorges to Oldham.   After going about twelve miles, they halted at a spot on the north side of the Charles, where they found a number of Indians belonging to that tribe, of which Standish and his party had there met some women in the visit of seven years before.[1]   The sachem of these Indians, afterwards known by the English as Sagamore John, was a son of the Nanepashemet whose grave had then been visited.   With Sagamore John's willing consent, the newcomers established themselves on a hill in the place called Mishawum, " where they found but one English palisadoed and thatched house, wherein lived Thomas Walford, a smith."

[1] *Supra,* 18.

The Spragues were soon followed by another and larger party from Salem, under the charge of Thomas Graves, the engineer of the company, especially " entertained " by it " to survey and set forth lands," and " to fortify and build a town." Evidently Endicott had wasted no time, for Graves could not have reached Salem before the 20th of June; and yet on the 24th of that month, or the 4th of July according to the calendar now in use, he and his party were at the mouth of the Mystic, where, in the course of the summer, a place was laid out under his direction, upon a plan approved by Endicott, and a large house built, which place was named Charlestown, and was intended to be the seat of government of the Massachusetts Bay.[1] The single great house, now put up by the servants of the company to accommodate such as were then expected shortly to come over, afterwards became the Charlestown meeting-house. In the autumn of 1629 about one hundred persons are supposed to have been living in the neighborhood of it.

The settlement of Charlestown was, therefore, no accident. Decided upon in England, it was intended to forestall a question of title, so far as such a question could be forestalled through actual occupation. It was a step taken, also, in pursuance of a policy which threatened to affect seriously the situation of the old planters about the bay, — those who had then been living there six years, and might be considered as securely established. The Massachusetts Bay company professed itself eager to deal fairly with these men ; but it had its own rules and regulations, not lacking in stringency, while Endicott, a man of domineering temper, who stood ready at any time to have

[1] *Mem. Hist. of Boston,* i. 385.

recourse to the pillory and the whipping-post, was instructed to enforce those rules. They related expressly to the trade in beaver and the cultivation of
tobacco. So far as the trade in furs was concerned,
there can be no question that it was the only really
profitable trade open to the old planters. They were
all engaged in it. Indeed, to such an extent were
they engaged in it that in Massachusetts beaver skins
were used as currency, just as tobacco was used in
Virginia. Of this trade, it has been stated already the
new colony proposed to make a government monopoly,
and, in the language of the letter of instructions written to Endicott by Cradock, on behalf of himself and
the Assistants, they would not willingly "permit any
to appropriate that to their own private lucre which
we, in our religious intentions, have dedicated to the
common charge of building houses for God's worship,
and forts to defend such as shall come thither to in-
habit."

So, also, as respects tobacco. Strange as it now
seems, those who first cultivated the soil on the shores
of Boston Bay seem to have looked upon the growing of tobacco as the most profitable use to which
they could put their labor. The promoters of the
new company, on the other hand, appear to have
shared, to the full extent, in King James' horror of
that weed, and some of the principal among them
even went so far as to declare themselves absolutely
unwilling to have any hand in the undertaking if it
was intended to permit tobacco to be grown. They
apparently looked upon it then much as opium is
looked upon now. When, therefore, the old planters
earnestly petitioned that they might not be cut off
from what they considered their most profitable crop,

the utmost concession they could get was that they might go on cultivating it for the present, in such manner and under such restrictions as Endicott and his council should think fitting, "having an especial care, with as much conveniency as may be, utterly to suppress the planting of it, except for mere necessity."

Under these circumstances, feeling the iron hand of Puritan authority at the very outset restricting, where it did not utterly suppress, the two branches of industry which they had always enjoyed, and which alone made life possible in the wilderness they had subdued and during years had occupied, — feeling this, and strongly suspecting that the title to the very land they tilled might next be called in question, it was small matter for wonder that the old planters looked with jealous eyes on their new neighbors. Indeed, certain of these ancient settlers did not hesitate in their apprehension to speak of themselves as slaves;[1] and, as the sequel showed, their fears, so far as some of them were concerned, did not prove to be groundless. Especially was this true of Thomas Walford.

While the tract granted to John Gorges was being occupied and Charlestown laid out in America, John Oldham, left far behind in the race for actual possession, seems to have fretted the time away in London. He was probably casting about in the effort to organize, with such aid as the Gorges family could give him, an expedition of his own; but, if this was the case, he was doomed to disappointment. The means with which to equip a vessel evidently were not forthcoming, and gradually the idea of an expedition, counter to that of the Massachusetts company, had to be

[1] Young, *Chron. of Mass.* 145; *Proc. Mass. Hist. Soc.* Series II. i. 239–40.

abandoned; but it was not until the next year that Oldham found his way back to America. He then seems to have accepted the situation, settling down at Watertown as one of the freemen of the colony, and in quiet subordination to its authority.

Meanwhile Thomas Morton was lost sight of. Bradford says that Morton "foold" Oldham and escaped, for aught they could learn at Plymouth, without so much as a rebuke even. This is very possible; for it would seem not at all unlikely that when he found himself, after his arrival at Plymouth, involved in negotiations with both John Gorges and the Massachusetts Bay company, Oldham had little time or thought to give to Morton, though Morton himself tells the story differently. According to his account the agent of the Plymouth people, whether Oldham or another, did his best and "used no little diligence" to have the deported prisoner proceeded against. Lawyers were consulted, and, as Morton expresses it, "a heape of gold" was laid before them; but they could find nothing to take hold of against him. Gorges undoubtedly could have brought any vendor to Indians of guns and ammunition to severe reckoning before the Star Chamber if nowhere else; and, furthermore, it was in the present instance his place to do it, for he was the representative man of the Council for New England, and to him, as such, Morton had been sent. In his defence of his patent before the House of Commons Gorges had especially dwelt on the heinousness of traders selling arms to the Indians, and, a little later, he had procured from the Privy Council a royal proclamation forbidding it; and now the chief offender in selling arms, who had treated the proclamation with contempt, denying even that it was law, had been arrested and delivered to him a prisoner. The Court of Star Chamber was but another name for the Privy Council. Gorges was a power in it. Undoubtedly, therefore, in the Star Chamber he could have taught Morton that royal proclamations, even if they were not law, at that time and so far as he was concerned, had much the force of law. But Gorges, apparently, had something else in view.

It has already been mentioned that, as Oldham had landed in Plymouth, where Gorges was royal governor, there can be no doubt that Bradford's letter was at once delivered to the latter, and the offences of which Morton stood charged explained to him. There can be equally little doubt that Gorges, after his wont, then proceeded to get all the information he could as to what was going on in New England from both Oldham and Morton. At first he may have been, and probably was, very indignant with the latter, and intent on having him punished; but if such was the case his anger soon cooled. The growing difficulties between the Massachusetts company and the Council for New England have just been described, and it called for no great degree of cunning on Morton's part to take advantage of these difficulties for the purpose of ingratiating himself with Gorges. That he did so appears clearly from the course of subsequent events. Like all the hangers-on at court, Gorges was a high-churchman; the promoters of the Massachusetts company were Puritans; the Plymouth people were Separatists. Under such circumstances Morton's course was clear. In giving his account of the events which had resulted in his appearing a prisoner at Plymouth, he represented himself as a victim of religious persecution; and it was not difficult then for him to show to the old knight and his son that he and they were interested together, as opposed to the old comers at Plymouth and the new comers at Salem.

Oldham, meanwhile, was at this very time taking from John Gorges a conveyance of territory, and could therefore hardly have seen his interest in pressing matters against Morton in that quarter. In this way it probably was that the master of Merry-Mount escaped without so much as a rebuke. Nevertheless there is reason to believe that his case was brought to the notice of the Governor and Assistants of the Massachusetts company, and that they now quietly made their arrangements to deal with him under certain future contingencies. None the less, for the present Morton was not only safe from all fear of molestation, but he was free to return to America. He was not slow in doing so.

At this time Isaac Allerton was in London as the agent of the Plymouth colony. The principal business he had in hand was to secure a new patent for the Plymouth people, covering by correct bounds a grant on the Kennebec; but, besides this, he was commissioned to obtain if possible a royal charter for Plymouth like that of the Massachusetts Bay company. In regard to the Kennebec patent he had to deal with the Council for New England; the charter could be obtained only from the King. The business gave Allerton much trouble. Indeed, as a correspondent wrote to Bradford, he " was so turrmoyled about it, as verily I would not nor could not have undergone it, if I might have had a thousand pounds." He found, too, that at King Charles' Court "many locks must be opened with the silver, nay, the golden key." He could make no headway except through favor, and the influence of Sir Ferdinando Gorges had to be secured. In securing it, not impossibly Morton proved himself a convenient go-between. In any event, when Allerton returned to New England in 1629 he astonished and scandalized the Plymouth community by bringing Morton back with him, " as it were to nose them," as Bradford indignantly put it. Allerton then lodged Morton in his own house, employing him as a clerk or scribe; an additional reason for inferring that he had in England been employed in a similar confidential way. It is easy as well as ludicrous to imagine the mixed disgust and dismay with which the sedate elders of Plymouth eyed the roystering lawyer as, like a counterfeit coin, he was returned on their hands; but it was in vain they protested at this undoing of the work of the previous year, and objected to Morton that he had not yet answered the charges laid to his door, for " hee onely made this modest reply, that hee did perceave they were willfull people, that would never be answered; and derided them for their practises and losse of laboure."

It does not appear how long Morton now remained at Plymouth; but it could not have been more than a few weeks before Allerton, who himself went back to England during the season, was, as Bradford puts it, " caused to pack him away." He then returned to Mt. Wollaston, where he found such of his old company as had not been dispersed by Standish, or frightened away by Endicott, — the more modest of them and those who had looked to their better walking; but hardly was he well back among them before he was in trouble with Endicott. It could not have been otherwise. For a loose, reckless roysterer, like Mor-

ton, to hope to live quietly side by side with the severe, God-fearing generation which had now sat down
at Salem was manifestly out of the question. In Virginia he would have been in his element ; in New
York he would have been unmolested ; indeed, anywhere else in the English colonies Morton would have
lived unnoticed and died unremembered. Fate threw
him among the intolerants of New England, and the
inevitable had to follow.

The first difficulty arose out of the jealousy which
the old settlers entertained towards the new. The
chief apprehension the leaders of the Massachusetts
company had felt in regard to what Oldham might do
had related to this jealousy. They feared he might
work on it, " and draw a party to himself, to the great
hindrance of the common quiet." This was exactly
what Morton now attempted. In the midst of the
scattered little community he was a Gorges intriguer
and a mischief-maker. As such he soon made his
presence felt. Some time in the latter part of 1629,
Endicott, in pursuance of instructions from London,
seems to have summoned all the settlers to meet together in a general court at Salem. There he doubtless informed them as to the general policy which the
company proposed to pursue ; and Morton says that
he then tendered to all present, for signature, certain
articles which he and the Rev. Samuel Skelton had
drawn up together. The purport of these articles
was that in all causes, ecclesiastical as well as political,
the tenor of God's word should be followed. The alternative was banishment.

Morton claims that he alone of all those present
refused to put his hand to this paper, insisting that a
proviso should first be added in these words, — " So as

nothing be done contrary, or repugnant to the Lawes
of the Kingdome of England." This is almost the exact language of King Charles' charter which had been
granted some six months before, and with the phraseology of which Morton was probably acquainted.
Whether the amendment thus proposed was accepted
by Endicott does not appear. It probably was,
though it is not difficult to imagine the grim dissatisfaction with which the suggestion of it must have been
received in view of the quarter from which it came.
The subject of regulating the trade in beaver skins
was next brought up, and it was proposed to enter
into a general partnership for the term of one year.
Morton says that on this matter also he stood out, and
it seems altogether probable that he did, for he was
there to make trouble on behalf of Gorges and Oldham. On the other hand, Endicott's instructions were
explicit. He was to see to it that " none be partakers
of [the company's] privileges and profits, but such as
be peaceable men, and of honest life and conversation,
and desirous to live amongst us, and conform themselves to good order and government." And further,
if any factious spirit developed itself, he was enjoined
" to suppress a mischief before it take too great a
head, . . . which if it may be done by a temperate
course, we much desire it, though with some inconvenience, so as our government and privileges be not
brought into contempt. . . . But if necessity require
a more severe course, when fair means will not prevail,
we pray you to deal as in your discretions you shall
think fittest." Instructions like these, in the hands
of a magistrate like Endicott, boded ill for such as
Thomas Morton.

Matters soon came to a crisis. Morton was proba-

bly emboldened to take the course he now took by the
belief that he would be supported in it by powerful
influence in London. He may have confidently hoped
to see Oldham's vessel appear at any time, with him on
board, come to take actual possession of the Robert
Gorges grant on the shore of the bay opposite to Mt.
Wollaston. In any event he refused to be bound by
the company's trade regulations, and seems to have
gone back to the less objectionable, at least, of his
old courses, — dealing with the savages as he saw fit,
openly expressing his contempt for Endicott's authority, and doing all he could to breed discontent
among the old planters. His own profits at this time
were, he says, six and seven fold. Such a state of
things could not continue. The affront daily put
upon the Governor was flagrant, and would have
stirred the anger of a patient man ; and John Endicott was not conspicuous for patience. Had he ig-
nored it, he might feel sure that his opponent would
take heart, and be emboldened to do him a far greater
injury thereafter. Accordingly, as the year drew to
its close, Endicott made an effort to arrest Morton ;
but the latter had learned by experience, and was not
to be twice caught in the same way. So, in some
way getting notice in advance of what was intended,
he concealed his ammunition and most necessary goods
in the forest ; and when the messengers, sent across
the bay to seize him, landed on the beach before his
house, he was nowhere to be found. The bird was
flown. This is his account of what then ensued : —

"The Commissioners entred the howse, and wilfully bent
against mine honest Host, that loved good hospitality.
After they had feasted their bodies with that they found
there, they carried all his corne away, with some other of

his goods, contrary to the Lawes of hospitality : a smale
parcell of refuse corne only excepted, which they left mine
Host to keepe Christmas with.

"But when they were gone, mine Host fell to make use
of his gunne, (as one that had a good faculty in the use of
that instrument,) and feasted his body neverthelesse with
fowle and venison, which hee purchased with the helpe of
that instrument, the plenty of the Country and the commo-
diousnes of the place affording meanes, by the blessing of
God ; and hee did but deride Captaine Littleworth, [Endi-
cott] that made his servants snap shorte in a Country so
much abounding with plenty of foode for an industrious
man, with greate variety."

Could Endicott now have laid hands on him,
there can be no doubt that Morton would have found
himself dealt with in summary fashion; but for the
present the Governor's attention was otherwise occupied, for this was that winter of 1629–30, during
which famine and sickness were rife at Salem. A
quarter part of those there died, and it was questionable whether the remainder, reduced by disease and
want of food, could struggle through until the coming
spring brought succor from England. Under such
circumstances, the magistrate had no time to think of
Morton. But not for that reason did he forget him.

With the following summer the great change came.
On the $\frac{30\text{th}}{9\text{th}}$ of $\frac{\text{May}}{\text{June}}$ the Mary & John, a ship of four
hundred tons measurement, commanded by Captain
Squeb, anchored off Hull, at the entrance of Boston
Bay. She had sailed from Plymouth on the $\frac{20\text{th}}{30\text{th}}$ of
the previous March, having on board about a hun-
dred and twenty passengers from the West of England. The agreement was that they were to be landed
at the mouth of the Charles River, Mishawum appar-

ently being the place intended; for those on board of
the Mary & John belonged to the Massachusetts
company, and must have been perfectly informed as
to what had already been done, and what was proposed. They were, in fact, the advance of the larger
body of emigrants who had embarked with Winthrop on the fleet at Southampton only two days
after Captain Squeb had got under weigh from Plymouth. The voyage of the Mary & John had been
entered upon by the "godly families," many in number and of good rank, who composed the bulk of the
passengers, by a solemn day spent in preaching and
praying and fasting, and had proved one of fair average quickness for those times, occupying seventy days.
They had come "through the deeps comfortably, having preaching or expounding of the word of God every
day for ten weeks together by [their] ministers."

Having now reached the entrance to the bay, the
captain informed the passengers that the voyage was
ended, and that they and their effects would be put on
shore there. Nantasket beach and the bold, swelling
headland of Hull must always in the month of June
have been an attractive place, and in 1630, as now,
the white, cool surf rolled in upon the sands at the
foot of hills green with the verdure of spring, amid
which wild strawberries ripened in profusion. As
the sea-wearied emigrants climbed to the summits of
hose hills they beheld from them a view of almost
unsurpassed beauty. On the one side lay the broad
harbor interspersed with green islands covered with
trees, while on the other was a boundless expanse of
ocean, the deep blue of which was here and there near
the shore broken by white waves rolling over isolated
rocks. Beyond the harbor lay the forest-clad uplands

of the promised land, with the Blue Hills looming
up hazily and yet boldly against the western horizon.
The air was soft and pure; the skies were serene.
Yet however attractive the place may have seemed to
those West of England rustics, cramped and wearied
by their long voyage, as a permanent home it was
manifestly far from inviting. A vivid glimpse of it,
as it then appeared to longer sojourners, is obtained
through a little episode which took place the year before Squeb's coming, and which is not only picturesque in itself, but full of suggestiveness in connection
with the early days of Massachusetts. As such it deserves to be told in detail.

This was the experience of Ralph Smith, a clergyman who had come over to Salem in company with
those who, in 1629, reinforced Endicott and settled
Charlestown. Smith wished to emigrate to New England, and the company readily enough granted him
permission to do so; but when his family and effects
were already embarked, and it was too late to put
him ashore, it came out that he differed " in judgment
in some things " from the company's own ministers.
Under the circumstances he was allowed to proceed,
but at the same time orders were sent to Endicott in
these words, — " Unless he will be conformable to
our government, you suffer him not to remain within
the limits of our grant." The unfortunate clergyman
had, in consequence, hardly landed at Salem when he
was shipped off again with his family and effects.
Bradford then takes up the narrative as follows : —

"Ther was one Mr. Ralfe Smith, and his wife and fami-
lie, that came over into the Bay of the Massachusets, and so-
journed at presente with some stragling people that lived at
Natascoe; here being a boat of this place putting in ther on

some occasion, he ernestly desired that they would give
him and his, passage for Plimoth, and some such things as
they could well carrie; having before heard that ther was
liklyhood he might procure house-roome for some time, till
he should resolve to setle ther, if he might, or els-wher as
God should disposs; for he was werie of being in that uncoth place, and in a poore house that would neither keep
him nor his goods drie. So, seeing him to be a grave man,
and understood he had been a minister, though they had no
order for any such thing, yet they presumed and brought
him. He was here accordingly kindly entertained and
housed, and had the rest of his goods and servants sente
for, and exercised his gifts amongst them, and afterwards
was chosen into the ministrie, and so remained for sundrie
years."

The incident not only reveals Nantasket, in 1629,
as an " uncoth place," occupied by " some stragling
people," but it vividly sets forth the difference, so
far as Christian toleration was concerned, between the
Separatists of Plymouth and the Puritans of Massachusetts Bay. The former kindly entertained the unfortunate outcast; and among them he exercised his
gifts, such as they were, for many years, being chosen
into their ministry. The latter, with much the same
idea of toleration as that court of High Commission
from which they had fled, cast him and his little children out into the wilderness, even as Sarah cast out
Hagar.

Such had been a newcomer's experience at Nantasket the summer before Captain Squeb landed there
his living freight of men, women and children. He,
at least, knew perfectly well that the place where he
had come to anchor was not the mouth of the Charles.
It was, indeed, roughly represented as being so on

Smith's map; but Squeb was no stranger on that coast. For years he had been connected with the Council for New England. In 1622 he had been formally commissioned by it as aid and assistant to its Admiral, Francis West, and had come out in command of the John & Francis of London. It is true, he had then apparently explored Mt. Desert; but there can be little doubt that, if he himself had not before been in Boston harbor, some of his present crew had been there, and when he landed his passengers at Hull he knew he was not fulfilling his contract. Nevertheless, land them there he did, and it only remained for them to huddle on the beach and shift for themselves. Borrowing a boat from the old settlers, the remnant of Oldham and Lyford's plantation, a well-armed party set out, a day or two after the landing, in search of their true destination. It would not be possible to recount the experience of this party in any language so expressive as that of Roger Clapp, one of its number : —

" We went in [the boat] unto Charlestown, where we found some wigwams and one house; and in the house there was a man which had a boiled bass, but no bread, that we see. But we did eat of his bass, and then went up Charles river until the river grew narrow and shallow, and there we landed our goods with much labor and toil, the bank being steep; and night coming on, we were informed that there were hard by us three hundred Indians. One Englishman, that could speak the Indian language, (an old planter,) went to them, and advised them not to come near us in the night; and they hearkened to his counsel, and came not. I myself was one of the sentinels that first night. Our captain was a Low Country soldier, one Mr. Southcot, a brave soldier. In the morning, some of the Indians came and stood at a distance off, looking at us, but came not near us. But when they had been a while in view, some of them came and held out a great bass towards us; so we sent a man with a biscuit, and changed the cake for the bass. Afterwards, they supplied us with bass, exchanging a bass for a biscuit cake, and were very friendly unto us. . . .

"We had not been there many days, (although by our diligence we had got up a kind of shelter to save our goods in,) but we had order to come away from that place, which was about Watertown, unto a place called Mattapan, now Dorchester, because there was a neck of land fit to keep our cattle on. So we removed and came to Mattapan. The Indians there also were kind unto us."

The old planter here referred to, who could speak the Indian tongue, was probably Blackstone, though it may have been Walford, at whose house at Mishawum they apparently stopped. One or the other of the two must, it would seem, have gone with them up the Charles as a guide. The place where they landed and encamped is supposed to have been the spot since occupied as a United States Arsenal in Watertown, and long known as the Dorchester fields. The locality to which they were recalled, and where the whole company finally settled down, was the historical Dorchester heights, now better known as South Boston.

Scarcely were they established here when, on the $\frac{17\text{th}}{27\text{th}}$ of June, Governor Winthrop, who had arrived at Salem five days before, came into the harbor, and went up the Mystic in search of a suitable place for settlement. Two days later, having sufficiently explored the country, as he thought, he returned to Salem, stopping on his way at Nantasket. The body of those who had come over in the Mary & John would still seem to have been there, as Winthrop says that he " sent for Captain Squib ashore and ended a difference between him and the passengers." Whereat the captain seems to have experienced quite a sense of relief, as he gave the Governor a salute of five guns as the latter headed away to Salem.

Winthrop had found the Charlestown settlers of the previous year in quite as severe straits as he had, a few days before, found the Salem people. Their supplies were wholly exhausted and they were reduced to living on mussels, fish and, when they could get it, Indian corn. But it was too late to consider what should be done, for the planting season was already over, the summer being now well advanced, and all that could at best be accomplished was to provide shelter against the rigor of the coming winter. Boston, or, as it was then called, Massachusetts Bay, had been fixed upon as the place where those who came with Winthrop were to land, and some provision for them had already been made at Charlestown. To Charlestown, therefore, the several vessels, twelve in number, came, and there the passengers and cargoes of household goods were at last put on shore. In the course of the month of July, the whole of the hill about the building which had been put up by Graves the year before was covered thick with tents, wigwams, booths and cottages. Governor Winthrop with his family, and Isaac Johnson, whose wife, the Lady Arbella, daughter of the Earl of Lincoln, had been left at Salem, probably occupied the one house, together with Mr. Wilson, the clergyman, and Increase Nowell, the elder. They had no church, and the preaching was in the open air under the sheltering leaves of a large tree.

A state of things better calculated to breed sickness could not well have existed. Several hundred men, women and children were crowded together in a narrow space, almost without shelter, and with unaccustomed and improper food. Never in their lives having seen anything but their English homes, they knew nothing of frontier life, to the new and strange conditions of which they were, after the manner of their race, unable readily to adapt themselves. Nor was this all. When they arrived they had been living for months on shipboard, fed on that salt meat which was then the only sea fare. Their systems had become reduced, and the scurvy had broken out. They were in no condition to bear exposure. Then, landed suddenly in midsummer, they had their first experience of a climate quite different from that which they had known before, — a climate of excessive heat and sudden change. Their clothing was not adapted to it. As a matter of course, dysentery and all sorts of bowel complaints began to appear. These they did not know how to treat, and they made things worse by the salt food to which they doubtless recurred when they found that an improper use of the berries and natural fruits of the country caused the disorders under which they suffered. Their camp, too, could not have been properly policed. We know what the sanitary condition of London and all large towns was in the first half of the seventeenth century, and how little attention was paid to growing piles of filth, even in the oldest and best-ordered communities. By degrees the hill at Charlestown, covered with decaying vegetable and animal matter, became unfit for human habitation; the air reeked with foul odors. It was easier to move away from the place than to cleanse it.

Unfortunately, Winthrop's contemporaneous account of this period of great trial has not been preserved. It was contained in the letters written to his wife, who had remained behind in England, while his whole journal record of the eighty-two days which intervened between his going to "Mattachusetts to find out a place for our sitting down," on the 17th of June, and the 7th of September, when the order was passed that "Trimountain shall be called Boston," fills but thirty-six printed lines, and nearly all of the memoranda contained even in those lines were made at a subsequent time. There were no days in Winthrop's life more trying to him, or of greater historical interest, than these; but their story was one of only discouragement and endurance. In the course of a few months, as he wrote to his wife, he lost twelve in his own family, including in the phrase "family" the servants he brought with him. When the ships returned to England in July, nearly one hundred went back in them, and at a later day others removed to Gorges' and Mason's plantation at Piscataqua. Those who remained do not seem to have been at all supplied with medicines, and their only doctor, "Mr. Gager, a right godly man, a skilful chirurgeon and one of the deacons of [the] congregation," himself died in September. The worthy Dr. Samuel Fuller, of Plymouth, visited the bay at this time, though he seems to have gone in his capacity of deacon rather than as a physician. The account he gave of the condition of affairs was graphic. The hand of God, he wrote back to Plymouth, was upon them, visiting them with sickness and not sparing the righteous. "Many are sick, and many are dead, the Lord in mercy look upon them! . . . I here but lose time and long to be at home. I

can do them no good, for I want drugs and things fitting to work with." Perhaps it was as well that Dr.
Fuller did go back to Plymouth, for the copious blood-
letting, to which in the absence of drugs he seems to
have had recourse,[1] could only have still further weakened systems already too much reduced. As human
aid could not be procured or seemed unavailing, the
divine protection was invoked, and, after the Puritan
fashion, days were set aside for fasting, humiliation
and prayer, the severe observance of which by individuals doubtless aggravated any tendency to disease
latent in them. The prevailing malady soon, of course,
became epidemic, and was supposed to be infectious.
The people of the poorer class, as being the less well
fed and the more exposed, naturally suffered the most
from it, and it fell heavily on the young; though the
more mature and the better-conditioned were by no
means exempt. The unfortunate Lady Arbella Johnson, coming direct " from a paradise of plenty and pleasure into a wilderness of wants," sickened in August
and early in September was dead. Her husband, one
of the Assistants, as they were called, or directors of
the company, followed her a month later. Another of
the Assistants, Edward Rossiter, died in October.
Coddington and Pynchon, also Assistants, lost their
wives; so did the Rev. George Phillips, pastor of the
church at Watertown, and George Alcock, deacon of
the church at Dorchester.

Under these circumstances, there being no family in
which there was not one dead, while in some families
there were many, a strong feeling of discontent with
the locality in which the settlers found themselves
placed naturally began to manifest itself. There were

[1] I. *Mass. Hist. Coll.* iii. 74.

in the neighborhood no living springs or running water, such as they remembered at home ; and to this fact the sickness was in great degree attributed. The single brackish water-source in the sands near the beach, to which they all went, did not half suffice to supply the general need. Accordingly, as the season advanced and the regions thereabout were more thoroughly explored, those at Charlestown broke up into small parties, seeking out different places of settlement. Some went to Medford, and sat down by the Mystic ; others to Roxbury, attracted by the fresh, clear waters of Smelt Brook. Watertown and Dorchester were already occupied. All this time William Blackstone, who had now been in the country seven years, was living alone as a hermit on the western slope of the peninsula, the three hills of which, across the channel to the south and west of Charlestown, lifted up their heads, bare of trees, in a neighborhood " very uneven, abounding in small hollows and swamps, covered with blueberries and other bushes." Knowing well, of course, the situation of affairs amongst the newcomers, and hearing the complaints of the insufficient supply of water, Blackstone's sympathies seem to have been moved, and he called Winthrop's attention to a fine spring on his own peninsula. Judging by the subsequent location of Winthrop's house and of the first church, this spring was slightly to the rear and on the east of the spot upon which the Old South Meeting-house was built a century later. It was fenced in at an early day, and the familiar name of " the Spring-gate " was long retained by its place of entrance ; [1] and later the passage-way across where the spring once flowed was called Spring Lane, the name it still retains. Black-

[1] Shurtleff, *Description of Boston*, 389.

stone now urged the Governor to move across and establish himself and his people there. Whereupon, early in October, much to the dissatisfaction of some of those who had with much labor got dwellings ready at Charlestown, Winthrop caused the frame of the house that was to have been built for him at Cambridge to be moved bodily to Shawmut, and set up opposite the southern corner of the present junction of School Street with Washington Street. With him went the Rev. Mr. Wilson and the greater part of his congregation. There they " began to build their houses against winter; and this place was called Boston."

CHAPTER XV.

THE FIRST ASSAULT ON KING CHARLES' CHARTER.

FAMINE, sickness and death at Salem; the confusion of settlement, together with the terror which accompanied and the sense of bereavement which followed pestilence, at Charlestown, — all these had given a reprieve to Thomas Morton; so, through the months of July and August, 1630, he lived undisturbed in his house at Mt. Wollaston. It was, indeed, a full year since his return there from Plymouth, when at last the hour for dealing with him came. Not improbably his was looked upon as a species of test case, through their treatment of which the magistrates of the new colony were to demonstrate to the old planters the fact that they, as magistrates, not only had the power to deal summarily with all whom they were pleased to regard as interlopers, but they would not hesitate to use that power. The spirit of discontent which smouldered among those who yet continued in the land, remnants of the Gorges failure of 1623, has already been referred to. If one or two of them were punished, it was felt that these would serve for an example to the others and reduce them at once to conformity. Morton was to furnish this example.

The first formal session of the magistrates, after the arrival of Winthrop at Charlestown, was not held until the $\frac{23d}{2d}$ of $\frac{August}{September}$. There can be little question that they met in the great house at Charlestown, and

the Governor, Deputy Governor Dudley, Sir Richard
Saltonstall, Pynchon, Bradstreet and others of the
Assistants whose names are less familiar, were present.   In disposing of business in hand, provision was
first made for the lodging and maintenance of the
clergy; and it was then ordered " that Morton, of
Mount Woolison, should presently be sent for by pro-
cesse."   Of the circumstances of his arrest, under
the warrant thus issued against him, Morton has left
us no account; but, two weeks later, on the $\frac{7th}{17th}$ of September, he was arraigned before the magistrates again
in session.   In addition to those at the previous meeting, Isaac Johnson — whose wife, the Lady Arbella,
then lay on her deathbed — and Endicott were there,
the latter having probably come from Salem expressly
to attend to the case of Morton.   To the prisoner it
must have been apparent from the first that the tribunal was one from which he had nothing to hope.
Of Endicott he had already had experience; and now,
at Endicott's side, sat the narrow-minded, intolerant
Dudley, with Pynchon and Bradstreet, all stern men
and harsh, typical Puritan magistrates.   Winthrop
was in the governor's chair.   Some business of detail
was first disposed of, and the officers then produced
their prisoner.   The proceedings which ensued could
not well have been more summary had they taken
place in the Star Chamber, or the Court of High
Commission; and Morton was soon made to realize
that he was not there to defend himself, but to receive, as best he might, a sentence which had already
been decided upon.   In vain did he challenge the jurisdiction of the court; in vain did he seek to humble
himself before its authority.   Neither challenge nor
submission was regarded.   Nor did the magistrates

waste their time in listening to a prolix defence. On
the contrary the argument of the accused, like his
protest and his submission, was peremptorily cut short
by impatient exclamations, and he was sternly bidden
to hold his peace and listen to the governor, while he
pronounced the decision of the court. And, indeed,
the prisoner could not but have listened in speechless
amazement and indignation while the following root-
and-branch sentence was passed upon him : —

"It is ordered by this present Court, that Thomas Morton, of Mount Wolliston, shall presently be set into the bil-
boes, and after sent prisoner into England, by the ship
called the Gift, now returning thither ; that all his goods
shall be seized upon to defray the charge of his transportation, payment of his debts, and to give satisfaction to the
Indians for a canoe he unjustly took away from them ; and
that his house, after his goods are taken out, shalt be burnt
down to the ground in the sight of the Indians, for their
satisfaction, for many wrongs he hath done them from time
to time."

This sentence spoke for itself then. It speaks for
itself now. Unfortunately Winthrop's admonitory
remarks in announcing it have not been handed down
to us, though we get in Morton's account of the proceedings a faint, far-away echo of what those remarks
were. It comes in the expression, which he makes a
part of the judgment, that his house was to be burned
" because the habitation of the wicked should no more
appear in Israel." This phrase could hardly but have
been Winthrop's. It has in it the true Puritan ring,
— the " thus saith the Lord " refrain. It was Bible
law, also, and illustrated to Morton in his own case
the significance of that Salem covenant, to which during the previous year he had refused to set his name,

that "in all causes, as well Ecclesiasticall, as Politi-
call, wee should follow the rule of God's word."

Neither was the sentence now promulgated an idle
one ; and, indeed, the Puritan magistrate was apt in
such cases to be as good as his word.   The Master of
Merry-Mount — Sachem of Passonagessit as he loved
to call himself, and Lord of Misrule as those of Plymouth called him — was ignominiously set in the stocks
before the great house at Charlestown, in the face of
the whole infant settlement; and there, he tells us
himself, the "harmeles salvages (his neighboures)"
came, "poore silly lambes," to look at him in blank
astonishment, wondering what it was all about.   The
sentence included, also, his banishment, and the burning of his house to the ground.   It was literally executed, though not without some delay.   The prisoner
was not sent back to England in the Gift, for the reason that the master of that vessel declined to take him,
on what ground does not appear ; nor was it until the
end of December — nearly, if not quite, four months
after his arrest — that a passage was obtained for him
in the Handmaid.   Even then, obdurate to the last,
Morton refused to go on board the vessel, declaring
that he had no call to go there, and so he had to be
hoisted on board by a tackle.   On the passage over,
also, he was nearly starved, no provision, except a
very inadequate one from his own stores, having been
made for his support, while the burning of his house
seems to have been dramatically arranged with that
curious vindictiveness which was characteristic of the
Puritans.   "The habitation of the wicked should no
more appear in Israel ;" but the destruction of it was
reserved until the "wicked" man was on his way into
banishment, and then it was burned down in his sight,

drearily lighting his outgoing path, " and nothing did
remain but the bare ashes as an emblem of their cruelty." [1]

The justice, and even the propriety, of Morton's
first arrest by the Plymouth authorities in 1628, cannot be successfully challenged. His own subsequent
pretence, that it was merely the means adopted by
them for breaking up a disagreeable competition in
the fur trade, is deserving of no more weight than his
other suggestion, that they disturbed him because of
much " enveying against the sacred booke of common
prayer, and mine host that used it in a laudable manner amongst his family, as a practise of piety." The
measure was, whether technically legal or not, a measure of self-preservation, pure and simple. That the
establishment at Mt. Wollaston was a disorderly one,
is apparent in every line of Morton's account of it.
A trade in firearms was there carried on. This was
distinctly charged, and Morton never, at the time or
later, denied it. That he would have denied it quickly
and emphatically enough, had it not been susceptible
of easy proof, admits of no doubt. In taking vigorous measures to suppress this traffic, by arresting and
sending to England the responsible promoter of it,
the Plymouth magistrates did only what they were

---

[1] There seems no question on this point. Samuel Maverick, writing
thirty years afterwards to the Earl of Clarendon, says : " They further ordered, as he was to sail in sight of his house, that it should be
fired " (*Coll. N. Y. Hist. Soc.* 1869, p. 40) ; while Morton himself
wrote that he " a farre of abourd a ship did there behold this wofull
spectacle." (*New English Canaan*, 164.) The sentence, that the
house should be " burnt down to the ground in the sight of the Indians," was passed at the session of the magistrates held on September 7 (*Records*, i. 75), and not until the close of December did the
Handmaid set sail. (Young, *Chron. of Mass.* 321.) See, also, *Proc.
Mass. Hist. Soc.* Series II. i. 238.

compelled to do ; and, in doing it, they acted with moderation and self-restraint. Their descendants, eight generations removed and upon a less remote frontier, would have disposed of the whole matter in a far more summary way, — in the way, in fact, which Morton says Miles Standish threatened to adopt.

Neither was the second arrest, that of 1630, under Winthrop's process, in itself a thing to be criticised. According to Morton's own account, he had been a thorn, both sharp and rankling, in Endicott's side ; not only had he refused to enter into any covenants, whether for trade or government, but he had openly derided the magistrate and eluded his messengers. This would not do. The company was right when it formally instructed Endicott that "all must live under government and a like law." It was necessary, therefore, that Morton should in good faith give in his submission, or that he should be compelled to take himself off. This position would have been correct ; but this position the magistrates did not take. Nothing was said in the sentence of any disregard of authority or disobedience to regulation. No reference was made to illicit dealings with the Indians. The trade in firearms the company had explicitly forbidden, directing that any one guilty of it should forthwith be apprehended and sent to England for punishment. But no renewal of this forbidden trade was now even charged against Morton. Again, the punishment inflicted upon him was one of extreme severity. He was set in the stocks ; his whole belongings were confiscated ; his habitation was burned to the ground before his eyes ; and he was banished the country. It could only be said that he was not whipped and he was not mutilated. Nothing less than a stubborn refusal to obey the authority of the colony would seem to have justified such severity.

On the other hand the charges actually made against him, and recited in his sentence, were of the most trivial character, — manifestly, trumped-up charges to serve a purpose. He had unjustly, it stands alleged, taken away a canoe from some Indians; he had fired a charge of shot among a troop of them, who would not bring a canoe across a river to him, wounding one and tearing a hole in the garments of another; he was "a proud, insolent man," against whom a "multitude of complaints were received" for injuries done by him both to the English and the Indians. Those specified, it is to be presumed, are examples of the rest. They amount absolutely to nothing. Samuel Maverick, writing long afterwards to Lord Clarendon, very fitly characterized them as mere pretences. Apparently conscious of this, Dudley, the deputy governor, in his letter to the Countess of Lincoln, adds that Morton was sent to England "for that my Lord Chief Justice there so required, that he might punish him capitally for fouler misdemeanours there perpetrated." Bradford, in his reference to this matter, further adds that Morton "was vehemently suspected for the murder of a man that had adventured moneys with him, when he came first into New England."

There would seem to be no doubt that there was a warrant in Winthrop's hands against Morton, bearing the sign manual of Nicholas Hyde, who at that time disgraced the office of Lord Chief Justice of the King's Bench; but, in view of Morton's subsequent immunity from all punishment, or even, so far as is known, from any criminal prosecution, a surmise would not

be forced that this paper had been procured, upon
some rumor of criminal conduct, by the lawyers of
the company before the fleet of 1630 set sail, in order
to have it ready for the contingency in which it was
actually used. In all historical probability, it was
nothing more or less than a seventeenth century English substitute for the French *lettre de cachet.*

Moreover, such a requisition, though it might have
warranted the return of Morton as a prisoner to England, certainly did not warrant the confiscation of his
goods and the burning of his house, in advance of
trial and conviction there. The confiscation and the
burning were unmistakable acts of high-handed oppression. As will frequently appear in these pages, it
is far too customary with the school of New England
historians to defend this, and the whole long record
of not dissimilar acts which disfigure the early annals
of Massachusetts, upon grounds which they are not
quick to accept when advanced in excuse of Wentworth, of Williams, or of Laud. It is argued that
the Puritans of the great migration were just, God-
fearing men, who had suffered persecution at home.
They had come to New England a weak, struggling
colony. Then it is assumed that unity of thought, as
well as of purpose and of action, was essential to the
existence of this colony. Freedom of opinion, it is
further assumed, was in those days synonymous with
internal dissension ; and internal dissension would
have jeopardized, if it had not destroyed, the colony.
Therefore the stern bigotry and savage intolerance
which made a hideous travesty of law and justice,
when exemplified in Archbishop Laud and his associates in the Court of High Commission, became not
only excusable in Governor Winthrop and his brother

magistrates, seated at their table in Boston, but constitute for them a new title to veneration.[1]

[1] " Religious intolerance, like every other public restraint, is criminal wherever it is not needful for the public safety; it is simply self-defence, whenever tolerance would be public ruin. . . . And the right [to exclude] becomes of yet more value, and the duty more imperative and inevitable, when the good in question is one of such vast worth as religious freedom, to be protected by the possessor, not only for himself, but for the myriads, living and to be born, of whom he assumes to be the pioneer and the champion." (Palfrey, i. 300, 301.)

" But, without detracting in the slightest degree from the lofty and enviable claims which have been made for [the younger Vane], it may well be more than doubted whether his views [of civil and religious liberty] were applicable to the condition of the colony at the time, and whether the little Commonwealth could have been held together in peace and prosperity — if held together at all — by any other policy than that which Winthrop defended.

"It was admirably said by the late Josiah Quincy on this subject, in his Centennial Discourse in 1830, that ' had our early ancestors adopted the course we at this day are apt to deem so easy and obvious, and placed their government on the basis of liberty for all sorts of consciences [the basis which Henry IV. adopted to a modified extent in the edict of Nantes], it would have been, in that age [what it was not found to be at all in France], a certain introduction of anarchy, [which was the exact argument advanced by Philip II., Louis XIV., and other historical persecutors].'" (R. C. Winthrop, in the *Mem. Hist. of Boston*, i. 127.)

The other side is always worth hearing. Referring to the language used by Prynne and Burton, Hook, Dean of Chichester, in his *Life of Laud* (187), says: " In the days of Henry VIII., Edward VI., Mary and Elizabeth, persons who ventured thus to speak of the constituted authorities would have been put to death. Papists had, when in power, executed Protestants, and Protestants had executed Papists; and Scotch Reformers, out of power, had recommended assassination. How the Puritans and ultra-Protestants in power were determined to act, their murder of Charles and of Laud, their king and their archbishop, would be sufficient to show. But the principles of the Puritans are more strongly marked in the laws they ordained for New England, where the intolerance of presbytery, the madness of the Anabaptists, and the extravagance of the Independents and Brownists reigned supreme. But they were in stern earnest, and their severity was not against religious errors, as they deemed them, only, but also against social crime. Capital punishment was adjudged for adultery,

But the question of religious tolerance is not now to be discussed ; and, so far as Morton is concerned, it does not then appear to have entered into the question. His was a case of civil persecution only. The man before them was a poor, lawless creature at best, and the Massachusetts magistrates had made up their minds in advance. They meant, in the preacher's holy phrase, to purge him from the land. He was not only what they termed a " libertine," but his presence at Mt. Wollaston was a standing menace to the company. The best use to which he could be devoted was that of an example to others. Doubtless, also, they suspected him even now of being an emissary of Gorges ; for they must, through Oldham, have known of the relations between the two during Morton's recent sojourn in England. If Winthrop and the rest entertained any such surmise, they were also quite correct in it. Morton was even then in correspondence with Sir Ferdinando. That he was an undesirable character to have about an infant colony, such as that presided over by Endicott and Winthrop, does not admit of question, and it was the avowed policy of the company to permit none regarded in this light to remain. Similar methods of dealing with improper and undesirable characters have since been not uncommon among the mining communities of the interior and the Pacific slope ; but it is somewhat singular that the rough camp-law there practised should find its earliest precedent on the first page of the records of Massachusetts Bay.

perjury and blasphemy. Those who lied, drank, or danced were to be publicly whipped. Heavy fines were laid upon such as swore or broke the Sabbath. At the same time, any Romish priest returning to the colony after banishment would be put to death." (*Lives of the Archbishops of Canterbury* (New Series), vi. 293.)

Whether Winthrop and his associates were or were
not justified in summarily banishing Morton in the
way they did, the so doing was none the less, as events
subsequently showed, a serious blunder. Their position was wholly different from that of the struggling
settlers of three years earlier. As Endicott had already shown, the magistrates of the company were
now perfectly able to enforce every regulation, whether
wise and necessary or the reverse, and they could suppress summarily all disorder. Under these circumstances they had much better have left Morton alone
under the harrow of their authority. At Mt. Wollaston, he was at worst nothing more than a nuisance.
They shipped him off to England, and at Whitehall
he rose to the large proportions of a formidable enemy. In New England he was under Winthrop's eye
and within reach of Endicott's hand ; in London he
became the ready tool of Gorges and inspired the
malignity of Laud.

Upon his arrival in England, Morton was committed to Exeter jail, but would not seem to have long
remained there. He probably communicated at once
with Sir Ferdinando Gorges, letters from whom to
him were then on their way to New England, and Sir
Ferdinando undoubtedly had sufficient influence to
procure the prisoner's speedy release. In any event,
the next year he was at liberty and busily concerned
in Gorges' intrigues for the overthrow of the Massachusetts colony ; and, in his efforts to accomplish that
result, he received the active assistance of two other
victims of New England's summary procedure. These
were Sir Christopher Gardiner and Philip Ratcliff.

There is no more singular and incongruous episode
in the first history of Massachusetts, save only that of

the May-pole of Merry-Mount, than the episode of Sir
Christopher Gardiner.   Who the man was, whence or
why he came, and whither he afterwards went, are
matters which have hitherto been wrapped in a mys-
tery which is not likely ever to be solved.   He seems
to have been of a Gloucester family, and he made
some claim of kinship to that famous Stephen Gar-
dyner, Bishop of Winchester in the days of Queen
Mary, whom Shakespeare has branded as a man of
" a cruel nature and a bloody."   The kinship thus
claimed is not impossible ; though it could scarcely
have been so near as that of uncle and nephew,
seeing that a full century, at least, must have intervened between the births of the two.[1]   However
related, Gardiner was evidently a man of education
and culture, and he had been an extensive traveller.
He appears to have received degrees, such as they
were, at some university ; and, having been a Protestant, he had, at some time before coming to New England, joined the Church of Rome.   His title was of a
doubtful character, and at times he is spoken of as a
Knight of the Holy Sepulchre, and then, again, as of
the Order of the Golden Melice ; but that he had a
right to some title would seem to be established by
the fact that at a later day he was referred to in England by Gorges, and in official proceedings, as Sir
Christopher Gardiner, Knight.

Whencesoever he may have received his title, he
first suddenly appeared in America, bearing it, about
a month before the arrival of Winthrop and his com-

---

[1] The Bishop of Winchester was born at Bury St. Edmunds in
1483. (Campbell, *Lord Chancellors*, ch. xl.) Sir Christopher Gardiner may have been forty-eight at the time of his misadventures in
New England in 1631. (Young, *Chron. of Mass.* 335.)

pany, having been hurried over probably, an agent of
Gorges, in advance of the colonists, in some vessel of
the fishing fleet. If he was such an agent, — and there
can be little doubt of the fact, — the exact purpose of
his coming at this time can only be surmised. It is
probable that he was commissioned to act for Sir Ferdinando, and to do whatever circumstances might require, or occasion make possible, to keep the Gorges
claims alive. He brought over with him a servant or
two, and was also accompanied by another companion,
"a comly yonge woman," as Bradford reports her,
whom he represented as being his cousin, but who
seems, in fact, to have been his mistress. For some
time after his first arrival he does not appear to have
been in any way molested. He came to the neighborhood of Boston Bay, and built for himself some sort of
a dwelling, though exactly where is not known. Deputy Governor Dudley simply says that it was seven
miles from Boston, and on the further side of a river.
Judging by the direction which Gardiner afterwards
took in his flight, it would seem most probable that
he lived on the Neponset, not far from its mouth, and
in close vicinity to the former "Massachusetts fields."
If he did live there, he was in the midst of Gorges'
adherents ; for Jeffreys and Morton were but a few
miles away, the former at Wessagusset and the latter
at Mt. Wollaston, while Blackstone, Maverick and
Walford were immediately across the bay about the
peninsula of Shawmut. It would further seem that
Gardiner could hardly have failed to meet Morton in
London during the summer of 1629, when both were
there and in constant communication with Gorges,
with whom, also, both were now in correspondence.

The presence of a man like Sir Christopher in the

neighborhood of a young settlement was an event which could not but attract notice. Furthermore, it called for explanation, as every one there had to give some account of himself. Gardiner claimed that he had come to the New World simply because he was weary of the Old, — that he sought here no preferment, but was willing to earn his living with the rest; and he even professed himself as desirous of joining some one of the churches. This account of himself seems to have been accepted as satisfactory ; perhaps, also, the magistrates were too much occupied to give much thought to him, and, not impossibly, they were awaiting further developments from their friends and agents in England. These came at last in March, 1631, about three months after Morton had been sent away, and from them it appeared that Gardiner was far from being a man of godly life. Two women claimed to be married to him, one of whom he had abandoned in Paris, the other in London. The former had then, apparently in hunting him up, found the latter, and a comparison of notes followed. It was known to them that Gardiner had gone to New England, and naturally the agents of the Massachusetts company were applied to for information as to his whereabouts. In due course of time letters from both wives were transmitted to Governor Winthrop, advising him of the facts in the case ; the first or Paris wife desiring her husband's return to her in hopes of his conversion to better things, while the second, or London, Lady Gardiner sought nothing less than the knight's "destruction for his foul abuse, and for robbing her of her estate, of a part whereof she sent an inventory hither, comprising therein many rich jewels, much plate, and costly linen." This wife of Sir Christopher further advised the Puritan magistrates that the "comly yonge woman whom he caled his cousin" was a "known harlot," Mary Grove by name, whose immediate sending back to England, in company with her husband, she also greatly desired. Altogether it was a scandalous case.

Accordingly, at a court held on February $\frac{18}{28}$, 1631, it was ordered that "Sir Christopher Gardiner shal be sent as prisoner into England by the shipp Lyon, nowe returneing thither," and steps were taken for his immediate apprehension. But it would seem that it was not in vain Sir Christopher had travelled in many lands and joined himself to the Church of Rome; for, apparently, he now had his own means of knowing what information came out from England, and what was proposed in Winthrop's council chamber. So he was on the watch; and when he saw the officers crossing the river, half a mile from his abode, he quietly put on his weapons and betook himself to the woods. Probably Morton's experience was fresh in his mind. His companion, Mary Grove, — if such was indeed her name, — the officers arrested, and took before the magistrates for examination, who found her an unwilling witness. A rigid questioning elicited little from her, and nothing at all to the detriment of Sir Christopher, except the fact that she was not married to him; which, indeed, had not been pretended. An order was accordingly made "to send her to the two wives in Old England, to search her further;" which order was not carried into effect.

Gardiner himself, meanwhile, lay concealed in the forest. The magistrates offered a reward for his capture, and, as the Massachusetts Indians asserted, gave them authority to kill him. This is improbable; but in any event he had gone beyond their reach, and was among what was left of the Pokánoket tribe, who, before the great sickness, occupied the region watered by the Taunton River, and lying between that stream and Massachusetts Bay. He was accordingly within the Plymouth jurisdiction. It is not very clear what his plan was, if, indeed, he had any. The Massachusetts magistrates thought that if he did not perish, as the chances were he would, from cold and hunger, he might try to make his way to Piscataqua or the stations in Maine; but he himself seems afterwards to have intimated that his idea was to get to New York and the Dutch settlement there. If such was his purpose, he soon found it impracticable; and so, for nearly a month, he wandered about in the neighborhood of the Taunton River, in what are now the towns of Middleborough and Bridgewater. At length some of the Indians living thereabouts, hearing of the price set upon him, went to Plymouth and told Governor Bradford where he was, asking if they might kill him : —

"But the Governor tould them no, they should not kill him, but watch their opportunitie and take him. And so they did, for when they light of him by a river side, he got into a canowe to get from them, and when they came nere him, whilst he presented his peece at them to keep them of, the streame carried the canow against a rock, and tumbled both him and his peece and rapier into the water; yet he got out, and having a litle dagger by his side, they durst not close with him, but getting longe pols, they soone beat his dagger out of his hand, so he was glad to yeeld; and they brought him to the Governor. But his hands and armes were swolen and very sore with the blowes they had given him. So he used him kindly, and sent him to a lodging wher his armes were bathed and anoynted, and he was quickly well againe, and blamed the Indeans for beating him so much. They said that they did but a litle whip him with sticks."

Meanwhile word of Gardiner's capture was sent to Winthrop, and presently Captain John Underhill and his lieutenant, Samuel Dudley, appeared to take charge of him. By them he was taken back in custody, reaching Boston on the $\frac{24th}{4th}$ of $\frac{April}{May}$.

It is not clear what now ensued. In his letter of acknowledgment to Bradford, written the day after Underhill got back with Gardiner, Winthrop denied that he ever "intended any hard measure to him, but to respect and use him according to his qualitie;" and, though Gardiner seems to have been kept for a time under close watch, he certainly never was tried or had any sentence inflicted upon him, nor was he even shipped back to England [1] under the magistrate's

---

[1] In his notes to Winthrop (ed. 1853, 65, n.) Savage says that the magistrates sent Mary Grove "for examination to London, in the same ship with Saltonstall, Coddington and Wilson." Palfrey (i. 329) says that it was "intended" to send Gardiner over in that vessel, but "the master of the Lion could not be persuaded to take charge of him, and it was some months longer before he could be gotten rid of." (Ib. 330.)

The thing is of no historical consequence whatever; but these statements are not correct. The Lion sailed from Salem April 1st (Young's *Chron. of Mass.* 340, n.), and Gardiner did not reach Boston in custody until May 4th. Gardiner was not "gotten rid of" either then, or some months later, but, as Winthrop himself says, "was kindly used, and dismissed in peace" (ii. 232). Finally, Mary Grove not only stayed in New England, but married at Boston, and not improbably descendants of hers may be living in Maine now. (III. *Mass. Hist. Coll.* viii. 321.)

Both Savage's and Palfrey's error arose from allowing themselves to infer too much from the entry in the Colony Records, and from Dudley's remark, in his letter to the Countess of Lincoln, that "we have taken order to send her to the two wives in England." Savage inferred that the woman was accordingly sent at once, naming the

order of February $\frac{18\text{th}}{28\text{th}}$.   On the contrary, when, six
weeks later, a sentence savage in its severity was
under the pressure of Endicott's influence imposed on
an offender, the execution of it was mitigated through
the intercession of Gardiner with Winthrop.

A few days after this, on $\frac{\text{June } 25\text{th}}{\text{July } 5\text{th}}$, a shallop reached
Boston from Piscataqua, bringing a package of letters
to Sir Christopher under cover to Governor Winthrop.
The confidence thus reposed in him the governor did
not hesitate to violate, any more than, seven years before, his brother governor at Plymouth had hesitated
to inform himself of the contents of the letters written
by the Rev. John Lyford.   Doubtless, too, Winthrop
held himself fully justified in so doing, for not only
was Gardiner a professed "ill-willer" to the colony,
but the magistrates, knowing that he belonged to the
Church of Rome, had inferred he was also an emissary
of the Pope, and engaged in some dark conspiracy
against "the poore churches here."   He was a snake
hiding in the tender grass, and to circumvent him all
means were justifiable.   So, receiving the letters,
Winthrop opened them.   The true significance of
Gardiner's presence in New England was then revealed.   The letters were from Sir Ferdinando Gorges,
and addressed to Gardiner as his agent, and in them
he referred to his claim to the land included in the

very vessel she was sent in; while Palfrey, including Gardiner also in
the order, apparently confused his case for the moment with that
of Morton, and the master of the Lion with the master of the Gift;
and, finally, in his general disapproval of Gardiner, caused the Boston
magistrates to be, as a matter of course, even more summary in their
way of disposing of him than they actually were.

In regard to Sir Christopher Gardiner and Mary Grove, and the singular body of poetry and romance which has grown up about them,
see the paper in the *Proc. of Mass. Hist. Soc.* xx. 60–88.

patent of 1622 to his son Robert, upon which land
the whole settlement at Charlestown and the governor's own farm of Ten Hills were located. A letter
from Gorges to Morton was also in the package.

It would seem altogether probable that Winthrop,
who was never deficient in shrewdness, now began to
realize that it was better not to send Gorges' agent
back to him full charged with anger and mischief.
Impressed by Gardiner's apparent rank, and Gorges'
recognition of it, the governor may also have thought
that it would be dangerous to provoke the knight too
far ; but, whatever the cause for leniency, matters
were not apparently further pressed against Sir Christopher, nor was he long deprived of his liberty of action. About this time Thomas Purchase, who had
come over in 1624, and later had settled on the An-
droscoggin, in what is now the town of Brunswick,
had occasion to be in Boston. He was a man of good
standing, and, whatever her previous relations with
Gardiner may have been, Mistress Mary Grove found
favor in his eyes. They were accordingly married in
Boston, some time in August, 1631. Purchase and his
wife then returned to his home in Maine, accompanied
by Gardiner, who, Winthrop says, was " dismissed in
peace," and professed himself under " much engagement for the great courtesy " with which he had been
treated. He remained at Brunswick, or thereabouts
in Maine, about a year longer, still acting, it is to be
presumed, as the agent of Gorges; and then, return-
ing to England, landed at Bristol on the $\frac{15\text{th}}{25\text{th}}$ of August, 1632. His former companion apparently threw
in her lot with New England, as Thomas Purchase's
wife Mary is recorded as having died in Boston on
the 7th of January, 1656.

It has been mentioned that in June, six weeks after his capture on the Taunton River, Gardiner had exerted himself in Boston to secure the mitigation of a sentence in course of execution on a criminal. This criminal was Philip Ratcliff, a servant of Governor Matthew Cradock. The offence for which he was punished was apparently committed at Salem, and, as recited in his sentence, was the "uttering mallitious and scandulous speeches against the government and the church" there. In another place it is referred to as a "most horible blasphemy," while Winthrop says he was "convict, *ore tenus*, of most foul scandalous invectives." The probability would seem to be that the poor wretch was a bondsman in a strange land and under a hard rule, — a man of unsettled mind, and no Puritan or religionist, — a coarse, crazy, homesick Englishman.[1] Morton, no very reliable authority on the point, gives a characteristic turn to the affair. He says that Ratcliff was a member of the Church of England : —

"And (to the end they might have some color against him) some of them practised to get into his debt; which he, not mistrusting, suffered : and gave credit for such commodity as he had sold at a price. When the day of payment came, instead of moneys, he being at that time sick and weak, and stood in need of the Beaver he had contracted for, he had an epistle full of zealous exhortations to provide for the soul, and not to mind these transitory things that perished with the body ; and to bethink himself whether his conscience would be so prompt to demand so great a sum of Beaver as had been contracted for. . . . The perusal of this (lap'd in the paper) was as bad as a potion to the creditor, — to see his debtor, Master Subtilety,

---

[1] In a letter from Edwards Howes to J. Winthrop, Jr., he is spoken of as "the lunatic man." (Savage in note to Winthrop, i. 56.)

a zealous professor, as he thought, to deride him in this extremity, — that he could not choose, in admiration of the
deceit, but cast out these words : —

"'Are these your members? — If they be all like these,
I believe the Devil was the setter-up of their Church.'"

Unfortunately for him, Ratcliff had to do with Endicott, and that magistrate seems at this time to have
been having a great deal of trouble. His methods
were peculiar. A few weeks before, he had got in a
wrangle with "goodman" Thomas Dexter at Salem.
Dexter is best known for his subsequent purchase of
Nahant, for a suit of clothes, from the Indian Black
William, who was afterwards hanged at Richmond's
Island for having a hand in the murder there of one
Walter Bagnall, "a wicked fellow [that] had much
wronged the Indians." Dexter himself does not seem
to have been a mild-mannered man ; for once, a few
years later, meeting on the road his neighbor Samuel
Hutchinson, between whom and himself there was
trouble, he jumped from his horse and bestowed on
the spot "about twenty blows" on his adversary's
"head and shoulders." However formidable he might
be to ordinary men like Hutchinson, Dexter was no
match for Endicott, who, as the result of their wrangle, gave him a beating out of hand. When called
to account for thus executing his own process, the
Salem magistrate had excused himself on the ground
of excessive aggravation, declaring to Winthrop that
"if you had seen the manner of his carriage, with
such daring of me with his arms on kembow, &c., it
would have provoked a very patient man." Nevertheless, he expressed his regret at having punished Dexter as he did, though he added significantly, — "If it
were lawful to try it at blows, and he a fit man for

me to deal with, you should not hear me complain."
The Court of Assistants took a different view of the
matter, and a jury impanelled at the session of April
23d found the irate magistrate guilty of "battry,"
and fined him forty shillings.[1]

These proceedings, which had occurred but a short
time before, and must have occasioned no little talk
at Salem, may have emboldened Ratcliff to set his
"arms on kembow," also, and to indulge in a little
"daring" of Endicott on his own account. If such
was the case, he reckoned badly. The magistrate did
not take the law into his own hands, but, with characteristic vehemence, he did carry the case before the
Court of Assistants, demanding, as Morton states it,
that the accused should be "made an example for all
carnall men, to presume to speake the least word that
might tend to the dishonor of the Church of Salem;
yea, the mother Church of all that holy Land." An
example he was certainly made; for he was sentenced
to be whipped, have his ears cut off, pay a fine of
forty pounds, and to be banished without the jurisdiction. So far the sentence passed upon him admits of
no doubt; but Morton adds that he was also to have
his tongue bored through, his nose slit, and his face
branded, and it was in these last respects that, through
Gardiner's expostulations with Winthrop, the sentence was mitigated in execution.

That for angrily inveighing against the church government and the magistracy of Salem this man was
whipped and banished, after being mutilated and
heavily fined, is matter of record, for Winthrop says
he was so sentenced, and that the sentence "was presently executed."[2] There has been, and very deservedly,

[1] Lewis, *Hist. of Lynn*, 39; Palfrey, i. 327, n.   [2] *History*, i. 56.

a considerable amount of denunciation expressed by modern historians of a certain sentence passed shortly after this time on one William Prynne by the Court of Star Chamber, in England. Prynne had published a book against the theatre, the tendency of which, according to Hallam, was more tiresome than seditious. For this he was ordered to stand twice in the pillory, to be branded on the forehead, to lose both his ears, to pay a fine of £5,000, and to suffer perpetual imprisonment. Prynne's sentence, like the very similar one passed on Ratcliff, was brutal in its cruelty. For it Archbishop Laud has most properly been held responsible; and for it he is now gibbeted in history: but the historians of New England have not felt called upon to visit the same severity of criticism upon the punishment inflicted on Ratcliff, or the magistrates who ordered it.[1]

---

[1] Palfrey, for instance, simply mentions the sentence in the words of the Records (vol. i. 351). Savage, in his notes to Winthrop, indulges in a note upon the subject, in which he finds himself "compelled to regret the cruelty of the punishment" (i. 68). In describing affairs and events then taking place on the other side of the Atlantic, these same authorities declare that this was the time when "the Star Chamber was rioting in barbarities." (Palfrey, i. 370.) In Massachusetts, "Thomas Fox is sentenced to be whipped for uttering scandalous speeches against the court" (ib. 326); Henry Lyon is "whipped and banished for writing into England falsely and maliciously against the execution of justice here" (ib. 352), etc., and these episodes are cited apparently to show how "minute and multifarious were the cares of the primeval magistrates of Massachusetts Bay." (Ib. 353.) In another place (ib. 563), the similarly barbarous outrages inflicted by Laud in the cases of Lilburne, Prynne and Leighton are described at length as examples of the "exasperating and intolerable abuses of ecclesiastical authority." But, while "Laud's special province lay in the enforcement of severe laws of uniformity" (ib. 562), Endicott, in pursuing an exactly similar course towards Morton, Ratcliff, Fox and Lyon, was protecting "religious freedom" by measures which were "simply self-defence," where tolerance would have been "public ruin." (Ib. 300.)

Thus Morton, Gardiner and Ratcliff had been dealt with in the space of a twelvemonth, — between September, 1630, when the first was set in the stocks, and June, 1631, when the last stood at the whipping-post. A year later they were all in England, bitterly denouncing the colony of Massachusetts Bay, and clamoring before the Privy Council for redress.

Nor, in dealing with them in a manner so summary and severe, could the Massachusetts magistrates have supposed that they had to do merely with obscure persons whose complaints were most unlikely ever to reach, much less affect, those high in English authority. On the contrary, it was well known that both Morton and Gardiner were in direct communication with Gorges, and they, of course, would secure for more obscure complainants a ready access to him. Under these circumstances, the course now pursued by Winthrop and his associates was little less than an open and intentional defiance of the Council for New England. Certainly the presence at this time in London of Morton, Gardiner and Ratcliff was a veritable godsend to Gorges, who, in company with Captain John Mason, the patentee of New Hampshire, was then exerting himself to the utmost to get the charter of the Massachusetts company revoked. The house in which Sir Ferdinando lived, as formerly it had been the point of gathering of all who had visited the coast of America, or could add anything to the stock of information concerning it, now became a head-quarters for those who had any complaint to make or charges to prefer against the magistracy of Massachusetts.

The attack was made on the 19th of December, 1632, and was a formidable one. It assumed the

shape of a petition to the Privy Council, asking the
Lords to inquire into the methods through which the
royal charter for the Massachusetts Bay had been
procured, and the abuses which had been practised
under it. Beside many injuries inflicted on individuals in their property and persons, the company was
also charged with seditious and rebellious designs,
subversive alike of church and state. The various
allegations were based on the affidavits of three witnesses, — Morton, Ratcliff and Gardiner, — and behind the allegations was the active influence of Gorges.
Had this petition been preserved, it could scarcely
have failed to throw a strange gleam of light on the
other and now unseen side of early Massachusetts
history; unfortunately, it is lost. It would have
been more peculiarly interesting from its curious insight into the future. In referring to it afterwards,
Winthrop said that it contained " some truths misre-
peated." Apart from severe judgments on individual
wrong-doers, taking the form of frequent whippings,
setting in the stocks, branding, ear-cropping, fining
and banishment, the real burden of charge lay in the
alleged disposition of the colony to throw off its allegiance to the mother country. There was in that wilderness already a church without a bishop; and it was
asserted in the petition that there was soon to be a
state without a king.

A harsh coloring was, doubtless, given to everything. So far as rebellion or independence was concerned, nothing is more certain than that neither the
leaders nor the common people of the Massachusetts
colony then entertained any thought of it; but it is
equally certain that the leaders, at least, were a stubborn, unyielding race of Commonwealth's-men, stern

of temper and with bitter tongues, who did continually
rail against state and church.   That even now they
only needed a little more consciousness of strength to
ripen on occasion into rebels, was probably asserted
in the lost document; and, however Winthrop might
deny it, the developments of three years later showed
conclusively that this assertion was true.   In the light
of their sympathies and sufferings, Gardiner and
Morton probably saw the real drift of what they had
heard said and seen done in New England a good
deal more clearly than Winthrop.

The result of the Gorges and Gardiner petition was
the appointment of a committee of twelve Lords of
the Council, to whom the whole matter was referred
for investigation and report.   The committee was empowered to send for persons and papers, and a long
and apparently warm hearing ensued.   The friends of
the company bestirred themselves at once.   Cradock
was, of course, in England; for, though he was at
one time governor of the company, he never went to
America.   Sir Richard Saltonstall was also there,
having returned in April of the year before.   With
them was John Humphrey, formerly deputy-governor,
and one of the original patentees of the company,
who had married a daughter of the Earl of Lincoln
and sister of the Lady Arbella, and was then preparing to come out to New England.[1]   Cradock, also,

---

[1] John Humphrey was subsequently one of the early settlers of
Swampscott. His wife, the Lady Susan, was never contented to live
in America, and at a later day the two returned to England, leaving
their children, among whom were ungrown daughters, here, — a proceeding which ultimately resulted in one of those loathsome scandals
with the details of which the pages of Winthrop and Bradford are
unpleasantly replete. The early settlers of New England were a
highly moral and correct race. They were none the less men and wo-

was Ratcliff's master, which fact was not without its bearing on the case. These three filed a written answer to the complaint; and at the hearing they received further assistance from Emanuel Downing, Winthrop's brother-in-law and a resident in London, and from Thomas Wiggin, who lived at Piscataqua, and had often been in Boston, but now most opportunely chanced to be in England.[1]

As Gorges had learned to his cost three years before, when at a critical moment the charter had been evoked, as by swift magic, from the innermost recesses of the palace, the company of Massachusetts Bay was by no means without influence in high quarters; and now recourse was had to every means of privately influencing the members of the committee. These unseen agencies were, in the London of the time of Charles I., and at his court, far more potent than written answers or counter allegations; nor, in the present instance, did the friends of the company labor in vain, for, to the astonishment of every one, the result of the proceedings was, that Gorges and his associates took nothing by them. The committee reported against any interference at that time, somewhat sophistically attributing to the " faults or fancies of particular men " those grounds of complaint which did not admit of explanation, but which they declared

men; and " wikednes being here more stopped by strict laws, and the same more nerly looked unto, so as it cannot rune in a comone road of liberty as it would, and is inclined, it searches every wher, and at last breaks out wher it getts vente." (Bradford, 385.) The details of the Humphrey scandal are given in Winthrop (ii. 45). See, also, Lewis, *Lynn* (p. 75), in which there is a very droll plate, supposed to represent Lady Susan Humphrey in the act of parting from her children.

[1] III. *Mass. Hist. Coll.* viii. 320.

were "in due time to be inquired into." This report, when made, was approved by King Charles, who had evidently also been labored with through the proper channels, inasmuch as he seems to have gone out of his way to further threaten with condign punishment those "who did abuse his governor and the plantation."

The immediate danger which threatened the infant settlement was thus averted; but the cloud, though it proved a passing one, had for a time looked black and ominous, nor was the more than possible outcome of it underestimated in Massachusetts. This Winthrop gave proof of through his actions; for when, in May, 1633, exact intelligence of the final action of the Council reached him, he at once wrote a letter gravely jubilant thereon to Governor Bradford at Plymouth, informing him of the glad tidings, and inviting him to join "in a day of thanks-giving to our mercifull God, who, as he hath humbled us by his late correction, so he hath lifted us up, by an abundante rejoysing, in our deliverance out of so desperate a danger." [1]

---

[1] Bradford, 297. See, also, for facts and authorities connected with the Council for New England and the conflict over King Charles' charter of 1629, Mr. Deane's two papers, "The Council for New England," Winsor, *Nar. and Crit. Hist. of Am.* iii. ch. ix.; and "The Struggle to Maintain the Charter of King Charles I.," *Mem. Hist. Boston,* i. ch. x.

CHAPTER XVI.

THE ASSAULT RENEWED.

SIR CHRISTOPHER GARDINER now disappears from the record. After the Privy Council hearing of January, 1633, his name is no more met with, and not improbably he again wandered off on his travels. Philip Ratcliff, on the contrary, Gorges would seem to have kept within easy reach, and at a later day he appeared again as a witness before the Council, — at least Thomas Morton says that he did so, and that on this occasion "he was comforted by their lordships with the cropping of Mr. Winthrop's ears." [1] Morton also was himself instant, active and persistent, for to return to New England remained henceforth the dream of his life; but, as he could hope to return there only after the ruin of the Massachusetts Bay colony, he now devoted himself to the work of accomplishing that ruin. To that end he became a hanger-on of Sir Ferdinando Gorges, whose fortunes for the rest of his life he seems in some degree to have shared; and, in sharing them, he at one time not without reason believed that the hour of triumph and of revenge was for him close at hand.

This was in 1634. During the fifteen months which had then passed since the attack on the charter in the winter of 1632–3, events had moved rapidly on both sides of the Atlantic. In New England, the colony

[1] Winthrop, ii. *191.

of Massachusetts Bay had taken firm hold of the soil, and already far exceeded in wealth and population the older settlement at Plymouth. In place of the straggling planters who lived in solitude about the bay in 1629, there were now upwards of four thousand English people distributed among twenty Massachusetts hamlets. Boston had grown into the semblance of a town, though it was still little more than a collection of log-huts and rude frame-houses built in straggling fashion on streets and lanes laid out regardless of symmetry, as the rough nature of the ground and the uneven holdings made convenient. The principal edifice was the meeting-house, as the place of worship was called, — a large, square building made out of rough-hewn lumber, the interstices of which were sealed with mud. It had no spire, and its sloping roof, like those of all the dwellings, was thatched with coarse grass cut from the marshes; it stood on one side, and close to the head of the short main street which led down to the principal wharf or landing-place of the town. Winthrop, still governor, though his hold on the office was weakening, dwelt not far from the meeting-house and nearly opposite the town spring, about which the better houses clustered. Above and behind the little town, in which may have lived some six or eight hundred souls, rose the bare, round top of Sentry Hill, on the back side of which, facing Charles River and the west, Blackstone still dwelt alone. The days of famine, sickness and trial were ended. The settlers had grown accustomed to their new surroundings, and the place was an active and prosperous one, — the seat of government of a colony which was full of confidence in its capacity to take care of itself in any contingencies likely to arise.

On the other side of the Atlantic, King Charles had now fairly entered upon his struggle with the people of England. In March, 1629, he had dissolved his third parliament; nor did he now mean ever to call another. He proposed to govern his kingdom as Philip II. had before governed Spain, and as Louis XIV. subsequently governed France. The king was to be the state. To bring this about he was having recourse to various extra-constitutional tribunals, — the Council of the North, the Star Chamber, the Court of High Commission. Questions relating to the colonies had hitherto been disposed of in the Privy Council, for they did not frequently arise and were regarded as of little account; but recently the large emigration to New England of "persons known to be ill-affected and discontented, as well with the civil as ecclesiastical government," had excited attention, and was looked upon with alarm. It was regarded as the gathering of a new plague-spot, from which deadly contagion might spread; for, both in Old and in New England fear was at the root of intolerance to a greater degree than either intellectual conviction or theological hate.[1] So, when in February, 1634, the fact was brought to the notice of the Council that several vessels loaded with passengers and stores destined for New England were then lying in the Thames, an order-in-council was issued staying the sailing of these vessels, and calling upon Cradock to produce the company's charter. Cradock replied that the charter was not in his possession, — that Winthrop had taken it with him to New England four years before. He was directed to send for it at once. Meanwhile the friends of the company in the Council prevailed so far that the vessels were allowed to

[1] Gardiner, *England*, 1603–1642, vii. 318; viii. 164–8.

sail, their masters entering into bonds to have the Book of Common Prayer used, during the voyage, at morning and evening service.

As special tribunals were now greatly in vogue, it was in certain quarters deemed best to organize one to take charge of colonial matters. The idea of such a tribunal seems to have grown out of the February order-in-council, and it was designed almost exclusively for the management of the affairs of New England, where "scandals" both in church and state were most rife. The year before, Laud had been made Archbishop of Canterbury, and now he was engaged with a whole heart in his lifelong war on Puritanism. In the Star Chamber and the High Commission his influence was supreme; and when, on the $\frac{1st}{11th}$ of April, a commission passed the great seal establishing a board with almost unlimited powers to regulate plantations, he was naturally at the head of it. There would even seem to be good reason for supposing that this tribunal was created at Laud's suggestion, and in consequence of the unsatisfactory action of the Privy Council in the matter of the vessels, two months before. A further inference from what went before and what followed is, that Laud's action in the matter was shaped and directed by Gorges. In other words, the organization of this colonial board, through Laud's influence and with Laud supreme in it, was Gorges' first move in the new attack he was now meditating on the charter of the Massachusetts Bay.

The historians of New England have exercised much ingenuity in devising reasons of state why King Charles granted the charter of 1629 at all, — why the attack upon it of 1632 came to nothing, — and why, two years later, it was renewed with so different result.

" Considering the character of the King on the one hand,
and the provisions of the charter on the other, it seems necessary to conclude, either that its tenor was not well known
to him when it received his assent, or else that his purpose
in granting it was to encourage the departure of Puritans
from England, at the time when he was entering upon
measures which might bring on a dangerous conflict with
that party. . . .

" The charter of the Massachusetts Company had passed
the seals almost simultaneously with the King's annuncia-
tion, after an exciting controversy with three Parliaments,
of his purpose to govern without Parliaments in future. It
might well appear to him, that, in the contests which perhaps were to follow, his task would be made easier if numbers of the patriots could be tempted to absent themselves
from the kingdom; and when he should have succeeded,
and the laws and liberties of England should be stricken
down, there would be nothing in his past grants to embar-
rass him in his treatment of the exiles, and his arm would
be long enough to reach and strong enough to crush them
in their distant hiding place. Or, if no scheme so definite
as this was entertained, the grant of the charter, inviting
attention to a distant object, might do something for his
present relief, by breaking up the dangerous concentration
of the thoughts of the Puritans on the state of affairs at
home." [1]

In writing history, as in dealing with the actual
affairs of life, it is as dangerous to see too far as
not to see far enough; and the historian who philoso-
phizes as to the possible deep motives of state which
may have influenced the action of a ruler, always pre-
supposes that the ruler in question was indeed influenced by deep motives. Of this in the case of
Charles I. there is no evidence. It would have been

[1] Palfrey, i. 391–2.

natural enough that broad and far-sighted considerations like those suggested should have entered into the mind and influenced the policy of Wentworth, for he was a man of capacity, a statesman of the Richelieu and Bismarck type. Laud also, though not a statesman, was a man who in his public action worked on a plan and to a given result. But there is nothing to connect Wentworth at any time with the course pursued by Charles in reference to the plantations in New England; and not until 1634 did Laud give any attention to them. In February, 1634, the Primate became the head of the tribunal then organized to attend to colonial affairs, and from that time forward the royal policy was clearly enough defined. A guidance both of head and hand becomes then apparent; but in 1629, when the charter was granted, Buckingham, who was as incapable of a consecutive policy as Charles himself, had been assassinated only the year before, and the place beside the throne made vacant by his death was not yet filled. Wentworth, just bought off from the patriot side, was busy in the North. Laud, still Bishop of London, was occupied with his ecclesiastical reforms. Thus, for the time being, the King governed by his own hand.

The character of Charles I. has been sufficiently discussed, nor is it necessary to speak of it here. An ordinary English gentleman of his time, correct in deportment and gifted with no little appreciation of finer things, he walked according to his lights in the sphere in which he was born. Unfortunately for him, he was born in the purple. Narrow-minded by nature, he was, except in matters of deportment, utterly unequal to his position; but this he never realized. Accordingly, feeling himself a king, he never questioned his own capacity to rule; and, after the manner of small, obstinate men, believing in few things he believed in them intensely. Chief among these was his own right divine. At his court all things went by royal favor. As a matter of course, such a very finite creature as he being the source of all bounties, the palace became from top to bottom a nest of corrupt intrigues; and, under these circumstances, it almost goes without saying that considerations of state policy had nothing to do with such trifles as the granting of the charter of the Massachusetts Bay company, or the outcome of the first assault upon it. As Allerton, while representing the Plymouth people in London at this very time, found out to their cost, when any favor at Whitehall was wanted, "by the way many riddles must be resolved, and many locks must be opened with the silver, nay, the golden key." So, when the charter of the Massachusetts company was granted, it was probably granted without particular consideration. The Earl of Warwick and Lord Dorchester, or more probably the Earl of Warwick through Lord Dorchester, asked for it, and the influence of the latter at court easily secured it. It may well be questioned whether the King gave a moment's serious thought to the matter. His idea of New England was probably much what ours of Alaska is now. It was a remote wilderness beyond the seas; and if any one, especially Puritans, wanted to try the experiment of living there, they were welcome to do so. They might also manage their affairs in their own way.

In like manner, after the charter was thus carelessly granted, and when the attack of 1632 was made, it again became a mere question of influence at court.

The King himself neither knew nor cared anything about the matter. His thoughts were absorbed in questions of tonnage and poundage, and royal monopolies; he was pondering over the war with Spain, and what Wentworth was doing in Ireland; he was devising vengeance against the opposition in England, and meditating upon the church system he meant to introduce into Scotland. So when Gardiner's and Morton's complaint was stirred before the Privy Council by Gorges, the decision turned not upon the right or wrong of the matter, or any possibilities of future empire beyond the seas, but it was a struggle for influence in the King's audience chamber. Cradock and Saltonstall and Downing there showed themselves better befriended than Gorges; and so the latter now suffered another " shrowd check."

But in this field of operations Sir Ferdinando was an opponent not safe to despise. The palace of Whitehall was a house with many ante-chambers, and if Warwick had influence in some of these, Gorges could secure it in others. He had been working through influence at court all his life. By means of it he had extricated himself from the Essex treason in 1601; and if influence at court could have brought it about, he would have become the ruler of a trans-Atlantic domain in 1623. As he had been in 1601 and in 1623, so was he in 1634. His plan of operations was, too, well conceived. He still meant to possess for himself and his descendants a principality in America, and to rule there as a royal governor. To bring this about he had to be strong at court; and he went to work to make himself strong at court just as he had gone to work twelve years before. He had then sought to influence James through Buckingham. He now influ-

enced Charles through Laud. He secured the ear of
the Primate, who hated a Puritan; and once he had
secured the ear of the Primate he was sure of that of
the King.

For thirty years Gorges had been ruining himself
in futile efforts to plant New England; and now the
planting of New England was accomplishing itself
not only without any aid from him, but in a way
which threatened his interests. As he expressed it,
"people of all sorts flocked thither in heaps;" and
those people, not content with refusing to recognize
his title to a domain, mutilated and abused his agents,
and drove them into exile. The Council for New
England was clearly not equal to the task of dealing
with such a crisis as this. It was necessary to proceed through some other agency, — to have recourse to
new expedients. The following scheme seems accordingly to have been devised: — The entire territory
still held under the grant of 1620, extending from
Maine to New Jersey, was to be again divided in severalty among the remaining members of the Council
for New England, and the letters-patent of the Council were then to be surrendered to the King, who
was to confirm the division just made. The Council being thus relegated to the domain of things for
which no further use exists, the King was to assume
the direct government of the whole territory, and appoint a governor-general to rule over it. Sir Ferdinando Gorges was then to be appointed the King's
governor-general. He would thus go out to his province clothed with full royal authority; and the question would then be, not between the settlers of
Massachusetts Bay, armed with a charter from the
King, and that "carcass in a manner breathless" the

Council for New England, but between a small body of disobedient colonists and the King's own representative. It was a well-devised scheme.

Here, at last, was a definite policy in regard to New England, and it was a policy which fitted in naturally with the great scheme of prerogative government which Wentworth and Laud were then welding into shape for the whole British Empire. It was " Thorough " applied to the colonies. Gorges was to do on a small scale in Massachusetts what Wentworth was already doing on a large scale in Ireland. The first step in carrying out the new policy — that policy which had its origin in the greed of Gorges, and found its motive force in Laud's bigotry — was the appointment of the royal commission for regulating plantations, with the Archbishop at its head. Save the lack of enforcing power, there was no limit to its authority. It could revoke charters ; it could remove and appoint governors ; it could even break settlements up if deemed best ; it could inflict punishment upon all offenders, either by imprisonment " or by loss of life or member." It was, in fact, a commission after Charles' own heart, for it represented Right Divine. In it the kingly authority stood out clean cut and absolute ; no earthly power intervened between the people and the royal will. The letters-patent bore date the 10th of April, 1634, and the new tribunal provided for in them was not slow in proceeding to its appointed work ; while the extent of Gorges' influence in it may be inferred from the fact that three weeks later Thomas Morton, Gorges' dependant, wrote to New England that the Massachusetts charter had already been brought in view, and, for manifest abuses there discovered, declared to be void. He further stated

that a general governor was to be sent over at once,
and with him he, Morton, was to return to America.
It is not quite clear whether the decisive hearing
which resulted in this decision took place before the
Privy Council and led to the appointment of the
commission, or whether it took place before the commission itself.[1] Wherever it took place, it seems to
have savored strongly of Star Chamber and High
Commission methods; and Cradock, Saltonstall and
Humphrey had there learned that influences were
at work not to be controlled by them. Indeed, the
first and last named would seem to have been be-
rated by Laud, in true High Commission style, as
a couple of impostors and knaves, and they "had
departed the council chamber with a pair of cold
shoulders." Ratcliff had again told his tale of wrong
and shown his scars to a tribunal, the members of
which, though not slow themselves in cropping of ears,
seem to have looked upon that form of mutilation
as a prerogative of their own. So far as Ratcliff

---

[1] Referring to the failure of the complaint to the Privy Council in
1634, Morton's language is: — " I have at this time taken more deliberation and brought the matter to a better pass. And it is thus brought
about, that the King hath taken the business into his own hands. The
Massachusetts patent, by order of the Council, was brought in view;
the privileges there granted well scanned upon, and at the Council
Board in public, and in the presence of Sir Richard Saltonstall and
the rest, it was declared, for manifest abuses there discovered, to be
void. The King hath reassumed the whole business into his own
hands, appointed a committee of the board, and given order for a
general governour of the whole territory to be sent over. The commission is passed the privy seal; I did see it, and the same was 1 mo.
Maii sent to the Lord Keeper to have it pass the great seal for confirmation." (Winthrop, ii. *190.)

This letter was dated the 1st of May. The hearing was presumably before the Privy Council, and the committee here spoken of
was the Laud Commission.

was concerned, they certainly had the will, and they did not seem to lack the power, to avenge him. He had described, apparently, the forms of marriage and the methods of preaching in use at Boston. It is needless to say that this had acted as a hot incentive on the Primate, who seems thereupon to have flamed forth in one of his outbursts of nervous anger, in which " he looked as though blood would have gushed out of his face, and did shake as if he had been haunted with an ague fit." In his wrath he now on the spot promised the witness, in retaliation for his own ears, the cropping of those of Governor Winthrop. Fortunately for John Winthrop and John Endicott the ocean rolled between Canterbury and themselves.

The production of the charter had already been ordered by a vote of the Privy Council of the 21st of February, — two months and a half before. Of this the Lord Commissioners were, of course, aware. In obedience to the injunction then laid upon him, Cradock had transmitted the order of the Council, accompanied by a letter of his own to Winthrop, who received both letter and order in July. Then began that struggle for the possession of the charter which continued for fifty years, and until the decisions of an English court had destroyed its political value. But the charter never went back to England. When this first demand for it reached him, Winthrop was no longer governor, for at the election in the previous May, Dudley had been chosen to supersede him. The new governor laid Cradock's letter, together with the order of the Council, before the Assistants, and after grave deliberation it was resolved to procrastinate. So the letter was treated as an unofficial one, and as such answered to Cradock; but as for the charter, it was replied that it could be transmitted only under the authority of the General Court of Massachusetts, which was not to meet until September. This missive was then entrusted to Governor Edward Winslow, of Plymouth, who at that time went out as joint agent of the two colonies, reaching London in the early autumn.

It was in Winslow's power only to say that he had not brought the charter; but its production does not seem to have been again immediately called for. Possibly the Lords Commissioners may have expected that the General Court would at its September session order it to be sent over; more probably, in view of the course which had then been decided upon, an examination of it was no longer considered necessary. The next spring, that of 1635, had been fixed upon by Gorges and Mason as the time for decisive action, when the charter was to be vacated, and Gorges, in the mean time appointed governor-general, was to go out to New England with a force sufficient to compel obedience. But all this implied a considerable equipment, and consequent outlay of money. Shipping had in the first place to be provided, and a large vessel was accordingly put upon the stocks. Rumor said, also, that the new governor-general was to take out with him a force of no less than a thousand soldiers. Whether this was true or not, there can be little doubt that all through the winter of 1634–5 active preparations were going on.

Meanwhile Winslow had other business in hand which took him before the Lords Commissioners of Plantations. He laid before them a petition on behalf of the colonies for authority to resist certain Dutch and French encroachments, — a proceeding which the cautious Winthrop thought not well advised, as it might seem to imply that such action on the part of the colonies needed to be authorized, and in this way it could be drawn into a precedent. Winslow none the less presented his petition, and several hearings were had upon it. Fully informed as to everything that went on before the Lords Commissioners, Gorges did not view this move with favor. It looked to military or diplomatic measures to be taken within his proposed jurisdiction, and the conduct of which should clearly be entrusted to him as governor-general. He accordingly went to work to circumvent Winslow, and what ensued threw a great deal of light on other things which took place at that time. It showed what a puppet Laud in these matters was in Gorges' hands, and how cunningly the latter pulled the strings.

Winslow, who long afterwards was described by Samuel Maverick [1] as " a Smooth tongued Cunning fellow, who soon got himselfe into Favour of those then in Supreme power, against whom it was in vaine to strive," apparently managed well the business he now had in hand. His suit prospered ; for he submitted to the Lords a plan for accomplishing the end desired, without any charge being imposed on the royal exchequer, and was on the point of receiving a favorable decision. Suddenly the voice of the Archbishop was heard. What followed was intensely characteristic, but Bradford best tells the story : —

" When Mr. Winslow should have had his suit granted, (as indeed upon the point it was), and should have been confirmed, the Archbishop put a stop upon it, and Mr.

[1] *Proc. Mass. Hist. Soc.* Series II. i. 240.

Winslow, thinking to get it freed, went to the board again;
but the Bishop, Sir Ferdinando, and Captain Mason, had,
as it seems, procured Morton (of whom mention is made
before, and his base carriage,) to complain ; to whose complaints Mr. Winslow made answer to the good satisfaction
of the board, who checked Morton and rebuked him sharply,
and also blamed Sir Ferdinando Gorges and Mason, for
countenancing him.   But the Bishop had a further end and
use of his presence, for he now began to question Mr.
Winslow of many things ; as of teaching in the church
publicly, of which Morton accused him, and gave evidence
that he had seen and heard him do it ; to which Mr. Winslow answered, that some time (wanting a minister) he did
exercise his gift to help the edification of his brethren, when
they wanted better means, which was not often.   Then
about marriage, the which he also confessed, that, having
been called to the place of magistracy, he had sometimes
married some ; and further told their lordships that marriage was a civil thing, and he found nowhere in the Word
of God that it was tied to ministry.   Again, they were
necessitated so to do, having for a long time together at first
no minister ; besides it was no new thing, for he had been
so married himself in Holland, by the magistrates in their
State-House.   But in the end (to be short), for these things,
the Bishop, by vehement importunity, got the board at last
to consent to his commitment ; so he was committed to the
Fleet, and lay there seventeen weeks, or thereabouts, before
he could get to be released.   And this was the end of this
petition and this business."

The friends and agents of the colonies being thus
disposed of, — Cradock, Saltonstall and Humphrey
having departed the Council Chamber with " a pair of
could shoulders," and Winslow, the " Smooth tongued
Cunning fellow, . . . against whom it was in vaine
to strive," being laid safely by the heels in the Fleet
prison, — the way for Gorges seemed clear.   His plan

was now rapidly developed. At a meeting of those still composing the Council, held at Lord Gorges' house on the 3d of February, a redivision of the sea-coast of New England was agreed upon. Sir Ferdinando and Captain Mason both were present, but, since the Gardiner-Ratcliff attack on the Massachu-setts Bay company two years before, the Earl of War-wick had apparently withdrawn from all connection with Gorges.[1] He was not, therefore, included in the redivision. This, like the original partition at the Greenwich lot-drawing of 1623, covered the entire North Atlantic coast, from New Jersey to Nova Sco-tia, all which was now divided into eight parcels and assigned to as many persons, among whom were the Marquis of Hamilton, and the Earls of Lenox, Surrey, Carlisle and Stirling. The coast of Massachusetts, from Narragansett Bay to Salem, fell to Lord Gorges; Sir Ferdinando received Maine as his share; and Captain Mason, New Hampshire and Cape Ann.

The division thus agreed upon was to take effect simultaneously with the surrender of the charter. Ten weeks later, at another meeting at Lord Gorges' house, a paper was read and entered upon the records, in which the reasons for surrendering the charter were stated at length. At a subsequent meeting, held on the 26th of April at the Earl of Carlisle's chamber at Whitehall, a petition to the King was submitted and approved, praying that separate patents might be issued securing to the associates in severalty the domains assigned them. A declaration from the King was also then read, in which his intention of appoint-ing Sir Ferdinando Gorges governor-general was for-mally announced; for the Primate of England and

[1] Winsor, *Nar. and Crit. Hist. of Am.* iii. 309, 370.

Chief of the Lords Commissioners for Plantations, speaking by the mouth of the King, did not propose "to suffer such numbers of people to runn to ruine, and to religious intents to languish for want of timely remedye and soveraigne assistance." New England was thus once more platted out among certain of the nobility and gentry about King Charles' court; and it only remained to pass the deeds before proceeding to eject the present occupants, — unless, indeed, these last should recognize the new titles, and make such compromise with their possessors as might yet be possible. In the matter of perfecting the new titles, matters were not allowed to rest. The details of the division had been arranged on the 3d of February, and on the 26th of April patents were petitioned for. Ten days later, Thomas Morton was "entertained to be Solliciter for confirmation of the said Deeds under the Great Seale, as also to prosecute suite at Law for the repealing of the Patent belonging to the Massachusetts Company. And is to have for fee twenty shillings a terme, and such further reward as those who are interested in the affaires of New England shall thinke him fitt to deserve upon the Judgement given in the Cause." A month afterwards, on the 7th of June, 1635, the formal resignation of the grand patent took place.

Returning now to the course of simultaneous events in New England, where great alarm prevailed, no sooner had Winslow, bearing the letter to Cradock, started on his voyage in July, 1634, than Governor Dudley and his brother magistrates went down to Castle Island, with "divers of the ministers and others," and took steps towards fortifying the entrance to Boston Harbor. The deputy, Roger Lud-

low, was appointed to oversee the work. A week
later, William Jeffrey came up from Wessagusset,
and, going to Winthrop's house, gave him a letter
which he had shortly before received from Thomas
Morton. It was dated on the 1st of May, — more
than two months after Cradock's letter, — and, written in a tone of high jubilation, contained new and
startling information. The writer began by addressing Jeffrey as " My very good Gossip," and doubtless
he had known him well in the olden days, when " the
owner of Passonagessit, to have the benefit of company, left his habitation in the winter and reposed at
Wessaguscus." The man to whom Morton exultingly
wrote had been one of those who contributed to the
charge of his first arrest by Standish, but now Morton gave him all the news, and most correctly, too.
Clearly the writer of the letter was in a position to be
well informed. Referring to the order for the immediate production of the charter, he described the
scenes before the Lords Commissioners. He declared
that the King had even then — a year before the
event took place — given order for a general governor
to be sent over ; " and I," he added, " now stay to return with the governour, by whom all complainants
shall have relief." Then he exclaimed, — " Repent,
you cruel separatists, repent, there are as yet but forty
days. If Jove vouchsafe to thunder, the charter and
kingdom of the separatists will fall asunder. Repent,
you cruel schismatics, repent." [1] He speaks signifi-

[1] It would seem that Morton intended this letter should reach Winthrop. It would also seem that the *New English Canaan* was not
written until after this letter, as in the last lines of the book he apparently alludes to it, repeating the very words quoted in the text
and adding that he used them in " letters returned into new Canaan,"
referring doubtless to this letter to Jeffrey, dated May 1, 1634.

cantly of Cradock's and Humphrey's " great friends,"
alluding, doubtless, to the Earls of Lincoln and of
Warwick, who had been unable longer to protect
them; and disclosed the source of his own influence
with the Archbishop by referring to " King Winthrop, with all his inventions and his Amsterdam
fantastical ordinances, his preachings, marriages, and
other abusive ceremonies, which do exemplify his detestation to the Church of England, and the contempt
of his Majesty's authority and wholesome laws."

There was a good deal of exaggeration in these tidings. Things only planned were, for instance, represented as having actually occurred. Doubtless, too,
as they read and re-read the letter, the magistrates
nursed themselves in the belief that the exaggerations
in it must be even greater than they really were. If
they did, they but deluded themselves. The General
Court met on the 25th of August, and, while it was
still in session, vessels arrived bringing despatches
which confirmed everything material that Morton had
written. A full copy of the order-in-council establishing the Lords Commissioners of Plantations was received, and private letters further advised the colonists
that ships were being fitted out, and soldiers got ready
for embarkation. Though ostensibly provided to send
a new governor to Virginia, these, as Winthrop wrote,
were " suspected to be against us, to compel us, by
force, to receive a new governour, and the discipline
of the Church of England, and the laws of the Commissioners."

Stirred by these tidings, the General Court took up
the matter of fortifications in a vigorous spirit. The
regular drilling of the train bands was provided for.
A council was chosen " for the managing and order-

ing of any war that might befall for the space of a
year next ensuing." Steps were taken to get arms
and ammunition together. Defences were ordered at
Dorchester and Charlestown, as well as at Castle
Island, and the magistrates were empowered to im-
press laborers to hurry them to completion.

It was in November, a few weeks after this court
adjourned, that Endicott mutilated the royal banner
at Salem, cutting from it the red cross. "Much matter," Winthrop wrote, "was made of this, as fearing
it would be taken as an act of rebellion, or of like
high nature, in defacing the King's colors; though
the truth were it was done upon this opinion, that the
red cross was given to the King of England by the
Pope as an ensign of victory, and so a superstitious
thing and relique of Antichrist."[1] None the less it
was a characteristic act, and the fittest answer Massachusetts could have made to the threatened encroachments of the Crown. Then, in January, just before the
Council for New England met in London to take the
steps which were to precede the surrender of its charter, all the ministers were summoned to Boston to hold
solemn conference with the Governor and the Assistants. The question was formally submitted to them, —
"What ought we to do if a general governor should
be sent out of England?" — and the clergy replied
with one voice that "we ought not to accept him, but
defend our lawful possessions if we are able." In
March, when the General Court met again, it was
ordered that the works on Castle Island should be
completed at once, and cannon mounted there. Up
to that time, the loftiest and most prominent of the
three rounding hills which composed in largest part

[1] Winthrop, i. *146.

the peninsula on which Boston now stood, — that one
of the three which, rising behind and between the
other two, whose broken bluffs shouldered the tide on
the bay front, gave from its triple peaks its original
name of Trimount to the place,[1] — this had been
known as Sentry Hill. It was now ordered that
"there should be forthwith a beacon set upon it," to
give notice to the country of any danger, and it was
thereafter known as Beacon Hill. At the same time
a military commission was established, with arbitrary
powers extending even to life and death, and the freeman's oath was exacted of every one. Maverick, who
still lived at Noddle's Island, and whose connection
with Gorges was not forgotten, under penalty of an
hundred pounds was ordered to remove himself and
his family to Boston ; and he was forbidden to entertain any stranger for more than a single night without
the leave of an Assistant. Shortly after April came
in " There was an Alarme presently given, [the town]
being informed by a Shallop that they had seen a
great shipe, and a smaller one goe into Cape Ann
Harbour, and early in the Morning, being Sabbath
day, all the Traine Bands in Boston, and Townes adjacent were in Armes in the streets, and posts were
sent to all other places to be in the same posture, in
which they continued untill by their scouts they found
her to be a small shipe of Plymouth and a shallope
that piloted her in. The generall and Publick report
was that it was to oppose the landing of an Enemie,
a Governour sent from England, and with that they
acquainted the Commanders." [2] It was but a false
alarm ; but, none the less, the prompt action taken

---

[1] Shurtleff, *Description of Boston*, 41 ; *Mem. Hist. of Boston*, i. 524.
[2] *Proc. Mass. Hist. Soc.* Series II. i. 240.

showed the sense of imminent danger which then prevailed. Meanwhile, all through these events and preparations a significant silence was preserved on the subject of the charter. The order for its immediate transmission to England lay on the table of the General Court; but that body met in session after session and took no notice of it. The people and the deputies, of one mind with the magistrates and the ministers, proposed to "defend their lawful possessions, if they were able."

So matters stood on either side of the ocean in 1635. Royal prerogative was arrayed against actual possession; but Sir Ferdinando Gorges was not destined to realize the dream of his life, and Winthrop saw in the failure a direct interposition of God's hand. The Lord, he said, "preserved and prospered his people here beyond ordinary ways of providence;" and then he pointed out how Mason, "a man in favor at court," had seen all his designs frustrated, and died bewailing his enmity against God's chosen people; and how Gorges never prospered, but, after being at large expense on account of his province here, "he lost all." The probability is that, in this last statement, the pious Governor touched on the true, though matter-of-fact, explanation of Gorges' failure and his own safety. Gorges kept attempting that which he did not have the means to carry out; and so failed, and "lost all." In this commonplace way, and in no other, "the Lord frustrated their design." The effort of 1634–5 was a mere repetition, on a somewhat larger and more resounding scale, of the effort of 1623. The latter had resulted in the expedition under Robert Gorges, and the former set all the courts in England in noisy motion. Neither of them brought anything

about. They both failed, too, from the same cause,
— want of money. The machinery in each case was
imposing, and there was a great deal of it; but, when
it came to doing anything in a practical way, it was apparent that behind the machinery there was nothing
but Sir Ferdinando Gorges, — an active-minded, adventurous soldier, skilled in court ways, persistent and
full of resource, but to the last degree impecunious.
And so, when action was at last necessary, the movement stopped in 1635, just as it had stopped in 1623.
In the later attempt Gorges had enlisted with him the
energetic Mason, and, probably through him, a ship
was to be provided. The building of this ship, without doubt, strained the resources of the two to the utmost; and when, in launching, it suffered a mishap, —
again probably from insufficient means, — they could
not repair the damage it had sustained. From the
King they could get commissions and commissioners,
— from the Archbishop they could get blessings for
themselves and bannings for their opponents, — but
when it came to men, to money and to supplies, neither King nor Archbishop had any to spare. Charles
was then seeking to keep the royal exchequer from
being absolutely empty by deriving an uncertain reve-
nue from the illegal imposition of taxes on trade, and
by the exaction of fines levied upon the great nobles
for encroachments on the royal forests; indeed, it was
in this very year, 1635, that the ship-money writs
were issued, and, the next year, public offices were
sold.[1] Yet notwithstanding all this the treasury of
the King was hardly less empty than that of the
Council for New England; and so Gorges found once
more that he had no one but himself to rely on. He

---

[1] Gardiner, *Hist. of Eng.*, 1603–1642, chs. lxxiv., lxxxii.

could go just so far, but no step further. His noble
associates would accept the domains he assigned them
on paper, but they would venture nothing for actual
possession. The hands of the King were full at home,
and the Primate was powerless out of England.

Of that "strong, new-built ship [which] in the very
launching fell all in pieces, no man knew how,"[1] nothing more was heard. It probably was sold for debt,
and repaired with no great trouble by its purchaser.
The King's governor-general did not go out to New
England; and he failed to go out for the simple reason
that he had not the means to go out, or, if he should
go out, the strength to sustain himself when he got
there. So the angry cloud in the east, after turning
Massachusetts into an armed camp, gradually vanished away in a distant rumble of harmless thunder
in the English courts of law.

In June, 1635, the attorney-general filed in the
King's Bench a writ of *quo warranto* against the
Massachusetts Bay company. This was the work
which Thomas Morton had a month before been "entertained to prosecute," and the promptness of the
attorney-general's action would seem to indicate that
the new agent for the Council had earned his fee for
that term at least, and even deserved some "further
reward." The scheme was to set the charter aside,
not because of any abuse of the powers lawfully conferred by it, but as being void *ab initio.* Every title
to land held under it would be thus vitiated. In due
course of law certain of the patentees appeared, denying the alleged usurpation on their part, and formal
judgments were entered against them. Cradock made
default, and was convicted of the usurpation charged.

---

[1] D'Ewes, *Autobiography*, ii. 118.

Judgment was then entered that the franchises should be taken into the King's hands. The patentees in New England made no appearance, and were outlawed. In the eye of the law, therefore, the charter was no longer anything more than a worthless parchment. In point of fact it was all that it had ever been; for the colonists disregarded the decision at Westminster, and Gorges was powerless. As for the King and the Primate, they were occupied with matters of more pressing urgency.

The summer of 1635 passed away, and the autumn found Gorges no nearer his governorship; but hope sprang eternal in his breast. Towards the end of November, a meeting of the associates of the dissolved Council for New England was held at the house of Lord Stirling, and a vote was passed that steps should be taken for getting particular patents issued as soon as possible for the land divisions agreed upon in the previous February. Morton was, in fact, reminded that things were not moving rapidly enough. It was also ordered that a petition be drawn, for presentation to the King in the Council's name, for an " allowance to be made for the maintenance and supportation of the Governour in such estate as might sort with the honour thereunto belonging."

But a heavy blow was now impending over Gorges. Captain John Mason, of New Hampshire, at this time died. Not improbably the meeting of the Council of November 26, and its action to hasten the issuing of the patents, was had in view of his condition, for his will is dated on that same day.[1] He died within the following month, and his death lopped away the right hand of Gorges' enterprise. Doubtless, after his na-

---

[1] Tuttle, *Captain John Mason,* 407.

ture, the old soldier, though now somewhat stricken in years, for in 1635 he was already verging towards threescore and ten, kept up a stout heart and looked forward to his departure to his government with each recurring spring. It was not to be. King Charles never had any money to spare to furnish forth expeditions against his stubborn subjects of the Massachusetts Bay. Their battle was to be fought out in England.

CHAPTER XVII.

EXIT GORGES.

WHAT has since come to be known as the solidarity
of the nations was not dreamed of in the state lore of
the seventeenth century; but, none the less, between
the years 1630 and 1640 it made itself very potently
felt. The insignificance of the Massachusetts colony
at the Whitehall of Charles I. has already been referred to.[1] That colony was, indeed, of such little
moment in the minds and eyes of the English people
and the English court, that few, except those engaged
in navigation, or for other reasons specially informed,
could have placed it on the map. Even Scotland was
then looked upon as a remote and unimportant region,
— so remote and so unimportant that Clarendon says,
— "No man ever inquired what was doing in Scotland, nor had that kingdom a place or mention in one
page of any gazette, so little the world heard or thought
of that people." Yet it is not possible to understand
why things chanced for Massachusetts as at this time
they did, without bearing constantly in mind the parallel course of events in England; while the course
of events, and the reason of men's action in England,
become enigmas quite insoluble, unless a key to them
is sought in the course of events in Scotland. Thus,
between 1635 and 1640 it was in Scotland that the

[1] *Supra*, 274.

immediate future of New England was receiving its shape.

To understand the sequence of the history now to be narrated it is necessary, therefore, to have clearly in mind the events that were taking place at the same time in several countries. It will be remembered that the Board of Lords Commissioners for Foreign Plantations, the origin and policy of which has just been described, was organized in April, 1634, and at the same time it had been decided to send out a governor-general to New England. Morton's jubilant letter to Jeffreys, announcing the fact, was written a few days later, on May $\frac{1st}{11th}$. At this very time Attorney-General Noy was turning over the musty bundles of records in the Tower, hunting up precedents for his new scheme of a ship-money tax, — " thinking that he could not give a clearer testimony that his knowledge in the law was greater than all other men's, than by making that law which all other men believed not to be so." [1] He died during the next summer, but Sir John Finch took the thing where the other left it, " and, being a judge, carried it up to that pinnacle from whence he almost broke his own neck." It was on the 20th of the following October that the first ship-money writ was issued; and on the 27th of the following month the Assistants met at Governor Dudley's house " to advise about the defacing of the cross in the ensign at Salem " by Endicott. Seven months later, in June, 1635, the Council for New England surrendered its patent, and King Charles, in accepting the surrender, declared it his intention to appoint Sir Ferdinando Gorges his governor-general. Simultaneously with this the attorney-general, Sir

[1] Clarendon (Oxford, 1849), B. I. §§ 157, 158.

John Banks, instituted his *quo warranto* proceedings against the Massachusetts company, to effect the overthrow of its charter; though it was two years later, and near the close of 1637, before judgment was entered up on these proceedings and the charter declared vacated. At the same term of the courts at which this judgment was entered, the great twenty-shilling ship-money case, in which Hampden was defendant, was argued through two entire weeks before the twelve judges; and, the succeeding month of June, judgment was rendered for the Crown. Between the argument in the ship-money case and the judgment, the tenor of which last was everywhere perfectly well known in advance, the Lords Commissioners for Plantations had sent out to Boston peremptory orders for the immediate transmission to London of the now vacated charter.

The direct issue had at last been made, and, to outward seeming, all things were moving smoothly to the desired end; but, in reality, grave doubts as to what was to be the outcome of all their efforts must already have crossed the minds of Gorges and Morton. Their confidence had touched full flood the year before; and, indeed, during the early months of that year all things had promised well for them. They, at least, had made no error of calculation, had fallen into no mistake of judgment, for they had attached themselves unreservedly to the party of Laud; and, whether in church or in state, the Primate was now supreme. They had done more than attach themselves to Laud's party; they had so played upon his prejudices as to enlist him heart and soul in their cause. Had the council chamber at Boston been within reach of the pursuivants of the High Commission, all matters would soon have been settled in complete accordance with the views of King Charles' "Governour Generall" and the "Sollicitor" of the Council for New England. But, in addition to being far removed from Massachusetts, the Archbishop at this time had a great deal to think of. There was, indeed, little in the three kingdoms, touching either church or state, to which he was not giving his personal attention.[1] He was regulating the most minute details of university discipline at Oxford, as its chancellor. He was also chancellor of the University of Dublin, for the better ordering of which he was securing a new charter and body of statutes. He was making it extremely uncomfortable for the foreign religious congregations in England on the one side, and for the Puritans on the other. In respect to both, he was allowing full swing to his passion for conformity. Then, he was in the heat of a great controversy in regard to the proper position of the communion-table in the churches ; but, nevertheless, he found time to attend to the important questions of copes, genuflexions and painted windows. He was in frequent correspondence with Wentworth, Lord-Lieutenant of Ireland, on affairs of state ; with Bishop Juxon, also, whom he had made Lord-Treasurer ; with the merchants of London, on questions of finance and trade. He was further causing a body of church canons to be prepared for Scotland, which kingdom he had decided must now be made to conform. In fact, when one reads the memoirs of those seething times, it seems as if there was nothing in which the venerable, well-meaning University Don did not concern himself ; and he always went to his

---

[1] Gardiner, *England*, 1603–1642, chs. xiv., lxix., lxxiii., lxxviii., lxxxiii. ; Green, *Hist. of English People*, B. VII. ch. vi.

work with that conscious rectitude of purpose, and infinite belief in his own wisdom, which ever have been
and ever will be the staff and the stay of the genuine
priest and inquisitor. Acute as well as vigorous in-
tellectually, he was the product of the cloister, placed
by his own unfortunate good fortune in the chair of
state. Devout and of untiring industry, he did his
whole duty, as he understood it, nor ever once flinched;
while, with that faith in regulating which is native to
men of little mind, he meddled with everything, and
marred everything with which he meddled. In the
broad, strong light of subsequent events, he seems to
have been put just where he was put by a providential
dispensation; for he was exquisitely calculated to lash
into open frenzy the latent tendencies of his time.[1] By
nature and in purpose the most conservative of men,
he was fated to be one of the most revolutionary factors of a revolutionary time.

As the head of the Board of Lords Commissioners
it, of course, devolved on the Archbishop to regulate
New England. Fortunately for New England and
the English-speaking race, — most unfortunately for
himself, — he at the same time undertook to regulate
Scotland. The result was as if a thunderbolt had
fallen from a clear sky. In the spring of 1637, when
the *quo warranto* proceedings against the Massachusetts company were drawing to their foregone conclusion in the Court of King's Bench, the cause of English constitutional government seemed fairly desperate.
The chances were at best heavily against it. No parliament had sat for eight years. It was believed that
none would ever sit again. It was a misdemeanor
even to petition the King to call one; and the country

---

[1] Gardiner, *England*, ii. 126.

meanwhile was enjoying a season of prosperity such
as there was no record of before. The leading patriots, having abandoned hope, were meditating voluntary exile. The Earl of Warwick secured the proprietorship of the Connecticut Valley; Hampden bought
a tract of land on Narragansett Bay; Lord Say and
Seale made arrangements to emigrate. The judges
had given their opinion in advance in favor of ship-
money; and Wentworth, supreme in Ireland, had
written to Laud, that, " since it is lawful for the King
to impose a tax for the equipment of the navy, it
must be equally so for the levy of an army : and the
same reason which authorizes him to levy an army to
resist, will authorize him to carry that army abroad
that he may prevent invasion. Moreover, what is law
in England is law also in Scotland and Ireland. The
decision of the judges will, therefore, make the King
absolute at home and formidable abroad." In June,
1637, King Charles and his court believed that he
was thenceforth free to govern at his will.[1]

One thing only was necessary, and that thing the
energetic, clear-seeing Wentworth fully appreciated
and emphasized in his letters : — " Let [the King] only
abstain from war for a few years that he may habitu-
ate his subjects to the payment of that tax." A brief
period of foreign peace and domestic plenty, — that
would clinch the matter. It was just this which Laud
was there to prevent. Without the slightest necessity for so doing, but acting after his nature, he suddenly broke, and broke forever, the spell of deathly
quiet which lay brooding over the kingdom. Busy-
body that he was, this, of all possible times, was the
time he selected for establishing in Scotland the
Church of England ceremonial.

---

[1] Green, *Hist. of Eng. People*, iii. 175.

Sunday, the 23d of July, 1637, was fixed upon for
the trial of the experiment. The result does not need
to be retold here. When Jenny Geddes flung that
mythical stool at the head of the Dean of Edinburgh
in the high church of St. Giles, she settled many
things besides the fate of episcopacy in Scotland.
Among those things was the danger then threatening the Massachusetts colony. Jenny Geddes' stool
struck Sir Ferdinando Gorges and Thomas Morton
quite as effectively as if the old crone had flung it
at them. It is one of the familiar incidents of the
history of that time that when Laud, on hearing the
first tidings of "Stony Sabbath,"[1] hurried over from
Lambeth to Whitehall to confer with Charles, he met
in the ante-chamber Archie Armstrong, the King's
jester, who saluted the angry Primate with the question, — "Who's the fool now, my Lord?" As the
jester soon found, to his cost, the author of that day's
mischief was in no mood to be joked about it; nor
did it turn out for either of the two fools — him of
the mitre, or him of the cap-and-bells — a laughing
matter. But it may well be questioned whether from
the day Laud was thus addressed, forward to the days
when he and the King both mounted the scaffold, any
adviser of Charles I. ever gave one hour's serious and
consecutive thought to the affairs of New England,
or what was going on there. As the Rev. John Cotton well put it in one of his discourses, — "God then
rocqued three nations, with shaking dispensations,
that he might procure some rest unto his people in
this wilderness."[2]

A few months before the "Casting of the Stools,"

---

[1] Or "Stonie-field Day." *Fairfax Correspondence*, i. 331.
[2] *Magnalia*, B. III. ch. i. § 33.

probably in anticipation of the results of Sir John
Banks' *quo warranto* proceedings, some sort of a
commission seems to have been prepared, by order of
the Lords Commissioners, creating a provisional government for New England, to act until final order
should be made as to the governor-generalship. A
copy of this commission was sent over to New England through one George Cleeve, who subsequently
played a part of sufficient prominence in the early
history of Maine to be now mentioned in it as " an
equivocal character," who in certain land transactions
" acted with great duplicity." [1]   Cleeve arrived at
Boston on the 26th of June, in the same ship with
the young Lord Ley, a youth of " lowly and familiar
carriage," son and heir of the Earl of Marlborough,
who had come over moved by curiosity to see the
country.   In addition to a copy of the commission for
the general government of New England, which was
probably addressed to Winthrop and others of the
colonial notables, Cleeve brought two other commissions.   One of these seems to have originated with
Morton, who at this time was in the pay of Cleeve,
as well as in that of the Council for New England.[2]
It was a patent under the privy seal, authorizing its
bearer to discover the great Lake Erocoise, of which
a most glowing account had been given in the " New
English Canaan."   The other was a commission from
Sir Ferdinando Gorges, empowering five or six of the
Massachusetts magistrates by name to govern his province of New Somersetshire in Maine, which extended
from Casco Bay to the Kennebec, and withal to oversee his servants and private affairs.   The last docu-

---

[1] Williamson, *Hist. of Maine*, i. 668.
[2] IV. *Mass. Hist. Coll.* vii. 331.

ment had decidedly the aspect of a missive from a
governor-general in possibility to his humbler but
faithful associates, and was looked on much askance
by Winthrop, who noted it "as a matter of no good
discretion." Whenever he did not wish to recognize
or obey a distasteful mandate, it was the custom of
the first governor of Massachusetts to take advantage
of any irregularity he could find in the form or super-
scription of the document, and pass it by in respectful silence. In this case the name of one of those mentioned in the commission was "mistaken, and another
[had] removed to Connecticut;" so he excused "our
not intermeddling," adding moreover, in his dryest
manner, "that it did not appear to us what authority
he had to grant such a commission."

If this commission was, as seems probable, issued
some time in April, 1637, Gorges had then for full two
years been publicly designated as the governor-general
for New England, and was only awaiting the close of
the *quo warranto* proceedings to be formally appointed. Had events then taken a different turn, and
the ship-money tax become actually leviable, instead
of merely declared legal, there can be little question
that he would speedily have come over in person on a
king's vessel. He probably now looked forward to
this with the utmost confidence, and the commission
which Cleeve bore to Winthrop and the rest, to oversee his private estate and affairs, Sir Ferdinando intended as a sort of vice-regal intimation of his confidence and friendliness of spirit. Three months later
the St. Giles liturgy riot took place in Scotland, and
from that time forward the King had no ships to spare
for New England. There are some indications that
the old courtier was now attempting a double and

well-nigh impossible game; having the Primate on
one side, and his future lieges in America on the
other, he sought to play upon the antipathy to all
Puritans of the former, and yet was most anxious to
conciliate the latter. The "New English Canaan"
was just issued from the press; and, while its effect
on the Archbishop would be most beneficial, it could
not fail deeply to incense the friends of the Massachusetts colony, who would be sure to transmit word
of it to New England. Accordingly, in September,
we find Gorges writing to Winthrop in a most conciliatory tone. There is in his letter no suggestion of
the governor-generalship. On the contrary " Ferde :
Gorges " assures his " much respected freindes," among
whom is " John Winthropp," that the former knows
nothing and can learn nothing of the commission for
governing New England, while as to Morton, he declares that the former " Sollicitor " is " wholely cash-
eerd from intermedlinge with anie our affaires hereafter." [1] But that such was really the case is, as will
presently be seen, at least open to doubt. It is far
more probable that in thus writing, the old knight
made use of a little of that Stuart kingcraft, which
in his younger days had been so much in vogue.

A year now elapsed during which Gorges made no
apparent headway. It was not in his nature to be in-
active, but such plans as from time to time he formed,
he must needs have unfolded to anxious and inatten-
tive ears; while of any futile attempts he may have
made at action, no record remains. At last, in the
spring of 1638, a few months after the close of the
quo warranto proceedings, the Board of Lords Commissioners gave feeble signs of life. On the 4th of

[1] IV. *Mass. Hist. Coll.* vii. 331.

April it met at Whitehall. The Primate sat at the
head of the table, and among those about it were the
Lord-Keeper Coventry, the Lord-Treasurer Juxon,
and the elder Vane, whose son had then recently
returned from New England. Calling to mind the
futile demand which four years before had been sent
through Cradock to Winthrop, and taking official
notice of the issue of the *quo warranto* proceedings,
the Board now passed an order directing the clerk
in attendance to send out to Governor Winthrop a
peremptory command for the immediate surrender of
the charter. It was to come back to London by the
return voyage of the ship which took the command
out, — " It being resolved," so the missive ran, " that,
in case of any further neglect or contempt by them
shewed therein, their lordships will cause a strict
course to be taken against them, and will move his
Majesty to reassume into his hands the whole plantation." [1]

This language certainly was not lacking in clear-
ness ; but the effect of it on those to whom it was
addressed must have been considerably impaired by
the fact that the ship which carried the missive to
New England was one of the fleet which also brought
out tidings of the fierce tumult of enthusiasm which
accompanied the signing of that solemn and famous
League and Covenant which worked the overthrow
of episcopacy in Scotland.[2] The signing of the Covenant had preceded the order for the return of the
charter by just one month.

None the less, when, in the early summer of 1638,

[1] Hutchinson, *State Papers*, 105 ; Ib. *History*, i. 86–7 ; Winthrop,
Life and Letters, ii. 224–8.
[2] Gardiner, *England*, 1603–1642, ch. lxxxvi.

the mandate of the Lords Commissioners reached Boston, it created no little alarm. There was nothing for it but to procrastinate ; but to procrastinate meant a great deal when six months had to elapse between each step of a process. Winthrop, also, was an adept in delay. With him in the governor's chair there was reason in the colonists' boast, that they could " easily spinne seven years out with writing at that distance, and before that be ended a change [might] come." [1] This work of fence exactly suited his calm, cautious tone of mind. Accordingly, when the order reached him, he at first merely placed it on file, — acting on the precedent established in the case of the similar order of four years before, that nothing could be done in the matter save by authority of the General Court, which did not meet until the following September, it being then perhaps the middle of June. When at last September came, bringing with it the General Court, " it was resolved to be best not to send [the patent], because then such of our friends and others in England would conceive it to be surrendered, and that thereupon we should be bound to receive such a governour and such orders as should be sent to us, and many bad minds, yea, and some weak ones, among ourselves, would think it lawful, if not necessary, to accept a general governour."

The latter portion of the reasons here assigned would have had a peculiar interest for Sir Ferdinando Gorges, but it is unnecessary to say that they were not incorporated in the formal reply, which was couched in the most humble and respectful language. There was about it no suggestion of disobedience, — not the most distant ring of defiance. Time and opportunity to

[1] *N. Y. Hist. Soc. Coll.* 1869, 85.

answer any charges which might be advanced against
the colony were asked for, and the utmost confidence
was expressed that all charges could be satisfactorily
met.   Finally, five several reasons were given why a
return of the charter should not be insisted on.   Two
of these were significant.   If the colonists, it was
argued, were forced to abandon their settlements, the
country would fall into the hands of the French or
Dutch ; or else (and in this alternative lay the significance) the " common people " would conceive that
they were freed from their allegiance and proceed
to confederate themselves under a new government,
" which will be of dangerous example unto other plantations and perilous to ourselves of incurring his
Majesty's displeasure, which we would by all means
avoid."

The long delayed reply, finished at last and bearing
on its every line the stamp of Winthrop's mind, was
presumably despatched early in September, for it
bore date as of the $\frac{6th}{16th}$ of that month.   In that case it
may have reached England in November.   If it did,
it probably received small attention there ; for it was
in that same November, five months after the formal
decision of the twelve judges had been rendered
against Hampden in the ship-money case, that the
King and Primate, to their utter surprise and discom-
fiture, found themselves forced, for the moment at
least, to yield to the Scotch insurgents.   Neither
money nor troops were available ; so the Covenant had
to be allowed, the liturgy was revoked, and a General
Assembly was summoned to meet at Glasgow.   It
met, — and, having met, would not submit to be dissolved.   So Charles and Laud, nursing their wrath
against a better occasion, had to look on from London

and see the patient work of years all undone in a
day. They, of course, at such a time gave no thought
to the Massachusetts charter, nor cared one straw
whether it was brought to London or was kept in
Boston. In all probability Gorges and Morton alone
conned over Winthrop's cautious reply as it lay on
the clerk's desk in the office at Whitehall.

When the next June came about, and the spring
fleet began to reach Boston, the Governor and all
his advisers were much concerned as to what answer
these vessels might bring to the reply of the previous
September. They knew well enough that complaints
had been frequently made, and that the deep displeasure of the Archbishop had been excited against them.
Rumors of his threats had reached their ears. "But
the Lord wrought for us beyond all expectation, for
the petition which we returned in answer of the order
sent for our patent, was read before the lords and well
accepted . . . ; and ships came to us, from England
and divers other parts, with great store of people and
provisions of all sorts." As for the good acceptance
of the petition, it would have required far more than
the skill in composition on which Winthrop here so
quietly plumed himself to have turned Laud a hair's
breadth from the path he had marked out, had circumstances been other than they were. But they were
what they were; and at the very time Winthrop in
Boston was complacently writing the words just quoted
from his journal, that ignominious military fiasco was
being enacted at Kelso, in Scotland, which proved for
both Charles and Laud the grotesque beginning of a
tragic end.

The first series of assaults on King Charles' charter had come to an end, and nothing more was heard

of the royalist plan of a general governorship. Not that Gorges then dismissed from his mind the dream of the latter, for to do so was not in his nature. He must have remained sanguine to the end; and even as late as 1640 we find him still deferring a visit to New England which he had confidently proposed for the spring of that year,[1] just as he had almost every year since 1623 deferred similar visits proposed with equal confidence. But Sir Ferdinando was now a man of over seventy years, and his remaining time was short. Nothing but a favorable turn in royal affairs could have helped him, and of that, after the summer of 1639, the prospect ever grew less. The idea of going out to New England in semi-royal state being in abeyance, his mind now characteristically turned to the development of his own private domain, — that region in Maine called New Somersetshire, which had fallen to his lot in the distribution of 1635. He had then sent out his nephew, William Gorges, in the capacity of governor to represent him there; and William Gorges had established himself at Saco, the most flourishing place north of the Massachusetts, and supposed to have then contained some one hundred and fifty inhabitants. He there, in 1636, organized the first regular government which went into operation within the limits of what, nearly two centuries later, became the State of Maine. His jurisdiction seems to have extended from what is now York to Penobscot Bay, within which region, it has been estimated, there already dwelt some fifteen hundred souls.

Governor William Gorges remained in America about two years, during which he showed himself to be a man of judgment and capacity, but in 1637 he

---

[1] Baxter, *Gorges*, i. 181; iii. 295-6.

had returned to England. After his return, and presumably acting upon his advice, Sir Ferdinando exerted himself to procure a royal patent covering a yet larger domain, and in this he at last succeeded; for, upon the 3d of April, 1639, he, his heirs and assigns, were by letters patent created absolute Lords Proprietors of the Province, or County, of Maine. The region thus conferred covered sixty miles of seacoast between the Piscataqua and the Kennebec, and extended one hundred and twenty miles into the interior. It was equal in extent to a sixth part of the present State. The powers and privileges enumerated in the charter were of the largest description, — larger, it has been asserted, than were ever granted by the crown to any other individual.[1]

The old man now gave free rein to his love of regulating; he showed that, had he ever been Governor-General of New England, he would in this respect have vied with his patron, the Archbishop. He divided his entire wilderness into " eight bailiwicks, or counties, and these again into sixteen several hundreds, consequently into parishes and tithings." He provided for a lieutenant, or deputy governor, to be the chief magistrate in his own absence, a chancellor, a treasurer, a marshal, an admiral, a master of the ordinance and a secretary. To these officials, all holding authority directly from himself as lord proprietor, he added eight deputies to be elected by the freeholders.[2] A mere paper government it was, of course, utterly unfitted for the time and place. But, such as it was, he sent it out to America, in 1640; and shortly after,

---

[1] Williamson, *Hist. of Maine*, i. 275; Baxter, *Gorges*, i. 180; ii. 123.

[2] *Briefe Narration*, B. II. chs. 3, 4.

Thomas Gorges — who, in a style regally grandiose,
he refers to as "my trusty and well beloved cousin"
— followed it, with a commission to be deputy-governor.
This gentleman, the son of Sir Ferdinando's
cousin Henry Gorges, was then twenty-two years of
age and had just finished his legal studies;[1] he impressed Winthrop on his arrival in New England as
being "sober and well disposed," and, stopping a few
days in Boston before going to his government, he
sought the advice of the magistrates there. When
he got to Maine, he found everything in a bad way,
— as bad indeed as well could be ; for an individual
known as the Rev. George Burdet had established
himself in supreme control. This Burdet — a most
unsavory character — had come to Salem in 1634,
where it is reported he at first made a favorable impression and preached for a year or more, "his natural
abilities [being] good, his manners specious, and his
scholarship much above mediocrity." Getting into
trouble there, he went to New Hampshire, and roundly
denounced the Massachusetts colony in letters to Archbishop Laud. In reply he was assured by that prelate
that he proposed at his first leisure moment to redress
the disorders referred to. As New Hampshire became
presently too warm for him, Burdet next moved into
Maine, where he soon managed to get the control of
everything into his hands. It would seem that he no
longer preached, as, selecting for his companions "the
wretchedest people of the country," he passed his
leisure time "in drinkinge, dauncinge [and] singinge
scurrulous songes." He had, in fact, "let loose the
reigns of liberty to his lusts, [so] that he grew very
notorious for his pride and adultery." At Agamen-

[1] Baxter, *Gorges*, ii. 186.

ticus, also, Deputy-Governor Gorges found the Lords Proprietors' buildings, — which had cost a large sum of money, and were intended to serve as a sort of government house, — not only dilapidated but thoroughly stripped, "nothing of his household-stuff remaining but an old pot, a pair of tongs, and a couple of cobirons." [1]

It was on Agamenticus, now York, the seat of government of his domain, that Sir Ferdinando next exercised his skill as a maker of charters. By an instrument bearing date April 10, 1641, he erected it into a town, or borough ; and by a further exercise of proprietary favor he the next year, March 1, 1642, created it a city, — the first on the American continent. He named it Gorgeana. Its magistracy was to consist of a mayor, twelve aldermen, twenty-four common-councilmen, and a recorder ; and, as Palfrey remarks, "probably as many as two thirds of the adult males were in places of authority." The forms of procedure in the recorder's court were to be copied from those of the British Chancery. This grave foolery was continued through more than ten years.[2] One, and not the least interesting point in connection with this charter, is that Thomas Morton attested it ; from which fact it may not unfairly be inferred, — for in Gorges' eyes the countersigning of his charter was no meaningless thing, — that Morton was then not at all in that disfavor which had been indicated in Sir Ferdinando's letter to Winthrop of four years before.[3]

Governor Thomas Gorges soon grew weary of his experience in the wilderness. His first trial of

[1] Williamson, *Maine*, 270, 283 ; Hubbard, *New England*, 263 ; Winthrop, ii. *10 ; iv. *Mass. Hist. Coll.* vii. 335.

[2] Palfrey, *New England*, i. 528.   [3] *Supra,* 303.

strength was with Burdet, and in this he soon showed
that he possessed energy, character and decision ; for
he caused the reverend transgressor to be promptly
arrested, and secured his conviction of divers offences,
— such as adultery, breaches of the peace, and
slanderous speeches. He in fact purged the country
of him, for Burdet shortly after went to England
breathing vengeance against his judges ; but, getting there after the outbreak of the Civil War, he
took the Royalist side, which resulted in his being at
once imprisoned by the Parliament.[1] Like so many
others, he then disappeared forever beneath the troubled waters. Having rid the country and himself
of this troublesome character, Gorges addressed himself in earnest to the work of his government, but
evidently found it a hopeless as well as a thankless
task. He held courts and punished offenders. Ruth
Gouch had to do penance " in a white sheet, publicly in
the congregation at Agamanticus, two several Sabbath
days." John Lander was fined " for swearing two
oaths," and Ivory Puddington for being drunk. The
general christening of all unbaptized children was ordered. While everything which related to the internal administration of his government was thus petty
and vexatious, the condition of external affairs was
perplexing. The Indians were restless ; there were
questions continually arising with the French ; a rival
title was set up to the easternmost portion of the
Lord Proprietors' domain. Under these circumstances,
when his commission as a deputy-governor expired, in
1643, Governor Thomas Gorges could not be induced
to remain longer in America.[2] Returning to England
he found the Civil War at its height; for in July of

[1] Winthrop, ii. 10.   [2] Baxter, *Gorges*, ii. 186.

that year Prince Rupert carried Bristol by assault,
and in September Lord Falkland was slain at New-
bury.

The struggle now going on had, of course, brought
all of Sir Ferdinando's projects to an end. He could
no longer entertain any idea of going out to New
England as its governor-general, and, indeed, all emigration thither had stopped. He could do nothing
towards peopling his domain. At home, it would
seem as if there could be no question as to which party
the old courtier would range himself with; yet later
on he is found writing that he had been for a time
" fearful to side with either party, as not able to judge
of so transcendent a difference ; " [1] but when he wrote
this the struggle was over, and he had made his submission, so it still remains open to question whether
the former political adherent of Laud and Strafford
had hesitated long in the beginning. Yet his age
might have excused him ; for, at the breaking out of
the Great Rebellion he could not have been less than
seventy-five, and it was now over fifty years since, in
the days of Elizabeth, he had led the soldiers of Essex
into the trench at Rouen.[2] Yet in 1641 he seems to
have taken some part in the military operations about
Bristol, in which town he dwelt when not at his country house at Ashton, five miles away ; and two years
later, in the summer of 1643, he planned in a letter to
King Charles the Royalist attack on Bristol, and Sir
Ferdinando's house was the farthest point reached by
the assailing forces, which there maintained themselves until forced to retreat. Subsequently Prince
Rupert captured the place ; but when, after Naseby,

[1] Baxter, *Gorges*, i. 196 ; iii. 298.
[2] Devereux, *Earls of Essex*, i. 271.

on the $\frac{10\text{th}}{20\text{th}}$ of September, 1645, Bristol was retaken by
Fairfax with " fierce and resolute storm," Gorges was
dwelling there, and became a prisoner of war.[1] Plun-
dered and put in confinement, he seems, though then
a man of nearly eighty, to have shared to the full the
hard fortunes of his Royalist friends; but later on he
found a protector in Fairfax, by whom his submission
was readily accepted, and he was allowed to return to
his home at Ashton.

But his troubles were not over. His title to the
larger portion of the province of Maine had been
called in question. There was a patent, called " the
Plough Patent," from the name of the ship in which
it was brought to New England, issued by the Council
for New England, earlier in date than Gorges' own
patent of 1639, and covering much of the same territory. Representing only what was characterized as a
" broken tytle," this buried and forgotten patent was
resuscitated by George Cleeve, who in some way got
scent of it in the course of his fruitless search for the
great Lake Erocoise. Cleeve had then gone to Europe, apparently for the express purpose of finding a
purchaser for the Lygonia claim, as it was called, and
finally induced Sir Alexander Rigby to buy it.[2] Sir
Alexander was a gentleman of wealth, who, besides
being a strong Puritan, was a member of the Long
Parliament, and at one time held the commission of
colonel in the Commonwealth army. Later on Cleeve

---

[1] Baxter, *Gorges*, i. 192–3; ii. 202; Belknap, *Am. Biog.* i. 389.

[2] " The Plough patent " is one of the enigmas of New England history, and continued so until, in the words of Winthrop applied to its
holders, it " vanished away." In regard to it see the *New English
Canaan* (Prince Soc. ed.), 84–5, n.; Baxter, *Cleeve of Casco Bay*, 116–
20, and map of patents, 150; Winsor, *Nar. and Crit. Hist. of Am.* iii.
322–3. Also, Banks, *Sir Alexander Rigby*, 27–39.

returned to America, as Rigby's agent; and, laying claim to the territory covered by the patent, at once brought about a collision of authority with the representative of Gorges. Meanwhile, in 1643, a parliamentary tribunal had succeeded to the powers of the Lords Commissioners of Foreign Plantations. At the head of this board sat, not Archbishop Laud, who was then a prisoner in the Tower, but Gorges' old associate in the Council for New England, the Puritan Earl of Warwick, with the title of governor-general. Among the members of the board were Say and Seale, Hazelrig, the younger Vane and Pym, and to it the question of the disputed title was referred. There could be little question as to what the decision of such a tribunal would be; as opposed to the Puritan colonel and member of Parliament, the broken-down old cavalier and prisoner of war had little consideration to expect. In the hands of its present holders the Plough Patent was of less than doubtful validity. In March, 1646, the commissioners rendered their decision accordingly, sustaining the Rigby title, and the Lord Proprietorship of Maine was at one swoop shorn of its fair proportions, — " a huge half-moon, a monstrous cantle out." [1]

In May of the following year Sir Ferdinando died at Long Ashton. He did not own the place; but for sixteen years he had lived there as the husband of Dame Elizabeth, relict of Sir Hugh Smith, who, receiving Long Ashton as her jointure, had in 1629 married Sir Ferdinando, himself a widower. He left

[1] The Gorges patent, of 1639, covered the region lying between the Piscataqua and the Kennebec; the Plough patent, of 1635, that between Cape Porpoise and Cape Elizabeth; the whole of the latter claim being included in the limits of the former. Deane, in *Nar. and Crit. Hist. of Am.* iii. 322-3; Baxter, *Gorges,* ii. 125; Ib. *Cleeve,* 150.

to his heirs what remained of his province, — the
region lying between the Piscataqua and Cape Porpoise, including the northernmost of the Isles of
Shoals. The subsequent history of the Gorges family, and of their Maine patent, is complicated and far
from interesting ; neither is it a necessary part of the
present narrative. It is sufficient to say that the validity of the grant was recognized, and long controversies arose between the Gorges family and the Massachusetts colony. At last, when Sir Ferdinando had
been thirty years in his grave, these controversies, and
the apparently endless litigation to which they gave
rise were brought to an unexpected close. A grand-
son, who also bore the name of Ferdinando, in consideration of the sum of £1,250, conveyed by deed, bearing date March 13, 1677–8, all his title and interest
under the patent, to the Governor and Company of
Massachusetts Bay, which thus became Lord Paramount of Maine. This £1,250 represented what remained as a net result to his descendants from Sir
Ferdinando's forty years of energetic devotion to his
American life-dream, backed by an actual expenditure
of over twenty thousand pounds sterling in money.[1]

The character of Gorges has been sufficiently por-
trayed in the course of this narrative. He belonged
to the time of Elizabeth, not to that of the Stuarts ;
and of the time of Elizabeth he was typical. At the
hands of the historian he has received scant justice,
for the dramatic intensity of the scene in Westminster
Hall when he was confronted with the despairing
Essex has burned itself into the record, and in doing
so has obliterated all else ;[2] it is forgotten that, more

[1] Baxter, *Gorges*, ii. 202, 204, 214.
[2] Doyle, *English in Am.; Puritan Colonies*, i. 21–3.

than twenty years later, the same Sir Ferdinando who
the Lords were then adjured by Essex to "look
upon," indignantly as an Englishman and a Protestant refused to obey when ordered before Rochelle to
deliver the ship under his command to the officers of
Richelieu to be used against the Huguenots, and, de-
spite the guns of his admiral, brought the Neptune,
alone of all the fleet, back in triumphant mutiny to
England.   Nor had Buckingham, all powerful as he
then was, dared to call him to account for the audacious act.[1]   Then and alway about Sir Ferdinando
Gorges there is something of the picturesqueness of
Essex and Sidney and Raleigh, and he seems out of
place in the company of Governor Winthrop, Mr.
Hampden and General Fairfax.   The whole scheme
of his life was Elizabethan, — large, undefined, adventurous.   There was about it no Puritan detail, —
no matter-of-fact, hard sense.   He dreamed of found-
ing a ready-made empire; accordingly he failed when
it came to planting a settlement.   To say that the
failure was inherent in the plan, is but to repeat an
historical commonplace.   Gorges built up, in his own
mind, an imaginary Mexico or Peru in New England.
In his confident belief, all that was required was once
to break the shell; and it took him his whole life to
find out that the thing did not exist.   None the less
he carried on through thirty years a sustained and
gallant struggle against fate; and, if his efforts could
not result in anything good for himself, they did very
nearly result in turning awry the course of New England history at a time when the colony was yet literally " but in the gristle and not yet hardened into the
bone " of even its infancy.   It has already been ob-

[1] Gardiner, *England*, v. 394.

served that, so far as America was concerned, Gorges
represented Charles' policy of prerogative, Laud's
conformity, and Wentworth's Thorough.   His scheme
of the governor-generalship and his attack on the
charter were the New England features of the Royalist programme.   They were as much part and parcel
of it as was the Court of High Commission or ship-
money, and came to nothing simply because both extra-
judicial tribunal and arbitrary tax were together bro-
·'ken down.   That these would have been broken down
had a Richelieu instead of a Laud shaped the King's
policy, is inconsistent with all that we now know of
the real condition of affairs in England at that time.
The scheme was a good scheme : but it was badly
handled ; and the handling of it was largely matter of
chance.   The world in no part of Europe had, in
1643, yet clearly outgrown the ancient order of things,
and there were no inherent conditions which caused
events in the British isles to take the course there
which they took elsewhere only a whole century and a
half afterwards.   For the time being it was throughout eastern Europe merely a question as to which
of two not unequally balanced but contending forces
most quickly evolved individual leadership and execu-
tive ability ; and, while Cromwell appeared on one
side of the Straits of Dover, on the other side of " the
silver thread " Richelieu stood forward.   Hence the
scene which took place in front of the Banqueting
House at Whitehall on the 30th of January, 1649,
was not reënacted in the Place de la Révolution until
the 21st of January, 1793.

But, even as it was, the scales of English fate long
trembled in the balance ; nor was the bad handling
which wrecked Strafford's well devised scheme of

" Thorough " seen in the execution of the New England portion of the plan. No mistake was made there. The courts did their work, and the charter was vacated. The governor-general was designated. Everything was ready; and then the other, and less distant, portions of the one great scheme collapsed. Pushed too far on a petty side issue, it met a stubborn obstacle, and at once it became apparent that the head and hand of him upon whom the conduct of the thing perforce devolved were unequal to the work. But nowhere was the danger greater than in New England. The infant settlement kept up a brave front, and would have kept it up to the end. It might even have put forth a feeble effort at resistance; but, in speaking of the Gorges schemes, a man as well informed on the true condition of those early New England affairs as Hutchinson does not hesitate to say : —

" We may make some conjectures what would have been the consequence of taking away the charter at this time. It is pretty certain, the body of the people would have left the country. Two years after, merely from a dissatisfaction with the soil and the climate, many did remove, and many more were on tip-toe and restrained only by the consideration of their engagements to stand by and support one another ; but where they would have removed is the question. . . . It is most likely they would have gone to the Dutch at Hudson's River. They had always kept up a friendly correspondence with them. In their religious principles and form of worship and church government, they were not very distant from one another. . . . If they had failed with the Dutch, such was their resolution, that they would have sought a *vacuum domicilium* (a favorite expression with them) in some part of the globe where they would, according to their apprehensions, have been

free from the control of any European power. In their
first migration most of them could say, *omnia mea mecum
porto.* All the difference as to the second would have been
that, so far as they had lessened their substance, so much
less room would have been necessary for the transportation
of what remained. Such a scheme would have consisted
very well with their notions of civil subjection."

The thought of America with Puritan New England left out is suggestive. But Sir Ferdinando
Gorges missed his destiny. He fought with the stars
in their courses.

CHAPTER XVIII.

THE FATE OF SIR FERDINANDO'S "PEOPLE AND PLANTERS."

IT remains to speak of the subsequent fate of those adherents of Gorges, — "servants, and certain other undertakers and tenants belonging unto some of us," the companions of Captain Robert Gorges in his expedition of 1623, and left by him in "charge and custody" of his "setled plantation" when he returned to England in the spring of 1624,[1] — the Episcopalian advance guard of the Puritan migration, those composing which had, when Winthrop first sailed into Boston Bay, already for seven years been living on its shores. The sites occupied by them have already been indicated. Starting from Wessagusset, where the main body still remained, individual settlers had built their dwelling-places and established themselves with their families and servants at Charlestown, East Boston and Boston; while Thomson's widow dwelt at Squantum, or on the island which still bears her husband's name. Morton's house at Mt. Wollaston was destroyed in the winter of 1630–1, in the way which has already been described, though he was himself destined to return to America to reckon again with Winthrop and the magistrates of Massachusetts. Sir Christopher Gardiner was a mere bird of passage.

[1] *Records of Council for N. E.* April 18, 1635.

A peculiar interest must always attach to William Blackstone as the first European occupant of the peninsula on which Boston stands, but of his life after the settlement not much is known.   When he pointed out to Winthrop the spring of fresh, pure water which welled out from the base of the hill on the opposite side of which he lived, he was a man of thirty-five. Winthrop was eight years older.   Blackstone had then been some five years at Shawmut.   For over three years more, until 1634, he continued to live in his hut on the west slope of Sentry Hill, as Beacon Hill was called, quite removed from the little community which clustered near the water and about the spring on the opposite slope, a mile or so away.   At first the new settlers did not press upon him, and he seems to have held friendly relations with Winthrop and the rest, who were in the habit of questioning him about the climate, the products of the soil, and the character of the country and of its natives.   On the 18th of May, 1631, he took the oath as a freeman.   But presently population increased, and the original settler began to feel its growing nearness.   Questions of title, also, arose.   Mather says that "by happening to sleep first in an hovel, upon a point of land there, [Blackstone] laid claim to all the ground, whereupon there now stands the metropolis of the whole English America, until the inhabitants gave him satisfaction." [1]   Whether or no he did indeed, as thus asserted, lay claim to "all the ground," no such claim was ever allowed; for at a court holden on the 1st of April, 1633, it was "agreed, that Mr. William Blackstone shall have fifty acres of ground set out for him near to his house in Boston, to enjoy for ever."

[1] *Magnalia* (Hartford, 1855), i. 243.

The next year affairs did not improve. Population was crowding more and more upon the recluse. He did not belong to the church ; he wore his old canonical gown. He was in fact "without ; " not of the Lord's people. As Mather goes on to say : — " This man was, indeed, of a particular humor, and he would never join himself to any of our churches, giving his reason for it : ' I came from England because I did not like the lord-bishops ; but I can't join with you, because I would not be under the lord-brethren.' " Accordingly, in 1634, reserving to himself only the six acres immediately about his hut, he sold to the town all his interest in the rest of the peninsula, including the fifty acres granted to him the year before. The consideration paid him was £30, which was raised by levying a rate of six shillings on each householder, " some paying less and some considerably more." Edmund Quincy, the first of the name in Massachusetts, was at the head of the committee appointed to assess this rate, as also at the same time " a rate for the cowes keeping, a rate for the goates keeping," etc. The tract of land thus purchased was subsequently devoted to public use as the town common.[1]

With a portion of the purchase-money of his land Blackstone bought some cattle, and then, packing his books and household goods upon them, he turned his face to the wilderness. He seems to have felt little disposition to go " further from the sun," as Hutchinson expressed it ; though at the time of his removal, or soon afterwards, he seriously thought of accepting an invitation to take charge of the church at Agamen-

---

[1] In regard to the location of Blackstone's dwelling and the bounds of the grant made to him, see *Memorial History of Boston*, i. 84, n., 552.

ticus. Indeed, the people there claimed that he promised to do so, but afterwards decided otherwise, his
hopes being " fed with the expectation of far greater
profit by his husbandry [in Rhode Island] then he
should have had by his ministry [in Maine] ; which
God only knows." [1] In any event, when he left Boston driving his little herd across the Neck through
Roxbury, he turned his back on the " very good house,
with an inclosure to it, for the planting of corn ; and
also a stipend of twenty pounds per annum," which
awaited his acceptance at Agamenticus, and directed
his steps southward out of the limits of the Massachusetts colony. Passing through the territory of the
Plymouth colony, he at last found a spot which pleased
him, on the banks of a river which emptied, at no great
distance further on, into Narragansett Bay. There,
setting himself down, he built another house and
planted a new orchard ; and there he passed the remainder of life. He revisited Boston several times,
riding, as tradition says, on a trained bull ; and on
one of these visits, in 1659, he took to himself, as
wife, the widow of John Stephenson, living in School
Street, not far from the house in which Governor
Winthrop had died ten years before.[2] They were
married on the 4th of July, Governor Endicott offi-
ciating as the magistrate, Blackstone being over sixty
at the time, while his wife could have been no longer
young, as her oldest child, by her former husband,
had been born sixteen years before. The two, nevertheless, had offspring. Blackstone's married life lasted

---

[1] iv. *Mass. Hist. Coll.* vii. 196.

[2] It is a singular fact that, though allusion is apparently once or
twice made to Blackstone by Winthrop in his history, no mention of
Blackstone name is there found.

fourteen years, his wife dying before him in June, 1673, while he survived her nearly two years, until the 26th of May, 1675. Roger Williams, writing a few days later to Governor John Winthrop, Jr., of Connecticut, gives these details of his end : —

"About a fortnight since your old acquaintance Mr. Blackstone departed this life in the fourscore year of his age : four days before his death he had a great pain in his breast, and back, and bowells : afterward he said he was well, had no paines, and should live, but he grew fainter, and yealded up his breath without a groane." [1]

He had been in America, at the time of his death, a few months only less than fifty-two years, forty of which he had passed at Study Hill, — by which name he called his Rhode Island home. At Study Hill, as at Boston before, he seems to have led a quiet, peaceable life ; yet, quiet as his life was, and much given up to that meditation of which he was so fond, it could not have been otherwise than laborious. Coming to America as he did, a young man of studious habits, — a graduate of a college, bringing his library with him, — it may be taken for granted that in those days he did not come unattended. He must have had one or more servants ; and, indeed, traditions to that effect survive. Yet he had to build houses and to exact a living from the soil. This implied labor ; and his days could not have been either wholly or in chief part given up to reading or to reflection. We also know that it was his custom in his latter years occasionally to preach at Providence, though what his exact tenets were does not appear; except that, though living near Roger Williams, he was reputed to be " far from his opinions." [2]

[1] IV. *Mass. Hist. Coll.* vi. 299.   [2] III. *Mass. Hist. Coll.* iii. 97.

Not a little has since been said and written of Blackstone, to the effect that he was " a memorable man," that he was " centuries in advance of the age " in which he lived, that his motto was " Toleration," and he " possessed qualifications which, under other circumstances, might have made him one of the foremost men of New England." This may or may not be so, but the simple fact is we have no means of forming any definite judgment about Blackstone's opinion, or intellectual power. He was a singular man ; and, as is apt to be the case with singular men when dead, he excites curiosity. The graduate of a university, he crossed the ocean almost immediately after taking his degree, and he carried with him into the wilderness his books and his studious habits. He then chanced to make his home on the site of a future great city, where he lived the life of a devout recluse, — almost a hermit. He disliked restraint and society ; but there is no reason whatever to suppose that he had a peculiarly active or a peculiarly vigorous mind. If he was gifted in that way, he succeeded most effectually in hiding his light from the world.

He died in good time. Just one month later King Philip's War broke out, and his home, with everything it contained, was among the first that went in the general destruction. Those rare Bibles, those large English and Latin folios, those quartos and duodecimos, more than one hundred and sixty in number, which had been the companions of a whole life of solitude, — and which would now, could they but have been preserved, be the most precious treasures of the library so fortunate as to possess them, — all perished. Not a leaf was saved. With the rest went " ten paper books " which in the inventory of the dead man's

property were valued at five shillings, or sixpence each.
It is not unfair to presume that these were the manuscript records of his life, — that at least they contained
that weather register which Winthrop referred to, as
his first winter's experience in Massachusetts was
drawing to a close. Had they been preserved, these
might have been among the most valuable and interesting of all the documents relating to early American history; but it is equally probable that consisting,
as has been suggested, wholly or in part of sermons of
his own composition,[1] they would have been among
the most disappointing. As a rule the meditations of
devout hermits have not proved peculiarly edifying to
subsequent generations. Morell and Blackstone, certainly companions, not improbably were also kindred
spirits, and Morell's poem would teach us not to put
too high a value on Blackstone's " paper books."

Blackstone himself seems never to have had trouble
with the Indians. He had lived all his life among
them, and, speaking their language, he understood
their character. Apparently, also, he possessed that
faculty of morally impressing himself on savage natures, which has since been so highly developed in
African explorers of the Livingstone type. It is
therefore possible, though hardly probable, that, had
he not died when he did, he and his might have escaped harm at the hands of Philip's people. Blackstone left a son and a daughter, neither of whom, at
the time of his death, could have been over fifteen
years of age. Both subsequently married, and the son
proved no credit to his parentage. A man of intemperate habits, he, with his wife Katherine, was in
1713 warned out of the town of Attleborough. He

---

[1] Amory, *William Blaxton, Coll. of Bostonian Society*, i. 5.

must then have been more than fifty years of age.
Subsequently he settled in Connecticut, and, dying,
left descendants who still perpetuate the Boston hermit's name ; but that will always be preserved in connection with the river whose waters, tired with moving the wheels of well-nigh innumerable factories,
flow forever by the spot which, through more than
forty years, was Blackstone's wilderness home and the
scene of his meditations.[1]

Much more is known of Samuel Maverick after the
settlement than is known of Blackstone, for at a later
period the former played a prominent part in the history of the colonies. To the end he retained the
church-and-state bias of the Gorges movement ; and,

[1] The facts in relation to Blackstone have been collected with much
care by Bliss in his *History of Rehoboth* (pp. 1–14), and by the Rev. F.
B. Da Costa, in his two papers printed in the *Churchman* of September
25 and October 2, 1880, and reprinted in pamphlet. A comprehensive list of other authorities relating to him is to be found in the ed-
itor's note in the *Memorial History of Boston*, i. 84. In regard to
Blackstone's English origin and descendants in America, see also Mr.
Amory's paper in *Coll. Bostonian Society*, i. 3–25. There is quite a
remarkable letter from the Rhode Island genealogist, S. C. Newman,
about Blackstone and his descendants, in the Appendix O, of the second volume (p. 568) of Arnold's *Rhode Island*. In it the writer says:
"William Blackstone was descended from a family of some distinction, who had long inhabited the vicinity of Salisbury, in the west of
England; he was born in 1595 ; entered Emanuel College, Cambridge,
England, and in 1617, took the degree of A. B. ; in 1621, received
the degree of A. M., and entered into Episcopal orders ; in 1623,
came to America with the expedition of Robert Gorges, whose objects were to establish an Episcopal colony."
This letter is dated December 3, 1859. It contains no reference to
authorities for the facts so absolutely stated in it, some of which have
been established only by documents published since the letter was
written. Williams' letter, for instance, in which he says that Blackstone died at fourscore in 1675, was first printed in 1863. In view of
these facts the accuracy of Mr. Newman's statements, so far as they
can yet be verified by generally attainable authorities, is most remarkable.

indeed, he became its last, as he was its most formidable, representative. But a brief sketch of the man's life will here suffice.[1] Born in 1602, in the county of Cornwall, when he came over to America Maverick was twenty-two years old, and he was but twenty-eight when Winthrop landed on the Charlestown shore. That when he came he was already married, and brought his young wife, Amias, with him, may be inferred from the fact that in 1648 he executed a deed of land to a son, who, being then of age, must have been born at least as early as 1627. Maverick probably came out to New England very much as David Thomson came out at nearly the same time. They were both young men, and both newly married; but, while Thomson established himself alone at Piscataqua, Maverick, more closely connected with the Gorges movement, went at once to Boston Bay; though it would appear he did not leave England in company with Robert Gorges, in 1623, but a year later.[2] Subsequently the two couples became near neighbors, and a first child may have been born at about the same time to each. It has been surmised that the Thomson child was born in 1625.[3]

Whether he came to New England in search of adventure, or looking for a home, it is clear that Maverick remained to trade. A man of gentle birth and good education, he was, as will presently be seen, noted for his hospitality; and his letters are as well

---

[1] All the facts and documents in relation to Samuel Maverick have been most patiently collected and sifted out by W. H. Sumner, in his *History of East Boston.* To him and his descendants that author devotes no less than a hundred pages of his work. Where no other authorities are indicated, reliance is placed, therefore, in the present account, on Mr. Sumner's book.

[2] *Supra,* 161.

[3] Deane in *Proc. Mass. Hist. Soc.* 1875–6, 373.

written as those of Winthrop or Bradford, or even as that famous History of the Rebellion, with the author of which Maverick carried on, at a later day, an active official correspondence. A generous liver, he was not himself a Puritan : nor does he ever seem to have had any liking for Puritans; as, certainly, they had none for him.

It has already been told how, when Winthrop and his party first sailed into Boston Bay, on the $\frac{17th}{27th}$ day of June, 1630, they found Maverick living in his fortified house at Winnisimmet, as what is now Chelsea was then called,[1] and the Governor passed the night with the "old planter," being entertained in a "very loving and courteous" manner. Though Maverick made application to be admitted a freeman on the $\frac{19th}{29th}$ of October, 1631, he for some reason did not take the oath until the $\frac{2d}{12th}$ of October of the next year. His "being strong for the Lordly Prelaticall power" may have stood in his way. Then, and long after, he was actively engaged in commerce, owning vessels and himself trading in them up and down the coast. He held, under a patent from Gorges, a tract of land on the Agamenticus; and in 1635-6 he passed an entire year in Virginia, coming back with his vessels loaded with goats and heifers, and telling the credulous Winthrop wonderful stories of the things he had seen. At other times, both Winthrop and Dudley were partners with him in his ventures.

There was evidently some connection between the long absence of Maverick in Virginia at this time, and the treatment he had undergone at the hands of the magistrates and colony during the governor-generalship panic of March, 1634. It will be remem-

[1] *Supra*, 161.

bered [1] that he had then not only been forbidden to
entertain strangers, but had been ordered by the General Court to prepare to remove from his house at
Noddle's Island to Boston.   As the alarm passed
away this order was rescinded, and it was during the
next year, while Gorges was still at work in London,
that Maverick went to Virginia.   Returning in August, 1636, he would seem to have resumed his old life
and hospitable ways; for when, in July, 1637, during
the full bitterness of the Hutchinsonian controversy,
Governor Winthrop invited young Harry Vane, whom
he had shortly before succeeded in office, to meet
the Lord Ley at a dinner given in honor of the latter, not only did the petulant and excitable heir of
Raby Castle refuse " to come (alleging by letter that
his conscience withheld him), but also, at the same
hour, he went over to Noddle's Island to dine with
Mr. Maverick, and carried the Lord Ley with him."

During the summer of 1638 an English gentleman
of ancient family and good education, John Josselyn
by name, visited America.   He was a son of Sir
Thomas Josselyn of Kent, and had a brother, one of
Gorges' people, living at Scarborough, Maine.   This
brother he was on his way to visit when he arrived at
Boston on the $\frac{3d}{13th}$ July.   In his account of what he
saw there at this time, he gives quaint glimpses of
Samuel Maverick.   Arriving upon the $\frac{3d}{13th}$, he says
that a week later, on the $\frac{10th}{20th}$: —

"I went ashore upon *Noddles Island* to Mr. *Samuel
Maverick* (for my passage) the only hospitable man in all
the Countrey, giving entertainment to all Comers *gratis*. . . .
Having refreshed myself for a day or two upon *Noddles-
Island*, I crossed the Bay in a small Boat to *Boston*, which

[1] *Supra*, 288.

then was rather a Village, than a Town, there being not
above Twenty or thirty houses; and presenting my respects
to Mr. *Winthorpe*, the Governour, and to Mr. *Cotton* the
Teacher of *Boston* Church, to whom I delivered from Mr.
Francis Quarles the poet, the Translation of the 16, 25, 51,
88, 113, and 137 Psalms into *English* Meeter, for his approbation; being civilly treated by all I had occasion to
converse with, I returned in the Evening to my lodging."

Remaining in Boston only two days at this time,
Mr. Josselyn, on the $\frac{12\text{th}}{22\text{d}}$ of July, set out for the eastward, where he passed the next two months, anchor-
ing in Boston Harbor again on the $\frac{27\text{th}}{7\text{th}}$ of $\frac{\text{September}}{\text{October}}$: —

"The Thirtieth day of *September* [Oct. 10, N. s.], I
went ashore upon *Noddles*-Island, where when I was come
to Mr. *Mavericks* he would not let me go aboard no more,
until the Ship was ready to set sail. . . .

"In the afternoon I walked into the Woods on the back
side of the house, and happening into a fine broad walk
(which was a sledgway) I wandered till I chanc't to spye
a fruit, as I thought, like a pine Apple plated with scales, it
was as big as the crown of a Womans hat; I made bold to
step unto it, with an intent to have gathered it, no sooner
had I toucht it, but hundreds of Wasps were about me; at
last I cleared myself from them, being stung only by one
upon the upper lip, glad I was that I scaped so well; But
by that time I was come into the house my lip was swell'd
so extreamly that they hardly knew me but by my Garments."

Eight days later Josselyn sailed for England. This
occurred during the autumn of 1638, and, for the next
six or eight years, Maverick continued to live on Noddle's Island, getting on with his neighbors as best he
could; but, in this matter, the best was badly enough.
An outspoken member of the Church of England, he

was living in the midst of Independents; and, among ascetics, he maintained a sometimes too generous hospitality. His relations with Winthrop were of the most friendly character, but he was so conscious of the hostile feeling which existed towards him generally that, as early even as 1640, he had made up his mind to follow the example of Blackstone, and, through a voluntary exile to escape the society of the "lord-brethren." [1] He did not then carry out this plan, and six years afterwards the always latent ill-feeling gathered to a head, taking the form of active persecution. This was in 1648, when the movement in direction of a reformed franchise and larger religious liberty first made itself felt in Massachusetts, finding expression in what is known as the Dr. Robert Childs memorial; and the ruthless way in which it was met and suppressed, by the constituted authorities, is one of those episodes in New England history which yet remain to be impartially recounted.

Maverick's name was one of those signed to the

[1] There is something almost touching in the isolation of one genial man in that intolerant and frozen social atmosphere, as revealed in the following extract from a letter which Maverick wrote to Winthrop at this time : — " I know there want not those which hunt after anything which may redound to my discredit. Yourself, ever honored Sir, and honest Capt. Gibbons, are the only men which ever dealt plainly with me, by way of reproof and admonition, when you have heard of anything in which I have been faulty, which I hope hath not been water spilt upon a stone, and by it you have much obliged me. There are those which take an inquisition-like course, by endeavoring to gather what they can from malcontented servants, or the like ; which course I conceive is not warrantable ; the former course is more commendable, and will work better effects. I hope God will enable me in some measure to walk inoffensively, but finding by ten years' experience that I am ever sore to divers here, I have seriously resolved to remove hence. . . . My well wishes shall ever attend the Plantation, and yourself and yours in particular, however. Be pleased to pass by my too long neglect of visiting you, having not been in Boston these four months." IV. *Mass. Hist. Coll.* vii. 308.

Childs memorial, and he had probably taken an active part in the political agitation, if such it could be called, which led to it. In any event, he soon found himself in serious trouble, for not only was he imprisoned, but he was ordered to pay a heavy fine. This he refused to do, and, as matter of precaution, gave a deed of Noddle's Island to his son. A little later, in 1650, he sold the island outright, and seems then at last, a man verging on fifty, to have moved away from the place which had been his home for twenty-five years. It does not appear where he passed the next ten years; but, when the Restoration took place, he found his way to England, and there labored strenuously at the court of Charles II. to have a commission appointed to supervise on the spot the affairs of the American colonies. It was the revival, in another form, of Gorges' scheme of the governor-generalship.

This time the effort was crowned with success, and in July, 1664, Maverick landed for the second time in New England, one of four royal commissioners, sent out with vessels of war and soldiers, to visit the colonies, and, in the King's name, to hear and determine all matters of complaint.

The proceedings of the Commission of 1664 are a portion of New England history, and it is not necessary to recount them here. As Maverick well knew when he came, he had to deal with a stubborn race. Doubtless he confidently believed that he should succeed, and that his former persecutors would at last submit their necks to the yoke; but, if he did indeed cherish any such belief, he was doomed to bitter disappointment. Not only did the magistrates and people of the Massachusetts Bay refuse the yoke, but, on the 24th of May, 1665, a trumpet was sounded at certain conspicuous points in the streets of Boston, and Maverick and his colleagues were publicly denounced in their own hearing as usurpers. This, too, was done by order of the General Court, and the commissioners were powerless; for, with the whole community arrayed against them, they had with them no armed alien force sufficient to compel obedience. So, presently, it was they who had to submit and go elsewhere, — probably deeming it more prudent in dealing with Massachusetts to bide their time. Their time never came.

His official duties as commissioner ultimately carried Maverick to New York, and he does not seem to have again made Boston his permanent home. Somewhere about 1668 the Duke of York, in consideration of his services and fidelity to the King, gave him a house "in the Broadway." Its exact locality is not known, but in it the stout-hearted old Episcopal royalist is supposed to have lived out the balance of his days. The exact time of his death is not known, but it was before the year 1676. He left, by his wife Amias, two sons and a daughter, whose descendants multiplied in the land which their ancestors were among the first to occupy.

Social lines were distinctly marked in the seventeenth century. Winthrop, in his state papers, writing as governor, talked of "the common people." The "common people" were whipped and set in the stocks when they misbehaved themselves; the gentry were fined and admonished.[1]   Blackstone and Maverick were men of family, education and property, —

[1] "43. No man shall be beaten with above forty stripes, nor shall any true gentlemen, nor any man equall to a gentleman, be punished with whipping, unless his crime be very shameful, and his course of life vitious and profligate." *Body of Liberties*, 1641, III. *Mass. Hist. Coll.* viii. 224.

gentlemen. They were called planters, and they owned servants. This was not the case with Thomas Walford. He was a blacksmith, — one of Winthrop's "common people." While, therefore, the Puritan magistrates showed some hesitation in their methods of dealing with the two former, they seem to have shown none whatever towards the latter. He was an Episcopalian. That he was also a worthy man, and had in him the making of a good citizen, is evident from the fact that afterwards, through thirty years and until his death in 1660, he was much esteemed at Portsmouth, to which place he moved when compelled to leave Charlestown. At Portsmouth he found a refuge and a welcome; grants of land were made to him, and in due time he was chosen one of the select-men, and a warden of the church. Very different seems to have been his treatment by the Massachusetts colony, the severity of which, though passed over as not deserving of remark by some of the historians of New England, has by the more liberal of them been referred to as an incident which "must be regretted." [1] Walford had lived long in that wilderness, and built himself a home there, in which he and his family dwelt in a rude and secure independence, and now, probably, he declined to conform; for he liked not the ways of the newcomers, and would not readily submit to their severe authority, — exercised in the most trivial matters, and especially in regard to Sabbath observances. Very possibly he had been brought up in the Sabbath observances, far from Puritanic, recommended in King James' Book of Sports. Accordingly, it was not long before he found himself in trouble, and at a court held on the $\frac{3d}{13th}$ of May, 1631,

[1] Savage in notes to Winthrop, i *53.

after ordering John Legge to be "severely whipped
this day at Boston, and afterwards, soe soone as con-
veniently may be, at Salem," the magistrates took up
the case of Thomas Walford. It was disposed of as
follows : —

"Tho: Walford, of Charlton, is ffyned 40 shillings, and
is injoyned, hee and his wife, to departe out of the lymits
of this pattent before the 20th day of October nexte, under
paine of confiscacion of his goods, for his contempt of au-
thoritie, and confrontinge officers, &c."

Then, after ordering Thomas Bartlett to be whipped,
and John Norman to be fined, the court had a jury
impanelled, and proceeded to dispose of the famous
assault and battery case of Dexter against Endicott,
which has already been alluded to.[1]

The fine Walford settled by killing a wolf ; but the
order of banishment does not seem to have been at
that time enforced, for, twenty-eight months later, the
court again orders "that the goods of Thomas Walford shal be sequestred, and remaine in the hands of
Anchient Gennison, to satisfie the debts hee owes in the
Bay to severall persons." On the 9th of the subsequent January (1634), his name still appears in the
list of inhabitants of Charlestown. Nevertheless, at
or about this time, Walford and his family left forever "the English palisadoed and thatched house"
which, "a little way up from Charles river side," had
for nearly ten years been their home, and journeyed
north to find, if a less congenial clime, more tolerant
at least if not more sympathetic neighbors.

The little settlement at Wessagusset would meanwhile seem to have pursued the even tenor of its life,

[1] *Supra,* 260.

undisturbed by the presence of the larger community
which had established itself on the other side of the
bay. The two were separated from each other by ten
miles of unbroken wilderness, through which ran one
not inconsiderable river, and the communication between them was wholly by water. In winter they
were practically cut off from each other. It was
years, also, before the intervening region began to fill
up; so that in September, 1634, Winthrop noted the
following incident in his journal: —

"About this time one Alderman, of Bear Cove [Hing-
ham], being about fifty years old, lost his way between Dorchester and Wessaguscus, and wandered in the woods and
swamps three days and two nights, without taking any food,
and, being near spent, God brought him to Scituate; but he
had torn his legs much."

In this remote, secluded little hamlet, dwelt a few
families, who in 1630 had been there seven years.
William Jeffreys and John Bursley were apparently
the two leading men of the place, and their names
only, among those of its inhabitants, have come down
to us. They neither of them seem to have had any
trouble with the Puritan authorities, and at a later
day Bursley was more than once a member of the
General Court, while Jeffreys acted as commissioner.
None of their descendants of the same name are now
to be found in Weymouth.

The first mention of the village, after the migration
of 1630, is met with in connection with a formal visit
made by the Massachusetts magistrates on those of
Plymouth. It took place between $\frac{\text{October 25th}}{\text{November 4th}}$ and November $\frac{\text{1st}}{\text{11th}}$, 1632, and Winthrop has left an account of
it. On the morning of the first-named day, he being
then governor, the Rev. Mr. Wilson and others went

aboard the Lyon, a vessel recently from England and lying in the harbor, and Mr. Pierce, its master, thereupon took them in a shallop, to Wessagusset. There they all passed the night, being " bountifully " entertained with store of turkeys, geese, ducks, etc. The next day Captain Pierce returned to his vessel, — in which, by the way, he was wrecked a few days later, on the capes of Virginia, — while Winthrop and the others trudged on to Plymouth, arriving there on the evening of the $\frac{26th}{5th}$ of $\frac{October}{November}$. Returning, the party left Plymouth on the morning of the $\frac{31st}{10th}$ of $\frac{October}{November}$, Governor Bradford, with the pastor and elder of the Plymouth church, "accompanying them near half a mile out of town in the dark ; " for, in order to finish their journey to Wessagusset that day, they had to start an hour before daylight : —

" When they came to the great river, they were carried over by one Luddam, their guide (as they had been when they came, the stream being very strong, and up to the crotch) ; so the governour called that passage Luddam's Ford. Thence they came to a place called Hue's Cross. The governour, being displeased at the name, in respect that such things might hereafter give the Papists occasion to say that their religion was first planted in these parts, changed the name, and called it Hue's Folly. So they came that evening to Wessaguscus, where they were entertained as before, and the next day came safe to Boston."

A year after this, Wessagusset.was described, by one who then visited it, as " but a small village ; yet it is very pleasant, and healthful, very good ground, and is well timbered, and hath good store of hayground." [1] In September, 1635, it was, by order of the General Court, made a plantation under the name

[1] Young, *Chron. of Mass.* 395.

of Weymouth, and twenty-one families from England were allowed there to establish themselves under the ministry of the Rev. Mr. Hull; but, even with this addition to its inhabitants, the place was the next year referred to in the records of the General Court as " a very small town." Exactly what this meant at that time, it is impossible now to say; but one year afterwards, during the Pequot War, Weymouth, as its portion of the general levy, was assessed £27 in money, and called upon to furnish five men. Under the system of computation adopted by the best New England authorities, this would indicate a total population of about three hundred and fifty souls.[1] A year later, in 1638, the little community came in for even more than its full share of the religious troubles of the period.

Indeed, for several years it seems to have existed in a state of incessant theological turmoil. A strong alien element made its presence felt, — other Blackstones, Mavericks and Walfords, — who would not take themselves off. The Rev. Mr. Hull and his families were newcomers, and not of the original settlement. Accordingly Mr. Hull soon found himself

---

[1] In 1634, the population of Massachusetts Bay is estimated to have been " between three and four thousand." (Palfrey, i. 383.) Winthrop, writing in May of that year, said, " in all, about four thousand souls and upward." (*Proc. of Mass. Hist. Soc.* December 14, 1882.) The great migration took place during the next few years. In June, 1634, there arrived in Boston " fourteen great ships, and one at Salem." (Winthrop, i. 134.) In one day in June, 1635, eleven ships came into the bay. (*Ib.* 192.) In 1640 the migration came to an end, and about four thousand families in all, or twenty-one thousand souls, had then come over (Palfrey, i. 584), of which fifteen thousand were settled in Massachusetts. It seems fair to estimate that three fourths of these came over before 1638. In that case, if the levy of Weymouth in 1637 was fairly proportionate (5:160), its total population would have been as stated in the text.

confronted in his ministry by a rival, the Rev. Mr.
Jenner.   Then, in 1637, the Rev. Mr. Lenthal put in
an appearance, followed in the succeeding year by the
Rev. Mr. Newman.   So grievous was the trouble that
in January, 1638, a party of elders from the Boston
church visited Weymouth in the rôle of peace-makers,
and although they were reported to have "had good
success of their prayers," it was only three months
later that the General Court itself took the matter in
hand.   Its method of procedure was not wanting in
vigor, and the Rev. Mr. Lenthal was made to see reason why he should publicly recant.   One of his followers was fined, and another whipped ; while yet a
third was significantly notified that the General Court
was "weary of him, unless he reform."   But it is not
necessary to here enter with any detail into the vexed
history of the Weymouth church.[1]   The policy of the
colony was a simple one, — those who would not conform could be silent, or they might go away.   Massachusetts was no place for dissentients.   Accordingly,
as the Wessagusset people either could not or would
not go away, their conforming was a mere question of
time ; and, as they were few in number and all plain,
simple folks, the process of absorption, when measured
in years, did not take long.   In 1644 it was over.   A
short experience of the pastoral care of one superior
man — the learned, faithful and devout Samuel Newman — had sufficed,   and   Weymouth   contentedly
merged itself in the Puritan community which was
pressing upon it from either side.   As years went on,
it even passed from memory that the original settle-

[1] But see the paper entitled "Conference of the Elders of Massachusetts," by J. Hammond Trumbull, relating to the Lenthal church
troubles in Weymouth, in *Congregational Quarterly Rev.* (April,
1877), xix. 232–48.

ment under Robert Gorges had proved a permanent one, and the closest historical scrutiny failed to detect, in record or tradition, a trace of Episcopal teachings. The leaven had been wholly worked out.

What became of the widow of David Thomson, after the settlement, nowhere appears. Apparently she continued in the occupation of the island which still bears her husband's name. Subsequently, in 1648, it was regularly granted by the General Court to her son, John Thomson, who had then recently attained his majority. He does not seem to have prospered; for, three years later, the island thus granted was seized for debt, and, after being sold twice or more in the intermediate time, it at length passed, in the year 1666, into the hands of the Lynde family, who held it for over a century.[1]

Like Blackstone, Maverick, Walford, Jeffreys, Bursley and all the other Gorges planters, David Thomson left descendants, who became merged for all time in the general Anglo-American community.

[1] Lynde *Diaries*, 32, n.

CHAPTER XIX.

OF THE SUBSEQUENT FORTUNES OF THOMAS MORTON, WALTER BAGNALL AND EDWARD GIBBONS, ONCE OF MERRY-MOUNT.

WITH three exceptions nothing is known of the subsequent lives of those who in 1625 sat down with Captain Wollaston at Passonagessit. These three were Thomas Morton, Walter Bagnall, of Richmond Island, Me., and Edward Gibbons, afterwards a prominent member of the Puritan community, and the commander-in-chief of its military establishment. It has already been noticed that Wollaston himself was a mere bird of passage.[1] Nothing more is heard of him, or of those who came with him, whether his partners and associates or his hired servants, excepting only the three who have been named.

Whether Gorges really did turn Morton adrift in 1637, as he asserted to Winthrop, or only professed to have done so, as would be inferred from the attestation of the Agamenticus charter of 1641, there can be little doubt that the fortunes of the latter steadily waned after the publication of the New English Canaan.[2] What became of him during the next few years does not appear, though probably he hung about London, a poor dependent on Gorges. Possibly when the Civil

[1] *Supra*, 162.
[2] For authorities, etc., in relation to Morton, see introductory matter to *New English Canaan*, Prince Soc. ed.

War broke out, and Sir Ferdinando sided with the King, Morton may, in the complications arising out of the Plough Patent, have turned against his old patron and attached himself to the Parliamentarians, Rigby and Cleeve; for, as early as 1637 Gorges speaks of him as Cleeve's agent, and at that time Morton would seem to have sent Cleeve to America in crazy search of "the great lake Erocoise." A certain amount of plausibility is given to the theory that he did thus desert Gorges, and seek the favor of his enemies, by the fact that Morton is next met with in Plymouth, pretending to be the agent of Rigby, the Puritan colonel and member of Parliament, and to hold from him a commission to look after his affairs in America. Morton even produced certain papers, claiming that he had a protection from the Parliament; but he took good care not to allow them to be examined. This was in the summer of 1643. His reappearance at Plymouth after thirteen years of absence naturally excited no little remark; for though there was apparently no copy of the New English Canaan in the Plymouth colony, the character of the book was perfectly well known, and it was considered "infamouse and scurillous." It would, indeed, have been not unnatural if the friends of Dr. Fuller, who had now been dead nine years, should have held the references to him in lively recollection. Governor Winslow, also, was then at Plymouth, and it is not probable that he had forgotten the seventeen weeks in the Fleet prison for which he was indebted to the author of the book.

The former Master of Mare-Mount and Lord of Misrule had, it would seem, now taken good care not to put himself within reach of the Massachusetts magistrates by landing at Boston; and even at Plym-

outh his petition that he might be permitted to tarry
there for a time was by no means acceded to as a matter of course.   One party was in favor of sending the
"petie-fogger of Furnefells Inne" out of the province
forthwith; but Governor Bradford, more merciful,
gave way so far as to consent that his old enemy might
pass the winter at Plymouth, but only on condition
that he took himself off with the opening of spring.
So there Morton remained.   It was twenty-one years
since he had first landed in New England, and he must
now have been well on in life.   He had been a wanderer and a free-liver.   His health was broken.   He
was poor too, — so poor that at Plymouth he was glad
to live "meanely at four shillings per week and content to drinke water, so he [might] dyet at that price."
Though he thus no longer enjoyed the good cheer of
Merry-Mount, the old man seems still to have retained
his love of field sports ; and once more he excited the
fierce wrath of Miles Standish by wandering gun in
hand over the Duxbury marshes.

Though the territory which Sir Alexander Rigby
claimed, and of which subsequently the Parliamentary commission put him in possession, lay wholly in
Maine, Morton either now was, or pretended to be,
engaged in some scheme of settlement at New Haven
or on the Narragansett.   His ostensible business at
Plymouth was to interest others in this project.   If
we accept Winslow's statement that he secured the
"promise of but one person who is old, weak and de-
crepid, a very atheist and fit companion for him," his
success was limited.

The next spring, in compliance apparently with the
condition imposed by Bradford, Morton left Plymouth.
He went at first to Maine, where the royalist party

was showing some signs of life, and on his way he even ventured within the Massachusetts jurisdiction, going by water to Gloucester. Endicott was on the watch, ready to pounce upon him like a hawk, and a warrant for his apprehension was quickly on its way to Cape Ann; but the bird seems to have taken flight to Maine in time to escape it. How long Morton remained at the eastward, or what he did there, does not appear, and he is next, in August of the same summer, heard of in Rhode Island, claiming now to be for the King, and glad to find there so many cavaliers. Winthrop all this time was watching him with curious eyes, and when the author of the New Canaan is next heard of he is within his old persecutor's grasp. What brought him to Boston now — whether he ventured there of his own free will, or was caught passing through the jurisdiction — is not known; but, under date of September $\frac{9\text{th}}{19\text{th}}$, 1644, five weeks after Coddington had spoken of him as being in Rhode Island, Winthrop wrote : —

"At the court of assistants, Thomas Morton was called forth presently after the lecture, that the country might be satisfied of the justice of our proceeding against him. There was laid to his charge his complaint against us at the council board, which he denied. Then we produced the copy of the bill exhibited by Sir Christopher Gardiner, etc., wherein we were charged with treason, rebellion, etc., wherein he was named as a party or witness. He denied that he had any hand in the information, only was called as a witness. To convince him to be the principal party, it was showed : 1. That Gardiner had no occasion to complain against us, for he was kindly used, and dismissed in peace, professing much engagement for the great courtesy he found here. 2. Morton had set forth a book against us, and had threatened us, and had prosecuted a *quo warranto* against

us.   3. His letter was produced, written soon after to Mr.
Jeffery, his old acquaintance and intimate friend."

Then followed Morton's jubilant letter of ten years
before, in which he tells of his assured and immediate
triumph, and of how Ratcliff " was comforted by their
lordships with the cropping of Mr. Winthrop's ears."
Since that letter was written, many things had happened.   " My Lord Canterbury," who then sat easily
first among " their lordships at the council board,"
had been nearly four years in the Tower, and was
on trial for his life.   Instead of subjecting Cradock
and Humphreys to his brutalities, the Archbishop was
now in his turn subjected to the even greater brutalities of Hugh Peters.[1]   Gorges, then designated by the
King as his governor-general in all America, was in
arms with Prince Rupert ; and — exactly " forty
days " before — " Jove " had indeed " vouchsafed to
thunder," for, at Marston Moor, King Charles had
been overthrown by Cromwell.   And here, in Boston,
was Morton, — not returning " with the governour,
by whom all complainants [were to] have relief," but
alone and penniless, confronting as best he might
" King Winthrop," sitting at the magistrates' table,
over which John Endicott — " the great swelling
fellow of Littleworth " of the New Canaan — presided
as governor, with the fatal letter to Jeffreys in his
hand.   A notable opportunity was thus offered for a
homily on the text, — " Let him that thinketh he
standeth take heed lest he fall."

There is something singularly *naif* and characteristic in Winthrop's record of what now took place, and
it illustrates very clearly one respect in which the early
Massachusetts magistrates enjoyed a marked advan-

[1] Hook, *Archbishops,* vi. 363.

tage over their successors. They carried the great
body of the law, especially of the criminal law, locked
up in their own breasts.[1] They were at once law-mak-
ers, law-expounders and the executors of the law. In
the same breath, as it were, they declared the crime,
condemned the criminal and inflicted the penalty. It
was small cause for wonder, therefore, that " the people . . . thought their condition very unsafe, while so
much power rested in the discretion of the magistrates." [2] In the case now in hand the prisoner at
their bar had fourteen years before been arrested, imprisoned and banished ; he had been set in the stocks,
fined to the extent of everything he possessed, and seen
his house burned down before his eyes. He had been
sent back to England, nominally to stand his trial for
crimes it was alleged he had committed ; and had
there been released from imprisonment, no accuser
appearing. Having returned to New England he was
now again arrested, and publicly arraigned before the
magistrates, " that the country might be satisfied of
the justice of our proceeding against him." As the
result of this " proceeding" he was imprisoned again
indefinitely, heavily fined, and narrowly escaped a
whipping. And what was the charge against him ? —
It was that he had made " a complaint against us at
the council board " !

"The council board," be it remembered, represented in those days the King in council. The complaint, therefore, in this case charged to have been
made, was made directly to the power from whence

---

[1] " In all criminall offences, where the law hath prescribed no certaine penaltie, the judges have power to inflict penalties, according to
the rule of Gods word." *Fundamentals of Mass.* 12 ; Hutchinson,
State Papers, 205.

[2] Palfrey, i. 442.

the charter of the colony emanated. It seems as if it
would have puzzled Winthrop and his associates, masters of political casuistry as they were, to point out to
the prisoner, or to the country they proposed to satisfy, any prescriptive law, much less any penal statute,
which made a criminal offence out of a representation
concerning them addressed to the acknowledged head
of the state. The thing charged, be it remembered,
was not an appeal in a judicial proceeding. Such
appeals the colonial magistrates always disallowed, and
claimed under their charter a right to disallow. The
thing charged was simply a " complaint " addressed
to the crown.

That any such view of the matter as the above ever
suggested itself to the mind of the court now sitting
in judgment is highly improbable ; nor does any such
view seem to have even been urged by the prisoner.
In point of fact, however it might be in reason or
in law, any questioning of the colonial magistrates,
whether in the way of appeal or otherwise, before king
or court or parliament, was then and long after looked
upon and treated in Massachusetts as a crime, and as
such was punished. Law or no law, the colonial magistrates did not propose to recognize any jurisdiction
superior to their own. To be fined, scourged, mutilated, imprisoned and banished, on the mere dictum
of a board of magistrates who pointed to no statute,
might be trying ; but such was the practice in early
New England, and as a matter of fact no one ever
improved matters for himself by carrying his complaints across the ocean. This Morton found out
now ; and Maverick and Childs found it out a little
later on. It certainly was not law ; perhaps it was
not justice. The stubborn spirit of independence be-

hind it was none the less what made New England; and, even in writing history, something must be pardoned to the spirit of liberty. Yet would Verres have dared to make a crime of the complaint a Roman citizen had proffered to the Senate and People of Rome?

The rest of Morton's story can be briefly told. Winthrop is the principal authority, and what he says throws a gleam of curious light on the thrift, as well as the charity, of those early times. To speak it plainly, Morton now was, in all human probability, a broken-down, disreputable sot; — he could not " procure the least respect amongst our people," is what Winslow says of him. He was certainly old, destitute and friendless, and Winthrop records the little that is known further of him in the following words : —

" Having been kept in prison about a year, in expectation of further evidence out of England, he was again called before the court, and after some debate what to do with him, he was fined one hundred pounds, and set at liberty. He was a charge to the country, for he had nothing, and we thought not fit to inflict corporal punishment upon him, being old and crazy, but thought better to fine him and give him his liberty, as if it had been to procure his fine, but indeed to leave him opportunity to go out of the jurisdiction, as he did soon after, and he went to Acomenticus, and living there poor and despised, he died within two years after."

Morton himself asserted that the harsh treatment he endured in prison, while waiting for that evidence from England which was to convict him of some crime, broke down his health and hastened his end. This, too, may well have been the case if he was indeed, as was subsequently charged, kept in jail and in fetters through a whole New England winter, without either

fire or bedding, even " to the decaying of his limbs." [1]
How he survived such exposure would seem to be the
only cause for wonder.

When describing in the New English Canaan the
forest beasts of New England, Morton incidentally
refers to a servant of his, who was reputed to have
made a thousand pounds in five years in the fur trade. [2]
He had then died, and Morton intimates that his possessions had mysteriously disappeared. This servant,
there is little room for doubt, was Walter Bagnall. [3] In
1627, and possibly a little earlier, Morton had visited
the coast of Maine, trading successfully for furs on
the Kennebec, and passing some time at Richmond
Island, near the entrance to Casco Bay. Indeed, it
would seem probable that he even then had a sort of
branch trading-station on this island, for he speaks
with much feeling of the rigor of its winter climate.
At the time of the arrest of Morton by Miles Standish, Bagnall was probably one of the four of the
Merry-Mount company who were away from home;

---

[1] Writing fifteen years later, Samuel Maverick said, — "Morton
was banished, his house fired before his face, and he sent prisoner to
England, but for what offence I know not; who, some years after
(nothing being laid to his charge) returned for New England, where
he was soon after apprehended and kept in the common Goale a whole
winter, nothing laid to his Charge but the writing of a Booke entituled
New Canaan, which indeed was the truest discription of New England
as then it was that ever I saw. The offence was he had touched them
too neere. They not proveing the charge, he was sett loose, but soone
after dyed, haveing as he said, and most believed, received his bane
by hard lodging and fare in prison. This was done by the Massachusetts Magistrats." *Proc. Mass. Hist. Soc.* Series II. i. 240.

[2] Prince Society edition of *New English Canaan*, 206, n., 218, n.

[3] In regard to Bagnall, in addition to the notes in the Prince Soci-
ety edition of the *New English Canaan*, already referred to, see also
Baxter's *George Cleeve of Casco Bay*, in the publications of the Gorges
Society.

and when he returned and found the place practically broken up, he was among those described as " the worst of the company," who dispersed, " the more modest" only remaining to keep the house.[1] Going back to Richmond Island, a dreary place some two hundred acres in extent, Bagnall there established himself ; and there he remained until 1631, engaged in trade with the savages, and known along the coast as " Great Watt." Winthrop describes him as " a wicked fellow [who] had much wronged the Indians," and the probabilities would seem to be that he carried the Merry-Mount methods with him to Maine, being wholly unscrupulous in his dealings. In any event, he prospered greatly, for at the time of his death he had amassed, according to Winthrop's estimate, — more reasonable than Morton's, though still large enough, — £400, mainly in goods. He was looking, also, to a larger and more permanent trade, and shortly before had made application for a patent to the Council for New England. On the 2d of December, 1631, just two months after he was killed, his request was granted, and Richmond Island, with fifteen hundred acres in addition thereto on the neighboring mainland, was allotted to him. Morton had then been nine months in England, and not improbably it was through his agency that Bagnall pressed his claim on Gorges.

On the 3d of October, 1631, an Indian called Squidrayset, a sagamore of the Casco tribe, was at Richmond Island with a party of his people. Whether he went there bent on violence, or to trade away his furs, is not known ; but possibly he already had wrongs to avenge, and a sudden quarrel on some new provocation may have arisen. Whatever the cause,

---

[1] Bradford, 243.

the result was that Bagnall, and the one other man
who lived on the island with him, the initial letter of
whose name alone is known, were set upon and murdered. The savages then burned the house and went
away, carrying off their victims' arms and goods.
When, a few days later, Captain Thomas Wiggin,
then at Piscataqua, received word of this outrage, he
hurried off a messenger to the Massachusetts magistrates, asking them at once to send a force of men
to avenge it; but they, excusing themselves on the
ground of the season and want of boats, showed small
disposition to follow the matter up. It was only a
year since they had finally suppressed the mother establishment at Mt. Wollaston, and, scarce nine months
before, Morton's house had by their orders been burned
to the ground; so now they evidently felt no great
call to disturb themselves if the savages had disposed
of the branch establishment on the coast of Maine in
a way not much more summary. Upwards of a year
afterwards, some pinnaces were sent out, carrying an
armed force to capture a gang of pirates then infest-
ing the waters of the Kennebec. In January they
returned, the cold putting a stop to an unsuccessful
search; but, on their way back, they landed on Richmond Island, and finding there Black Will, a Lynn
Indian, hanged him out of hand. So far as now appears, there would not seem to have been any reason
to suppose that Black Will was concerned in the mur-
ders of fifteen months before, the real perpetrators of
which are said to have been at Presumpscot Falls, not
five miles away, at the very time of his hanging; but,
in accordance with the frontier code, one outrage was
thus offset against another. Bagnall's goods had disappeared among the Indians; but, more than two cen-

turies after his death, the ploughshare turned up, on Richmond Island, a stone pot of ancient form, in which were found some forty pieces of money of Elizabethan and Stuart coinage. Those most competent to judge were strong in the belief that this money was a portion of the murdered Englishman's hoard.

Edward Gibbons was more fortunate than his companions, Morton and Bagnall. The career of this man was, indeed, so varied and curious, — so strangely illustrative of early colonial life and manners, — that it is well worth while to recount it in the language, so far as may be, of the time. It is merely necessary to premise that Gibbons was probably not one of those who came in Captain Wollaston's company, or an original member of it. He may have been a relative of Ambrose Gibbons of Piscataqua, and would seem to have lived there for a time. Bradford intimates that Morton's establishment became the resort of "all the scume of the countrie," and Edward Gibbons was a young man of reckless, roving disposition; so that, a kindred spirit, he may have found his way to Merry-Mount during the time of Morton's ascendency there.

However this may be, Gibbons was, in all probability, like Bagnall, absent from Mt. Wollaston at the time of Morton's arrest in 1628; and after that he may have been accounted one of "the more modest" of the crew, who remained about the place. If so, he must have been a looker-on at the hewing down of the May-pole, under Endicott's eye, in the ensuing September, and hearkened also to the magistrate's stern admonition that he and his companions should "look there should be better walking." But even before that event, Gibbons would seem to have experienced a change of heart. On this subject, Joshua Scottow,

who wrote about forty years after Gibbons' death, and
referred to a manuscript he had left behind him, is the
principal authority. He is as quaint as he is incoherent, and, referring to the famous gathering of the
Salem church on the $\frac{6th}{16th}$ of August, 1629, he tells
the story thus : —

" At which Convention, the Testimony which the Lord of
all the Earth bore unto it, is wonderfully memorable, by a Saving Work upon a Gentleman of Quality, who afterwards was the Chieftain and Flower
of *New England's* Militia, and an Eminent Instrument
both in Church and Commonwealth ; he being the younger
Brother of the House of an Honourable Extract, his Ambition exceeding what he could expect at home, Rambled
hither : Before one Stone was laid in this Structure, or our
Van Currier's Arrival, he was no Debauchee, but of a Jo-
cund Temper, and one of the Merry Mount Society, who
chose rather to Dance about a *May pole*, first Erected to
the Honour of *Strumpet Flora*, than to hear a good Sermon ; who hearing of this Meeting, though above Twenty
Miles distant from it, and desirous to see the Mode and
Novel of a Churches Gathering ; with great studiousness, he
applyed himself to be at it ; where beholding their orderly
procedure, and their method of standing forth, to declare
the Work of God upon their Souls, being pricked at the
Heart, he sprung forth among them, desirous to be one of
the Society, who though otherwise well accomplished, yet
divinely illiterate, was then convinc'd and judged before all ;
the secrets of his heart being made manifest, fell down and
Worshipped God, to their astonishment, saying, That God
was in them of a truth."

*Major
General
Gibbins.*

Subsequent and more reliable authorities add that,
though the Salem preachers encouraged their pros-
elyte in his good intentions, they very prudently
" chose to have some evidence of his sincerity ; "[1] and

[1] Eliot, *Biog. Dict.* 216.

the next record concerning the convert is indicative of
backsliding, and seems quite to justify this hesitation
on the preachers' part, savoring far more of Merry-
Mount than of the Salem church. At the Court of
Assistants held at Boston on the 16th of August,
1631.

"It is ordered, that Mr Shepheerd and Robte Coles
shalbe ffyned 5 marks a peece, and Edward Gibbons XXˢ,
for abuseing themselves disorderly with drinkeing to much
stronge drinke aboard the Frendshipp, and att Mr. Maver-
icke his howse at Winettsemet."

In connection with this most unmistakable debauch,
it is interesting to know, on the authority of Governor Bradford, that the "stronge drinke" in question was "meatheglin," — a liquor made of honey and
water, boiled and fermented, — of which there were
two hogsheads in the cargo of the Friendship. This
liquor belonged to Plymouth parties, but, the Friendship going to Boston, the contents of the hogsheads
were there transferred into wooden "flackets." "But
when these flackets came to be received [at Plymouth]
ther was left but six gallons of the two hogsheads, it
being drunke up under the name leackage, and so
lost." [1] How large a portion of this "leackage" Gibbons and his friends were responsible for, does not
appear; but it would seem to have been enough to
lead to their "abuseing themselves disorderly."

Afterwards Gibbons married, became a selectman
and commissioner, and was frequently a delegate to
the General Court, besides being one of the most active merchants in Boston. His military turn began
to show itself as early as 1634, and in 1645 he was

[1] Bradford, 269.

captain of the Boston train-band. Meanwhile, it is
very much to be feared that he for a time tried his
hand at buccaneering. Certainly, in 1636–7, he
passed a number of months in the West Indies, in a
small pinnace of thirty tons, those aboard of which,
for some unexplained reason, did not dare to touch at
any inhabited place; preferring to land in unfre-
quented harbors, and subsist on turtles and hogs.
Gibbons had been given up for lost in Boston, when
suddenly he reappeared there, in June, 1637, bringing with him a vessel, his possession of which he accounted for in a most singular way, for he asserted
that, being forced into some harbor of the West Indies,
he would infallibly have been captured by a French
man-of-war lying there, had not the captain of the
man-of-war, "one Petfree," who had formerly lived at
Piscataqua, been acquainted with him.[1] Accordingly,
instead of being captured, Gibbons found himself
"used curteously," his commodities exchanged for a
home freight, and his vessel finally sent back to Boston, taking with her a prize belonging to the French
captain, which Gibbons was authorized by its captor
to sell "for a small price to be paid in New England."
Winthrop adds that Gibbons on this occasion brought
home an "aligarto, which he gave the governour."
Though the explanation thus given must naturally have
suggested further inquiry, not only does it seem to have
passed unchallenged in Boston, but time subsequently
gave to it a sort of religious coloring, — what might,
perhaps, be termed a New England theological glow;
and it was recorded by Cotton Mather in his Magnalia among remarkable sea-deliverances, as " *the wonderful story of Major* Gibbons." [2] According to this

[1] Palfrey, ii. 226, n.; Winthrop, i. 270.   [2] B. I. ch. i. § 3.

version, Gibbons' vessel, owing to the continuance of
contrary winds, got out of provisions, and those on
board would have been reduced to the necessity of
eating each other, had not God, in answer to " their
importunate prayers," caused first " a mighty fish "
to leap into their boat, and then " a great bird " to
light upon its mast. Both of these were captured,
and then, as the still famishing company was about to
have recourse " to the heart-breaking task of slaying
the person under designation," a third miracle occurs,
and they fall in with the courteous " French pirate,"
and so made " a comfortable end of their voyage."
Satisfied with the results of this singular experience,
Gibbons does not appear to have had anything further
to do with either pirates or piracy ; but, settling down
as a merchant in Boston, he had a house on what is
now Washington Street, opposite the foot of Cornhill,
and a farm in the country at Pullen Point, as Point
Shirley was then called.[1] At a later day he was
concerned in the LaTour d'Aulnay complications in
Acadia ; and when, in 1645, d'Aulnay captured La
Tour's fort at St. John " by assault and scalado,"
Major Gibbons, who had involved himself in La Tour's
schemes to the extent of more than £2,000, " by this
last was now quite undone." He still seems, none
the less, to have been a man of substance, for, in a
very life-like description of a visit of d'Aulnay to
Boston in August, 1646, Winthrop says the French
guests lodged at " the house of Major Gibbons, where
they were entertained that night."

D'Aulnay's visit to Boston took place in October,
1646, at which time Gibbons had risen to be commanding officer of the Suffolk Regiment, with the title of

---

[1] *Mem. Hist. of Boston*, i. 578, n.

sergeant-major. He had then held the position for two years, having been chosen to it in 1644, when the militia was first organized and the office created; for there were now four regiments altogether in the colony, each commanded by a sergeant-major, and the whole by a major-general. Thomas Dudley was the first to hold the latter position, " whose faithfulness and great zeal and love to the truths of Christ, caused the people to choose him to this office, although he were far stricken in years." Dudley the next year (1645) was chosen governor, and John Endicott was appointed major-general in his place. He, also, was chosen governor, in 1649, and then Sergeant-major Gibbons succeeded to the major-generalcy, and held the office until his death, on the 9th of December, 1652.

His only approach to active service seems to have been in 1645, when " it clearly appeared that God called the Colonies to a war " with the Narragansetts. A force of three hundred men, whereof Massachusetts furnished one hundred and ninety, was then put into the field, with Major Gibbons in supreme command. Among his lieutenants were the redoubtable Captain Miles Standish, of Plymouth, and the no less redoubtable Captain John Mason, of Connecticut, each in command of a contingent of forty men; but the mere spectacle of so formidable an array proved too much for the savages, and the frightened sons of Canonicus made haste to send in their submission. Though he saw no active fighting, Major-General Gibbons, none the less, impressed his contemporaries as a soldier of prowess; and Captain Edward Johnson, of Woburn, has handed him down to posterity, through the Wonder-Working Providence, as

" A man of a resolute spirit, bold as a Lion, being wholly tutor'd up in New-England Discipline, very generous, and forward to promote all military matters ; his forts are well contrived, and batteries strong, and in good repair, his great Artillery well mounted, and cleanly kept, half Canon, Culverins and Sakers, as also field-pieces of brass very ready for service."

II.

THE ANTINOMIAN CONTROVERSY.

THE ANTINOMIAN CONTROVERSY.

CHAPTER I.

THE REV. JOHN WHEELWRIGHT OF "THE MOUNT."

THOMAS MORTON'S house at Merry-Mount was burned to the ground in December, 1630, and its occupants were driven away. For several years thereafter the region between the Neponset and the Monatoquit — the seaward slope of the Blue Hill range — was without other inhabitants than the few Indians of Chickatabot's following, who, the sole representatives in those parts of the Massachusetts tribe, flit to and fro across the pages of the record, and haunt " the Massachusetts Fields," the mere ghosts of their race.

Indeed, for a short space of time, and yet one measured by years, the Neponset seems to have been looked upon as practically the southern boundary of Massachusetts. Starting from Salem, and making their first lodgment on the shores of Boston Bay at Charlestown, the outposts of what is known in New England history as the Great Migration had pushed their way up the valleys of the Charles and the Mystic, and south as far as the Neponset ; but at the Neponset the southerly movement paused. It was a barrier in the way, — the first and the smallest of many barriers of the same kind which New England civilization was destined to surmount.

It was in this unoccupied region — a region some five miles or so across, between Dorchester on the north and Wessagusset on the south — that in 1634 Alderman of Bear Cove, as Hingham was then called, losing his way, wandered through woods and swamps for three days and two nights without encountering a human being;[1] for, though it was known to have a fertile soil, clear of trees, and to be well adapted to farming purposes, the border land, as it then was, seems to have been under a sort of ban. Morton's doings had given it an evil name. It was no fit home for godly families.

This state of affairs was not likely to continue long. The early settlers of Massachusetts Bay, unlike those of Plymouth, were many of them men of substance. At home the associates of Carver and Bradford had been plain people, while, of those who came with Winthrop and Saltonstall, many had belonged to the gentry; and these last brought with them to the New World the English passion for landed possessions, — that land-hunger which they inherited direct from Germanic and Norman ancestors, and which they left unimpaired and unsatisfied to their descendants. Every man of mark among them was eager, as soon as he set foot in New England, to secure a domain for himself and his descendants. The peninsula of Boston was small, — "too small to contain many," as Wood described it only three years after the settlement; so that those living there were " constrained to take farms in the country." Accordingly, Governor Winthrop had the Ten-Hill farm of 600 acres in Medford, besides some 1,200 acres more "about six miles from Concord northwards." Governor Dudley

---

[1] *Supra*, 337.

had 1,700 acres, — 200 on the west side of the Charles over against Cambridge, 500 on the easterly side of the river, above the falls, and 1,000 from Concord northwards. Sir Richard Saltonstall had 1,600 acres, part in Watertown, part in Natick, and, later, part in Springfield. So it went on; and it naturally resulted that, as immigration increased, the land-hunger, which was quite as well developed in the new as in the old comers, could find in more remote parts only that on which to feed.

Then it was that people began to look across the Neponset; and accordingly, at the session of the General Court, held in May, 1634, it was ordered " that Boston shall have convenient enlargement at Mt. Wollaston." Six months later that territory was formally annexed to Boston as a sort of outlying dependency, Dorchester intervening between the two, and the process of dividing it up among private owners, in estates of from 200 to 700 acres, was begun. On the 14th of December a committee of five was appointed to go out and assign " what may be sufficient for William Coddington and Edmund Quincy to have for their particular farms there." Quincy was the progenitor of the family after a member of which the town in which the Mount lay received its name a century and a half later; Coddington afterwards became the father of Rhode Island. The Mt. Wollaston bay-front was now assigned to the two, — the place where Morton's house had stood subsequently falling to Coddington, though it finally passed by purchase and descent into the hands of a Quincy.

Allotments to others were at the same time made, but they are not to the present purpose. It is necessary to pass over a couple of years before coming to

two names — William Hutchinson and John Wheelwright [1] — which are associated not only with holdings
at the Mount, but with controversies that for a time
seemed to threaten the very existence of the colony.
Its life was spared; but through more than a century
and a half its history bears the deep pit-marks of
those controversies, much as men of those early days
bore from childhood scars of the smallpox.

Theological controversies are as a rule among the
most barren of the many barren fields of historical
research; and the literature of which they were so
fruitful may, so far as the reader of to-day is concerned, best be described by the single word impossible. Among modern writers Hallam had to acquaint
himself with it in at least a general way; and even
Hallam, who was not wont to flinch at an array of
books and authors, was appalled, not more by the
mass than by the aridity of those devoted to this
particular branch of learning. More than once he
refers to the subject, with a touch of sadness as well
as a warmth of imagery not usual with him. "Our
public libraries," he in one place remarks, "are cem-
eteries of departed reputation; and the dust accu-
mulating upon their untouched volumes speaks as

---

[1] The allotment to William Hutchinson was made by votes of Jan-
uary $\frac{4}{14}$, 1636 and January $\frac{8}{18}$, 1637, and included 600 acres of land,
lying in what is now North Quincy, "betwixt Dorchester bounds and
Mount Woollistone ryver." (*Second Report of Boston Record Com's*,
(1877), 7, 14.) The Wheelwright allotment was made by vote of
$\frac{\text{February } 20}{\text{March } 2}$, and April $\frac{2}{12}$, 1637. It included 250 acres lying south of Mt.
Wollaston, and "extended into the countrye." (*Ib.* 15, 17, 45, 46.)
The Rev. John Wilson's and the Rev. John Wheelwright's holdings
at "the Mount" seem to have been contiguous, and what Lechford remarked of Blackstone and Williams might have been remarked of Wheelwright: — " He lives neere master, *Wilson*, but is far
from his opinions." (*Supra*, 325.)

forcibly as the grass that waves over the ruins of
Babylon ; " and again, speaking of the wordy " cham-
pions of a long war," he declares of their writings that
" they belong no more to man, but to the worm, the
moth, and the spider. Their dark and ribbed backs,
their yellow leaves, their thousand folio pages, do not
more repel us than the unprofitableness of their substance."

So far as its substance was concerned, the great
New England religious controversy of 1637 forms no
exception to the general truth of Hallam's criticism.
Not only were the points in dispute obscure, but the
discussion was carried on in a jargon which has become unintelligible; and, from a theological point of
view, it is now devoid of interest. At most, it can
excite only a faint curiosity as one more example of
that childish excitement over trifles by which communities everywhere and at all times are liable to be
swept away from the moorings of common sense. But
the, so-called, Antinomian controversy was in reality
not a religious dispute, which was but the form it
took. In its essence that controversy was a great deal
more than a religious dispute ; it was the first of the
many New England quickenings in the direction of
social, intellectual and political development, — New
England's earliest protest against formulas. The
movement of sap in a young tree was not more natural,
and the form the quickening took, and the individuals
who participated in it were the only matters of chance.
It was designed by no one. No one at the time realized its significance. It was to that community just
what the first questioning of an active mind is to a
child brought up in the strictest observance of purely
conventional forms. So viewed, the mis-called Anti-

nomian controversy becomes, in the light of subsequent history, full of interest. As an illustration of the men and manners and modes of thought of a civilization wholly unlike any which now exists, it is replete with life and incident.

John Wheelwright was the third minister of the gospel who regularly preached within the limits fixed in the Massachusetts patent south of the Neponset. William Morell and Joseph Hull of Weymouth alone preceded him; and when Wheelwright's voice was first heard in that wilderness, the voice of Morell had been silent for more than twelve years, while Hull had taken up his work only a twelvemonth before. Wheelwright was in his day esteemed a learned and eloquent divine, and he was also a very famous one ; for it was his fortune, by a discourse delivered on a day of public fasting and prayer in January, 1637, to throw the Massachusetts community into a state of commotion without a parallel in its history. It was, perhaps, the most momentous single sermon ever preached from the American pulpit; and, indeed, in this respect to be compared only with the yet more famous Sacheverell sermons, preached seventy years later in London.

The author of this memorable fást-day deliverance was born in 1592 at Saleby, a little hamlet of the market-town of Alford, some twenty-four miles from the English Boston, in the region known as the fens of Lincolnshire. This region has the reputation of being one of the least interesting in England. Saturated with water through one half of the year, through the other half it is a dreary flat ; and yet, towards the close of the sixteenth century, the fens of Lincolnshire seem to have been somewhat prolific of men destined to play prominent parts in the settlement of America.

The names of all the fen hamlets terminate with *by*, indicative of their Danish origin ; and at Willoughby, only a few miles from Saleby, and a little over thirty from the yet more famous Scrooby, in the next county of Notts, John Smith was born thirteen years before Wheelwright. Of the latter's youthful days not much is known. His father, a landholder of the middle class, gave the son a good education, and in due course of time he became a student at Cambridge. There is a tradition that he and Oliver Cromwell knew each other well in their college days. The story is to the effect that in later years the Protector once said : — " I remember the time when I was more afraid of meeting Wheelwright at football than I have been since of meeting an army in the field, for I was infallibly sure of being tripped up by him." This, like most utterances resting on tradition, has an apocryphal ring ; but it is an established fact that Cromwell esteemed Wheelwright highly, and showed him marked favor at a subsequent time.[1] Taking his degree at Cambridge in 1618, Wheelwright five years later, in 1623, having married in the meanwhile, succeeded his wife's father in the vicarage of Bilsby, one of a cluster of hamlets close to the spot of his birth. The great religious movement against dogmas and ritualism was then fast developing in England, and assuming more and more strongly the Puritan phase. Wheelwright was married, possessed of some property, and secure in a comfortable living ; but he was a born controversialist, and seems to have entered into the spirit of the rising protest with all the superfluous energy of

[1] Bell, *John Wheelwright*, Prince Society Publications. Where other authorities are not specified, reference for statements relating to Wheelwright should be made to Bell's work.

youth. Before 1633 the crisis with him had come ; he was already silenced for non-conformity, and, though he had neither resigned nor been removed, his vicarage had been treated as vacant, and into it a successor inducted. During the next three years he ministered privately, but with an ever-increasing reputation, and in April, 1636, embarked for New England.

Before this Wheelwright's first wife had died, and he had married Mary, a daughter of Edward Hutchinson of Alford, and sister of one William Hutchinson. This William Hutchinson had, with his wife Anne, gone to America in 1634, and landed in Boston in September, thus preceding Wheelwright by about two years. Arriving on the $\frac{25\text{th}}{6\text{th}}$ of $\frac{\text{June}}{\text{July}}$, 1636, on the $\frac{12\text{th}}{22\text{d}}$ of the next month Wheelwright was admitted to the church, being then in his forty-fifth year. In 1636, and, indeed, for years after that, there was but one meeting-house in Boston, — the rude, one-story barrack already described. In this edifice were gathered together each Sabbath and lecture-day all the inhabitants of Boston who were neither too young profitably to attend divine worship, nor incapacitated for some good and sufficient reason. The Rev. John Wilson, first pastor of the church, ministered to the flock, though somewhat overshadowed by the greater eminence in public estimation of his colleague, — or teacher, as he was called, — the Rev. John Cotton.

Wheelwright had not been many weeks a member of the church before some of its more active members began to agitate the question of installing him by Cotton's side as an additional teacher. The suggestion was first publicly made on Sunday, November $\frac{2}{12}$, 1636, at the church-meeting which regularly followed the services ; and a week later it assumed formal shape.

A decided opposition was at once developed, at the head of which were Wilson, the pastor, and Winthrop, the ex-governor, while the whole movement, as was natural enough in so small a community, soon connected itself with the political situation. To understand how this came about, and the close bearing it had on all that followed, a retrospect is necessary.

The popularity of Winthrop, not only in the colony at large but in his own town and church of Boston, had for some time been on the decline. This was due to no fault of his; but would rather seem to have been one of those inexplicable, temporary eclipses which nearly every prominent public man is at some time in the course of his career fated to pass through. With or without cause the community wearies of him, and then, perhaps, presently returns to him; nor in either case can any one say why. The smaller the community, also, the more liable it is to this ebb and flow of popular favor. Accordingly, at the election of 1634, the freemen, without ostensible reason, but in supposed reply to a famous discourse of John Cotton's on the tenure of office by magistrates, had quietly relegated Winthrop to private life, and chosen Dudley governor in his stead. A year later again they chose Haynes, who had then only recently come over, to succeed Dudley.

Among the many newcomers during the terms of these two governors were three persons destined to play parts of especial prominence in the early history of the colony; these three were Anne Hutchinson, Henry Vane and Hugh Peters. It will be necessary to speak in some detail of Mrs. Hutchinson at a later point in the narrative, and her presence in Boston was not at once felt. With the other two it was different. From

the moment they set foot on Massachusetts soil, both
Vane and Peters became leading factors in the development of the colony.

Naturally enough both the people of Massachusetts
and Massachusetts writers have always taken a peculiar interest in the younger Vane. He figures in the
list of those who were governors of the Colony and
the State, and not only was he subsequently prominent among the statesmen of the English Commonwealth, but the romance which hangs about his death
on the scaffold casts a strong gleam of light as well
as a tragic shadow upon what is otherwise rather a
matter of fact and commonplace record of names,
few indeed of which are more than locally remembered. The hand of either the assassin or the headsman is apt, also, to exercise a perturbing and, at
times, even a transmuting influence on the judgments
of history; and this has been especially so in the case
of Vane. At best, his personality is far from being of
the distinct kind; if, indeed, so far as Massachusetts
is concerned, he has not so long been held up as the
ideal of an etherealized Puritan, youthful and poetic,
gracefully wearing his halo of martyrdom, that at last
effusiveness of sentiment has had more to do with
the popular estimate in which he is held, than calm
judgment backed by adequate knowledge. Judged, on
the other hand, in the ordinary way and by what he did
and what he left behind him, " young Sir Harry Vane "
was a born parliamentary leader, and an administrator
who on occasion did not fear to combine with his energy a sufficiency of guile; while, as a thinker and
writer, he was undoubtedly a man of large and aspiring
mind, nourishing lofty ideas far in advance of his time,
but with a faculty of expression by no means equal-

ling the fineness of his thought. Consequently his writings are not only mystical, but they are so involved and dull that Hume was fully justified in pronouncing them unintelligible and devoid of common sense; and now they are read only by the closest students of political history, nor always clearly understood even by them. In the minds and memories of the great majority of well-informed persons of his own country, Vane is associated chiefly with the sonnet addressed to him by Milton, and with Cromwell's ejaculation, as characteristic as it was contemptuous, when he turned the Long Parliament out of doors. It is also remembered that he met with calm courage a death no less cruel than early and undeserved.

When he landed in Boston, in October, 1635, young Vane was scarcely more than a boy. He would seem to have been what in ordinary life is known as an ingenuous youth, in eager sympathy with the most advanced thought of his day. As such he was full of high purpose; but his judgment was by no means mature, and accordingly he was petulant and indiscreet, — at times overbearing. From the outset he impressed himself deeply on the colonists. There was a glamour about him. A solemn sedateness of manner was then in vogue; but the winning faculty none the less made itself felt, and Vane was in person a handsome young patrician, — a man of unusual aspect, as Clarendon phrases it. His zeal and youthful piety, his manifest simplicity and directness of purpose, won all hearts. Furthermore, at this time Massachusetts was sorely pressed by the machinations of Gorges and Laud, and stood in utmost need of friends at court; Vane was the son of a privy-councillor, one of the King's most influential advisers, and, naturally

enough, the colonists, overwhelmed by a sense of their
own littleness, were inclined to magnify out of all
due proportion any possible influence at Whitehall.
Everything therefore contributed and combined to
lend importance to young Vane. His father's son, he
represented also Lords Brooke and Say, the Puritan
patentees of Connecticut; and he had come to New
England upon the express license and command of
King Charles. The result was, that before this "noble young gentleman of excellent parts," as Winthrop
describes him, had been two months in America, the
inhabitants of Boston, at a general meeting upon
public notice, agreed that none of them should sue one
another at law " before that Mr. Henry Vane and the
two elders have had the hearing and deciding of the
cause, if they can." It is no matter for wonder if
such adulation turned the head of the recipient, especially when that recipient was a youth yet in his
twenty-fourth year.

Hugh Peters, the companion of Vane in his outward voyage, was a man of wholly different stamp.
While " young Sir Harry " was innately a patrician,
Peters, though he had been educated at Cambridge,
was of the people. There was more than an absence
of natural fineness in his composition ; he was coarse-
grained. Over ten years Vane's senior, tall and thin,
nervous and active both in mind and in body, Peters
was voluble in speech and afraid of nothing. With
his strong voice and fiery zeal, he was looked upon in
his day as the typical Puritan fanatic and preacher ;
and already, before coming to New England, he was
famous for the success with which he swayed great
audiences. He had himself experienced persecution ;
yet it was not in his nature to brook opposition from

others.   Not long after his arrival at Boston, the banishment of Roger Williams made vacant the Salem
pulpit, and Peters was called to fill it.   This he did
most acceptably through five years, making himself
conspicuous not only for the strict church discipline
he enforced upon his people, but for the bustling out-
door energy with which he devised new business out-
lets for them.   Subsequently, in 1641, he was sent back
to England as a sort of agent of the colony, and during the Civil War he became a fighting chaplain in the
army of the Parliament.   Eliot says that he then " beat
the pulpit drum " for Cromwell ; and Burnet describes
him as " a sort of an enthusiastical buffoon preacher."
He certainly fought, preached and carried despatches
by turns ; now stimulating the soldiery by his wild
eloquence, and now rushing in with them to the sack
of Winchester and Basing House.   When Laud, a
broken, weak old man, was leaving the peers' chamber after his arraignment, Peters overwhelmed him
with abuse, and, had he not been restrained, would
have struck him.   He preached by special appointment before Cromwell and the Commons at the Solemn
Fast during the sittings of the High Court of Justice,
and during the trial he was conspicuous for his exer-
tions among the soldiery to incite them to clamor for
the execution of the King.   Whatever it may have been
at Salem, his oratory at this time was famous for its
extravagance of language, and for the coarse, familiar
interpretations of Scripture by means of which he
was wont to stir his audience and raise a solemn
laugh.   At the funeral of the Protector, he walked by
Milton's side.   Thus, when the Restoration took place,
he had won for himself a dangerous prominence, and
was even looked upon as " the most notorious incen-

diary of all the rebels." As such he was marked for destruction. His trial may be read among those of the Regicides, and he was butchered at Charing Cross on the 16th of October, 1660.[1]

Landing in Boston in October, Vane was admitted to membership of the Boston Church on the $\frac{1st}{11th}$ of November, and during the same month Peters was preaching a sort of commercial crusade in Boston and at Salem, moving the country to organize a fishing company. In January the two, acting apparently in

---

[1] The word "butchered" is here used advisedly, for the details of the execution are incredible in their brutality. John Cook and Hugh Peters were tried and executed together. They were dragged from the gaol to the scaffold on hurdles, the head of Harrison, who had been executed before, being fastened on Cook's hurdle, looking towards him. Peters' courage, alone of those that suffered, did not rise to the occasion. "He was in great amazement and confusion, sitting upon the hurdle like a sot all the way he went, and either plucking the straws or gnawing the fingers of his gloves;" and "he was observed all the while to be drinking some cordial liquors to keep him from fainting." Cook suffered first, bearing himself exultingly, but expressing the wish that Peters "might have been reprieved for some time, as not being prepared or fit to die." When Cook was "cut down and brought to be quartered, one they called Colonel Turner called to the sheriff's men to bring Mr. Peters near, that he might see it, and by and by the hangman came to him, all besmeared in blood, and rubbing his bloody hands together, he (tauntingly) asked, 'Come, how do you like this, Mr. Peters? How do you like this work?' To whom he replied, 'I am not (I thank God) terrified at it, you may do your worst.'" Presently he ascended the ladder, and, "after he had stood stupidly for a while, he put his hand before his eyes and prayed for a short space; and the hangman often remembering him to make haste by checking him with the rope, at last, very unwillingly he was turned off the ladder."

Another account says that "he smiled when he went away," but what he said "either in speech or prayer, it could not be taken, in regard his voice was low at that time, and the people uncivil."

Such was a public political execution at Charing Cross, in the most crowded streets of London, in the year of grace. 1660. See, also, on this subject note (5) in Baxter's *Memoir of Sir Ferdinando Gorges*, 6.

concert, went still further in their efforts for the well-
being of the colony. "Finding some distraction in
the Commonwealth, arising from some difference in
judgment, and withal some alienation of affection
among the magistrates and some other persons of
quality, they procured a meeting at Boston of the
governor [Haynes], the deputy [Bellingham], Mr.
Cotton, Mr. Hooker, Mr. Wilson, and there was present Mr. Winthrop, Mr. Dudley and themselves." The
real cause of the trouble thus mysteriously referred
to, though well understood, by all, could not readily be
set forth in an open, public way, for it was nothing
more nor less than Dudley's jealousy of Winthrop.
This had broken out as early as 1633, and had then
culminated in the famous interview at Charlestown, at
which the former charged the latter with exceeding
his authority as governor. Winthrop, in reply, challenged his critic to show wherein he had so exceeded,
"and speaking this somewhat apprehensively, the deputy began to be in a passion, and told the governor
that, if he were so round, he would be round too. The
governor bad him be round, if he would. So the
deputy rose up in great fury and passion, and the
governor grew very hot also, so as they both fell into
bitterness." A half reconciliation was then effected
through the mediation of the clergy, but the two men
were of different disposition, and Dudley could not
well help criticising Winthrop ; for while Winthrop,
of a calm temper and naturally tolerant, inclined to
the ways of mercy and forbearance, Dudley, a man of
thoroughly intolerant nature, was ever harsh and severe.
Narrow in mind and rough of speech, with all a
narrow-minded man's contempt for opinions different
from his own, "the deputy" was as outspoken as he

was courageous. Accordingly in the Charlestown interview of 1633 he had not hesitated to attack Winthrop for the too great leniency of his administration. Heavier fines, severer whippings, more frequent banishments, were called for; and as this view strongly commended itself to the average Puritan, and especially to the average Puritan divine, it had contributed in no small degree to the decline of Winthrop's popularity, and Dudley's final substitution for him in the position of governor.[1] And so, as Winthrop put it, " factions began to grow among the people, some adhering more to the old governor, and others to the late governor, Mr. Dudley, — the former carrying matters with more lenity, and the latter with more severity."

The meeting now arranged by Vane and Peters

[1] Winthrop has been regarded by most of the native New England historians, and notably by Palfrey, with a veneration which has impaired respect for their judgment whenever the authority of the first governor is invoked. They see things only through his eyes, and the ordinary scrutiny of modern historical criticism is laid aside where he is involved. Repeated instances of this indiscriminate adulation will be referred to in the course of this narrative. Nevertheless the difficulty of Winthrop's position, and the skill and high-minded rectitude with which he on the whole demeaned himself, should always be borne in mind. On this point the evidence of a foreign student and investigator carries more weight than that of one to the manor born : — " Every page in the early history of New England bears witness to the patience, the firmness, the far-seeing wisdom of Winthrop. But to estimate these qualities as they deserve, we must never forget what the men were with whom, and in some measure by whom, he worked. To guard the Commonwealth against the attacks of courtiers, churchmen and speculators, was no small task. But it was an even greater achievement to keep impracticable fanatics like Dudley and Endicott within the bounds of reason, and to use for the preservation of the state those headstrong passions which at every turn threatened to rend it asunder." Doyle, *English in America; the Puritan Colonies,* i. 165.

with a view to healing these factions was highly characteristic. The Lord was first sought. The prayer
over, Vane declared the occasion of the meeting and
the result sought to be obtained from it; which he
described as "a more firm and friendly uniting of
minds, especially of Mr. Dudley and Mr. Winthrop."

It must at first have been somewhat awkward for
the officious youth, as both Winthrop and Dudley professed an utter unconsciousness of any ill-feeling or
jealousy. They did not deny that there had been
something of the sort long previous, but Winthrop
professed "solemnly that he knew not of any breach
between his brother Dudley and himself:" while Dudley comfortably remarked "that for his part he came
thither a mere patient; and so left it to others to
utter their own complaints." Fortunately for Vane,
the existing governor, Haynes, then came to his aid,
and, after a certain amount of clumsy circumlocution,
proceeded, "as his manner ever was," to deal with
Winthrop "openly and freely," specifying certain
cases in which the latter had, as he expressed it,
"dealt too remissly in point of justice." To this
Winthrop replied, and, after partly excusing and explaining, came at last to the real point at issue. He
"professed that it was his judgment that, in the infancy of plantation, justice should be administered
with more lenity than in a settled state, because people
were then more apt to transgress, partly of ignorance
of new laws and orders, partly through oppression of
business and other straits; but, if it might be made
clear to him that it was an error, he would be ready
to take up a stricter course." The aid of the clergy
was then invoked. The matter was referred to the
ministers present, — Cotton, Hooker and Wilson, —

to be considered overnight, and the next day they were to report a rule for the future guidance of the magistrates ; and this they did, all agreeing in one conclusion, " that strict discipline, both in criminal offences and in martial affairs, was more needful in plantations than in a settled state, as tending to the honor and safety of the gospel." Winthrop thereupon professed himself satisfied. He admitted that he had theretofore " failed in overmuch lenity and remissness," but promised that he would " endeavor (by God's assistance) to take a more strict course hereafter. Whereupon there was a renewal of love amongst them."

This took place on January $\frac{18}{28}$ and $\frac{19}{29}$, 1636, and in the following May young Vane was chosen governor to succeed John Haynes. He was chosen on the 25th of the month, or what is now the 4th of June. The day following John Wheelwright landed in Boston.

CHAPTER II.

MISTRESS ANNE HUTCHINSON.

WHEN Wheelwright found himself on New England soil, it must have been to the house of his brother-in-law, William Hutchinson, that he first directed his steps. It was the reunion of a family; for not only was Mrs. Wheelwright a sister of Hutchinson, but their mother also had now come over. Nor was Wheelwright himself welcomed there as a relative merely; he was looked upon as another eminent man added to the colony, — a new pulpit light. He at once plunged into whatever of religious or political life the little settlement contained; for of that life the house of William Hutchinson, or rather the house of his wife, Anne Hutchinson, had then for some time been the centre.

It has already been mentioned that the Hutchinsons had come over to New England in 1634, about two years before Wheelwright. Of this couple their contemporaries tell us that the husband was "a man of very mild temper and weak parts, and wholly guided by his wife;" while she was a woman "of a haughty and fierce carriage, of a nimble wit and active spirit,[1] and a very voluble tongue, more bold than a man, though in understanding and judgment inferior to many women." This vigorous bit of pen portraiture shows at least what the "Father of Massa-

---

[1] "Of a ready wit and bold spirit." Winthrop, i. 239, 296.

chusetts " was capable of in that line when thoroughly
aroused ; nor is it necessary here to inquire into its
truth to nature. Suffice it now to say that during the
two years which intervened between her own arrival
in Boston and the arrival of her husband's brother-
in-law, Mistress Anne Hutchinson, as she was called,
slowly, skilfully, conscientiously, had been accumulat-
ing, in the heart of the little, nascent community into
which she had come, that mass of combustible material which was soon to kindle into a fierce blaze.
Wittingly or unwittingly, though probably the latter,
she had entered upon a desperate undertaking, which
she was destined to carry forward with a degree of
courage and persistence, combined with feminine
tact, which made the infant commonwealth throb
through its whole being. She had attempted a premature revolt against an organized and firmly-rooted
oligarchy of theocrats.

The early Massachusetts community was in its essence a religious organization. Church and state
were one ; and the church dominated the state. The
franchise was an incident to church membership.
The minister — the " unworthy prophet of the Lord "
— was the head of the church. There was a deep significance, as there may have been a bitter sneer, in
Blackstone's parting shot as he left Boston, in which
the " lord-bishops " were joined with " the lord-
brethren." At the point it had now reached, the
Reformation of the previous century had resulted in
practically substituting for a time many little popes
and little bishops for the one pope and the few great
bishops. The fundamental principle of that Reformation had been the paramount authority of the Holy
Scriptures as a rule or guide in life, as opposed to the

dictation of popes, synods and councils. The human
mind after centuries of implicit obedience had re-
volted; and, in the revolt, the reaction as usual was
complete. Instead of unquestioning submission to
human authority, no human authority whatever was
allowed to intervene between man and God's Word.
The issue could not be put more forcibly than it was
by John Knox in one of his discussions with Queen
Mary. She said to him : — "You interpret Scripture
after one manner, the Pope and cardinals after another; whom shall I believe, or who shall be judge?"
— and Knox at once replied — "Ye shall believe God,
that plainly speaketh in His Word; and further than
the Word teaches you, ye neither shall believe the
one nor the other. The Word of God is plain; and
if there appear any obscurity in one place, the Holy
Ghost, which is never contrarious to Himself, explains
the same more closely in other places; so that there
can remain no doubt but unto such as obstinately
remain ignorant."

Thus God's Word was beyond question, and it only
remained to interpret it and declare its meaning in
any given case; but the interpreting and the declaring were the function of the clergy. The " lord-brethren " had thus been substituted for the " lord-bishops,"
— many local popes for the one at Rome. The casuistry to which the early New England clergy gravely
had recourse in defending the position thus assumed
might have moved the admiration of a Jesuit. When
earnestly adjured by brethren, more liberal as well as
more logical, not to make men hypocrites by compelling an outward conformity, thus practising that in
exile which they themselves went into exile to escape,
— when thus adjured, they replied that they had fled

from man's inventions; but there was a wide difference between man's inventions and God's institutions,
and they compelled a conformity only to the latter.
The institution being of God, the sin was not in the
magistrate who compelled, but in his perverse will
who stood in need of compulsion.[1] And so the final
"thus saith the Lord" had passed from Rome to
Massachusetts. Priest and inquisition had given way
to bishop and high-commission, and they in their turn
to minister and magistrate.

It is true, this system, unlike that of Rome, carried
within it the seeds of its own decay, for it rested on
discussion, and no final, inspired authority was recognized when irreconcilable differences of opinion arose.
The minister carried with him only such weight as
belonged to his individual character and learning,
and to his ordained position; though "the unworthy
prophet of the Lord," God had not touched that
prophet's lips with fire, nor did he claim to be in
direct communication with Him. Neither were any
intermediates recognized. Early New England ab-
jured all Saints. But when it came to the interpre-
tation of the Scriptures, — the inspired Word, the
one guide both on earth and heavenward, — though
open and almost endless discussion was allowed and
even encouraged, and that discussion, bristling with
dialectics and casuistry, was overlaid with a rubbish
of learning, yet it has not in the result always been
at once apparent wherein the minister differed from

---

[1] "Christ doth not persecute Christ in New England. . . . For
though Christ may and doth afflict his own members; yet he doth
not afflict (much less persecute) Christ in them, but that which is
left of old Adam in them, or that which is found of the seed of
the serpent in them." Cotton, in *Publications of Narragansett Club,*
ii. 27–8.

the priest.   Both priest and minister had recourse to
civil persecution to compel religious conformity ; and,
while the fagots that consumed Servetus and Savon-
arola were not unlike, they forever bear witness to a
strong family resemblance between Romish cowl and
bands of Geneva.

Not unnaturally, therefore, it has of late been somewhat the fashion to ignore this difference between
priest and clergyman, and, indeed, some have even
been disposed to deny its existence.   Like Milton,
they have claimed that after all, — " New Presbyter
[was] but old Priest writ large."   And yet, practically and in point of fact, the difference was not to
be measured, for in itself it was great, and in its logical consequences vital.   It was the same difference
in spiritual matters which exists politically between
an absolute ruler under right divine, and a civil authority exercised under the restrictions of a written
constitution.   In the spiritual contests of the sixteenth and seventeenth centuries the Pope represented
divine right ; the Bible, the written constitution.
The constitution was, it is true, indisputably vague,
and everything depended on the construction given
to its provisions.   Except in certain small localities
like Holland, or among a few most advanced thinkers
of the day, who, like Roger Williams, were looked
upon as visionaries, the conception of spiritual freedom and religious toleration had no more footing in
the mind of the seventeenth century than the idea
of freedom in crime and immunity from its legal penalties has now.   Human thought had not yet grasped
the distinction between personal liberty where the
rights of others are not involved, and license where
those rights are involved ; so far, indeed, from having

grasped this distinction, one of the plainly stated contentions of the more advanced advocates of religious tolerance was, if a man conscientiously disbelieved in the right of any human authority, he ought not to be forced to obey it. None the less, the first great step towards educating the human mind to the difference between spiritual freedom and criminal license was taken when Bible law was substituted for papal dictum. The written word then became matter for judicial construction; but, like any other written law, when once construed and its meaning ascertained by competent and recognized authority, it was held by common consent to be the rule in force. It only remained to compel obedience to it, just as now obedience is compelled to the criminal law. When, therefore, Cotton argued that, while it was wrong to persecute man against conscience, no man's conscience compelled him to reject the truth; and therefore to force the truth upon him could be no violation of conscience, — when he argued in this way he uttered that which to us is foolishness; but, from his standpoint of time and light, he was merely asserting that on points of doubtful construction the law must be established by the tribunal of last resort, and, when once established, must be uniformly obeyed by all or enforced upon all. The fallacy which lurked between his premises and his conclusion did not suggest itself to him. A spiritual authority and a spiritual law were deemed just as necessary as a criminal authority and a criminal law.

Nevertheless, though the divine of the reformed church of the sixteenth century did set himself up as the ordained expounder of the written law, the importance of the ground gained when a written law was

substituted for an inspired dictum must not be lost
sight of. All else followed in due time. In the
searching discussion which ensued, the learning, the
common sense, and finally even the authority and
commission of those who comprised the tribunal, were
questioned; and at last the law itself, and the necessity
of any law, or of general conformity to it, was openly
denied. " This was some time a paradox, but now
the time gives it proof; " but two centuries and a half
ago, to the early New England Puritans, it was worse
than a paradox, — it was a blasphemy. As well doubt
the existence of God himself as question the binding
authority of His Word.

The Hebrew Bible was, then, the fundamental religious law — the spiritual constitution, as it were —
of the Puritan community. The clergy were the ordained and constituted expounders of that law, — the
Supreme Theological Court. Before them and by them
as a tribunal each point at issue was elaborately and
learnedly discussed; reasons were advanced and authorities cited for each decision they rendered. Behind
their decisions was the Word; and behind the Word
was God and His Hereafter. The spiritual organization was complete.

The religion of the Puritan was, also, realistic in all
its parts, — so realistic, indeed, as to be a practical
piece of machinery, — human, mundane machinery.
There was God, the Constitution and the Court —
and the clergy were the Court. But to the men and
women composing the Puritan community, the Court
was no more a reality — hardly more a visible thing
— than the Supreme Being himself; for in those days
religion meant a great deal. It was no sentiment or
abstraction. The superstition which prevailed is to

the modern mind well-nigh inconceivable. All shared
in it. Sleeping and waking, at bed and board, in the
pulpit, in the field or at the work-bench, God and his
providences, the Devil and his snares, were ever present. Their direct interposition was seen in events
the most trivial. A harmless reptile crawls bewildered among the elders at a synod and is killed by
one of them, " and out of doubt the Lord discovered
somewhat of his mind in it ; " so the serpent personi-
fied the Devil, and the synod the churches of Christ,
while Faith was represented by that elder who crushed
the head of the Evil One. There takes place " a great
combat between a mouse and a snake, in the view of
divers witnesses ; " and the pastor of the first church
of Boston interprets the portent to his people, while
the governor of the colony records his words. The
snake is again the Devil, while the mouse becomes
" a poor contemptible people, which God had brought
hither, which should overcome Satan here and dispos-
sess him of his kingdom." Two unfortunate men are
drowned while raking for oysters ; " it was an evident
judgment of God upon them, for they were wicked
persons." The hand of God was heavy also on those
who spake " ill of this good land and the Lord's people here ; " some were taken by the Turks, and they
and their wives and their little ones sold as slaves ;
others were forsaken of their friends, or their daughters went mad or were debauched, or their children
died of the plague, or their ships blew up with all on
board. Soon or late, some ill befell them or theirs ;
and through that ill the finger of the Lord was revealed. A poor barber, called hastily to perform a
dentist's office, and bewildered in a storm of snow
between Boston and Roxbury, is found frozen **to**

death; and presently it is remembered he had been a theological adherent of Mrs. Hutchinson. There befalls a great freshet, and the Indians "being pow-wowing in this tempest, the Devil came and fetched away five of them." A father, industrious or inter-ested in his task, works one hour after Saturday's sunset, and the next day his little child of five years is drowned; and he sees in his misfortune only " the righteous hand of God, for his profaning His holy day against the checks of his own conscience." A wife is suspected of the murder of her husband, a mother of killing her illegitimate child, and as they touched them " the blood came fresh " into the dead faces, and the bodies " bled abundantly." And when the most terrible misfortunes incident to maternity be-fell Anne Hutchinson and her friend, the no less un-happy Mary Dyer, the grave magistrates and clergy, gloating in blasphemous words over each lying detail of the monstrous fruit of their wombs, saw therein " God himself bring in his own vote and suffrage from heaven."

But it is needless to multiply instances. The records of the time are full of them; for even angry men in their disputes would treasure up in memory every trivial or ludicrous mishap which befell their opponents, and, while so doing, they were said to be busy " gathering Providences." The finger of an om-nipresent Almighty was thus visible everywhere and at all times; now meting out rewards and punish-ments while reversing the action of the wind and tide, and then revealing itself in terror through strange portents in the sky.

Among a people educated to this high pitch of fer-vor, theological controversy was the chief end towards

which the higher branches of education were directed.
The Scriptures, and the volumes of commentary upon
them, were the sole literary nutriment; while they
were studied only that scholars might, with gloomy
joy, dispute over the unknowable.   Not that there were
then no other books in the world.   It is true, there
was no light current literature in the modern sense of
the term; but the great body of the classics existed,
and every man and every woman of good education
had a familiarity with them now possessed by few.
They were "the humanities" of the time.   Of the
great names in modern letters, also, the greatest were
already known.   Boccaccio, Dante, Ariosto and Tasso
were familiar in the Italian.   Don Quixote is alluded
to in the New Canaan as a book with which every
one was acquainted.   Rabelais had died nearly a
century before, and the third reprint of Montaigne's
Essays, in its English translation, had appeared in
1632.   Bacon, Shakspeare, Spenser and Ben Jonson
had done their work; Milton was doing his, for it was
in 1634 that Comus was set upon the stage: but, to
the New England Puritan, Spenser was an idle rhyme-
ster, Jonson a profane scoffer, and Shakspeare a wan-
ton playwright.   As to Boccaccio and Rabelais, copies
of their works would in primitive Massachusetts have
been rooted out as Devil's tares.   That there were
French books, as well as Latin, in Governor Winthrop's library, we know; and it is possible to imagine him sitting in his library in primitive Boston
with a volume of Montaigne in his hand: but to Endicott or Dudley and the rest, while those writings of
Cotton, which to us are as devoid of life as they are
of value, were full of interest, the pages of the French
humorist would have seemed idle words.   Fanaticism

is no less destructive to the capacity of general literary enjoyment than a diseased appetite is to a delicate taste. Drunkards crave alcohol, and communities exalted with religious fervor care only for books on theology. Early New England had no others. Some adequate idea of the utter intellectual aridity which consequently prevailed may be derived from the Sewall diary. Sixty years after the Antinomian controversy, Pole's Synopsis, and the expositions of Calvin and Caryl, were the companions of the reading man's leisure, while the Theopolis Americana and the Magnalia were the ripe fruits of the author's brain.

Fortunately, the New Englander came of a hardheaded stock. Though individuals at times lashed themselves into a state of spiritual excitement bordering close upon insanity, and occasionally crossed the line, this was not common. When all was said and done, there was in the early settlers a basis of practical, English common sense, — a habit of composed thought and sober action, which enabled them to bear up with steady gait under draughts of fanaticism sufficiently deep and strong to have sent more volatile brains reeling through paroxysms of delirium. Only twice or thrice in all their history have New Englanders as a mass lost their self-control; and because they lost it then, other communities, with whom losing it has been matter of too frequent occurrence to excite remark, have never forgotten those occasions, nor allowed New Englanders to forget them. Such an occasion was the Antinomian controversy, and such again was the witchcraft mania.

Among this people, — strong, practical, self-contained and tenacious, burning with a superstitious zeal which evinced itself in no sharp, fiery crackle, but in a

steady glow, as of white heat, which two centuries did
not suffice wholly to cool, — among this people stood
the clergy, a class by themselves, almost a caste.
Learned in things theological, highly moral, deeply imbued with a sense both of the dignity and the duties
of their calling, the first generation of New England
divines was no less bigoted as a class than men with
minds at once narrow and strong are wont to be. That
they were to the last degree intolerant needs not be
said, for all men are intolerant who, in their own conceit, know they are right; and upon this point doubt
never entered the minds of the typical divines of that
generation. Their pride of calling was intense. Not
only in their pulpits, but in their daily lives they
were expected to and did make a peculiar sanctification obtrusively manifest. They were not as other
men ; and to this, not only their garments, but their
Scriptural phrase and severe visage bore constant witness. And in these last characteristics — the dress,
the speech and the faces of the clergy — lay the heart
and the heat of the great Antinomian controversy.
The ministers were the privileged class of that community, — " God's unworthy prophets," as they phrased
it. Living in the full odor of sanctity among God's
people, — His chosen people, whom He "preserved
and prospered beyond ordinary ways of Providence,"
— they constituted a powerful governing order. And
now, suddenly, a woman came, and calmly and persistently intimated that, as a class, God's prophets in
New England were not what they seemed. No longer
were they unworthy in their own mouths alone.

Though she is said to have been a cousin of John
Dryden, little is known of Mrs. Hutchinson's ante-
cedents in England; nor is it necessary that much

should be known. Her husband was the owner of an
estate at Alford, and descended from a family the
genealogy of which has since been traced with results
more curious than valuable. Though Alford was so
far from the English Boston that Mrs. Hutchinson
could hardly have been a constant attendant at St.
Botolph's Church, she seems to have been such an
ardent admirer of the Rev. John Cotton that, when
"he kept close for a time, and fitted himself to go to
New England," she prepared to follow. Born about
the year 1600, during the time she lived in Boston —
a little less than four years — Anne Hutchinson was
a woman in the full vigor of life. She had a strong
religious instinct, which caused her to verge closely on
the enthusiast, and a remarkably well-developed con-
troversial talent. But above all else Anne Hutchinson, though devoid of attractiveness of person, was
wonderfully endowed with the indescribable quality
known as magnetism, — that subtle power by which
certain human beings — themselves not knowing how
they do it — irresistibly attract others, and infuse them
with their own individuality. Among the many well-
known phases of emotional religion, that of direct intercourse with the Almighty has not been the least
uncommon ; and, if Mistress Hutchinson did not actually pretend to this, she verged dangerously near it.
She certainly in moments of deep spiritual enthusiasm
felt movements which she professed to regard as direct
divine revelations. Not that she actually claimed to
be inspired, or to speak as one prophesying ; but at
intervals she professed to feel that the Spirit of God
was upon her, and then she was not as her ordinary
self, or as other women. The exact line between this
and inspiration is one not easy to draw ; yet probably

some shadowy line did exist in her mind. However this may be, the mere suggestion of such a thing was enough with the early Massachusetts divines. The doctrine of an inward light was to them peculiarly hateful, and they regarded such a light rather as a gleam of hell fire than as a heaven-born beam. That they themselves were not in any way inspired was a cardinal point in their religious faith.[1] They had for their guide the written Word; and that only. For any one to claim to have more, — to be in direct spiritual communication with the Almighty, — was to assert a superiority in what was the very soul of their calling. They were " unworthy prophets " of the Lord; and here was one who claimed to be more nearly than they in the Master's confidence. But the God they worshipped was that same Jehovah with whom direct and personal intercourse had been held by the prophets of old. He was not a metaphysical abstraction. Freely pictured in glass and on canvas, the awe with which a finer sense has since surrounded Him did not surround Him then. Always present, always in that human form in which He revealed himself to Moses, his face might well be seen at any moment, even as his voice was often heard and his hand felt. But to them, his servants, He had given only his Scriptures through which to ascertain his will. When, therefore, Mistress Hutchinson claimed, through a process of introspection, to evolve a know-

---

[1] This was explicitly set forth in the Westminster Confession of 1643: " The whole Council of God concerning all things necessary for his own Glory, Men's Salvation, Faith and Life, is either expressly set down in Scripture, or by good and necessary Consequence may be deduced from Scripture: Unto which nothing at any time is to be added, whether by new Revelations of the Spirit, or Traditions of Men." See, also, Ellis, *The Puritan Age in Massachusetts,* 124–166.

ledge of the divine will from her own inner consciousness, she not only, in the eyes of the ministers, began
to share in the blasphemies of Knipperdolling and
John of Leyden, but she did so through the assertion
of a most impudent and irritating superiority. If she
did not directly say it, her every act was a repetition
of the phrase, " I am holier than thou ! "

Thus Mrs. Hutchinson's whole course in Massachusetts was a direct and insulting challenge to the body
of the clergy. Bad enough in itself from their point
of view, it was aggravated by the feminine ingenuity
with which she made herself disagreeable. She belonged to a type of her sex for the production of
which New England has since achieved a considerable
notoriety. She seems to have been essentially transcendental. She might perhaps not inaptly be termed
the great prototype of that misty school. She knew
much ; but she talked out of all proportion to her
knowledge. She had thought a good deal, and by
no means clearly ; having not infrequently mistaken
words for ideas, as persons with more inclination than
aptitude for controversy are wont to do. To confute
her was not easy, for her disputation was involved in
a mist of language which gave the vagueness of a
shadow to whatever she might be supposed to assert.
Nevertheless, here was this eloquent mystic lifting up
her voice under the very eaves of the sanctuary, and
throwing the subtle charm of her magnetism over the
hearts of God's people.

Boston was in 1637 the village capital of an infant
colony. It was a very small place, — so small that
when Josselyn visited it, a year later, he spoke of it as
containing not above twenty or thirty houses. In this
he must have been mistaken, as a stranger often is, in

roughly estimating the size of a town new to him; for, even then, Boston must have numbered about two thousand inhabitants of all ages.[1] The original huts and cabins, of rough-hewn logs, were fast giving place to a better class of frame houses, the Elizabethan fronts and overhanging gables of which looked out on crooked, unpaved lanes, something more than cow-paths, but not yet streets. No building in the town was eight years old, and the new brick house of Mr. Coddington, the treasurer of the province, was the only one of the kind. It was a hard-working little community; but, when work was done, only religion remained upon which social and intellectual cravings could expend themselves. There were no newspapers, — no dances, parties, concerts, theatres or libraries. They had the Sabbath services, followed by the church-meetings, and the Thursday lectures. The wedding was a civil service; the funeral a sombre observance.[2] In a state of society such as this it was inevitable that the love of excitement, common to all mankind, should take a morbid shape. There must be religious sensations, seeing there could be no other; and the place

[1] It is difficult to see how, with the strict church attendance then exacted, so large a population could have been accommodated in one meeting-house. Yet in 1638 Boston was called upon to furnish twenty-six men for the Pequot War, out of a total levy of one hundred and sixty. The population of Massachusetts in 1637 could not well have been less than twelve thousand. (See *supra*, 340, n.) It was probably more than that. If the levy was proportional, it would indicate for Boston a population of at least one thousand nine hundred and fifty.

[2] " Marriages are solemnized and done by the Magistrates, and not by the Ministers. At burials, nothing is read, nor any funeral Sermon made, but all the neighborhood, or a good company of them, come together by tolling of the bell, and carry the dead solemnly to his grave, and there stand by him while he is buried. The ministers are not commonly present." Lechford, *Plain Dealing*, 94.

was so small that a moderate-sized sensation absorbed
it wholly.   Though the stage was far from large, Mrs.
Hutchinson found it admirably prepared for her; the
audience craved excitement, every eye was upon her,
her voice filled the theatre.

During her earlier life in Boston she seems to have
acquired a well-deserved popularity by her considerate
spirit and skill as a nurse and adviser in cases of child-
birth, and ailments peculiar to her sex.   She was evidently gentle, and by nature sympathetic.   Then she
began to meddle with theology, to which, from the
first, she had shown herself much inclined.   Even on
her voyage her utterances had excited doubts as to her
orthodoxy in the mind of the Rev. Zachariah Symmes, a
devout man who had come with her; and his warnings
to the magistrates for a time delayed her admission to
the church.   But admitted she was at last, and about
two years later she began to make her presence felt.
Her husband's house stood in what might be called
the fashionable quarter of the town, — a good stone's
throw to the south of the church and behind it, not far
from the town spring, and nearly opposite the house
of Governor Winthrop.[1]   Here, and at the homes of
certain of her acquaintances, she presently began to
hold a series of exclusively female gatherings, and
later of gatherings composed of both sexes.   At the
earlier of these she herself presided, and in all she was
the leading spirit.   These meetings were numerously
attended, and at those held exclusively for women,
forty, sixty, and even eighty would be present.   The
original idea was to recapitulate, for the benefit of

---

[1] It occupied the Old Corner Bookstore lot, now so called, on Washington and School streets, extending up the latter to the present City
Hall enclosure. *Memorial History of Boston*, i. 174, n., 579, n.

such as had been unable to attend Sabbath services,
the substance of the recent discourses of the clergy,
and more particularly of Cotton. Small private gatherings of a similar character had been not uncommon
ever since the beginning of the settlement; but, though
the idea was not new with Mrs. Hutchinson, she developed it. Under her inspiration the germ grew
rapidly; or, as she might herself have said, it came
up in a night, even as the gourd came up which God
prepared for Jonah. The woman was in fact a born
social leader. Her meetings were the events of a primitive season.

At first the elders and magistrates favored them
and smiled upon her. It looked like an awakening;
souls were being drawn to Christ. It soon became
what would now be known as a revival. But Anne
Hutchinson was light-headed as well as voluble. She
had an unruly tongue as well as an insatiable ambition,
and, not long contenting herself with the mere repetition of sermons, she began to comment upon them, to
interpret and to criticise. In other words, she set up
as a preacher on her own account. The women were
not accustomed to hear one of their own sex " exercise," and she was popular among them; so they
flocked to her more and more. A community living
in a state of religious exaltation is of course predis-
posed to mental epidemics. Accordingly, to the utter
dismay of the clergy and the old magistrates, every one
near enough to feel her influence was soon running
after the new light. " It was a wonder," wrote Winthrop, " upon what a sudden the whole church of Boston (some few excepted) were become her new con-
verts, and many also out of the church, and of other
churches also ; yea ! many profane persons became of

her opinion." And in another place he asserts that
" she had more resort to her for counsell about matter
of conscience than any minister (I might say all the
elders) in the country." To the same effect the Rev.
Thomas Weld declared that she " had some of all sorts
and quality in all places to defend and patronize " her
opinions ; " some of the magistrates, some gentlemen,
some scholars and men of learning, some burgesses of
our General Court, some of our captains and soldiers,
some chief men in towns, and some men eminent for
religion, parts and wit." Then Mrs. Hutchinson's
head turned. She had a calling to be a religious enthusiast, and it would seem that visions of political
greatness also began to float before her. In imag-
ination she saw her husband seated in the chair of
Winthrop and of Vane, with herself by his side, " a
prophetess, raised up of God for some great work now
at hand, as the calling of the Jews."

Unfortunately for Mistress Hutchinson, what has
since been known as " the emancipation of woman "
had not in the first half of the seventeenth century
been formulated among political issues, and the more
conservative soon began to look upon her much as
Governor Winthrop subsequently looked on crazy
Mistress Ann Hopkins, — " a godly young woman
and of special parts," who had lost her understanding
" by occasion of her giving herself wholly to reading and writing ; " whereas, " if she had attended her
household affairs, and such things as belong to women,
and not gone out of her way and calling to meddle
in such things as are proper for men, whose minds
are stronger, etc., she had kept her wits, and might
have improved them usefully and honorably in the
place God had set her."

But at first Mrs. Hutchinson was encouraged. In modern language, she was even fashionable ; her *séances* were in vogue. Not only did the thoughtful and the half-crazed, but the very parasites flocked to them. Side by side with young Harry Vane were Richard Gridley, " an honest, poore man, but very apt to meddle in publike affaires, beyond his calling or skill," and canny Jane Hawkins, " notorious for familiarity with the Devil." [1] Indeed, there have not come down to us from those times many touches of nature more life-like than Wheelwright's description of the grounds of " goodwife Hawkins's " Antinomianism. The Rev. Thomas Weld had accused her, in the language just quoted, of being a witch ; whereupon Wheelwright very sensibly replied that she was —

" A poore, silly woman, yet having so much wit as, perceiving Mrs. Hutchinson ambitious of proselytes, to supply her wants she attended on her weekly lecture (as it is called), where, when Mrs. Hutchinson broached any new doctrine, she would be the first would taste of it : And being demanded whether it were not clear to her, though she understood it not, yet would say, *Oh yes, very clear.* By which means she got, through Mrs. Hutchinson's affection to her, some good victuals, insomuch that some said she followed Christ for loaves. Now seeing those things were so, me thinks our Author need not have been so rigid in his opinion of her . . . when, as it appears, she complied with her patroness, not so much out of love to her positions as possets, — being guilty, I think, of no other sorcery, unless it were conjuring the spirit of Error into a Cordial." [2]

[1] Weld, *Short Story*, 31. The unfortunate Jane Hawkins' proclivities to the Evil One gave Governor Winthrop much trouble ; for " she grew into great suspicion to be a witch " (Winthrop, i. *263). Where no other sources of information are cited, Winthrop's *History*, and Weld's *Short Story* are the authorities for the narrative.

[2] Bell, *John Wheelwright*, 198.

For the severe old theocrats it was a serious matter to have a school of criticism — a *vivâ voce* weekly religious review, as it were — thus spring into life, under the very eaves of the meeting-house. They had been accustomed to have their teachings accepted as oracles; but those teachings now no longer passed unchallenged, nor were the voices of the critics hushed even at the gates of the tabernacle. On the contrary both Mrs. Hutchinson and her disciples audaciously carried their war into Africa. She herself publicly left the congregation when the pastor, Wilson, rose to preach. Others followed her example, contemptuously turning their backs on their ministers; while it was plaintively observed that "the most of them were women, and they pretended many excuses for their going out, which it was not easy to convince of falsehood in them, or of their contempt" of the pastor.[1] Yet others boldly and in open meeting challenged the minister's words almost before they had passed his lips. So that the Rev. Thomas Weld was driven lugubriously to exclaim, with a degree of feeling which speaks volumes as to his own individual experiences in that kind, —

"Now, after our sermons were ended at our public lectures, you might have seen half a dozen pistols discharged at the face of the preacher (I mean) so many objections made by the opinionists in the open assembly against our doctrine delivered, if it suited not their new fancies, to the marvellous weakening of holy truths delivered. . . . Now the faithful ministers of Christ must have dung cast on their faces, and be no better than legal preachers, Baal's priests, Popish factors, Scribes, Pharisees, and opposers of Christ himself! Now they must be pointed at, as it were with the finger, and reproached by name."

[1] Cotton, *Way Cleared,* 61.

The cup was indeed a bitter one. Yet, bitter at best, it was administered with a perverse ingenuity which distilled it to gall. Mistress Hutchinson professed what was called, in the theological parlance of the time, the Covenant of Grace, as distinguished from the Covenant of Works. Without going into any detailed explanation of long-forgotten seventeenth century theology, it is sufficient for present purposes to say that the relations of the Creator with mankind seem in it to have been largely based on the analogy of a human landlord and tenant. To mankind the earth had been given; not outright, but on certain terms and conditions, all of which were expressed in the Hebrew Bible. These terms, as primarily set forth, had been violated by Adam, and the original covenant between Creator and created, known as the Covenant of Works, had then ceased to be binding, and been terminated by one party to it. Under this covenant all of the seed of Adam would have been saved, and enjoyed after mundane death an eternity of heavenly life. When the original Covenant of Works was thus cancelled, the Creator, instead of, so to speak, ejecting and destroying Adam, made, out of a spirit of pure mercy, a new covenant with him and his seed, under which not all of the sons of man would be saved, but only such of them as the Creator might see fit to spare, — the Lord's elect. And this was known as the Covenant of Grace.[1]

---

[1] " To open and clear this matter the following *Positions* may be laid down.

1. " *It has pleased God all along from the beginning of the World to transact with man in a Covenant way.* This is an effect of God's good pleasure towards him. God could be no debtor to his creature, till he made himself so by his own *promise.* He might, if he had so pleas'd, stood upon his Sovereignty, and challenged the Obedience

Originally, therefore, for one to be under a Covenant of Works meant to be of those left under the original and violated compact, and consequently not included among those admitted to the benefits of the new compact, or Covenant of Grace.   In other words, those under a Covenant of Works were the unregenerate seed of Adam, — not the Lord's elect; those under a Covenant of Grace were the regenerate seed. The whole question went back to the third chapter of the book of Genesis, — the garden, the serpent, original sin and the fall of man.

The theory of the two covenants, starting from this far-away origin, underwent during the fierce religious controversies of the reformation an outward change at

from him that was due to him, without engaging any reward for it. But to shew his *goodness* and bounty to man, he has been pleas'd to bind himself to him by Covenant.

2. "*GOD never has made but two Covenants with man:* which are ordinarily distinguish'd into, the *Covenant of Works*, and the *Covenant of Grace*. The Covenant of Works, was that which God made with *Adam* in a state of Innocence; in which all *his* seed were comprehended with him: and under which, he as their *Head* stood a probationer for life, upon the condition of perfect obedience. Of this Covenant we have an account in many places of Scripture. The *Covenant of Grace* is with *man fallen:* the first revelation whereof was made presently after God had past sentence upon him; and the first account we have of it is in that *promise*, Gen. 3. 15. And was more and more *explain'd* as God saw fit at *divers times*, and in *divers ways* to the *fathers* by the *Prophets:* but especially to *Abraham* and the Church of *Israel;* as the writings of the *Prophets* fully shew." Williams, *Essay to Prove the Interest of the Children of Believers in the Covenant* (1727), 5–6.

Winthrop says that Mrs. Hutchinson "brought over with her two dangerous errors: 1. That the person of the Holy Ghost dwells in a justified person. 2. That no sanctification can help to evidence to us our justification. From these two grew many branches; as, 1, Our union with the Holy Ghost, so as a Christian remains dead to every spiritual action, and hath no gifts nor graces, other than such as are in hypocrites, nor any other sanctification but the Holy Ghost himself." (i. *200.) This is Winthrop's first mention of Mrs. Hutchinson.

the hands of Luther. It was, indeed, a necessary part
of the reaction against mediæval Romanism that heart-
piety and spiritual exaltation, or justification by faith
as it was termed, should be opposed to the tests of
confession, penance, pilgrimages, legacies to the church,
masses, Ave Marias, etc., all constituting justification
by works. In the theological parlance of the sixteenth
and seventeenth centuries, therefore, neither grace nor
works, as applied to the two covenants, signified what
they signified in the beginning, or what they signify
now.   Grace was no longer an act of supreme mercy,
as at first, nor was it conscientious carriage in life, as
now; but it implied a certain vague and mystic exaltation and serenity of soul arising from the consciousness of a Heaven-directed heart, — a serenity not to
be attained by the most exact observance of the formalities of religion; the word works, on the other
hand, did not imply, as now it would, the idea of a
life devoted to good deeds, as distinguished from one
of mere empty professions, but it meant simply a rigid
and exact compliance with the forms of pietism, — its
fastings, its prayers, its sanctimoniousness and harsh
discipline, — in a word, with all external observances
involving continuous mortification of soul as well as
body.[1]   Viewed from a modern point of view the seventeenth century Covenant of Grace was as mystic, indefinable and delusive as its Covenant of Works was
harsh, material and repulsive.

Nevertheless, there the two covenants were, the very
corner-stones of theology, — recorded and set forth
from the beginning of the world, accepted by all. The
single question was as to the elect, — which among

[1] This difficult subject is fully discussed by Dr. G. E. Ellis in his
Puritan Age in Massachusetts, 300–362.

the living seed of Adam were, through the Covenant of Grace, to enjoy life everlasting? — and which, walking under the Covenant of Works, were damned to an eternity of Hell fire? When, dead in the flesh, the immortal soul of the believer appeared before God's judgment seat, how justify the life which had been lived? What pleas for salvation would be listened to? And one class of religionists insisted that a record of faithfully observed rules of conduct, a careful regard for the decalogue, alms, fasts, Sabbath attendance, — all this was but to claim the advantage of the abrogated Covenant of Works. Hell yawned for such. On the other hand was infinite faith, a love of Christ unlimited, an inward sweetness and light, — and these, in their case they proclaimed, meant a justification through Grace.

The only certain elements in the awful problem were death and the judgment. The situation, accordingly, is not one conceivable now; but it was very real among those dwelling in Massachusetts in 1636, when Mistress Anne Hutchinson proceeded to draw the line. With her it may be said to have been a question of afflatus, for she contended that the divine spirit dwelt in every true believer; but that the fact of any single person — even though such person might be a minister of the gospel, of extraordinary gifts — being a true believer, could not with any certainty be inferred either from a demeanor of sanctity or from conduct in life. Mrs. Hutchinson's Covenant of Grace is, perhaps, most nearly expressed in modern religious cant as a " condition of true inwardness." But with her it further implied the actual indwelling of the Spirit of the Lord. He in whom that Spirit dwelt was of the elect. He in whom it did not dwell might be a very worthy man, and what we would call a good conventional minister; but God's seal was not on his lips.

The conclusion to be drawn from all this was painfully apparent. To say that a grave divine was under a Covenant of Works was a gentle paraphrase for calling him a "whited sepulchre." This certainly was bold enough; but Mrs. Hutchinson did not stop here. With great cunningness of aggravation — with an almost unsurpassed faculty of making herself innocently offensive — she then proceeded, not to designate particular divines as being under a Covenant of Works, but to single out two of their whole order as walking in a Covenant of Grace. These two were John Cotton, and, after his arrival, John Wheelwright. The others were necessarily left to make the best of an obvious inference.

Looked at even after the lapse of two centuries and a half, and in the cold perspective of history, it must be conceded that this was more than the meekest of human flesh could be expected quietly to endure; but the early clergy were not conspicuous for meekness. Nor had they come to New England with this end in view. On the contrary, they had come expecting God's people to be there ruled by God's Word; and that Word God's ministers were to interpret. And now, on the very threshold of this theocracy, the sanctity of His mouthpiece was disputed. They loved controversy dearly; but this was no case for controversy. God's kingdom was threatened from within; the serpent was among them. The head of the serpent must be crushed. So they sternly girded themselves for the fray: and opposed to them was one woman only; but her tongue was as a sword, and she had her sex for a shield.

CHAPTER III.

A QUARREL IN A VESTRY.

IT was not until it reached its later stages that what has passed into New England's history as the Antinomian controversy involved the whole province of Massachusetts. At first it was confined to the church in Boston, — a family affair, so to speak. Mrs. Hutchinson, like many other women before and since, did not fancy her minister. He failed to appeal to her. The cause of her dislike is not known. Most probably it lay upon the surface and was of a personal character; for the Rev. John Wilson, though doubtless in his way a worthy, well-intentioned man of the commonplace, conventional kind, had about him little that was either sympathetic or attractive. Harsh in feature and thick of utterance,[1] he was coarse of fibre, — hard, matter-of-fact, unimaginative. In his home and church life he is reputed to have been a not unkindly man, and a " devoted friend and helper to those who needed his love and care; " while in his pulpit he was more remarkable for his strength of faith and zeal for ordinances than for his talents as a preacher. On the other hand, he was by nature stern, unrelenting, bigoted; a man " than whom orthodoxy in New England had no champion more cruel and more ungenerous." [2] Of his conduct and bearing in the Antinomian con-

[1] Johnson, *Wonder-Working Providence*, 40.
[2] J. A. Doyle, *English in America: The Puritan Colonies*, i. 419.

troversy of 1637 much will need to be said in these
pages, while in the Baptist persecution of twenty years
later his zeal and passion led him to revile and even
strike prisoners being led away from the judgment
seat; [1] and, in 1659, when the two Quakers, William
Robinson and Marmaduke Stevenson, were hanged on
Boston Common, the aged pastor of the First Church
not only denounced them fiercely from his pulpit, but
he even railed at them from the foot of the gallows.[2]

[1] " Upon the pronouncing of [my sentence] as I went from the Bar,
I exprest myself in these words : ' I blesse God I am counted worthy to
suffer for the name of Iesus ; ' whereupon Iohn Wilson (their Pastor as
they call him) strook me before the Iudgment Seat, and cursed me,
saying, ' The Curse of God, or Iesus, goe with thee ; ' so we were carried to the Prison." Letter from Obadiah Holmes in *Ill Newes from
New England,* IV. *Mass. Hist. Soc. Coll.* ii. 47.

[2] With these two was Mary Dyer, who will be often referred to in
this narrative. She was reprieved, and, when the others were hanged,
sat on the steps of the scaffold. The story is most characteristic of
the time and people under discussion, but can only be told in the
quaint language of the original chronicle : —
" Then Mary Dyar was called, and your Governour said to her, to
this effect, — Mary Dyar, you shall go to the place whence you came,
and from thence to the place of Execution, and be hanged there until
you are Dead : — To which she replied, The Will of the Lord be
done. — Then your Governour said, Take her away, Marshal : She
Answered, Yea, joyfully shall I go. — So she was brought to the
House of Correction again, and there continued, with her other two
Friends, in Prison, till the 27th of the same Month ; . . . And on the
27th of the 8th Month, aforesaid, ye caus'd the Drums to beat, to
gather your Soldiers together for the Execution ; and after your Worship was ended, your Drums beat again, and your Captain, James Oliver, came with his Band of Men, and the Marshal, and some others,
to the Prison, and the Doors were opened, and your Marshal and Jay-
lor call'd for W. Robinson and M. Stevenson, and had them out of the
Prison, and Mary Dyar out of the House of Correction, . . . and your
Captain, with his Band of Men, led them the back way (it seems you
were afraid of the fore-way, lest it should affect the People too much)
to the Place of Execution, and caused the Drums to beat, when they
attempted to speak (hard Work) and plac'd them near the Drums, for
that purpose, that when they spake, the People might not hear them.

In such a man as this, however useful he might be
for much of the coarser though necessary work of life,
there was little to attract a person of delicate percep-
who in great Multitudes flock'd about them. . . . I say, your Captain
caused his Drums to Beat, when they sought to speak; and his Drums
he would not cease beating, tho' they spake to him, whilst they were
speaking. (A Barbarous Inhumanity never heard of before in the
English Nation, to be used to suffering People.) And as he led them
to the place of Execution, your old bloody Priest, Wilson, your High-
Priest of Boston (who was so old in Blood, that he would have had
Samuel Gorton, and those with him, long ago to be put to Death, for
their Differing in Religion ; and when but one Vote parted it, was so
Mad, that he openly inveighed against them who did it, saying in the
Pulpit, Because thou hast let go the Man, whom I have appointed to
Destruction, Thy Life shall go for his Life, and thy People for his
People ; Preaching from that Text, who said, — He would carry Fire
in one Hand, and Faggots in the other, to Burn all the Quakers in
the World. — Who having some of those Peoples Books in his Hand,
as they were burning the Books of Friends by your Order, threw them
in the Fire, saying, — From the Devil they came, (Blasphemous
Wretch !) and to the Devil let them go. — He who said to ye, when
ye sat on the Blood of these Men, — Hang them,[1] or else (drawing
his Finger athwart his Throat, so making Signs for it to be cut, if ye
did it not) I say, this your bloody old High-Priest, with others of his
Brethren in Iniquity, and in persecuting the Just, met them in your
Train-Field ; and, instead of having a sense upon him suitable to such
an Occasion, and as is usual with Men of any Tenderness, he fell a
Taunting at W. Robinson, and shaking his Hand in a light Scoffing
manner, said, — Shall such Jacks as you come in before Authority
with your Hats on ? — with many other taunting words. To which
W. Robinson replied, — Mind you, mind you, It is for the not putting
off the Hat, we are put to Death. — And when W. Robinson went
cheerfully up the Ladder, to the topmost round above the Gallows,
and spake to the People, — That they suffered not as evil Doers, but
as those who testified and manifested the Truth, and that this was the
Day of their Visitation, and therefore desired them to mind the Light

[1] " This is that Priest Wilson, whom C. Mather, in his late History of New England, so much commends, and with his Brother in Iniquity, John Norton (of whom
more hereafter) ranks with John Cotton (a Man of a better Spirit, in his Day) under the Title of Reverend and Renowned Ministers of the Gospel, comparing him
to David and John the Apostle ; and calls, That Great Saint and Worthy Man, that
was such an irreverent, unworthy and blood-thirsty Persecutor of the People of
God : But, let him know, That Sinners are no Saints ; nor, no Murtherer hath Eternal Life abiding in him, 1 John 3. 15."

tion like Mistress Hutchinson, — nay, more, there must have been in him much that was absolutely repulsive to her. The antipathy clearly was not on the pastor's side. Indeed, at first, in his heavy, mannish way, he seems to have been disposed to patronize his female parishioner, so much his intellectual superior. He encouraged her meetings, manifesting his goodwill whenever occasion offered, and bearing cheerful witness to the ways of free grace. He was not a man to entertain a secret, instinctive distrust; for, though compounded of a clay less fine, he was by nature frank, open and outspoken. Presently his suspicions were aroused. He was human, too, and undoubtedly he began to feel jealous. To the pastor, this constant and public adulation of the teacher could not be altogether grateful. Indeed, it was plainly meant to be otherwise than grateful to him. To bear and forbear was not in the man's nature; so by degrees he passed from open approval to silent disapproval, and then it was not long before he began to speak out. So far as his side of the case was concerned, this did

that was in them, the Light of Christ, of which he Testified, and was now going to Seal it with his Blood. — This old Priest in much Wickedness said, — Hold thy Tongue, be silent, Thou art going to Dye with a Lye in thy Mouth. . . . So, being come to the place of Execution, Hand in Hand, all three of them, as to a Wedding day, with great cheerfulness of Heart; and having taken leave of each other, with the dear Embraces of one another, in the Love of the Lord, your Executioner put W. Robinson to Death, and after him M. Stevenson . . . and, to make up all, when they were thus Martyr'd by your Order, your said Priest, Wilson, made a Ballad of those whom ye had Martyr'd. . . . Three also of Priest Wilson's Grand-Children died within a short time after ye had put these two Servants of the Lord to Death, as something upon his Head, who cared not how he bereaved the Mother, of her Son, and the Children, of their Father, and the Wife, of her Husband. The Judgment of the Lord in . . . which, is to be taken Notice of." *New England Judged* (1661,) pp. 122–5, 126, 136.

not mend matters; for as an antagonist — in what
might be called the socio-parochial fence of that day —
John Wilson was wholly at the mercy of Anne Hutchinson. She was as quick as he was clumsy, and his
grave censure was met with a contempt which was at
once ingenious and studied. Presently she found that
he stood in her way. In Boston there was but one
church; and clearly that church was not large enough
for both. Cotton was Mrs. Hutchinson's favorite
preacher. At his feet she had sat at home; when he
came to New England she soon followed. Next to
Cotton's, she set most store on the teachings of her
husband's kinsman, Wheelwright; and when Wheelwright landed in Boston her influence was at its height.

The church was already split into factions. On
the one side was the pastor, supported by Winthrop
— then deputy — and a few others; on the other
side was Mrs. Hutchinson, carrying with her the
whole body of the members, with the governor, Vane,
at their head. The teacher, Cotton, also notoriously
inclined to her. The young sap was moving in the
tree, and Boston, at least, was ripe for revolt against
the old order of men and of things; but hostilities had
not yet begun.

The coming of Wheelwright brought on a crisis.
It was Mrs. Hutchinson, doubtless, who now conceived
the idea — if indeed she had not already for some time
been entertaining it — of having Wheelwright in-
stalled as an assistant teacher by Cotton's side. This
could not, of course, be agreeable to Wilson, who for
some time must have had cause to realize that his own
religious influence was on the wane; just as he had
seen the political influence of his life-long friend and
patron, Winthrop, wane before. He and his friends

accordingly, if they did not actually oppose the suggestion, received it with coldness. Then Mrs. Hutchinson seems to have begun hostilities. She struck; and she struck none the less hard because the blow was given in a woman's way. She intimated that the pastor of the church was, after all, not an able minister of che New Testament; he was not sealed with the spirit; he was under a Covenant of Works. The conflict now began to rage fiercely all through the little town. Wilson was struggling for what to him was worth more than life, — a minister, he was struggling to sustain himself in his pulpit and before his people. With him was Winthrop. Opposed to him was all Boston. Indeed, the members of his parish seem even now to have been as men infatuated; they acted as those might act who were subject to the wiles of a sorceress.

Meanwhile, outside of Boston all was comparatively quiet. The contagion of the new opinions had, indeed, spread to Roxbury and a few other of the neighboring towns, church-members of which had doubtless attended Mrs. Hutchinson's gatherings; but, as a whole, the rest of the province pursued the even tenor of its way, though the air was full of rumors as to the strange uproar going on in Boston, — the new ideas advanced there, the dissensions in the church; the quarrel between Mr. Wilson and his people, the dubious attitude of Cotton. The sympathies of the other ministers were wholly with Wilson. Not only was he a member of their order of the regular, conventional type, but he was receiving harsh treatment; for the course of Mrs. Hutchinson and those who followed her was as unprovoked and cruel as it was ingenious and feminine.

Presently, therefore, the ministers of the outlying towns determined to intervene, in their brother's behalf, and endeavor to restore peace to his distracted church.   A meeting of the General Court was to take place in October, and it was arranged that the ministers should then come to Boston and hold a conference on these matters among themselves and with the members of the Court.   They did so Tuesday, the 25th, and, Cotton and Wheelwright both taking part with the rest, some progress into the incomprehensible was made.   They agreed on the point of sanctification, " so as they all did hold that sanctification did help to evidence justification ; " but they were not all of a mind as to the "indwelling of the person of the Holy Ghost ; " and none of the ministers were disposed to go the length of asserting " a union of the person of the Holy Ghost, so as to amount to a personal union ; " though it was understood that Mrs. Hutchinson and Governor Vane held even this advanced tenet.   However unintelligible the discussion might be in other respects, one thing was clear, — if the last proposition was admitted, inspiration followed.   The way was open for the appearance of a brood of God's prophets in New England.

The conference resulted in nothing, and the open move, already referred to, was made in favor of Wheelwright as an assistant teacher.   This had already been proposed at the meeting of the Boston church held after the services of the previous Sabbath ; and now on Sunday, the 30th, five days after the conference of the clergy, the proposal was brought up for final action.   The meeting was one of far more than ordinary interest, for it was felt that something decisive was at hand ; and presently, when the ser-

vices were ended, the calling of Wheelwright was formally propounded. It is easy·to imagine the silence
which for a brief space prevailed in the crowded meeting-house. It was at last broken by Winthrop, who
rose and said that he could not give his assent to the
thing proposed. He spoke with much feeling, and
referred to the fact that the church was already well
provided with able ministers, " whose spirits they
knew, and whose labors God had blessed in much love
and sweet peace; " while he objected to Wheel
wright, as being a man " whose spirit they knew not,
and one who seemed to dissent in judgment." He
then proceeded to specify certain questionable doctrines supposed to be entertained by the new candidate, having reference to a distinction between " creatures " and " believers," and the relations of either, or
both, with the Holy Ghost. Vane immediately followed on the other side, and " marvelled " at the point
just made ; quoting the high authority of Cotton in
support of the doctrine in question. This reference
naturally brought Cotton to his feet, who proceeded
to demur and define ; and in closing called upon
Wheelwright to explain himself on a few controverted
points of theology. This the latter then proceeded
to do. When he had finished, Winthrop closed the
debate, for the time being, by declaring that, although
he personally felt the utmost respect for Mr. Wheelwright, yet he could not consent to choose him an
associate teacher, " seeing he was apt to raise doubtful
disputations."

The matter was taken up again the next day. In
the little village community, anything which affected
the church affected every member of it. The proposal
to make Mr. Wheelwright an associate teacher, and

the discussion to which it had given rise, had all that Sunday evening and the next morning been the one subject talked about in every household and at each street corner. A good deal of feeling was evinced also over the position taken by Winthrop; and more yet at the warmth with which he had maintained it. For the last, when the debate was renewed, he made an ample apology. He then went on to state at considerable length his views upon certain " words and phrases, which were of human invention, and tended to doubtful disputation rather than to edification." When he had finished, a profound silence seems to have pervaded the grave, well-ordered assembly. No one rose to reply to him, or to continue the discussion; and here the whole matter was allowed to drop. No factious spirit was shown. According to the rule of the Boston church, it was sufficient that grave opposition had been expressed. The selection of Wheelwright was urged no further.

But Wheelwright was too active and able a man to remain long without a call, and a large and very influential portion of the Boston church was in close sympathy with him. Among these were Coddington, Hutchinson, Hough and others, who held the large allotments, which have been referred to, at the Mount. Those dwelling in that region, though few in number, had for some time been complaining of the hardships their remote and isolated position imposed upon them. They were mainly poor men with families. Ten or twelve miles from the meeting-house, this distance they had to traverse each Sabbath, or else fail to participate in worship. Accordingly the gathering of a new church at the Mount had been for some time under discussion. The chief objection was that such

action would apparently defeat the very end for which
Boston had received " enlargement," — the upholding
of the town and the original church, — for the loss of
so many leading members of both, as would move
away if a new society was gathered, could not but be
severely felt.   To meet this objection it had been arranged in the September previous that those dwelling
at the Mount should pay a yearly town and church
rate to Boston of sixpence an acre for such lands as
lay within a mile of the water, and threepence an acre
for such as lay inland.   It was a species of non-resi-
dent commutation tax.   This arrangement imposed in
turn on the Boston church a well-understood obligation to make adequate provision for the spiritual well-
fare of those thus tributary to it.   In the days of
sparse settlement the situation could not but occur,
and the natural way of meeting it was to establish
branch churches, or " chappels of ease," as they were
termed in the English church, for the accommodation
of the outlying precincts.[1] Some elder, or gifted
brother, was wont to hold forth, or to prophesy, as it
was phrased, at these each ordinary Sabbath, while
the sacrament was administered at stated periods in
the mother church.

As soon as Winthrop's dissent had put a final stop
to the plan of choosing Wheelwright associate teacher,
the friends of the latter from the Mount had recourse
to this plan.   At the very meeting at which Winthrop insisted on his objection, the records of the
First Church show that " Our brother, Mr. John
Wheelwright, was granted unto for the preparing for
a church gathering at Mount Woollystone, upon a
petition from some of them that were resident there."

[1] III. *Mass. Hist. Coll.* iii. 75.

This vote was passed on the 30th of October. On the 20th of February following, an allotment of two hundred and fifty acres of land at the Mount was made to the new pastor, to be located " where may be most convenient, without prejudice to setting up a towne there." Wheelwright seems to have ministered faithfully and acceptably to those settled immediately beyond the Neponset, during a period of almost ex-actly one year.

Chosen to his ministry, if such it might be called, in what are now the earlier days of November, the new pastor may, during the winter's inclemency, have ministered at the homes of his little congregation, and the following spring and summer preached " abroad under a tree," like Phillips and Wilson at Charles-town seven years before ; but in all probability during the succeeding summer of 1637, for John Wheel-wright and under his supervision, the rude meeting-house was built, which afterwards stood for years in Braintree " over the old Bridge " and just south of it, on the rising ground where the road, or trail rather as it then was, between Boston and Plymouth crossed the little streamlet subsequently known as the town brook.[1]

[1] Wilson, 250*th Commemorative Services*, 26, 41 ; *Braintree Records*, 2, 9 ; Pattee, *Old Braintree and Quincy*, 228 ; Lunt, 200*th Anniversary Discourses*, 121-2 ; Adams, *Address in Braintree* (1858), 74.

CHAPTER IV.

A PROVINCE IN A TURMOIL.

THE settlement of Wheelwright at the Mount did not serve to restore theological tranquillity either to the Boston church or to the province. On the contrary, the action of the ministers at their October conference, and the sympathy they had then shown for their brother Wilson, only stimulated Mrs. Hutchinson. Her tongue was more active than ever, and her followers more noisily aggressive. So far from being overawed by authority, she met authority with what sounded very like defiance; for now she declared that his brethren were no better than Wilson. None of them were sealed; none of them were able ministers of the New Testament. They, as well as he, were all under a Covenant of Works; they were Legalists, to a man.

During the month of November, 1636, a long controversy was carried on between Vane and Winthrop, arising out of the discussion at the time of Wheelwright's proposed appointment. Vane, it has been seen, went with Mrs. Hutchinson the full length of maintaining " a personal union with the Holy Ghost." He was not content with Cotton's belief in " the indwelling of the person of the Holy Ghost in a believer." He was apparently disposed to contend that a believer, truly justified, was himself the Holy Ghost. The discussion turned on a metaphysical abstraction,

which the disputants sought to solve by quoting at
each other the English rendering of Hebrew or Greek
texts, and scraps of Patristic learning. Conducted
in writing " for the peace sake of the church, which
all were tender of," it covered the first " three hundred years after Christ " and was, of necessity, absolutely sterile. Both parties to it agreed that the
Holy Ghost was God, and that it dwelt in believers ;
but in what way nowhere appeared, " seeing the Scripture doth not declare it." Winthrop, therefore, earnestly entreated Vane that in the phrase " indwelling
of the person of the Holy Ghost " the " word ' person '
might be forborn, being a term of human invention
and tending to doubtful disputation in this case."

As the rumors of this controversy, and of Vane's
ardent support of the new opinions, spread through
the province, Winthrop's popularity underwent a sudden revival. He was recognized as the champion of
the old theocracy, the defender of the true faith, the
clergy and the ancient order of things. His too great
leniency was forgotten. He was the opponent of
Vane ; he alone in Boston had been faithful found
among the faithless many. Vane, on the other hand,
was rapidly getting his first lesson in realities, and he
did not relish it. From being the umpire in all disputes, — the blessed peacemaker, — he was now, everywhere outside of Boston, looked at askance, as the
great sower of the seeds of dissension in God's vineyard. The most scandalous motives were freely imputed to him ; these troubles were all to promote his
selfish ends. Conscious of the purest purpose only,
young Sir Harry was of a sensitive nature, easily
wrought upon. He probably felt his intellectual superiority to those about him; he knew that his views

were broader than theirs, that he had a larger and firmer grasp of principle. But, after all, a callow youth, he had yet to learn how to bear up successfully against the hard, practical tests to which, fortunately, day-dreams of human progress are wont to be subjected. His nerves, therefore, soon completely got the better of his judgment; and in December, receiving letters from England, he informed his brother magistrates that his immediate return was necessary. At once the General Court was called together to arrange for his departure.

The magistrates and deputies being assembled at Boston, on the $\frac{7th}{17th}$ of December, the Governor made known his intentions. The nature of the urgent demands upon him from England were not publicly stated, but certain of the magistrates to whom the letters had been shown agreed that they were imperative, " though not fit to be imparted to the whole court." Accordingly the members of the Court, after looking at one another for some time in grave perplexity, decided to hold the matter under advisement overnight; and so adjourned. When they met the next morning, one of the magistrates rose and made a speech expressive of the deep regret felt by all at losing such a governor in a time of so great peril, referring more particularly to the Pequot troubles then impending. This either proved too much for the excitable and overwrought Vane, or it afforded him the opportunity for which he was waiting. Suddenly, bursting into a flood of tears before the astonished assembly, he blurted out the true facts in the case, declaring that the causes assigned for his departure were not the real causes, — that even though they involved his whole worldly ruin, they would not have induced him then to depart, if it were not for the wicked accusations advanced against him, as if he were the cause of the dissensions and differences which rent the colony, and which he feared must soon bring down a judgment of God upon them all. This singular confession naturally changed the aspect of the case. Urgent private business in England might afford a governor sufficient reason for vacating his office ; a conviction on his part of impending public disaster was wholly another thing. Accordingly, when Vane had calmed himself and wiped away his tears, the deputies very properly said that if such were his reasons for going, they did not feel bound to give their assent. Vane then went on to protest that what had escaped from him during his recent outburst had been dictated rather by feeling than judgment, — that the private reasons contained in his letters seemed to him imperative, and that he must insist upon receiving leave to depart.

There can be little question that a large majority of the Court were quite willing events should take this course, and, indeed, would have been only too glad to be thus rid of their too impressionable governor. Accordingly a general and respectful silence indicated that assent which it would have been awkward, at least, formally to announce. After some further debate it was then decided to choose a new governor in Vane's place, instead of having the deputy succeed him, and that day week was fixed for holding the court of elections. The matter seemed to be disposed of, and the way was open for the conservatives quietly to resume political control. Winthrop was to replace Vane.

This arrangement wholly failed to meet the views

of the friends of Mrs. Hutchinson. No sooner, therefore, were the tidings generally known in Boston, than the town was alive with excitement. A meeting of certain of the more prominent among the church-members was at once held, and it was decided that Vane must not be permitted to go, — that they did not apprehend the necessity of his departure upon the reasons alleged; and a committee was appointed to wait upon the Court, and present this view of the case. Whereupon Vane, whether quietly or with more tears and passion does not appear, " expressed himself to be an obedient child to the church, and therefore, notwithstanding the license of the court, yet, without the leave of the church, he durst not go away." But the fact would seem to be, that Vane's somewhat transparent *coup de théâtre* failed. The deputies evinced an unanticipated readiness to take him at his word; and so his friends of the church had to help him out of an awkward predicament.

When the day fixed for the new election came, it was merely voted not to proceed, and the election was deferred until the regular time in May. Meanwhile Vane's troubles were by no means lessened by his vacillating and puerile course. The clergy whom he had offended might be narrow-minded bigots; but they were none the less men, stern and determined. A number of them had come to Boston, at the time the new election was to have taken place, to advise with Winthrop and their other friends in the Court as to what course should now be pursued to put an end to the dissensions. They were especially anxious to win Cotton over from the Opinionists, as the followers of Mrs. Hutchinson were called. They were anxious to win him over for two reasons: not only was he the

most eminent man of their order, and as such respected and even revered by them all, but his great
name and authority were a tower of strength to their
opponents, making their cause respectable and shield-
ing it from attack. So Weld, Peters and the rest
now drew up under specific heads the points on which
it was understood Cotton differed from them, and submitted the paper to him, asking for a direct answer
of assent or dissent on every point. Cotton took the
paper and promised a speedy reply.

When Vane heard of this meeting he was deeply
offended, for it had been held without his knowledge.
A day or two later the ministers and the Court met
to consider the situation. The Governor of course
presided, and opened the proceedings by stating in a
general way why they were there gathered. Then
Dudley and others, after the usual practice, exhorted
all to speak freely ; whereupon Vane pointedly remarked, from his place at the head of the table, that,
for his part, he would be content to do so, but that he
understood the ministers were already settling matters
in private and in a church way, among themselves.
Then another scene took place. Hugh Peters stood
up and proceeded sternly to rebuke the Governor.
In language of the utmost plainness he told Vane that,
with all due reverence, it " sadded the ministers' spirits " to see him jealous of their meetings, or apparently
seeking to restrain their liberty. As the loud-voiced
fanatic began to warm in his exhortation, the unfortunate young Governor realized the mistake he had
made and tried to avert the gathering tempest ; he
explained that he had spoken unadvisedly and under
a mistake. Peters could not thus be stopped, and
what ensued was intensely characteristic of the Pres-

byterian and Puritan times. It vividly recalls to mind
those parallel scenes, which only a few years before had
been so common between the ministers of the Scottish
Kirk and the son of Mary Stuart, when they were
wont to scold him from their pulpits, and bid him "to
his knees;" so that once when — as Vane had now
done — James complained of some meeting of theirs as
being without warrant, "Mr. Andrew Melville could
not abide it, but broke off upon the King in so zealous, powerful and unresistible a manner that, howbeit
the King used his authority in most crabbed and
choleric manner, yet Mr. Andrew bore him down,
and uttered the commission as from the mighty God,
calling the King but 'God's silly vassal;'" and,
taking him by the sleeve, told him that there were
"two kings and two kingdoms in Scotland. There
is Christ Jesus the King, and his kingdom the kirk,
whose subject James the Sixth is, and of whose kingdom not a king, nor a lord, nor a head, but a member." And all this he had said to him "divers times
before." So now in New England, Hugh Peters —
speaking, it may safely be assumed, after his wont,
with much vehemency — plainly told Governor Vane
that until he came, less than two years before, the
now troubled churches were at peace. Again the
Governor broke in with the text that the light of the
gospel brings a sword. In reply Peters besought
him "humbly to consider his youth and short experience in the things of God, and to beware of peremptory conclusions, which he perceived him to be very
apt unto." Then the Salem minister launched into
a long discourse on the causes of the new opinions
and divisions, leaving the discomforted chief magis-

trate of Massachusetts to meditate on the consequences
of juvenile indiscretion.[1]

Later in the proceedings Wilson rose and seems to
have relieved his feelings by what Winthrop describes
as " a very sad speech." It would appear indeed to
have been a veritable jeremiad. The pastor of the
church of Boston deplored the condition of things,
and predicted the disintegration of the settlement
unless existing troubles were speedily settled. He
touched upon doctrinal points, and took direct issue
with Cotton, who only that very day had, in a sermon
before the Court, laid down the principle that " sanctification was an evidence of justification." Wilson
now denied this, — though apparently the metaphysical issues involved became at this point too subtle to
be grasped by Winthrop, who alone has given an
account of the debate ; and it is obvious that in this
regard the ordained theological combatants were quite
as much in the dark as those of the laity who strove
to follow them. While one learned divine asserted
a thesis beyond human intelligence to comprehend,
another denied it ; and the lay members of the congregation listened, and tried to look wise over the
spiritual issues involved. As to the practical issues,
no illumination was needed and, in regard to them,
all were sufficiently in earnest ; for, when it came
to trouble in the churches, Mr. Wilson had ground
to stand upon. That did exist ; especially, as his
listeners knew, in his own church. And he attributed
it all to the " new opinions risen up amongst us."
At the conclusion of this diatribe, which evidently

---

[1] Subsequently in England, during the time of the Commmon-
wealth, Vane and Peters would seem to have sustained very friendly
relations towards each other. (Yonge, *Life of Peters*, 5.)

called forth marks of decided approval from the audience, some expression of opinion was taken, and it was found that all the magistrates excepting Vane, Coddington and Hough, and all the ministers excepting Cotton and Wheelwright, were in sympathy with the Boston pastor.

In the way of conferences this month of December, 1636, was a busy time in Boston. Not content with dealing first with Cotton and then with Vane, the visiting clergy appear to have gone to the fountain-head of the trouble, seeking an exchange of views with Mrs. Hutchinson herself.[1] She was nothing loath, and the occasion could not have been otherwise than edifying in the extreme. Being summoned to the place where the ministers were already met, she there found Wilson, Peters, Weld and others of those opposed to her; and of her friends, Cotton, Wheelwright, Leverett (the elder of the Boston church) and a few more. Peters acted as spokesman for the ministers, while Wilson busied himself with taking notes. Addressing Mrs. Hutchinson "with much vehemency and intreaty," Peters urged her, as the source from which all difference had arisen, to explain why she conceived that he and his brethren were different from Cotton

---

[1] This must have been the time of the meeting, though the date of it nowhere appears. Peters, however, in his evidence, says: — "We did address ourselves to the teacher of the church [Cotton] and the court then assembled . . . our desire to the teacher was to tell us wherein the difference lay between him and us. . . . He said that he thought it not according to God to commend this to the magistrates, but to take some other course, and so . . . we thought it good to send for this gentlewoman." (Hutchinson, ii. 490.) Here is a very distinct reference to the conference between his brother ministers and Cotton, which took place, as appears in the text, on December $\frac{1}{2}$ or $\frac{1}{3}$, 1636, and was followed immediately by the interview, described at the trial, between them and Mrs. Hutchinson.

in their ministry, and why she so openly asserted that they taught a Covenant of Works. At first Mrs. Hutchinson would seem, as well she might, to have been somewhat appalled at the presence in which she found herself, and the directness of her arraignment. She was even disposed to deny what was charged. But, when they offered proof, she presently recovered her courage, and even assumed her rôle of prophetess, exclaiming, — "The fear of man is a snare; why should I be afraid?" Then, in reply to Peters' questions, she asserted that there was indeed a wide and broad difference between Cotton and the others, that he preached a Covenant of Grace, and they a Covenant of Works; and, moreover, that they could not preach a Covenant of Grace, because they were not sealed, and were no more able ministers of the gospel than were the disciples before the resurrection of Christ. Cotton, in whose presence all this was said, found his position becoming uncomfortable, and accordingly broke in, objecting to the comparison. But she insisted upon it. Then she instanced Shepard of Cambridge and Weld of Roxbury, as neither of them preaching a Covenant of Grace clearly. The former, she said, was not sealed. "Why do you say that?" he asked. "Because," she replied, "you put love for an evidence." Presently Mr. Phillips of Watertown, observing how reckless her criticisms were, and bethinking himself that she had never heard. him preach, asked her in what his ministry differed from that of Cotton. She apparently asserted that he too was not sealed. As Peters afterwards remarked : — "There was a double seal found out that day," — a broad seal and a little seal, — "which never was." Then the discussion seems to have run off into the unintelligible ;

and, when at last they parted, all were not quite clear
whether what had taken place tended, as a whole, to
allay exasperation or to increase it.

But no such doubt rested on Wilson's speech before
the General Court. That had amounted to nothing
less than an angry arraignment of almost the whole
body of his own people, including both Cotton and
Vane. It excited, therefore, great anger among them,
and at once the contest was transferred back from the
General Court to the Boston church. It was there
proposed to admonish him. Again Winthrop came
to his defence, claiming that, whatever the pastor
might have said before the Court, it was general in
its application, and of a privileged nature. When
called upon to explain what he meant by his statements, and to name those he referred to in them, Wilson did not appear well. He equivocated, in fact,
most barefacedly, professing that he had not intended
to reflect on the Boston church or its members, any
more than upon others. Every one who listened to
him knew that this was not so. Vane and Mrs.
Hutchinson were members of his church. It was
they to whom he had referred ; and what he now said
was not true.

It was at last determined to proceed against him
publicly, and on Tuesday, the $\frac{31st}{10th}$ of $\frac{January}{February}$, the Boston
pastor was arraigned before his flock and in his own
meeting-house. Vane led the attack ; and, after his
nature at that time, he did it violently. Then the
whole congregation followed, pouring bitter and re-
proachful words upon their minister's head. Winthrop and one or two others alone said anything in
the pastor's behalf, and in his journal Winthrop remarked that " it was strange to see how the common

people were led by example to condemn him in that which, it was very probable, divers of them did not understand, nor the rule which he was supposed to have broken; and that such as had known him so long, and what good he had done for the church, should fall upon him with such bitterness for justifying himself in a good cause." Wilson bore the ordeal meekly, answering as best he could, but to little purpose. The great majority were in favor of immediately passing a vote of censure. Throughout Cotton had sympathized with the church, expressing himself with a good deal of feeling; but he had not failed to preserve a certain judgment and moderation. He now intervened, saying that he could not at that time proceed to censure, as the usage of the Boston church required unanimity, and some were opposed to it; nevertheless he did administer a grave exhortation. That the teacher should thus rebuke the pastor, in the presence of the whole congregation, was probably a thing unexampled, and a picture at once suggests itself, of a venerable man standing up, with white hair uncovered before his people, to be reprimanded by his junior. It is, therefore, well to bear in mind that the facts were quite otherwise. Though Wilson was pastor and Cotton teacher, the former was a man not yet fifty, and with a large share of health and vigor; while the latter was not only several years the older of the two, but recognized by all as much the more eminent. Nevertheless, the proceeding was outrageous and unjustifiable. Deeply mortified as he must have been, Wilson bore himself with manly dignity. He took his scolding before his flock in silence, and, going quietly on in his duties, he bided his time. And his time came.

Throughout the next forty days the storm continued to rage with ever-increasing violence. Winthrop and Cotton engaged in a written controversy over the proceedings in Wilson's case, which correspondence Winthrop says was loving and gentle, though in it he " dealt very plainly " with the teacher. A whole brood of new heresies was meanwhile currently alleged to be cropping out in Boston. It was even asserted that such opinions were publicly expressed, " as that the Holy Ghost dwelt in a believer as he is in heaven ; that a man is justified before he believes ; and that faith is no cause for justification." That heresies such as these should be tolerated in any well-ordered Christian community was looked upon by the body of the clergy as wholly out of the question. After due consultation among themselves, therefore, they determined to labor with Cotton once more. He himself afterwards asserted that, through all these times, Mrs. Hutchinson seldom resorted to him, and was never in Vane's confidence or in his. Indeed, he added, probably with a good deal of insight into the woman's character, even when Mistress Hutchinson " did come to me, it was seldom or never, that I can tell of, that she tarried long. I rather think she was loath to resort much to me, or to confer long with me, lest she might seem to learn somewhat from me." [1] But the general report was otherwise ; and so his brethren drew up another schedule of differences, this time under sixteen heads : —

This they " gave to him, entreating him to deliver his judgment directly [on the sixteen points ;] which accordingly he did, and many copies thereof were dispersed about. Some doubts he well cleared, but in some things he gave

[1] *Way Cleared*, 88.

not satisfaction.   The rest of the ministers replied to these
answers, and at large showed their dissent, and the grounds
thereof; and, at the next General Court, held 9th of the
1st, they all assembled at Boston, and agreed to put off all
lectures for three weeks, that they might bring things to
some issue."

CHAPTER V.

THE FAST-DAY SERMON.

SUCH was the condition of affairs in Boston and in the province of Massachusetts when the year 1637 opened. "Every occasion," says Winthrop, "increased the contention, and caused great alienation of minds; and the members of Boston [church], frequenting the lectures of other ministers, did make much disturbance by public questions, and objections to their doctrines, which did any way disagree from their opinions; and it began to be as common here to distinguish between men, by being under a Covenant of Grace or a Covenant of Works, as in other countries between Protestants and Papists."

From the depths of one of the now forgotten controversies in which Luther was a chief participant, the Orthodox faction had exhumed a term of opprobrium to be applied to their opponents; for then to say that a man was an Antinomian or an Anabaptist was even more offensive and injurious than it would be in the present day to speak of him as a communist or a free-lover. It was merely another way of calling him a lawless libertine or a ferocious revolutionist. It would be mere waste of space to go into the history of a religious sect which seems to have existed from the earliest days of the Christian era; suffice it to say that the name Antinomian was coined by Luther and applied to the adherents of John Agricola. It meant, as its derivation implies, that those designated by it set themselves against and above law and denied its restricting force, — though law, it should be added, meant in the religious disputations of the days of Luther the Mosaic code as revealed in the Old Testament, and more especially set forth in the decalogue. In other words, Antinomianism was merely another phase of the same old dispute over the one true and only path to salvation. The idea of the arraignment at the bar of final judgment, universally accepted in those days and that community, has already been alluded to. It was in no way vague, remote or mystical as it has now become. The doctrine that a pure, straightforward, conscientious performance of duty in this life is the best preparation for the life to come, which, under these conditions, may safely be left to take care of itself, — this modern doctrine of justification and salvation had then no vogue. On the contrary the judgment seat was a sternly realistic, matter-of-fact tribunal, fashioned on human models, but never absent from thought, — a living, abiding terror. It was, in the minds of the men and women who then lived, just as much an ordeal to be looked forward to and be prepared for as, with certain classes, the admission to an academy or college or a profession is looked forward to and prepared for now : only, in the former case the question at issue was all-important, and the decision was one from which there was no appeal ; for behind the judgment seat were the gates of Heaven and Hell, — life everlasting or endless torments. As already has been said, — What plea in justification would be accepted at that tribunal ? — The Church of Rome preached the doctrine of works, — obedience to the law as expounded by authority, observance of ceremonies, conformity in life : — the Lutheran, on the other hand, abjuring all forms and ceremonials, put his trust in faith, implicit and unquestioning, and in divine grace.

So far all was simple. The issue was easy to comprehend. But the revealed Word now presented itself, and to it the pitiless logic of Calvin was applied. The biblical dogmas of creation, original sin and redemption through God's grace had to be brought into some accordance with the actualities of this life and the revelation as to the life to come ; omnipotence, omniscience, prevision and predestination were to be accepted and disposed of. Logic gave way under the strain, and human reason sought refuge in the inconceivable. What was right and good and just among men was, necessarily, neither just nor good nor right with God. He was a law unto himself.

Then followed the dogma of the elect. As prescience was a necessary, and so admitted, attribute of the omnipotent God, everything was ordained in advance, and consequently all men were predestined from the beginning, — many would be lost, a few would be saved ; — but, whether lost or saved, the decision had been reached from the beginning and could in no way be influenced. It is difficult to see how what was called Antinomianism did not follow of necessity from these premises. The elect were superior to the restraints of law; and this Luther distinctly asserted. Antinomianism was therefore the refuge of the libertine : — if he was destined to be saved, he would be saved, all possible misdeeds to the contrary notwithstanding; if he was doomed to be lost, the rectitude of a life of restraint would avail him nothing.

As applied to Anne Hutchinson, Henry Vane and John Wheelwright the term Antinomian was, therefore, an intentional misnomer.[1] About them there was no trace of license, no suggestion of immorality or hypocrisy; nor, it must be added, was there any disposition to protestantism, or even increased liberality in religion. They accepted both law and gospel. They denied none of the tenets of Calvin. They merely undertook to graft upon the stern, human logic of those tenets certain most illogical, spiritual offshoots of their own. In other words, they also, like their teacher and prototype the transcendentalists of that earlier day, were in their own estimation the elect of God. Conscious of the indwelling of the Holy Ghost, they, and they only, could look forward with confidence to the inevitable time when, standing before the judgment seat, they should plead in justification the Covenant of Grace.

Such was New England Antinomianism and such was the spiritual issue the Antinomian presented, — an issue harmless enough in our days, though not so wholly devoid of harm then; an issue not easy now to comprehend, nor calculated to excite a feeling of sympathy. Ordinarily it would be dismissed as merely one more phase of religious exaltation. But in the case of Anne Hutchinson and her following, with the spiritual was combined a political issue, and with both yet other issues, social, parochial and individual, until together they made up a drama in which almost no element was wanting. The theological struggle was

---

[1] In his Fast-day sermon, now to be referred to, Wheelwright expressly enjoined his hearers and sympathizers " to have care that we give not occasion to others to say we are libertines or Antinomians." Bell, *Wheelwright*, 175.

between Anne Hutchinson and John Wilson, and it
was over Cotton; the political struggle was between
Vane and Winthrop. Cotton, both factions hoped
to secure. That he now sympathized with those who
preached the new Covenant of Grace, or the Antinomians as their opponents designated them, was apparent; but his brother ministers looked upon him as
a very precious brand which it might yet be given
unto them to snatch from the burning. Anne Hutchinson, with whom the church-people of Boston were
literally infatuated, outside of Boston was regarded
with hate, — and a hate not of the mere conventional
kind, but of that exquisitely rancorous description
which has been set apart by itself and regularly classi-
fied as the *odium theologicum*. Though Wheelwright
had moved to Mount Wollaston, and for several weeks
been ministering to the scattered farmers thereabouts,
his position in the controversy was well understood.
Too sensible and cool-headed to go the whole length
Mrs. Hutchinson went, he did not believe in her misty
transcendental revelations; but, as regards the dogmas of sanctification and the personal presence of the
Holy Ghost in the true believer, he stood in advance
probably of Cotton, and by the side of Vane. None
the less, by classing him with Cotton, as alone being
sealed and preaching a Covenant of Grace, his sister-
in-law had conferred on the minister at the Mount a
dangerous prominence. His position was not like that
of Cotton. He did not enjoy the same reputation or
equal authority. He did not even have a distinct settlement of his own. He rested moreover under the
imputation of inclining to novel and questionable
doctrines. Everything combined, therefore, to centre
upon Wheelwright the angry eyes of his brethren.

He was the representative, the kinsman, the favored preacher of her whom they called the " virago," the " she-Gamaliel," the " American Jezebel." She was a woman, and her sex could not but shield her somewhat. He was a man, and a contentious one ; and as such he invited assault. So over his head the clouds began to gather, black and ominous. An occasion for their bursting only was needed ; and for that his enemies had not long to wait.

On the $\frac{19\text{th}}{29\text{th}}$ of January a solemn fast was held, because of " the miserable estate of the churches in Germany " and in England, the growing Pequot troubles, and the dissensions nearer home. Wheelwright may have preached to his own people at Mount Wollaston on the morning of that day ; but later he seems to have gone to Boston, where in the afternoon he attended church services and listened to a discourse from Cotton. After Cotton had finished, Wheelwright was called upon " to exercise as a private brother ; " and he improved the occasion by delivering his famous sermon.[1] There is strong presumptive evidence that, even on this day of penitential humiliation, certain of God's unworthy prophets were cunningly lying in wait one for another; for, as he held forth, some one among those who listened to him was rapidly taking down a verbatim report of all that he uttered.

Once hostilities are decided upon, a pretext for open war is never far to seek. In itself there was assuredly nothing in that Fast-day sermon which would have attracted any general public notice. It had a very direct bearing on things then exercising the public mind ; but this is usual in occasional discourses. As a matter of taste, so sharp an arraignment of those

[1] Bell, *Wheelwright*, 13, 15, notes 21 and 25.

walking in a Covenant of Works was at that time decidedly out of place, especially when preached from Mr. Wilson's pulpit. Though the congregation, with less than half a dozen exceptions, entirely sympathized in it, yet they all knew, and Mr. Wilson knew, that he, the minister of the church, was receiving an exhortation. It was this apparently which gave the affair what zest it had. In fact the whole thing would seem to have been arranged beforehand between Mrs. Hutchinson and Wheelwright. It bore on its face traits highly suggestive of her handiwork. The Lord, it was seen, might be made to deliver Wilson into the hands of his enemies on the Fast-day; and so Wheelwright stood ready to smite, and spare not.

In common with most writers of his time, and especially theological writers, Wheelwright was always involved and obscure in expression. How, in fact, the congregations of those days understood and followed the pulpit utterances is incomprehensible now. Possibly there was an inspiration of fanaticism then about, which has since passed away; but, more probably, much that was said was not taken in at all, and religious fervor supplied the place of comprehension. The Fast-day sermon is no better calculated for easy comprehension by an audience, or for that matter by a reader even, than are the other productions of Wheelwright's pen. Couched in that peculiar scriptural language in which the Puritan and the Covenanter delighted, and of which the most familiar specimen — *plus Arabe que l'Arabie* — is the address of Ephraim McBriar after the skirmish at Drumclog, it is, except in parts, a very dull performance; and, if delivered to a modern congregation, would hardly excite in those composing it any sensations except curiosity,

soon followed by drowsiness and impatience. But, so
far as phraseology and the corresponding delivery of
the speaker are concerned, the following extracts from
Wheelwright's discourse might well have been the
original which inspired the more brilliant imitation of
Scott : —

"The way we must take, if so be we will not have the
Lord Jesus Christ taken from us, is this, — We must all
prepare for a spiritual combat, — we must put on the whole
armor of God, and must have our loins girt and be ready to
fight. Behold the bed that is Solomon's ; there is threescore
valiant men about it, — valiant men of Israel. Every one
hath his sword in his hand and, being expert in war, hath
his sword girt on his thigh, because of fear in the night. If
we will not fight for the Lord Jesus Christ, Christ may come
to be surprised. Solomon lyeth in his bed; and there is
such men about the bed of Solomon; and they watch over
Solomon, and will not suffer Solomon to be taken away.
And who is this Solomon but the Lord Jesus Christ; and
what is the bed but the church of true believers; and who
are those valiant men of Israel but all the children of God !
They ought to show themselves valiant; they should have
their swords ready ; they must fight, and fight with spiritual
weapons, for the weapons of our warfare are not carnal but
spiritual. And, therefore, wheresoever we live, if we would
have the Lord Jesus Christ to be abundantly present with
us, we must all of us prepare for battle, and come out
against the enemies of the Lord ; and, if we do not strive,
those under a Covenant of Works will prevail. We must
have a special care, therefore, to show ourselves courageous.
All the valiant men of David and all the men of Israel, —
Barak, and Deborah, and Jael, — all must out and fight for
Christ. Curse ye Meroz, because they came not out to help
the Lord against the mighty ! — Therefore, if we will keep
the Lord Jesus Christ and his presence and power amongst
us, we must fight. . . .

" When Christ is thus holden forth to be all in all, — all in the root, all in the branch, all in all, — this is the gospel. This is that fountain open for the inhabitants of Judah and Jerusalem for sin and for uncleanness ; and this is the well, of which the wells under the old testament were certain types. This same well must be kept open. If the Philistines fill it with earth, with the earth of their own inventions, those that are the servants of Isaak, — true believers, — the servants of the Lord, — must open the wells again. This is the light that holdeth forth a great light, that lighteth every one that cometh into the world. And if we mean to keep Christ, we must hold forth this light.

. . . .

" The second action we must perform and the second way we must take is, — When enemies to the truth oppose the ways of God, we must lay hold upon them, we must kill them with the Word of the Lord. The Lord hath given true believers power over the nations, and they shall break them in pieces as shivered with a rod of iron. And what rod of iron is this but the word of the Lord ; — and such honor have all his saints. The Lord hath made us as threshing instruments with teeth, and we must beat the hills as chaff. Therefore, in the fear of God handle the sword of the spirit, the word of God ; — for it is a two-edged sword, and this word of God cutteth men to the heart." [1]

---

[1] In his references to Wheelwright and the Fast-day discourse, Dr. Palfrey, in his History, evinces even more than his usual spirit of reverence for the fathers of New England, and less than his usual accuracy. He speaks of the sermon as " a composition of that character which is common to skilful agitators. Along with disclaimers of the purpose to excite to physical violence, it abounds in language suited to bring about that result. . . . Another art of demagogues Wheelwright perfectly understood. By exhorting his hearers to prepare themselves to be martyrs, he gave them to understand that they were in danger of being so, and that, if they preferred not to be, they must take their measures accordingly." (i. 479, n.) He also remarks that " it was perhaps well that this sermon was delivered at Braintree, and

Though at the time of their delivery these utterances do not seem to have excited any particular remark, they did soon after afford a pretext for open
strife between the factions into which the province
was divided. As the weeks passed on, it became
apparent that a struggle was to take place in the next
General Court. This met on the $\frac{9th}{19th}$ of March, nearly
seven weeks after the fast, and was attended by an
advisory council of clergymen. It has been seen that
all lectures were then deferred for three weeks, that

that the angry men whom it stimulated did not pass Winthrop's house
in returning to their homes.''

The fact is, the sermon was delivered, not at Braintree, but in Boston, and within a stone's throw of Winthrop's house; while there can
be very little doubt that Winthrop was himself among the audience
which listened to it. In their anxiety to justify the subsequent proceedings of the magistrates and clergy, the New England historians
have imagined a condition of affairs existing in Massachusetts in
1635–7 which the evidence does not warrant. They have transformed
the self-contained little New England community into something very
like a French or German mob. The Wheelwright discourse neither
led, nor was intended to lead, to any outbreak of " angry men." Indeed, it did not at the moment excite enough remark to cause Winthrop, after listening to it, to make any mention of it in his journal.
It dealt in no rhetoric or figures of speech which were not usual in the
pulpit oratory of those days.

That Wheelwright was a strong-willed and ambitious divine, prone
to controversy and eager for notoriety, is evident enough; but the
record of his earlier no less than of his later life stamps him as a
thoroughly pure and conscientious man. Every believing controversialist is of necessity an agitator; but " demagogues " rarely enjoy
convictions for the sake of which they suffer, as did Wheelwright
and his friends, persecution and banishment. In the Antinomian controversy the record of Wheelwright is far more creditable to him
than those of Cotton and Winthrop are to them. Finally, there is no
reason whatever to question the judgment of Mather, pronounced
long after the controversy had subsided, that Wheelwright " was a
man of the most unspotted morals and unblemished reputation; "
and that " his worst enemies never looked on him as chargeable with
the least ill practices.''

nothing might hinder the ministers from giving their exclusive attention, during the sessions of the Court, to the one subject uppermost in the minds of all.

Although the opponents of Mrs. Hutchinson controlled every church, and consequently every town in the province outside of Boston, yet the legislature — as then organized under the governorship of Vane — was not unequally divided. A preliminary struggle between the two parties took place over the case of one Stephen Greensmith, who had ventured to express, somewhere and at some time, the opinion that all the ministers, with the exception of Cotton, Wheelwright, "and, as he thought, Mr. Hooker," were under a Covenant of Works, — in other words, were "whited sepulchres." Being adjudged guilty of this sweeping criticism, Greensmith was fined £40, and required to give sureties of £100 for the payment thereof. Who the man was, or why he was thus utilized for example's sake, does not appear. The Court, having in this way indicated its disapproval of the new doctrines, next went on to emphasize its approval of the old. The proceedings of the Boston church against Wilson, because of his jeremiad before the December Court, were reviewed. Winthrop says that they "could not fasten upon such as had prejudiced him," and would seem to imply that it was for this reason — because they could not be fastened upon — that these persons escaped punishment with Greensmith. Yet Winthrop had himself recorded how, on the 31st of December at the church-meeting, "the governor [young Harry Vane] pressed it violently" against the pastor. The chief offender in the case happened, therefore, to be the presiding officer of the Court which thus failed to "fasten upon" him.

Nevertheless the subject was discussed and evidently with warmth, for the ministers were called on to advise upon it. They took the correct ground, laying down the principle that no member of a court, and consequently no person by request advising a court, could be publicly questioned elsewhere for anything said to it. The spirit and tenor of Wilson's speech were then approved by an emphatic majority, this action being, of course, intended as a pointed rebuke to Vane.

So far it was mere skirmishing. The parties were measuring strength before they grappled over the real issue. It had probably now been determined among the ministers that Wheelwright was to be called to a sharp account. His position invited attack ; and his utterances in private, there is every reason to suppose, as well as in public, afforded ready pretext for it. He was the man set up against Wilson, by Wilson's own people, in his own meeting-house. Wilson had there been called to account for a speech made before the Court ; and now the Court proposed to call Wheelwright to like account for a sermon delivered before Wilson's church. No sooner, therefore, had the Court approved of what Wilson had said in December, than it went on to consider what Wheelwright had said in January. The matter of the Fast-day sermon was brought up. In answer to a summons Wheelwright presently appeared, the notes of his discourse, taken at the time of its delivery, were produced, and he was asked if he admitted their correctness. In reply he laid before the Court his own manuscript, and was then dismissed. The next day he was again summoned.

Less than twenty-four hours had elapsed, but during that brief space of time the Court had received a very distinct intimation that the course upon which it seemed to be entering was not to pass unchallenged. It came in the form of a petition, signed by nearly all the members of the Boston church, praying that proceedings in judicial cases should be conducted publicly, and that matters of conscience might be left for the church to deal with. The Court was, in other words, respectfully invited to attend to the matters which properly concerned it, and not to meddle in the affairs of the Boston church. This paper was at once ordered to be returned to those from whom it came, with an indorsement upon it to the effect that the Court considered it presumptuous. The examination of Wheelwright was then proceeded with behind closed doors. His sermon being produced he justified it, and asked to be informed of what, and by whom, he was accused. He was answered that, the sermon being acknowledged by him, the Court would proceed *ex officio*, as it was termed. In other words, it would examine him inquisitorially under oath. This proposal immediately called forth loud expressions of disapproval from those of the members who were friendly to the accused. Voices were heard exclaiming that these were but the methods of the High Commission, and as such were associated in the minds of all with the worst measures of that persecution which had harried them and their brethren out of England. Wheelwright thereupon declined to answer any further questions, and the proceedings for the moment came to a standstill.

The anti-clerical party in the Court now carried their point, in so far that what more was to be done was ordered to be done in public. This decided,

Wheelwright, later in the day, was again summoned.
The room was now thronged, nearly all the clergy of
the colony being among those present, and, his Fast-
day discourse having been again produced, Wheelwright proceeded to justify it, — declaring that he
meant to include in his animadversions "all who
walked in such a way" as he had described to be a
Covenant of Works. The matter was then referred
to the ministers of the other churches, who were
called upon to state whether " they in their ministry
did walk in such a way." As a method of securing
at once evidence, and a verdict upon it, this was ingenious, and worked most satisfactorily. There was
little room for doubt what the answer would be, and
when the Court met the next morning it was ready.
One and all, — Cotton only excepted, — the ministers
replied, they did consider they walked in such a way.

The verdict was thus rendered. But the record was
not to be made up without a further struggle. It yet
remained to declare the judgment of the Court that
Wheelwright was guilty of contempt and sedition.
The doors were again closed, and behind them a debate which lasted two entire days was entered upon.
Nothing is known of its details, except that Winthrop
and Vane were the leaders of the opposing forces, and
the result hung long in the balance. For a time it
seemed as if the extremists would be thwarted by a
small preponderance of voices ; but at last, to quote
the words of one most active in the struggle, " the
priests got two of the magistrates on their side," and
so secured a majority.[1]

The judgment of the Court was announced. But
not even then did Vane abandon the struggle. He

[1] Coddington to Fretwell; cited in Felt's *Eccles. Hist.* ii. 611.

tendered a protest against the action just taken. This protest the Court refused to spread upon its record, on the ground that in it the proceedings were condemned and the convicted divine wholly justified. Another petition from the church of Boston was now presented, which, at a later stage of the struggle, came into sinister prominence. It was a singularly well-drawn paper. Respectful in tone, it was simple, brief, direct and logical. It was, of course, an earnest protest against the action of the Court, and breathed a deep sympathy with the condemned; but at the time no exception was taken to its tone. It seems to have been received as a matter of course, and was placed upon the files of the Court. To it were appended above threescore names.

The conservatives had carried their point. None the less, the struggle had been so severe, the resistance at every point so obstinate and the majorities so small, that the victors were not in a position to follow up their success. Accordingly the sentence upon Wheelwright was deferred to the next General Court, before which he was ordered to appear. So far as he was concerned, therefore, it only remained to decide whether he should, during the interim, be silenced as a preacher. This, also, being a question of church discipline, the magistrates referred to the ministers for their advice; and they naturally hesitated to have recourse to a proceeding so irresistibly suggestive of bitter English memories. Though angry and bigoted, they were honest; and they could not at once, even with Hugh Peters and Thomas Weld as their leaders, introduce into this, their place of refuge from Laud's pursuivants, the most odious features of Laud's ecclesiastical machinery. Weld himself, in-

deed, had good cause to know what it was to be silenced. Six years before, in company with Thomas
Shepard who now again sat by his side, he had stood
before the hated Archbishop, even as Wheelwright
now stood before them. With what face could they
now measure out to him as "that lion" had then
meted out to them? Accordingly the magistrates
were advised not to silence Wheelwright, but to commend his case to the church of Boston, to be dealt
with spiritually. In view of the remonstrance from
members of that church which had just been presented, this course certainly was a forbearing one. It
opened a door to conciliation.

As was the custom, the sessions of the Court had
been held in Boston. But Boston swarmed like an
angry ant-hill with the adherents of those who professed the Covenant of Grace. The influence of an
intense local, though outside, public opinion, all setting strongly one way, had made itself unmistakably
felt throughout the recent stormy sittings, and had
greatly modified the conclusions arrived at by the
deputies. Action taken behind closed doors had been
met within a few hours by earnest protests over long
lists of well-known names. The conservative party,
though in the majority, was none the less the opposition, so long as Vane remained governor. Naturally,
therefore, those composing it felt anxious to have all
further operations conducted amid less uncongenial
surroundings. If it was necessary to proceed to ex-
tremities, it would be expedient, at least, to secure
the removal of the seat of government from Boston
to some other place, at any rate for a time. Accordingly, when all other business was disposed of, the
final move of that session on the part of the con-

servatives was made in the form of a proposition that
the next General Court should meet at Cambridge,
or Newetowne as it was then called.

Though the suggestion was unprecedented, it was
by no means unjustifiable. It was fairly open to
question whether, under the circumstances of intense
excitement then prevailing, the action of the Court
could be looked upon as wholly free from outside
restraint so long as its sittings were in Boston. It
was true there had been no tumult as yet, and the
law-abiding habits of the people made tumults improbable. But the province, though made up of a
tolerably compact body of settlements, was without
any system of mails or public conveyance, — without
newspaper, newsletter, or printing-press. The only
means of communication was by word-of-mouth, or by
letter sent through chance occasion. The boat, the
saddle and the farm-wagon were the forms of carriage ; and he who could command none of these
might either find his way on foot or stay at home.
This was an important fact, not to be disregarded in
any attempt to forecast the result of an impending
election. It was true, the charter-officers of the company were no longer chosen by those only of the freemen who were present and actually voting in the general assembly which elected them. Heretofore this had
been the practice ; but, naturally, the inconvenience
incident to such a system had made itself more and
more felt as the settlements spread over a wider territorial surface, and this inconvenience had been temporarily met by the passage of a recent law permitting
the freemen to send in their votes by proxy, which
law was now to go into operation for the first time.
Still the votes were not to be cast in the towns where

the freemen dwelt, and then canvassed. They were
simply held in the form of proxies to be used in the
case of formal balloting by a deliberative body. That
the coming election would be hotly contested was well
known. It was to take place, as before, in a general
assembly of the freemen ; and, in the course of a contested election held in this way, it was inevitable that
points of order and procedure would arise. These
points, as they arose, would have to be decided by
those actually present, voting *vivâ voce*, or by count
of uplifted hands. If the election was held in Boston, every Boston freeman would assuredly be present, and his vote would count. The freemen from
the other towns would be in a strange place ; they
would be overawed and silenced by the unanimity of
those who felt themselves at home. If riot or violence should occur, the case would be yet worse, for
every advantage would be on one side ; all the dis-
advantages on the other. Then, after the magistrates
were chosen, the sessions of the Court were to be
held. At these sessions matters were to be discussed
and issues were to be decided in regard to which
intense feeling existed. Under such circumstances, a
legislative assembly, which was supreme, could hardly
be expected to hold its sittings in a place where the
whole public sentiment was bitterly opposed to those
composing a majority of that assembly, and where the
local church constituted itself a sort of board of revis-
ion over any action taken.

Though all this was obvious enough, Vane declined
to see it. He was the presiding officer of the Court,
and he met a formal motion for a change of the place
in which its next sessions were to be held, not as a
governor and presiding officer should, but again with

the angry petulance of a displeased boy. He flatly refused to entertain it. Apparently he had not yet learned that those with whom he was dealing were men, — and men quite as decided as he, and a good deal more mature. They were of the class which produced Eliot and Pym, Hampden and Cromwell; and it was not likely they would now be turned from their course by childish opposition: so, when Winthrop, the deputy-governor, hesitated to usurp the presiding officer's functions, upon the ground that he was himself also an inhabitant of Boston, the stern Endicott was equal to the occasion. He submitted the question to a vote, and declared it carried. The Court then adjourned.

CHAPTER VI.

A HOUSE DIVIDED AGAINST ITSELF.

THE charter-election was this year to be held on the $\frac{17\text{th}}{27\text{th}}$ of May, and the time which intervened between the adjournment of the Court in March and that day was one of great excitement. Not only was each party to the theological dispute striving to secure the control of the government, but the fear of an impending war with the dreaded Pequot tribe was in every mind. So far as the church of Boston was concerned, there were no signs whatever that the dissensions which rent it were subsiding. Mr. Wilson and Mrs. Hutchinson could not be brought together. They were separated by something far more insuperable than even theological tenets, — by an extreme personal antipathy.

As the election day drew near, Winthrop and Vane were put forward as opposing candidates, and the adherents of neither neglected any precaution likely to influence the result; while the deep interest felt in that result of itself insured not only a full vote, but a large personal attendance. Though recorded as of May 17, 1637, it is to be borne in mind that the events now to be described really took place on what is with us the 27th of the month, so that, as spring was merging into early summer, the verdure was far advanced. The day was clear and warm, when at one o'clock the freemen gathered in groups about a large oak-tree which stood on the north side of what is now Cambridge Common, where Governor Vane, in English fashion and beneath the open sky, announced the purpose of the meeting, — the annual charter-election. Most of the notabilities of the province, whether magistrates or clergy, were among the large number present. As soon as the meeting was declared ready for business, a parliamentary contest was opened over a petition offered on behalf of many inhabitants of Boston. It was in effect an appeal, in the case of Wheelwright, taken from the deputies to the body of freemen themselves, in General Court assembled. As such, its presentation at that time was clearly not in order ; for, as the day was specially set apart for the choice of magistrates, the choice of magistrates took precedence over everything. If other business could be thrust on the meeting first, it was obvious an election might in this way be defeated, and the colony left without a government. Vane took advantage of his place as presiding officer to insist upon having the paper read. To this Winthrop objected, contending very properly that the special business of the day should first of all be disposed of. As Vane stood firm, an angry debate ensued, and the significance of the change in locality became at once apparent. Had the Court met in Boston, there can be little doubt that Vane, who had forgotten the magistrate in the party leader, would have been sustained in his arbitrary rulings by the voices of those actually present. The position assumed by the youthful governor was striking and dramatic enough; but it was also suggestive of memories connected with that greater and more turbulent forum, in which Gracchus and Sulpicius appealed directly from the senate to the

people of Rome. That, under the strain to which
the eager and too zealous patrician now subjected it,
the meeting did not break into riot, was due only to
the self-control and respect for law and form — the
inherited political habit — of those who composed it.

Separated as the two places were by a broad arm
of the sea, and the adjoining flats and marshes, Boston
was then a long way from Cambridge. Indeed, it is
not easy to realize that the two cities — now so closely
connected by direct, broad thoroughfares, running between continuous rows of buildings — could, even two
centuries and a half ago, have been so far apart that
the passage from one to the other was not only long
and tedious, but at times fraught with peril. Yet
such was the fact. Only a few months after the election of 1637, Winthrop recorded how a young man,
coming alone from Cambridge to Boston in a storm,
perished, and was found dead in his boat ; and, more
than sixty years later, the wife of the president of the
college, having her children with her, was in great
danger while making the same passage, and found her
way to Boston at last over Roxbury neck, after being
driven ashore on the Brookline marshes.[1] On the
4th of July, 1711, Judge Sewall noted down that he
" went to Commencement by Water in a sloop," and
in May, 1637, the most direct way of going to Newetowne from the vicinity of Mr. Wilson's church, at
the head of State Street in Boston, was unquestionably by boat, taken probably at Long Wharf. In a
good shallop, with a favoring breeze and a flood tide,
it was a pleasant sail ; but if the journey was to be
made by land, it would be necessary to cross over to
Charlestown, or go many miles about by way of Bos-

---

[1] Sewall, *Diary*, ii. 74.

ton neck, through Roxbury and Watertown, for there
was as yet no ferry from the foot of the hill below
William Blackstone's house. Accordingly, as had
doubtless been intended when the place was chosen, it
had proved much easier for the freemen of Roxbury,
Watertown, Charlestown and the northern towns to
assemble on Cambridge Common than for those of
Boston; and it speedily became manifest that the
larger number of those present sided with Winthrop.
This fact held in check the friends of Vane. None
the less, threatening speeches drew forth angry words,
and a few of the more hot-headed were on the verge
of coming to blows; some, indeed, did lay hands upon
each other. In the midst of the tumult the pastor
Wilson — his gravity of calling, the stoutness of his
person and his fifty years of age notwithstanding —
clambered up against the trunk of the spreading oak,
and, clinging to one of its branches, began vehemently
to harangue the meeting, exhorting the freemen there
present to look to their charter, and to consider of
the present work of the day, which was therein set
apart for the choosing their magistrates. In reply to
this sudden appeal, a loud cry was raised of " Election! Election!! " in response to which Winthrop, as
deputy-governor, cut the knot by declaring that the
greater number should decide on the course to be
pursued. He then put the question himself. The
response did not admit of doubt. The majority were
clearly in favor of proceeding to an immediate election.

Vane still refused to comply. Then, at last, Winthrop flatly told him that, if he would not go on, they
would go on without him. Remembering how Endicott had dealt with him under very similar circum-

stances only two months before, Vane now gave way
to the inevitable, and the election was allowed to proceed. It resulted in the complete defeat of his party.
He was himself left out of the magistracy, as also
were Wheelwright's two parishioners at the Mount,
Coddington and Hough. The conservative party resumed complete political control under Winthrop as
governor, with the stern and intolerant Dudley as his
deputy. As if also to indicate in a special way their
approval of Endicott's decided course throughout
these proceedings, the deputies, among their first acts
when they met, chose him a member of the standing
council for the term of his life, — an honor which a
year before, in plain defiance of the charter, had been
conferred upon Winthrop and Dudley, the governor
and deputy now elected, and which never was conferred on any except these three. The reaction was
complete.

The freemen of Boston meanwhile had anxiously
watched the election, intentionally deferring the choice
of their own delegates to the new Court, in order that
they might be free to act as events should seem to
make expedient. They now at once, on the morning
of the day after the election, chose as their representatives the defeated candidates for the magistracy, —
Vane, Coddington and Hough. The Court saw fit to
look upon this action as an affront, and, declaring the
election " undue," ordered a new one to be had. A
pretext for this foolish course was found in an alleged
failure to notify two of the Boston freemen of the
meeting to elect. A new warrant was immediately
issued, and notice then given by " private and particular warning from house to house," as a result of
which the contumacious town returned the same three

men. And now the Court, " not finding how they
might reject them," admitted them to their seats.
This was on the $\frac{19th}{29th}$ of May, two days after the general election, — so simple and prompt was the early
procedure.

The Massachusetts General Court of 1637 consisted
of eleven magistrates elected by the freemen of the
colony at large, and thirty-two deputies chosen by the
fourteen towns, and representing them. Magistrates
and deputies sat and voted together, — the separation
into two chambers, as the result of the controversy
between Goodwife Sherman and Captain Keayne over
the slaughtered hog of the latter, not taking place
until five years later, in 1642. Of this body, consisting, all told, of forty-three members, the opponents of
Mrs. Hutchinson had complete control ; might was
wholly on their side, for the opposition was limited to
the three Boston representatives. At first the dominant party used their power sparingly, and an earnest
attempt seems even to have been made to put an end
to strife. It came, too, from influential quarters. The
clergy was not wholly made up of fanatics like Peters,
or of bigots like Weld, or of those by nature contentious, like Wheelwright, and the better class of
them, men like Shepard and Cotton, now evinced a
real desire to reach some common ground. There was
no printing-press in the land, and it was only through
sermons, lectures, disputations, and manuscript writings circulating from hand to hand, that the discussion could be carried on ; but, by the industrious use
of these means, the subtle questions in dispute were
reduced to so fine a point that Winthrop, tolerably
versed as he was in the metaphysico-theologies of the
time, very distinctly intimated that the issues involved

were beyond his comprehension. " Except men of
good understanding," said he, " and such as knew the
bottom of the tenets of those of the other party, few
could see where the difference was." Wheelwright
even, stubborn as he was, showed some signs of yield-
ing. And thus the stumbling-block, the single obstacle which apparently stood in the way of complete
reconciliation, was reduced to this curious thesis, —
to the average modern reader, pure foolishness, —
" Whether the first assurance be by an absolute promise always, and not by a conditional also ; and whether
a man could have any true assurance, without sight of
some such work in his soul as no hypocrite could
attain unto." Translated into modern speech this
meant simply that, Vane and Cotton, representing the
Boston church, accepted the Calvinistic tenet of predestination, and denied that conduct in life, or works,
could be a plea for salvation. In other words, in the
elect, salvation was not conditional ; such were born
to be saved, else Omnipotence was not prescient.
From this logic there seemed, humanly speaking, no
escape, and Antinomianism apparently followed ; but
it was then added that, practically, no one could be
of the elect, or have any real assurance of salvation,
without such genuine moral elevation as was wholly
inconsistent with hypocrisy or licentiousness in life.

There would seem to be nothing in metaphysical
subtleties of this description calculated of necessity to
render those who saw fit to indulge in them an element
of civil danger in the state. Winthrop seems to have
reached some such common-sense conclusion, and at
first his councils prevailed. So presently when, in
the order of legislative business, Wheelwright's case
was taken up, and he again presented himself before

the Court, he was merely dismissed until its next session; though with a significant admonition that in the interval it would be well for him to bethink himself of retracting and reforming his error, if he hoped to receive favor. His answer was thoroughly characteristic of the man and of the times. He boldly declared that if he had been guilty of sedition he ought to be put to death; but that, if the Court meant to proceed against him, he should take his appeal to the King. As for retraction, he had nothing to retract.

Although the more moderate portion of the dominant party were reluctant to go to extremes, and still hoped that some way would open itself to peace and reconciliation, they were not disposed to run any risk of letting the fruits of their victory escape them. They held the magistracy, and they did not propose to be driven from it. The franchise, it has already been mentioned, was an incident to church-membership; and all the churches in the province, save one only, could safely be counted upon. Though such a condition of affairs would seem to have afforded assurance enough, it did not satisfy the dominant party; so it was determined to make assurance doubly sure. With this end in view the General Court now passed an alien law, which may safely be set down as one of the most curious of the many curiosities of partisan legislation.

As is usually the case with legislation of this nature, the alien law of 1637 was intended to meet a particular case. Framed as a general law, it was designed for special application. The tide of immigration to New England was then at its flood. With the rest, Wheelwright and his friends were looking for a large addition to their number in the speedy arrival of a

portion of the church of a Mr. Brierly in England,
who possibly may have been Wheelwright's successor
at Bilsby. One party was already on its way; for,
while the Court sat in June, in July, only a month
later, some of Hutchinson's kinsfolk landed with others
at Boston. Not improbably they were of the Brierly
church. Had they been permitted to remain within
the limits of the patent, there can hardly be any question these people would have settled at the Mount,
where Wheelwright ministered and where William
Hutchinson's farm lay. In the existing state of public opinion they could not, indeed, have very well settled anywhere else. It was with a view to this rein-
forcement of the minority that the General Court in
May passed that alien law of 1637, which imposed
heavy penalties in case strangers were harbored or
allowed to remain in the province above three weeks
without a magistrate's permission. The peculiar point
and hardship of the law lay, of course, in the fact that
all the magistrates, without exception, belonged to one
party in the state, and were wholly devoted to it.[1]

---

[1] The original germ of this law is found in the entry of 30th November, 1635, of the Boston records (*Second Report of Boston Record
Commissioners*, 5). But the act passed by the General Court of 1637
is so singular, and so large a body of Massachusetts town legislation
seems to have originated from it, that it is here printed in full. Its
passage led at the time to a series of papers, attacking and defending
it, from the pens of Vane and Winthrop. These are included in the
Hutchinson Papers. There is an abstract of the discussion in Up-
ham's Life of Vane in Sparks' American Biography (N. S. vol. iv.).
The text of the law (*Records*, i. 196) reads as follows: —
  " It is ordered, that no towne or person shall receive any stranger,
resorting hither with intent to reside in this jurisdiction, nor shall
allow any lot or habitation to any, or entertain any such above three
weeks, except such person shall have allowance under the hands of
some one of the council, or of two other of the magistrates, upon pain
that every town that shall give or sell any lot or habitation to any

When the body of immigrants from the Brierly church landed, they were confronted with this new ordinance. So far as appeared, they were all God-fearing, well disposed, English men and women, and in Boston their friends were in a large majority; yet their friends could not entertain them above three weeks, nor could Boston give or sell them a lot or habitation, under a heavy and recurring penalty. Presently others came, and among them Mrs. Hutchinson's brother.[1] A delay of four months only in the enforcement of the law could be obtained for them from Winthrop. At the expiration of that time they must be without the jurisdiction. They submitted, for they could not help themselves; nor is it now known where they went, though probably they settled in Exeter, in New Hampshire.

Party feeling already ran dangerously high, evincing itself in ways not to be mistaken. The debates in the General Court had been violent and angry; as Winthrop says, even insolent speeches had been delivered. When the result of the election at Cam-

such, not so allowed, shall forfeit £100 for every offence, and every person receiving any such, for longer time than is here expressed, (or than shall be allowed in some special cases, as before, or in case of entertainment of friends resorting from some other parts of this country for a convenient time,) shall forfeit for every offence £40; and for every month after such person shall there continue £20; provided, that if any inhabitant shall not consent to the entertainment of any such person, and shall give notice thereof to any of the magistrates within one month after, such inhabitant shall not be liable to any part of this penalty. This order to continue till the end of the next Court of Elections, and no longer, except it be then confirmed."

[1] Winthrop speaks of "a brother of Mrs. Hutchinson" (i. 278), but he probably meant a brother-in-law. It was apparently Samuel Hutchinson, who received permission to remain in Boston through the winter of 1637 (*Records*, i. 207), and who the next spring accompanied Wheelwright to New Hampshire. (Bell, *Wheelwright*, 34.)

bridge was declared, the sergeants who, as was then
the custom, were in official attendance upon Vane,
armed with swords and halberds, refused to escort
his successor.   They were all Boston men, and their
conduct is the best possible evidence of the unanimity as well as the intensity of the feeling there.   Laying down their halberds they went home, leaving
Winthrop, the newly elected governor, to do the same,
unattended.   When at this time, also, Boston was
called upon to supply her portion of the levy for service in the Pequot campaign, not a church-member
would consent to be mustered; and the refusal was
based on the fact that their own pastor, selected from
among the clergy by lot as the chaplain to accompany
the contingent, walked in a Covenant of Works.   Military service, especially of a somewhat desperate character in savage warfare, is not usually coveted, and in
this case a prudent regard for their own scalps may
at the same time have dulled martial ardor and quickened conscientious doubts in the minds of the church-
members in question; but none the less this holding
back made at the time a deep impression throughout
the other towns of the province, giving "great discouragement to the service," and the apologists for
the subsequent persecution have not failed to put due
emphasis on it since.[1]

As the June days passed away, the alien law was
under discussion at Cambridge, and the excitement in
Boston increased rather than grew less.   From the
time of his first coming, Vane had always occupied at
church a seat of honor among the magistrates, whether
he was one of them or not.   But on the Sabbath after
the election, instead of taking his usual place, he

[1] Palfrey, i. 492.

and Coddington went and sat with the deacons, in a way calculated to excite the utmost possible public notice ; and when Winthrop, noticing this, courteously sent to them to resume their old places, they pointedly declined to do so. As governor, Vane had walked to church in state, accompanied by four of the town's sergeants. They now refused to attend Winthrop, alleging that their attendance on his predecessor had been merely out of personal devotion to him. This could not but have been deeply mortifying to Winthrop; and it occasioned so much scandal that the colony took notice of it, and offered to furnish men, from the neighboring towns in turn, to carry the halberds as usual. Upon this Boston professed itself willing to furnish halberd-bearers, though not the sergeants, and the Governor at last was fain to use two of his own servants, and so settle the matter. Nor were Vane's discourtesies to Winthrop confined to official acts or questions of church etiquette. They touched social relations also. It has already been seen how in June the Governor undertook to give a dinner party to young Lord Ley, and among others sent an invitation to Vane; and how Vane declined to come on the extraordinary ground that " his conscience withheld him ; " but, at the time named for the entertainment, " went over to Noddle's Island to dine with Mr. Maverick, and carried the Lord Ley with him." Besides being the recognized leader of the opposition, Vane was a defeated candidate for office ; and, as such, it was peculiarly incumbent upon him to behave with dignity and self-restraint. Winthrop had already set him a lofty example in this respect: but Winthrop never appeared to such advantage as when bearing up against political defeat,

while Vane now demeaned himself rather like an
angry, sulking schoolboy than like the head of a party
in the state ; and his followers undoubtedly imitated
him.   Consequently, all through the summer of 1637
Winthrop's position must have been most· trying.
Wilson, who had he been there would have shared
the general opprobrium with him, was absent with the
soldiers of the Pequot expedition.   Hence the Governor found himself in Boston — Boston, his home
and the town he had founded — with the whole community as one man against him.   Vane would not go
to his house.   The town officers refused to attend
upon him.   A bitter controversy was going on over
the alien law, which excited so much feeling that Cotton seriously thought of moving out of the province,
while not even the relief and exultation over the triumphant close of the Pequot war drew men's thoughts
away from it.   Nor was this to be wondered at.   The
news of Mason's victories in Connecticut and the
storming of the Pequot fort reached Boston at the
very time when Winthrop, acting under that alien
law, refused to permit Samuel Hutchinson to remain
in the province.   In the hour of common triumph,
therefore, the people of Boston saw their friends, relatives and sympathizers, who had just finished the
weary voyage which joined them in exile, refused even
a resting-place, much more an asylum, — and refused
it, also, merely on the ground that they were the
friends, relatives and sympathizers of the people of
Boston.   Such a stretch of government authority not
only must have seemed an outrage, but it was an
outrage.   It compelled a denial of those rights of
common hospitality which even savages respect, and
as persecution it was not less bitter than any prac-

tised in England. Looked at even now, after the lapse of two hundred years and more, to be forced to send one's brother or sister, at their first coming into a new land, out into the wilderness — even as Abraham sent Hagar — was a sore test of patience. The minority in Boston would have been either more or less than human had they meekly submitted to it. They did not meekly submit to it ; and so, when midsummer was come, there were " many hot speeches given forth," and angry threats were freely made.

Early in August the posture of the opposing factions underwent a change ; Wheelwright lost a potent friend and ally, and the party of the clericals gained one. On the $\frac{3d}{13th}$ Vane sailed for England, and his friends took advantage of his departure to make a political demonstration. The ship he was to go in lay at anchor well down the harbor, opposite Long Island. As the hour for embarking drew near, his political adherents and those who sympathized in his theological views collected together, and formally accompanied their departing leader to his boat. They were under arms, and some cannon had been brought out ; and, as the barges bearing him and a company of friends were rowed out into the stream, they were saluted again and again by volleys of small arms and ordnance. Winthrop was not there to bid his rival farewell ; nor, in view of Vane's studied discourtesies to him, was he to be blamed for his absence. None the less he was mindful of the occasion and what was due to it, and, as the party swept by Castle Island, the salute from the town was taken up by the fort and repeated.

Vane never came back to Boston ; nor, judging by his course while there, is the fact greatly to be

regretted. Doubtless he improved, and, as he grew
older, he became more self-restrained; none the less
he was born an agitator and always remained one,
and it is of men of this description that new countries
stand in least need. Unquestionably as respects the
issues involved in the so-called Antinomian controversy, Vane was, in the abstract, more — much more
— nearly right than Winthrop. But, while his mind
was destructive in its temper, that of Winthrop was
constructive. In new countries everything is to be built
up, and there is little to pull down. In the Massachusetts of 1637, there was nothing but the clergy.
Vane was the popular leader in the first movement
against their supremacy, and the fight he made showed
he possessed parliamentary qualities of a high order;
but, as was apparent in the result of it, the movement itself was premature. After the failure of that
movement its leader would have proved wholly out of
place in New England, while in England he found
ample field for the exercise of all his powers. In the
world's advance every one cannot be on the skirmish
line; nor is the sharp-shooter necessarily a more useful soldier than he who advances only just in front of
the solid line of battle, — even though the latter be
less keen of sight and wide of vision. As compared
with Winthrop, the younger Vane was a man of
larger and more active mind, of more varied and brilliant qualities. What is now known as an advanced
thinker, he instinctively looked deeper into the heart
of his subject. Winthrop, it is true, shared in the
darkness and the superstition, and even — in his calm,
moderate way — in the intolerance of his time; but
it was just that sharing in the weakness as well as the
strength — the superstitions as well as the faith — of

his time which made him so valuable in the place chance called upon him to fill. He was in sympathy with his surroundings, — just enough in the advance, and not too much. In 1637 — persecution or no persecution, momentarily right or momentarily wrong — Massachusetts could far better spare Henry Vane from its councils than it could have spared John Winthrop.

Vane's departure was none the less an irreparable loss, almost a fatal blow, to John Wheelwright, for by it he was deprived of his protector, and left, naked and bound, in the hands of his enemies. Nor did they long delay over the course they would take with him. The Pequot war was ended; for in July the last remnant of the doomed tribe had been destroyed in the swamp fight at New Haven, and now grave magistrates and elders were bringing to Boston from the Connecticut the skins and the scalps of Sassacus and his sachems, ghastly trophies of the savage fight. They arrived on the $\frac{5th}{15th}$ of August, Vane having sailed on the $\frac{3d}{13th}$, and the same day the party of the clericals was reinforced by the return of Mr. Wilson. Having been absent some seven weeks, with the Massachusetts contingent under Stoughton's command, he had been sent for to return at once. In response to the summons Stoughton — then at New London, and preparing to cross over to Block Island — immediately dismissed his chaplain, "albeit," he wrote, "we conceived we had special interest in him, and count ourselves naked without him;" but he bethought himself that "we could enjoy him but one Sabbath more." And so Wilson returned by way of Providence, in company with the Rev. Thomas Hooker and the Rev. Samuel Stone, respectively the minister and the teacher of the church at Hartford, both close disputants as well as famous divines.   All the clergy of the province and neighboring settlements were in fact now directing their steps towards Boston ; and the spirit of theological controversy aroused itself, quickened and refreshed by two months of thought diverted to carnal warfare.   A synod was to be held.

CHAPTER VII.

VÆ VICTIS.

SYNODS and convocations are the last recourse of perplexed theologians. A high authority in matters connected with Puritan history and theology, after referring to them as "the bane and scourge of Christendom," adds that, while "called to promote harmony and uniformity, they have invariably resulted in variance, discord and a widening of previous breaches."[1] The synod of 1637 was the first thing of the sort attempted in America; and, under the circumstances, and in the absence of all the usual machinery for carrying on discussion, it was perhaps as good a method of bringing opposing parties together as could have been devised. When brought together, even if no agreement could be reached, they might at least find out each where the other stood; and, if the chances were that in its results a synod would embitter rather than allay strife, this risk had to be taken. The meeting was fixed for the $\frac{30\text{th}}{9\text{th}}$ of $\frac{\text{August}}{\text{September}}$, and a busy three weeks, crowded with meetings and lectures, Days of Humiliation and Days of Thanksgiving, preceded. Some of the elders, evidently much troubled at the gravity of the situation, busied themselves to bring about an understanding between Wilson and Wheelwright and Cotton. So far as Cotton was concerned they were not unsuc-

[1] Ellis, *The Puritan Age*, 219; Savage, *Winthrop*, i. *240, n.

cessful, for, now that Vane was gone, the eloquent teacher of the Boston church began to find his position a trying one. He had, indeed, seriously thought of turning his back on the dust and turmoil of Boston, — political as well as theological, — and seeking refuge and quiet elsewhere; but the idea did not commend itself to him. He was no longer young, and, perhaps, his nerves gave way before the prospect of again facing the wilderness, a banished man; perhaps also he was over-persuaded by the members of his church. Accordingly a sensation was excited in the Boston meeting-house when, on the Sunday following Wilson's return, Cotton announced to the congregation that the minister had explained certain words, used by him in his discourse before the Court in the previous October, as applying not to any pulpit doctrines uttered by the teacher himself or by his brother Wheelwright, but to some opinions " privately carried." As it was quite well known that Mr. Wilson had long before made this very equivocal concession, the sudden change in his own mind, indicated by Cotton's announcement, excited no little comment. He was evidently opening a way for retreat.

The following Thursday Mr. Davenport delivered the lecture at Boston. He was a famous controversialist, and had in Holland borne earnest witness against what he termed " promiscuous baptism," holding rigidly to the tenet that children of communicants only should be admitted to that holy institution. Having only recently come to New England, Mr. Davenport had no settlement within the patent; but, nevertheless, out of deference to his great fame, he had been urged to attend the Synod, and he now lectured on the nature and danger of divisions, while at the same time he " clearly discovered his judgment against the new opinions." It was another indication of the set of the tide. The 24th of the month was kept as a Fast-day in all the churches; and on the 26th, amidst much rejoicing, Stoughton and his soldiers returned from their Pequot campaign and were feasted. Then came $\frac{\text{August 30th}}{\text{September 9th}}$, and the Synod.

It met at Cambridge, and was composed of some twenty-five ministers, being " all the teaching elders through the country," with whom were Davenport and others freshly arrived. When to these were added the lay members and the body of the magistrates, it will be seen that the attendance was large. The deliberations were in public. Among those present were some few of Shepard's conciliatory temper, but the majority and the leaders were men of the type of Ward, Weld and Peters. They were there to stamp a heresy out; and they proposed to do it just as effectually in New England as Archbishop Laud, at that same time, was proposing to do it in the mother country. From the first, a well-developed spirit of theological hate showed itself in easy control of everything. Mather says that " at the beginning of the assembly, after much discourse against the unscriptural enthusiasms and revelations then by some contended for, Mr. Wilson proposed : 'You that are against these things, and that are for the spirit and the word together, hold up your hands !' And the multitude of hands then held up was a comfortable and encouraging introduction unto the other proceedings." The other proceedings were in perfect keeping with the introduction. There was in them no trace of wisdom, of conciliation or of charity, — nothing but priestly intolerance, stimulated by blind zeal.

No sooner was it organized and ready for business than the Synod proceeded to throw out a sort of general drag-net designed to sweep up all conceivable heretical opinions. The work was thoroughly done, and soon there were spread upon the record no less than eighty-two " opinions, some blasphemous, others erroneous, and all unsafe," besides nine " unwholesome expressions." [1]   As all the twenty-five ministers — with one exception, or possibly two — were of the same way of thinking, the proceedings were reasonably harmonious.   Certain of the lay members from among the Boston delegates were indeed outspoken in their expressions of disgust that such a huge body of heresies should be paraded without any pretence of their being entertained by any one ; but Wheelwright seems discreetly to have held his peace, taking the ground that, as they were not imputed to him, they were none of his concern.   Consequently, when the indignant Bostonians got up and left the assembly, he remained behind, nor jarred upon the spirit of unbroken harmony which for a time followed their departure.   After every conceivable abstract opinion and expression had been raked up, the entire pile was most appropriately disposed of by the Rev. Mr. Wilson with one sweep of the theological dung-fork.   In reply to the gasping inquiry of one of his brethren as to what should be done with such a dispensation of

[1] As the term "unwholesome expressions" hardly conveys a clear idea to modern readers, a statement of one of those now spread upon the record, and of its synodical confutation, may not be out of place :—

"S. Peter more leaned to a Covenant of Works than Paul, Pauls doctrine does more for free grace than Peters.

"ANSW. To oppose these persons and the doctrine of these two Apostles of Christ, who were guided by one and the same Spirit in preaching and penning thereof, in such a point as the Covenant of workes and grace, is little lesse than blasphemy."

heterodoxies, the pastor of the Boston church exclaimed, no less vigorously than conclusively : — " Let them go to the devil of hell, from whence they came ! "

Having in this way very comfortably disposed of preliminaries, the Synod settled itself down to real business. The work in hand was to devise some form of words which Cotton and Wheelwright on the one side, and the body of their brethren on the other, would assent to as an expression of common belief. There were five points nominally in question, which were subsequently reduced to three. To appreciate the whole absurdity of the jargon, in which metaphysics lent confusion to theology, these must be stated in full : —

" 1. That the new creature is not the person of a believer, but a body of saving graces in such a one ; and that Christ, as a head, doth enliven or quicken, preserve or act the same, but Christ himself is no part of this new creature.

" 2. That though, in effectual calling (in which the answer of the soul is by active faith, wrought at the same instant by the Spirit,) justification and sanctification be all together in them ; yet God doth not justify a man, before he be effectually called, and so a believer.

" 3. That Christ and his benefits may be offered and exhibited to a man under a Covenant of Works, but not in or by a Covenant of Works."

It is not easy to realize now that strong, matter-of-fact, reasoning men could ever have been educated to the point of inflicting — and, what is far more curious, of enduring — persecution, banishment and torture in the propagation or in the defence of such incomprehensible formulas. They furnish in themselves at once the strongest evidence and the most striking illustration of the singular condition of religious and

theological craze in which early New England existed.
As the modern investigator puzzles over these articles
of a once living faith, in vain trying to find out in
what lay their importance, — even conceding their
truth, — the Synod, and the outcome of its wrestlings,
calls to mind nothing so much as that passage from
the poem of the greatest of its co-religionists, wherein,
with bitter mockery, one portion of " the host of Hell "
is represented as sitting on a hill apart, where they

> " reason'd high
> Of Providence, foreknowledge, will, and fate,
> Fix'd fate, free will, foreknowledge absolute;
> And found no end, in wand'ring mazes lost."

The difference between Milton's devils and the early
New England divines seems to have been that, while
the one and the other lost themselves in the same
mazes of the unknowable, the former evinced much
the more Christian spirit of the two in their methods
of conducting the debate.   Both were suffering banishment from their former homes; but, while the
Synod of the fallen angels in their place of exile
amicably discussed points of abstract difference, the
similar Synod of New England ministers betrayed,
throughout their proceedings, all " the exquisite rancor
of theological hate."

After much discussion, written as well as oral, of
the controverted points, Cotton, with a degree of
worldly wisdom which did credit to his head, declared
at last that he saw light.   Whether he really did so
or not is of little consequence.   It is clear that no one
in the assembly had any distinct conception of what
they were talking about; and it was certainly nothing
against any one that he professed to see the nebulous
idealities, at which they were all gazing through the

dense mist of words, in the same way that the majority saw them. Wheelwright was of a less accommodating spirit. To him the cloud looked neither like a whale nor like a weasel. He would not say that it did. So far as he was concerned. therefore, the Synod resulted exactly as his enemies desired. He was now completely isolated ; he had lost Cotton as well as Vane.

The sessions continued through twenty-four days. At first arguments were delivered in writing and read in the assembly, and answers followed in the same way ; but as this method of procedure occupied too much time, recourse was had to oral disputation. Then the questions at issue were speedily determined. Finally, all other business being disposed of, Mrs. Hutchinson's female symposiums were voted a nuisance, or, in the language of the day, " agreed to be disorderly and without rule ; " and then, on the $\frac{22d}{2d}$ of $\frac{September}{October}$, the convocation broke up amid general congratulations " that matters had been carried on so peaceably, and concluded so comfortably in all love." The result of it all was that " Mr. Cotton and they agreed, but Mr. Wheelwright did not."

From the day of adjournment onward, therefore, Wheelwright was to confront his opponents alone ; and in the number of his opponents were included the whole body of the clergy and the whole body of the magistracy. The Synod had done its work in two ways ; not only was Cotton saved, but, the efforts at conciliation having failed, it only remained to leave the refractory to be dealt with by the arm of the civil authority. The General Court, elected at the time of the stormy Cambridge gathering in May, had shown little disposition to grapple in earnest with the Antinomian issue. As often as that issue presented itself it was postponed; and the course of the deputies would seem to warrant an inference that, elected as they had been while the parties were not unevenly divided, the Court contained a representation of each side sufficient to hold the other side in check. Whether this was so or not, on the $\frac{26\text{th}}{6\text{th}}$ of $\frac{\text{September}}{\text{October}}$ — just four days after the adjournment of the Synod — the Court, which had been elected for the entire year, was suddenly dissolved, and a new election ordered.

The cause of so unusual a proceeding can only be inferred; yet it would seem but reasonable to suppose that the legislature, as then made up, was not considered equal to doing the work in hand; and, certainly, the new Court was a very different body from the old one. Of the twenty-seven delegates who met at Cambridge on the day the May Court was dissolved, twelve only were reelected; and of the thirty-three members of the Court chosen in October, no less than twenty-one were new men. Among those left out was Wheelwright's stanch friend and parishioner, Atherton Hough; but Coddington, Aspinwall and Coggeshall were returned by Boston, and constituted at least a nucleus of opposition.

The new Court met on the $\frac{2\text{d}}{12\text{th}}$ of November. Those composing it found both Wheelwright and Mrs. Hutchinson still obdurate. The former, just as if no Synod had ascertained the whole everlasting truth and expressed it in plain language, was preaching the Covenant of Grace to all who would hear him at the Mount; while the latter continued her weekly female gatherings, and put no bridle on her tongue. With the clouds lowering heavily over them, they maintained a bold front. They did more than this, — they even went out to meet the danger, openly rejecting all thought of compromise, with a loud assertion that the difference between them and their opponents was as that between heaven and hell, — a gulf too deep to fill, too wide to bridge. In later days, under similar circumstances, persons feeling in this way would quietly have been permitted to set up a conventicle of their own, at which they could have mouthed their rubbish until they wearied. A schism in the church would have restored quiet to the community. But this was not the rule of primitive New England. That rule was one of rigid conformity, — the rule of the " lord-brethren " in place of the rule of the " lord-bishops." So, as Winthrop expressed it, those in the majority, " finding, upon consultation, that two so opposite parties could not continue in the same body without apparent hazard of ruin to the whole, agreed to send away some of the principal." A somewhat similar conclusion had previously been reached in regard to Spain and the Netherlands by Philip II., and was subsequently reached in regard to France by Louis XIV.

Having decided upon extreme measures the leaders of the dominant party now proceeded in a business-like manner. Those composing the minority were to be thoroughly disciplined. There was no difficulty in dealing with Wheelwright and Mrs. Hutchinson. They were doomed. But the men who were in the ascendant — the Welds, the Peters, the Bulkleys and the Symmes of the colonial pulpit — had no idea of contenting themselves with that small measure of atonement. The heresy was to be extirpated, root and branch. " Thorough " was then the word at Whitehall; and " Thorough " was the idea, if not the word, in Massachusetts. But a species of sweep-net was now needed which should bring the followers no less than the leaders under the ban of the law. The successful prosecution of Wheelwright afforded the necessary hint. Wheelwright had been brought within the clutches of the civil authorities by a species of *ex post facto* legal chicanery. Even his most bitter opponents did not pretend to allege that he had preached his Fast-day sermon with the intent to bring about any disturbance of the peace. They only claimed that his utterances tended to make such a result probable, and that his own observation ought to have convinced him of the fact.[1] Therefore, they argued, although it was true that no breach of the peace had actually taken place, and although the preacher had no intent to excite to a breach of the peace, yet he was none the less guilty of constructive sedition. Constructive sedition was now made to do the same work in New England which constructive treason, both before and after, was made to do elsewhere. It was a most excellent device; and a pretext, or "fair opportunity," as Winthrop expresses it, for its application was found in that remonstrance of the 9th of the previous March, which, signed by sixty of the leading inhabitants of Boston, had now quietly reposed among the records of the colony through four sessions of two separate legislatures. The paper speaks for itself.[2] The single passage in it to which even a theologian's acuteness could give a color of

[1] This point is of importance, and Winthrop's language is explicit in regard to it:—"If his intent were not to stirre up to open force and armes (neither do we suspect him of any such purpose, otherwise than by consequent) yet his reading and experience might have told him, how dangerous it is to heat people's affections against their opposites." *Short Story*, 53.

[2] See Appendix to Savage's *Winthrop* (ed. 1853), i. 481-3.

sedition was couched in these words : — " Thirdly, if you look at the effects of his Doctrine upon the hearers, it hath not stirred up sedition in us, not so much as by accident; we have not drawn the sword, as sometime Peter did, rashly, neither have we rescued our innocent brother, as sometime the Israelites did Jonathan, and yet they did not seditiously." The last six words are those which Governor Winthrop, and the subsequent apologists of what now took place,[1] dwell upon as in themselves sufficient to make the drawing up or signing of this paper an offence for which banishment was a mild and hardly adequate penalty ; and this, too, in face of the fact that the remonstrance immediately went on as follows : — " The covenant of free grace held forth by our brother hath taught us rather to become humble suppliants to your Worships, and if we should not prevail, we would rather with patience give our cheeks to the smiters."

Even had this paper been of a seditious character, it was presented to a former Court, and not to the one which now passed judgment upon it. The Court elected in November, 1637, had no more to do with the Boston remonstrance of the preceding March than with any other paper, the character of which, as it slept among the dusty archives, some deputy might chance not to fancy. Those to whom it was addressed had considered it a respectful and proper document ; and it was reserved for a body to which it was not addressed to hunt it up on the files, in order to declare it a contempt and make it the basis of a proscription.

The Court met on the $\frac{2d}{12th}$ of November. No sooner was it organized than it became apparent it was to be

---

[1] Palfrey, i. 492.

purged; in it the elements of opposition were few, but
those few were to be weeded out. It has already been
mentioned that Coddington, Aspinwall and Coggeshall were the deputies from Boston. They were all
three adherents of the Covenant of Grace, friends of
Mrs. Hutchinson and supporters of Wheelwright;
while Coddington's name stood first among those
affixed to the remonstrance now pronounced seditious.
Coddington was a magistrate, an old and honored
official, — a man classed, in popular estimation, with
Winthrop and Endicott as one of the founders of the
colony. Him they did not like to attack; and there
is also reason to believe that Winthrop exerted himself to shield his old associate. No such safeguards
surrounded Aspinwall and Coggeshall. The record of
the Court shows that it was at once demanded of the
former whether he still adhered to the sentiments expressed in the remonstrance. He replied that he did.
A vote expelling him from his seat was immediately
passed. Indignant at the expulsion of his colleague,
Coggeshall then rose in his place and declared his
approbation of the remonstrance, though his name
was not among those signed to it; and he added that,
if the course taken with Aspinwall was to be followed
towards others, they " had best make one work of all."
He was taken at his word, and forthwith expelled.
Other deputies had then to be elected. The freemen
of Boston would have been indeed devoid of any feelings of manliness, much more of pride, had such treatment of their representatives not excited indignation
among them, and at first they proposed to return to
the Court the same deputies to whom seats had just
been refused. This action must at once have brought
on the crisis, and Cotton prevented it; for he was

still looked upon as friendly to the defeated party, —
indeed, in heart, he was so, — and among the church-
members, who alone were freeholders, their teacher's
influence was great. Instead of Coggeshall and Aspinwall, accordingly, William Colburn and John
Oliver were chosen, and the next day appeared to
take their seats. But an examination of the remonstrance revealed Oliver's name upon it; and, when
questioned, he justified the paper. Permission to
take his seat was consequently refused him, and the
election of another in his place ordered. The freemen of Boston took no notice of the new warrant.

The Court being now purged of all his friends,
Coddington only excepted, Wheelwright's case was
taken up. He appeared in answer to the summons ;
but, when asked if he was yet prepared to confess
his errors, he stubbornly refused so to do, protesting
his entire innocence of what was charged against
him. He could not be induced to admit that he had
been guilty either of sedition or of contempt, and he
asserted that the doctrine preached by him in his
Fast-day discourse was sound ; while, as to any individual application which had been made of it, he was
not accountable. Then followed a long wrangle, reaching far into the night and continued the next day,
during which the natural obstinacy of Wheelwright's
temper must have been sorely tried. At his door was
laid the responsibility for all the internal dissensions
of the province. He was the fruitful source of those
village and parish ills ; and every ground of complaint
was gone over, from the lax response of Boston to
the call for men for the Pequot war to the slight
put by his church upon Wilson, and by the halber-
diers upon Winthrop. To such an indictment de-

fence was impossible ; and so, in due time, the Court
proceeded to its sentence. It was disfranchisement
and exile. As it was already what is the middle of
our November, the date of the exile's departure was
at first postponed until March, when the severity of
the winter would be over ; in the mean time, as a
preacher, he was to be silenced. From this sentence
Wheelwright took an appeal to the King, which the
Court at once refused to allow. Twenty-four hours
later, after a night of reflection, he withdrew his appeal, offering to accept a sentence of simple banishment, but refusing absolutely to be silenced. He was
then at last permitted to return to his own house at
Mt. Wollaston, and his sentence stands recorded as
follows : —

"Mr. John Wheelwright, being formally convicted of
contempt and sedition, and now justifying himself and his
former practice, being to the disturbance of the civil peace,
he is by the Court disfranchised and banished, having fourteen days to settle his affairs ; and, if within that time he
depart not the patent, he promiseth to render himself to
Mr. Stoughton, at his house, to be kept till he be disposed
of ; and Mr. Hough undertook to satisfy any charge that
he, Mr. Stoughton, or the country should be at."

Unlike Mrs. Hutchinson and the body of those
who were to follow him into banishment, Wheelwright did not direct his steps towards Rhode Island.
On the contrary, after preaching a farewell sermon
to his little congregation, in which there was no word
of retraction, he turned his face to the northward,
and with all the courage and tenacity of purpose
which throughout had marked his action, in spite of
the inclement season and the impending winter, within
his allotted fourteen days he was on his way to the

Piscataqua. He went alone through the deepening snow, which that winter lay from November to the end of March " a yard deep," according to Winthrop, beyond the Merrimac, and " the more north the deeper," while the mercury ranged so low that the exile himself, with a grim effort at humor, drearily remarked that he believed had he been filled with " the very extracted spirits of sedition and contempt, they would have been frozen up and indisposed for action." [1] Not until April did his wife, bringing with her his mother-in-law and their children, undertake to follow him to the spot where he and a few others had founded what has since become the academic town of Exeter. It is merely curious now to reflect on the intense bitterness, and sense of wrong and of unending persecution which must have nerved the steps of the former vicar of Bilsby, when, at forty-five years of age, he turned his back on Mt. Wollaston, and sternly sought refuge from his brethren in Christ amid the snow and ice of bleak, unfertile New Hampshire.

[1] *Mercurius Americanus*, Bell, 228.

CHAPTER VIII.

HAVING disposed of Wheelwright's case the General Court, without stopping to take breath, at once proceeded to that of Mistress Hutchinson, — " the breeder and nourisher of all these distempers." In the language of the time, she was "convented for traducing the ministers and their ministry in this country ; " and these words most happily set forth her offence. It could not be charged against her that she had signed the remonstrance, for her name was not among those appended to it ; she had preached no sedition ; being a woman, she could bear no hand in any apprehended tumult. She had criticised the clergy ; and for that she was now arraigned.

Though, as will presently appear, the proceedings were in no way lacking in interest, there was about them nothing either solemn or imposing. Indeed, all the external surroundings, as well as the physical conditions, were so very matter-of-fact and harsh, that any attempt at pomp or state would have been quite out of keeping ; everything, without as well as within, was dreary and repellent, — in a word, New England wintry. The Court was still sitting at Newetowne, as it was called ; for the name was not changed to Cambridge until a year later, though the college was at this very session ordered to be fixed there. It was a crude, straggling settlement,

made up of some sixty or seventy log-cabins, or
poor frame-houses, which only eighteen months before had been mainly abandoned by their occupants,
who, under the lead of their pastor, Thomas Hooker,
had then migrated in a body to the banks of the Connecticut.   The Rev. Thomas Shepard, with those who
had just come over with him, had bought the empty
tenements and moved into them.   An inscription cut
in the granite foundation wall of a modern bake-
house, on the busy Mt. Auburn thoroughfare, now
marks the spot where the church, or meeting-house
rather, stood on the upland, not far from the narrow
fringe of marshes which there skirted the devious
channel of the Charles.   In front of it ran the main
village street, ending in a foot-bridge leading down
to low-water mark at the ferry, while a ladder was
secured to the steep further bank of the river for
"convenience of landing."   Close to the meeting-
house, but nearer to the ferry, was the dwelling built
for himself by Governor Dudley in 1630, and in
which, at the breaking-up of the sharp winter of 1631,
he wrote his letter to Bridget, Countess of Lincoln,
"having got no table, or other room to write in than
by the fireside upon my knee."   Laid out with some
regard for symmetry and orderly arrangement, Newetowne was looked upon as "one of the neatest and
best compacted towns in New England, having many
fair   structures,   with   many   handsome   contrived
streets."   The river being to the south, on the northern side of the village there stretched away a comparatively broad and level plain, covering many
hundred acres, then used as a common pasture-
ground and fenced in by a paling of a mile and a
half in length.   A year or two later, the college build-

ing was erected on the southern limit of this plain;
while a third of a mile or so to the north stood the
great oak under which had been held that May election which resulted in the defeat of Vane, and in
Winthrop's return to office.[1]

Of the meeting-house itself no description has been
preserved. It seems to have been a rude frame building, built of rough-hewn boards, the crevices of which
were sealed with mud. Its roof, sloping down from
a long ridge-pole, on which was perched a bell, had,
it is supposed, at first been thatched, but was now
covered with slate or boards; and the narrow dimen-
sions of the primitive edifice may be inferred from
the fact that when, a dozen years afterwards, it no
longer sufficed for a prospering community, the new
and more commodious one which succeeded it was
but forty feet square. Such as it was, the meeting-
house was the single building of a public sort in the
place, and within it the sessions of the Court were
now held, as those of the Synod had been held there
shortly before.

The season was one of unusual severity, and the
days among the shortest of the year. Though November, according to the calendar then in use, was not
yet half over, there had nearly a week before been a
considerable fall of snow, which still whitened the
ground, while the ice had begun to make, piling itself up along the river's bank.[2] No pretence even
was made of warming the barrack-like edifice; and,
dark at best in the November day, it could not be

---

[1] Higginson, 250*th Ann. of Cambridge,* 48; Mackenzie, *First Church
in Cambridge,* Lect. II.; Paige, *Cambridge,* 18, 37; Young, *Chron. of
Mass.* 402.

[2] Winthrop, i. *243–4, *264.

lighted at all after dusk. Its furniture consisted
only of rude wooden benches, on which the deputies
and those in attendance sat, and a table and chairs for
the Governor and the magistrates. All told, the Court
consisted of some forty members, nine of whom were
magistrates; but the little church was thronged, for
the outside attendance was large, almost every person
of note in the province being there. Indeed, nothing
in the history of Massachusetts, up to this time, had
ever excited so great an interest. The clergy, in
point of fact not only the prosecutors in the case
but also the witnesses against the accused, were necessarily present in full ranks. Wilson and Cotton
both were there from Boston: the former bent on the
utter destruction of her who, sowing dissension between his people and himself, had, with feminine
ingenuity, strewed his path with thorns; the latter
not yet terrified into a complete abandonment of those
who looked to him as their mentor. The fanatical
Peters had come from Salem; and he and Thomas
Weld of Roxbury, having been the most active promoters of the prosecution, were now to appear as chief
witnesses against the accused. With the pastor,
Weld, had come Eliot, the teacher at Roxbury, — now
only thirty-four, and not for nine years yet to begin
those labors among the Indians which were to earn
for his name the prefix of "the Apostle." He too
was unrelenting in his hostility to the new opinions.
There also were George Phillips of Watertown, " one
of the first saints of New England;"[1] Zachariah

[1] George Phillips was the common ancestor of that Phillips family
subsequently so prominent in the history of Boston. Cotton Mather,
with even more than his usual quaintness, says of him that "he la-
boured under many bodily infirmities: but was especially liable to
the cholick; the extremity of one fit whereof, was the wind which
carried him afore it, into the haven of eternal rest."

Symmes of Charlestown, who himself knew what it was to suffer for " conscientious nonconformity ; " and finally Thomas Shepard of Cambridge, " a poore, weake, pale-complectioned man " of thirty-four, but yet " holy, heavenly, sweet-affecting and soul-ravishing." And indeed Shepard alone of them all seems to have borne in mind, in the proceedings which were to follow, that charity, long-suffering and forgiveness entered into the Master's precepts. Winthrop presided over the deliberations of the Court, acting at once as judge and prosecuting attorney. At his side, foremost among the magistrates, sat Dudley and Endicott, — men whose rough English nature had been narrowed and hardened by a Puritan education.

Such was the Court. The culprit before it for trial was a woman of some forty-six or seven years of age.[1] Slight of frame, and now in manifestly delicate health, there was in her bearing nothing masculine or defiant ; though, seemingly, she faced a tribunal — in which, so far as now appears, she could have found but two friendly faces — with calmness and self-possession. She had no counsel, nor was the trial conducted according to any established rules of procedure. It was a mere hearing in open legislative session. Of its details, one — himself an eminent New England clergyman not versed in legal technicalities or familiar with rules of evidence or the methods of courts — has said that the treatment which the accused then underwent " deserves the severest epithets of censure," and that " the united civil wisdom and Christian piety of the fathers of Massachusetts make but a sorry fig-

---

[1] The exact date of Mrs. Hutchinson's birth has not been ascertained. She was married at St. Mary Woolnoth, London, 9 August, 1612.

ure." [1] Certainly, if what there took place had taken
place in England at the trial of some patriot or non-
conformer before the courts — ecclesiastical, civil or
criminal — of any of the Stuarts, the historians of
New England would not have been sparing in their
denunciations. But the record best speaks for itself.
From that record it will appear that the accused,
unprovided with counsel, was not only examined and
cross-examined by the magistrates, her judges, but
badgered, insulted and sneered at, and made to give
evidence against herself. The witnesses in her behalf
were browbeaten and silenced in careless disregard
both of decency and a manly sense of fair play. Her
few advocates among the members of the court were
rudely rebuked, and listened to with an impatience
which it was not attempted to conceal ; while, throughout, the so-called trial was, in fact, no trial at all, but
a mockery of justice rather, — a bare-faced inquisitorial proceeding. And all this will appear from the
record.

The Court met, and presently the accused, in obedience to its summons, appeared before it. At first,
though it must have been manifest she was shortly to
become a mother, she was not even bidden to sit
down, but soon " her countenance discovered some
bodily infirmity," and a chair was provided for her.

[1] Dr. George E. Ellis, in the biography of Anne Hutchinson.
(Sparks' *American Biography,* N. S. vi. 277.) Dr. Ellis' life of Mrs.
Hutchinson was written in 1845 ; in 1888, after an interval of over
forty years, he reviewed the whole subject of the Antinomian Controversy in his work entitled *The Puritan Age in Massachusetts* (300–62).
He there says (336) : — "We have to fall back upon our profound im-
pressions of the deep sincerity and integrity of [Winthrop's] character
. . . to read without some faltering or misgiving of approval, not to
say with regret and reproach, the method with which he conducted
the examination of this gifted and troublesome woman."

The offence of which she had been really guilty, —
the breeding of a faction in the Boston church against
the pastor, Wilson, and, when his brethren came to
his aid, not hesitating to criticise them also, — this
offence it was somewhat embarrassing to formulate in
fitting words. It could not well be bluntly charged.
Winthrop therefore began with a general arraignment, in which he more particularly accused the prisoner of having meetings at her house, "a thing not
tolerable nor comely in the sight of God nor fitting
for [her] sex;" and, further, with justifying Mr.
Wheelwright's Fast-day sermon and the Boston petition. Mrs. Hutchinson now showed herself quite able
to hold her own in the casuistical fence of the time,
and this part of the case resulted disastrously for the
prosecution. Indeed, the logic made use of by Winthrop was of a kind which exposed him badly. He
contended that the accused had transgressed the law
of God commanding her to honor her father and
mother. The magistrates were the fathers of the
commonwealth; and therefore, in adhering to those
who signed the remonstrance, even though she did not
sign it herself, she dishonored the magistrates, and
was justly punishable. Coming from the mouth of
the Archbishop of Canterbury in 1637 this would be
pronounced sophistical rubbish; it was equally sophistical rubbish when uttered by the Governor of Massachusetts Bay for the same year. Mrs. Hutchinson
disposed of the allegation with dignity and point in
these words : — "I do acknowledge no such thing;
neither do I think that I ever put any dishonor upon
you."

The next count in the indictment pressed upon her
related to the meetings of women held at her house.

Here, too, the prosecution fared badly. Mrs. Hutchinson was asked by what warrant she held such meetings; she cited in reply the usage which she found prevailing in Boston at her coming, and the Scriptural rule in the second chapter of Titus, that the elder women should instruct the younger. The following altercation then ensued : —

"GOVERNOR WINTHROP. You know that there is no rule [in the Scriptures] which crosses another ; but this rule [in Titus] crosses that in the Corinthians. You must therefore take [the rule in Titus] in this sense, that the elder women must instruct the younger about their business, and to love their husbands, and not to make them to clash.

"MRS. HUTCHINSON. I do not conceive but that it is meant also for some public times.

"GOVERNOR. Well, have you no more to say but this ?

"MRS. H. I have said sufficient for my practice.

"GOVERNOR. Your course is not to be suffered ; for, besides that we find such a course as this greatly prejudicial to the State, . . . we see not that any should have authority to set up any other exercises besides what authority hath already set up ; and so what hurt comes of this you will be guilty of, and we for suffering you.

"MRS. H. Sir, I do not believe that to be so.

"GOVERNOR. Well, we see how it is. We must therefore put it away from you ; or restrain you from maintaining this course.

"MRS. H. If you have a rule for it from God's Word, you may.

"GOVERNOR. We are your judges, and not you ours. And we must compel you to it.

"MRS. H. If it please you by authority to put it down, I will freely let you. For I am subject to your authority."

For a moment, these words as Winthrop uttered them must have jarred with a strange and yet famil-

iar sound on the ears of the listening clergy, hardly
one of whom had in England escaped being silenced
by the prelates; and now they heard the same principles of rigid conformity laid down in their place of
refuge, — freedom of conscience was once for all there
denied. The preliminaries were now brought to a
close, and the trial proceeded to the real issue involved. The charge was explicit. Mrs. Hutchinson,
it was alleged, had publicly said that Mr. Cotton
alone of the ministers preached a Covenant of Grace;
the others, not having received the seal of the Spirit,
were consequently not able ministers of the New Testament, and preached a Covenant of Works. To this
count in the indictment against her she was at first
invited to plead guilty; which she declined to do.
Governor Winthrop then permitted himself to indulge
in a sneer, which was met with a prompt and digni-
fied rejoinder. Both sneer and rejoinder stand thus
recorded : —

"GOVERNOR WINTHROP. It is well discerned to the
Court that Mrs. Hutchinson can tell when to speak and
when to hold her tongue. Upon the answering of a question which we desire her to tell her thoughts of, she desires
to be pardoned.

"MRS. HUTCHINSON. It is one thing for me to come before a public magistracy, and there to speak what they
would have me to speak; and another when a man comes
to me in a way of friendship, privately. There is a difference in that."

Possibly it was at this point in the trial that, stung
by Winthrop's slur, the anger of the accused flashed
up and found expression in hot words; for Weld tells
us that once, "her reputation being a little touched,
. . . she vented her impatience with so fierce speech

and countenance, as one would hardly have guessed
her to have been an Antitype of Daniel, but rather of
the lions, after they were let loose." However this
may be, the witnesses for the prosecution, Peters,
Weld, Eliot, Symmes and the others, who up to this
time had been watching the case in grim silence, were
now called upon, and, one after another, gave their
evidence. Though the question at issue was sufficiently
plain, the discussion then soon passed into the unintelligible. It has been seen that, at a certain point
in the growth of differences in the Boston church,
the ministers of the adjoining towns had been called
upon to interpose, and a conference had then taken
place between the two sides, — the visiting elders and
Mr. Wilson representing one, and Mrs. Hutchinson,
Cotton and Wheelwright the other.[1] The evidence
now given related to what had then taken place. The
ministers all asserted that the conference was a formal
one of a public nature, and so understood at the time.
This Mrs. Hutchinson denied, — thus making the
point that she had been guilty of no open disparagement of the clergy, but that, whatever she had said,
had been drawn from her in private discourse by
those now seeking to persecute her for it. As to the
Covenant of Works, while they asserted that she had
charged them with being under such a covenant, she
insisted that she had done nothing of the sort ; though
she admitted that she probably had said that they
" preached a covenant of works, as did the apostles
before the Ascension. But to preach a covenant of
works, and to be under a covenant of works, are two
different things." She did not deny that she had
singled out Mr. Cotton from among them all as alone

[1] *Supra,* 426–8.

being sealed with the seal of the Spirit, and therefore preaching a Covenant of Grace, which bit of jargon was explained as meaning that one so sealed enjoyed a full assurance of God's favor by the Holy Ghost. Here at last, in this special assurance attributed to Cotton, was the rock of offence from which flowed those waters of bitterness, the cup of which Wilson and Weld and Peters and the rest had been forced to drain to the last drop. A woman's preference among preachers was somehow to be transmuted into a crime against the state.

It would be neither easy nor profitable to attempt to follow the trial into the metaphysico-theological stage to which it now passed. Cotton Mather says that " the mother opinion of the [Antinomian heresy] was, that a Christian should not fetch any evidence of his good state before God, from the sight of any inherent qualification in him ; or from any conditional promise made unto such a qualification." [1] This being the mother opinion, and itself not translucent, all the parties to the proceedings now began to obscure it by talking about " witnesses of the spirit " and " the seal of the spirit," and " a broad seal " and " a little seal," and the " assurance of God's favor " and " the graces wanting to evidence it," and " the difference between the state of the apostles before the Ascension, and their state after it." The real difficulty lay in the fact that the words and phrases to which they attached an all-important significance did not admit of definition, and, consequently, were devoid of exact meaning. They were simply engaged in hot wrangling over the unknowable : but, while Court and clergy and accused wallowed and floundered in the mire of their own

[1] *Magnalia*, B. III. P. II. ch. v. § 12.

learning, belaboring each other with contradictory
texts and with shadowy distinctions, under it all there
lay the hard substratum of injured pride and personal hate; and on that, as on the rock of ages, their
firm feet rested secure.

Six of the ministers testified in succession, Hugh
Peters first. Their evidence was tolerably concurrent
that Mrs. Hutchinson had at the Boston church conference spoken freely, saying that they all taught a
Covenant of Works, — that they were not able ministers of the New Testament, not being sealed, — and,
finally, that Mr. Cotton alone among them preached a
Covenant of Grace. This testimony, and the subsequent wrangle, occupied what remained of the first
day of the trial, before the growing dusk compelled
an adjournment. The next morning, as soon as Governor Winthrop had opened the hearing, Mrs. Hutchinson stated that, since the night before, she had
looked over certain notes which had been taken at
the time of the conference, and that she did "find
things not to be as hath been alleged," and accordingly she now demanded that, as the ministers were
testifying in their own cause, they should do so under
oath. This demand caused much excitement in the
Court, and was looked upon as a fresh insult heaped
upon the clergy. Winthrop held that, the case not
being one for a jury, the evidence need not be under
oath; while other of the magistrates thought that, in
a cause exciting so much interest, sworn testimony
would better satisfy the country. The accused insisted. "An oath, sir," she exclaimed to Stoughton,
" is an end of all strife; and it is God's ordinance."
Then Endicott broke in sneeringly: — " A sign it is
what respect she has to [the ministers'] words;" and

presently again : — "You lifted up your eyes as if
you took God to witness you came to entrap none, —
and yet you will have them swear ! " Finally, Winthrop, that all might be satisfied, expressed himself as
willing to administer the oath if the elders would take
it ; though, said he, " I see no necessity of an oath in
this thing, seeing it is true and the substance of the
matter confirmed by divers." The deputy-governor,
Dudley, then turned the discussion off by crying out :
— " Mark what a flourish Mrs. Hutchinson puts upon
the business that she had witnesses to disprove what
was said ; and here is no man in Court ! " To which
bit of characteristic brutality the accused seems quietly
to have rejoined by saying : —" If you will not call
them in, that is nothing to me."

The ministers now professed themselves as ready
to be sworn. At this point Mr. Coggeshall, the dismissed delegate from Boston, apparently with a view
to preventing a conflict of evidence, ventured to suggest to the Court that the ministers should confer
with Cotton before testifying. The suggestion was
not well received, and Mr. Coggeshall found himself
summarily suppressed ; indeed, three of the judges
did not hesitate to deliver themselves in respect to
him and the accused as follows : —

" GOVERNOR WINTHROP. Shall we not believe so many
godly elders, in a cause wherein we know the mind of the
party without their testimony ?

" MR. ENDICOTT (addressing Mr. Coggeshall). I will
tell you what I say. I think that this carriage of yours
tends to further casting dirt upon the face of the judges.

" MR. HARLAKENDEN. Her carriage doth the same. For
she doth not object an essential thing ; but she goes upon
circumstances, — and yet would have them sworn ! "

But before the elders were again called on to testify, Mrs. Hutchinson was told to produce her own witnesses. Of these Mr. Coggeshall was one. He rose when his name was called, and his examination is reported in full and as follows : —

" GOVERNOR WINTHROP. Mr. Coggeshall was not present [at the conference between Mrs. Hutchinson and the elders].

" MR. COGGESHALL. Yes, but I was. Only I desired to be silent till I should be called [to testify].

" GOVERNOR. Will you, Mr. Coggeshall, say that she did not say [what has been testified to]?

" MR. COGGESHALL. Yes. I dare say that she did not say all that which they lay against her.

" MR. PETERS (interrupting). How dare you look into [the face of] the Court to say such a word.

" MR. COGGESHALL. Mr. Peters takes upon him to forbid me. I shall be silent."

The first witness for the defence having been thus effectually disposed of, the second, Mr. Leverett, was called. He testified that he was present at the discussion between the ministers and Mrs. Hutchinson ; that Mr. Peters had then, " with much vehemency and intreaty," urged the accused to specify the difference between his own teachings and those of Mr. Cotton ; and, in reply, she had stated the difference to be in the fact that, just as the Apostles themselves before the Ascension had not received the seal of the Spirit, so Peters and his brethren, not having the same assurance of God's favor as Mr. Cotton, could not preach a Covenant of Grace so clearly as he. When he had finished his statement a brief altercation took place between Weld and Mrs. Hutchinson, at the close of which Governor Winthrop called on

Mr. Cotton to give his recollection of what had taken place.

Mrs. Hutchinson had been less fortunate in her management of the latter than of the earlier portions of her case. Since the question had turned on what took place at the conference, she had found herself pressed by evidence, and beyond her depth. As is apt to be the case with voluble persons under such circumstances, she had then had recourse to small points, — making issues over the order in which events occurred, or the exact words used, and pressing meaningless distinctions, — cavilling even, and equivocating. By so doing she had injured her case, giving Peters a chance to exclaim: — "We do not desire to be so narrow to the Court and the gentlewoman about times and seasons, whether first or last;" while Harlakenden had, as it has been seen, broken out in disgust: — "She doth not object any essential thing, but she goes upon circumstances." The demand that the ministers should be sworn was another mistake. It was an affront to the elders, the most revered class in the community, and it both angered them and shocked the audience. A blasphemy would hardly have angered or shocked them more. Not only did it excite sympathy for the prosecutors and prejudice against the accused, but there was nothing to be gained by it. The ministers had not given false testimony; and she knew it. The only result, therefore, of her demand of an oath was that they gave their testimony twice instead of once, and insomuch impressed it the more on the minds and memories of all. Mrs. Hutchinson, consequently, was fast doing the work of the prosecution, and convicting herself.

But her cause now passed into far abler hands.
Cotton's sympathies were strongly with her, and he
seems to have been quite ready to show it.   When
called upon to listen to the evidence of his brethren,
he had seated himself by Mrs. Hutchinson's side ;
and he now rose in answer to Winthrop's summons,
and proceeded to give his account of what had passed
at the conference.   Silencing the accused and soothing
the Court, he soon showed very clearly that the qualities
which made him an eminent pulpit orator would also
have made him an excellent jury lawyer.   With no
little ingenuity and skill he went on explaining things
away, and putting a new gloss upon them, until, when
he got through, the prosecution had very little left to
work on.   In summing up, he said that at the close
of the conference it had not seemed to him " to be
so ill taken as [now] it is.   And our brethren did
say, also, that they would not so easily believe reports
as they had done ; and, withal, mentioned that they
would speak no more of it.   And afterwards some of
them did say they were less satisfied than before.
And I must say that I did not find her saying they
were under a Covenant of Works, nor that she said
they did preach a Covenant of Works."

A discussion then ensued between Cotton and the
other ministers, — calm in outward tone, but, on their
part at least, full of suppressed feeling.   Peters took
the lead in it ; but even he was not equal to an attempt at browbeating the renowned teacher of the
Boston church from the witness-stand, as he had
browbeaten Coggeshall from it a few minutes before.
Finally Dudley put this direct question : — " They
affirm that Mrs. Hutchinson did say they were not
able ministers of the New Testament."   It touched

the vital point in the accusation.   The whole audience
must have awaited the response in breathless silence.
It came in these words : — " I do not remember it."

The prosecution had broken down.   It apparently
only remained to let the accused go free, or to condemn and punish her on general principles, in utter
disregard of law and evidence.   Silence and discretion alone were now needed in the conduct of the
defence.   Then it was that, in the triumphant words
of her bitterest enemy, " her own mouth" delivered
Anne Hutchinson " into the power of the Court, as
guilty of that which all suspected her for, but were
not furnished with proof sufficient to proceed against
her."   But modern paraphrase cannot here equal the
terse, quaint language of the original reports.   Cotton had just sat down, after giving his answer to
Dudley's question.   Some among the audience were
drawing a deep breath of relief, while others of the
magistrates and clergy were looking at one another
in surprise and dismay.   The record then goes on as
follows : —

" Upon this she began to speak her mind, and to tell of
the manner of God's dealing with her, and how he revealed
himself to her, and made her know what she had to do.
The Governor perceiving whereabout she went, interrupted
her, and would have kept her to the matter in hand ; but,
seeing her very unwilling to be taken off, he permitted her
to proceed.   Her speech was to this effect : —

"'When I was in old England I was much troubled at
the constitution of the churches there, — so far troubled,
indeed, that I had liked to have turned Separatist.   Whereupon I set apart a day of solemn humiliation by myself,
that I might ponder of the thing and seek direction from
God.   And on that day God discovered unto me the un-

faithfulness of the churches, and the danger of them, and
that none of those Ministers could preach the Lord Jesus
aright; for he brought to my mind this scripture : — " And
every spirit that confesseth not that Jesus Christ is come in
the flesh is not of God ; and this is that spirit of antichrist,
whereof ye have heard that it should come ; and even now
already it is in the world." I marvelled what this should
mean ; and in considering I found that the Papists did not
deny that Christ was come in the flesh, nor did we deny it.
Who then was antichrist? Was it the Turk only? Now I
had none to open scripture to me but the Lord. He must
be the prophet. And it pleased the Lord then to bring to
my mind another scripture : — " For where a testament is,
there must also of necessity be the death of the testator ; "
and he that denies the testament denies the death of the
testator. And in this the Lord did open unto me and give
me to see that every one that did not preach the new covenant denies the death of the testator, and has the spirit of
antichrist. And upon this it was revealed unto me that the
ministers of England were these antichrists. But I knew
not how to bear this ; I did in my heart rise up against it.
Then I begged of the Lord this atheism might not be in me.
After I had begged for light a twelve-month together, the
Lord at last let me see how I did oppose Christ Jesus, and
he revealed to me that scripture in Isaiah : — " Hearken
unto me ye that are far from righteousness : I bring near
my righteousness ; it shall not be far off, and my salvation shall not tarry ; " and from thence he showed me the
atheism of my own heart, and how I did turn in upon a
Covenant of Works, and did oppose Christ Jesus. And
ever since I bless the Lord, — he hath let me see which was
the clear ministry and which the wrong, and to know what
voice I heard, — which was the voice of Moses, which of
John Baptist, and which of Christ. The voice of my beloved I have distinguished from the voice of strangers.
And thenceforth I was more choice whom I heard ; for,

after our teacher, Mr. Cotton, and my brother Wheelwright were put down, there was none in England that I durst hear. Then it pleased God to reveal himself to me in that scripture of Isaiah : — " And though the Lord give you the bread of adversity and the water of affliction, yet shall not thy teachers be removed into a corner any more, but thine eyes shall see thy teachers." The Lord giving me this promise, and Mr. Cotton being gone to New England, I was much troubled. And it was revealed to me that I must go thither also, and that there I should be persecuted and suffer much trouble. I will give you another scripture : — " Fear thou not, O Jacob my servant, saith the Lord : for I am with thee ; for I will make a full end of all the nations whither I have driven thee : but I will not make a full end of thee ; " and then the Lord did reveal himself to me, sitting upon a Throne of Justice, and all the world appearing before him, and, though I must come to New England, yet I must not fear nor be dismayed. And I could not be at rest but I must come hither. The Lord brought another scripture to me : — " For the Lord spake thus to me with a strong hand, and instructed me that I should not walk in the way of this people."

" ' I will give you one more place which the Lord brought to me by immediate revelations ; and that doth concern you all. It is in the sixth chapter of Daniel. When the Presidents and Princes could find nothing against Daniel, because he was faithfull, they sought matter against him concerning the Law of his God, to cast him into the lions' den. So it was revealed to me that they should plot against me ; the Lord bade me not to fear, for he that delivered Daniel and the three children, his hand was not shortened. And, behold ! this scripture is fulfilled this day in my eyes. Therefore take heed what ye go about to do unto me. You have power over my body, but the Lord Jesus hath power over my body and soul ; neither can you do me any harm, for I am in the hands of the eternal Jehovah, my Saviour.

I am at his appointment, for the bounds of my habitation are cast in Heaven, and no further do I esteem of any mortal man than creatures in his hand. I fear none but the great Jehovah, which hath foretold me of these things, and I do verily believe that he will deliver me out of your hands. Therefore take heed how you proceed against me ; for I know that for this you go about to do to me, God will ruin you and your posterity, and this whole State.'

" Mr. Nowell. How do you know that it was God that did reveal these things to you, and not Satan ?

" Mrs. Hutchinson. How did Abraham know that it was God that bid him offer his son, being a breach of the sixth commandment ?

" Deputy-Governor Dudley. By an immediate voice.

" Mrs. Hutchinson. So to me by an immediate revelation.

" Deputy-Governor. How ! an immediate revelation ?

" Mrs. Hutchinson. By the voice of his own spirit to my soul.

" Governor Winthrop. Daniel was delivered by miracle ; do you think to be delivered so too ?

" Mrs. Hutchinson. I do here speak it before the Court. I look that the Lord should deliver me by his providence." [1]

At once, the current of the trial now took a new direction. The dangerous topics of special revelation and miraculous action had been opened up. The feeling which existed with respect to these in the Puritanic mind has already been referred to.[2] That

---

[1] The utterances of Mrs. Hutchinson as here given are taken from both reports of the trial. That in the *Short Story* is at this stage much the more detailed, and it is supplemented by that in Hutchinson's *History*. Though in this narrative the two reports have been woven into one, nothing has been interpolated, and the original phrases and forms of expression have all been carefully preserved. Some of the texts suggest doubts as to the accuracy of the reports.

[2] *Supra*, 387-9.

it was illogical did not matter. It was there. No one for an instant doubted the immediate presence of the Almighty, or his care of his Chosen People, or his Special Providences which they so much loved to note. In the minds of Winthrop or Dudley or Endicott, to question that He was there at that trial in the Cambridge meeting-house, guiding every detail of their proceedings, would have fallen but little short of blasphemy. Had it chanced to thunder during those November days, or had the Northern Lights flashed somewhat brighter than was their wont, His voice would have been heard therein, and His hand seen. They fully believed that in the ordinary events of daily life He shielded some, while on others He visited His wrath. But, when it came to revelations and miracles, they drew the line distinctly and deep. Special Providences? yes! Miracles? — no! Portents? — yes! Revelations? — no! Mrs. Hutchinson accordingly had now opened the vials of puritanic wrath, and they were freely emptied upon her head. Nor were they emptied on her head alone. Cotton himself was no longer spared. At first he took no part in the broken and heated discussion which followed the prophetic and defiant outpouring of the accused, but some allusion to him was soon made, and then Endicott called on " her reverend teacher . . . to speak freely whether he doth condescend to such speeches or revelations as have been here spoken of."

Cotton in reply endeavored to discriminate between utterances which were " fantastical and leading to danger," and those which came " flying upon the wings of the spirit." As to miracles, he said that he was not sure that he understood Mrs. Hutchinson; but, he added : — " If she doth expect a deliverance

in a way of Providence, then I cannot deny it." Here
Dudley interposed, exclaiming : — "No, sir, we did
not speak of that." Cotton then added : — "If it be
by way of miracle, then I would suspect it." Later
on he again recurred to the subject, now speaking
of miracles and "revelations without the Word" as
things he could not assent to and looked upon as de-
lusions ; adding kindly, "and I think so doth she too,
as I understand her." Then Dudley broke rudely in,
remarking : — "Sir, you weary me and do not satisfy
me." The current had now set strongly in one direction, and Cotton was not only powerless to stem it,
but was indeed in some danger, as Dudley's remark
showed, of himself being swept away by it. All pretence of an orderly conduct of proceedings was abandoned, and magistrates, clergy and deputies vied with
each other in denunciation and invective, Winthrop
himself setting the bad example.

"GOVERNOR WINTHROP. The case is altered and will
not stand with us now, but I see a marvellous providence of
God [it will be remembered that the offence of the accused
was looking for a deliverance through a 'providence of
God'] to bring things to this pass that they are. We have
been hearkening about trial of this thing, and now the
mercy of God by a providence hath answered our desires
and made her to lay open herself and the ground of all
these disturbances to be by revelations, . . . and this hath
been the ground of all these tumults and troubles ; and I
would that those were all cut off from us that trouble us,
for this is the thing that hath been the root of all the mischief. . . . Aye ! it is the most desperate enthusiasm in the
world, for nothing but a word comes to her mind, and then
an application is made which is nothing to the purpose, and
this is her revelations ! . . .

"MR. NOWELL. I think it is a devilish delusion.

"GOVERNOR WINTHROP. Of all the revelations that ever I read of, I never read the like ground raised as is for this. The Enthusiasts and Anabaptists had never the like. . . .

"DEPUTY-GOVERNOR DUDLEY. I never saw such revelations as these among the Anabaptists; therefore am sorry that Mr. Cotton should stand to justify her.

"MR. PETERS. I can say the same, and this runs to enthusiasm, and I think that is very disputable which our brother Cotton hath spoken. . . .

"GOVERNOR WINTHROP. It overthrows all.

"DEPUTY-GOVERNOR DUDLEY. These disturbances that have come among the Germans have been all grounded upon revelations; and so they that have vented them have stirred up their hearers to take up arms against their prince and to cut the throats of one another; and these have been the fruits of them. And whether the devil may inspire the same into their hearts here I know not; for I am fully persuaded that Mrs. Hutchinson is deluded by the devil, because the spirit of God speaks truth in all his servants.

"GOVERNOR WINTHROP. I am persuaded that the revelation she brings forth is delusion.

"All the Court but some two or three ministers here cried out, — We all believe it! We all believe it!! . . .

"MR. BARTHOLOMEW. My wife hath said that Mr. Wheelwright was not acquainted with this way until that she imparted it unto him.

"MR. BROWN. . . . I think she deserves no less a censure than hath been already passed, but rather something more; for this is the foundation of all mischief; and of all those bastardly things which have been overthrown by that great meeting [the Synod]. They have all come out from this cursed fountain."

The Governor now forthwith proceeded to put the question. As he was in the midst of doing it, Mr. Coddington, who had hitherto preserved silence, arose and asked to be heard. Referring then to the meetings at Mrs. Hutchinson's house, he asked whether, supposing those meetings to have been designed for the religious edification of her own family, no others might have been present? "If," replied Winthrop, "you have nothing else to say but that, it is pity, Mr. Coddington, that you should interrupt us in proceeding to censure." But Coddington on this occasion showed true courage; for, though in a hopeless minority, he went on — undeterred by Winthrop's rebuke, and regardless of the impatience of his weary and excited audience — to point out that absolutely nothing had been proved against Mrs. Hutchinson, except that she had asserted the other ministers did not teach a Covenant of Grace so clearly as Cotton, and that they were in the state of the apostles before the Ascension. "Why!" he added, "I hope this may not be offensive nor any wrong to them."

Then again Winthrop broke in, declaring that her own speech, just made in Court, afforded ample ground to proceed upon, even admitting that nothing had been proved. Coddington then closed with these forcible and eloquently plain words : —

"I beseech you do not speak so to force things along ; for I do not for my own part see any equity in the Court in all your proceedings. Here is no law of God that she hath broken ; nor any law of the country that she hath broken. Therefore she deserves no censure. Be it granted that Mrs. Hutchinson did say the elders preach as the apostles did, — why, they preached a Covenant of Grace. What wrong then is that to the elders? It is without question that the apostles did preach a Covenant of Grace before the Ascension, though not with that power they did after they received the manifestation of the spirit. Therefore, I pray consider what you do, for here is no law of God or man broken."

The Court had now been many hours in unbroken session. The members of it were so exhausted and hungry that Dudley impatiently exclaimed : — " We shall all be sick with fasting ! " Nevertheless the intervention of Coddington, and the scruples of one or two of the deputies, led to the swearing of two of the witnesses for the prosecution, and the colleagues, Weld and Eliot, were called upon by the Governor to take the oath. When they rose and held up their hands, Peters rose and held up his hand also. They testified again that at the meeting in Boston the accused had said there was a broad difference between Cotton and themselves, — that he preached a Covenant of Grace, and they of Works, and that they were not sealed ; and, added Eliot, " I do further remember this also, that she said we were not able ministers of the gospel, because we were but like the apostles before the Ascension." " This," said Coddington, " was I hope no disparagement to you. Methinks the comparison is very good." And Winthrop then interjected : — " Well, we see in the Court that she doth continually say and unsay things."

The hesitating deputies now pronounced themselves fully satisfied, and Winthrop put the question. The record closes as follows : —

" GOVERNOR WINTHROP. The Court hath already declared themselves satisfied concerning the things you hear, and concerning the troublesomeness of her spirit, and the danger of her course amongst us, which is not to be suffered. Therefore if it be the mind of the Court that Mrs. Hutchinson, for these things that appear before us, is unfit for our society, — and if it be the mind of the Court that she shall be banished out of our liberties, and imprisoned till she be sent away, let them hold up their hands.

" All but three held up their hands.

" Those that are contrary minded hold up yours.

" Mr. Coddington and Mr. Colburn only.

" Mr. Jennison. I cannot hold up my hand one way or the other, and I shall give my reason if the Court require it.

" Governor Winthrop. Mrs. Hutchinson, you hear the sentence of the Court. It is that you are banished from out our jurisdiction as being a woman not fit for our society. And you are to be imprisoned till the Court send you away.

" Mrs. Hutchinson. I desire to know wherefore I am banished.

" Governor Winthrop. Say no more. The Court knows wherefore, and is satisfied."

In the Colony Records of Massachusetts the sentence reads as follows : —

" Mrs. Hutchinson, (the wife of Mr. William Hutchinson,) being convented for traducing the ministers, and their ministry in this country, shee declared voluntarily her revelations for her ground, and that shee should bee delivred, and the Court ruined, with their posterity ; and thereupon was banished, and the mean while was committed to Mr. Joseph Weld untill the Court shall dispose of her."

CHAPTER IX.

THE EXCOMMUNICATION.

THE case of Wheelwright had been disposed of by the Court on what was then the 4th and is now the 14th of the month, while that of Mrs. Hutchinson had occupied the 7th and 8th, now the 17th and 18th. During the proceedings in the latter case Wheelwright was at his home at the Mount, and it is small matter for surprise that when he heard of them he made haste to quit the soil of Massachusetts. Less able to face a winter in the wilderness, Mrs. Hutchinson was to wait until spring, not in Boston at her own house and among friends and sympathizers, but at Roxbury, under the watch and ward of Thomas Weld, in the house of his brother Joseph. The remaining events of the controversy can be quickly narrated.

Immediately after passing sentence on Mistress Hutchinson, the Court, worn out with excitement, long sessions, cold and fasting, seems to have indulged itself in a recess of several days. It met again on the $\frac{15\text{th}}{25\text{th}}$, and, refreshed by the brief cessation from labor, took up its work vigorously at the point where it had been dropped. The sergeants, who in the previous May had laid down their halberds when Vane failed of his reëlection, and had refused to attend Winthrop home, were " convented." The names of both were " on the seditious libel called a remonstrance or petition." They were discharged from

office, disfranchised, and fined respectively twenty and
forty pounds. One of them, Edward Hutchinson, —
he who was fined forty pounds, — turned himself contemptuously when his sentence was pronounced, telling the Court that if they took away his means they
must support his family. He was promptly imprisoned ; but, after a night's reflection, humbled himself
and was released. William Balston, the other, was
apparently a man of the outspoken English type,
with the courage of his convictions. When confronted with his signature to the petition he at once
acknowledged it, and bluntly told the Court " that he
knew that if such a petition had been made in any
other place in the world, there would have been no
fault found with it." Subsequently the fines of both
were remitted on condition they departed the province ; and they were among those who the next March
went to Rhode Island.

One after another the signers of the Boston remonstrance of the previous March were then summoned
to the bar of the Court. The choice offered them was
simple, — they could acknowledge themselves in fault
and withdraw their names from the offensive document, or they could pass under the ban of the law.
A few, some ten in number, recanted ; some five or
six of the more obdurate were at once disfranchised.
Among these was John Underhill, then captain of the
train-band and a salaried officer of the colony. The
order now made by the Court in regard to him was
terse and did not admit of misconstruction. It ran
in these words, — " Capt. Underhill, being convicted
for having his hand to the seditious writing, is disfranchised, and put from the captains place " ; but
ten months were yet to elapse before he was banished.

Throughout, Underhill's case was peculiar, and, as will presently be seen, the solemn way in which Winthrop recorded the man's religious buffoonery throws a gleam of genuine humor over one page at least of a dreary record.

Though not now banished, Underhill's name heads the list of the "opinionists" of Boston, fifty-eight in all, who were, at the same November session of the Court which banished Wheelwright and Mrs. Hutchinson, ordered within ten days to bring their arms to the house of Captain Robert Keayne, and there deliver them up to him. Besides the fifty-eight in Boston, seventeen others, in five different towns, — in all seventy-five persons, — the recognized leaders of the minority, were disarmed, and, under a heavy money penalty, forbidden to buy, to borrow or to have in their possession either weapon or ammunition, until the Court should take further action. The ground for this measure, in which the agitation culminated, was set forth in the order promulgating it. It was a "just cause of suspition, that they, as others in Germany, in former times, may, upon some revelation, make some suddaine irruption upon those that differ from them in judgment." The decree, needless to say, excited deep indignation among those named in it. It was in fact a mild proscription. Those proscribed were powerless, and they proved themselves law-abiding. In the words of Winthrop, — "When they saw no remedy, they obeyed."

Plainly, also, there was "no remedy." Throughout all the proceedings which had taken place, the Boston church had been the stronghold of the secular faction in the state; and now even when generally disarmed and with its leading members disfranchised and

marked for exile, there were those in it who were
earnest to have their brother Winthrop called to
account and dealt with in a church way for his course
as governor.   Obviously, such an attempt would only
have made matters worse, and those of the elders, to
whom appeal had been made, showed no zeal in their
action, — they were not forward in the matter.   Then
Winthrop, fully understanding the situation, wisely as
well as boldly took the initiative, making a formal
address to the congregation.   In this he laid down
the correct rule clearly and forcibly, with numerous
scriptural references to chapter and verse in Luke and
Matthew, and fortifying himself with precedents drawn
from the action in similar circumstances of Uzzia and
Asa and Salam : — if a magistrate, he said, acting
in his private capacity, should take away the goods
of another, or despoil his servant, the church could
properly call him to account for so doing; yet if he
was guilty of such conduct in his official character, he
was not accountable to the church, no matter how
unjust his action might be.   In the present case, the
Governor went on to declare, whatever he had done
had been done by him with the advice and under the
direction of Cotton and other of the church's elders,
and he would now give but a single reason in his own
justification, — that single reason was that the brethren singled out for exile were so divided from the rest
of the country in their judgment and practice that
their presence in the community was, in his opinion,
not consistent with the public peace.   "So, by the
example of Lot in Abraham's family, and after Hagar
and Ishmael, he saw they must be sent away."

This action and discourse of Winthrop's was not
without importance, and it bore fruit; for it was the

theocratic period in Massachusetts, and the church was too much inclined to meddle in the affairs of state. The clergy were now supreme. They had converted the General Court into a mere machine for the civil enforcement of their own inquisitorial decrees; Mrs. Hutchinson had been banished for " traducing the ministers," and it was not proposed to allow further freedom of religious thought in Massachusetts. It was the clergy, not the churches, who constituted the power behind the throne. The principle that the magistrate was not amenable to the church for acts done in his official capacity was sound, and could be most appropriately asserted by one speaking with authority. The enunciation of the further principle, that the magistrate should be equally free from what may be called a politico-theological coercion, whether exercised by priests or ministers, was unfortunately deferred to a long subsequent period.

Mrs. Hutchinson meanwhile, separated from her family, was wearing away the long winter in semi-imprisonment at Roxbury. At first she labored under a good deal of mental depression, natural enough under the circumstances; for not only must the re-action from the excitement of the trial have been great, but she was soon to give birth to a child. Her despondency did not last long; and, indeed, she was now thoroughly in her element. Though secluded from the rest of the world for fear of the injury she might do in the way of spreading pernicious heresies, she was still the most noted woman in the province; and as such she was literally beset by the clergy, and by Mr. Thomas Weld in particular. They were far from being done with her yet. After the manner of their kind also, in every age and in all countries, the Massachusetts ministers, having secured an absolute supremacy in the state, were now busy hunting out "foul errors" about inherent righteousness, the immortality of the soul, the resurrection, the sanctity of the Sabbath, etc., etc., such heresies being very rife; for, as Winthrop sagely observed, it could not be expected that "Satan would lose the opportunity of making choice of so fit an instrument [as Mistress Hutchinson], so long as any hope remained to attain his mischievous end in darkening the saving truth of the Lord Jesus, and disturbing the peace of his churches." It was now that Cotton not only abandoned his old allies to their fate, but became one of their leading persecutors. He probably knew his brethren. At the trial at Cambridge he had seen it wanted but little to cause Peters and Weld to throw off all restraint, and open the cry on him as they had upon Wheelwright. Indeed both Endicott and Dudley had there addressed him in a way he was little accustomed to, using language both insulting and brow-beating; while Winthrop, on one occasion at least, seemed to feel the necessity of diverting attention from him.[1] Having at the close of the Synod ceased from all antagonism to his brethren, Cotton had since sought to occupy a neutral attitude as peacemaker. He now realized that this was not enough. He had professed he was persuaded; he must furnish proof of it by works also. He made up his mind to do it. One feeble effort, as will be seen, he yet made in behalf of Mrs. Hutchinson, and it was creditable to him; in other respects, from this time onward, the position in the controversy held by the teacher of the Boston church was simply pitiable, — the ignominious

---

[1] Hutchinson, *Massachusetts*, i. 74.

page in an otherwise worthy life.   He made haste to
walk in a Covenant of Works, — and the walk was a
very dirty one.   None the less he trudged sturdily on
in it, now declaring that he had been abused and
made use of as a "stalking horse," and now bewailing
his sloth and credulity.   And thus " did [he] spend
most of his time both publicly and privately," engaged in the inquisitor's work of unearthing heretics
and heresies.   A little later he even allowed himself
to be put forward as the mouthpiece of his order, to
pass judgment on his old associates and to pronounce
filial sympathy a crime.

Mrs. Hutchinson was soon found to be the one root
from whence had sprung the many heresies now un-
earthed ; when traced, they all ran back to her.   Hereupon the ministers " resorted to her many times,
labouring to convince her, but in vain ; yet they resorted to her still, to the end they might either re-
claim her from her errors, or that they might bear
witness against them if occasion were."   For now a
new ordeal awaited her.   She was to undergo the discipline of the church in which she was a sister.

In careful preparation for this, a species of ecclesiastical indictment was drawn up by the brethren, setting forth the utterances of the prisoner, as taken down
from her own lips.   Containing some thirty several
counts, it was altogether a formidable document.[1]   A

---

[1] A few of these counts will suffice to give a general idea of the
whole : —

" 8. The Image of God wherein Adam was made [Mrs. Hutchinson]
could see no Scripture to warrant that it consisteth in holinesse, but
conceived it to be in that he was made like to Christ's manhood."

" 12. There is no evidence to be had of our good estate, either from
absolute or conditional promises."

" 15. There is first engraffing into Christ before union, from which
a man might fall away."

copy of it was then sent to the church at Boston, and that church in due course applied to the magistrates to allow Mrs. Hutchinson to appear and answer to the accusation. Leave was of course granted, and at length, in what would now be the latter part of March, Joseph Weld's prisoner returned once more to her own house. But her husband was not there to meet her. He and her brother, and indeed all those whom she could look to for countenance and support, were away seeking out a new home, against their impending exile; nor did her opponents fail to attribute their absence to "the good providence of God," who thus removed opposition.

The proceedings were appointed for the $\frac{15th}{25th}$ of March. They excited the deepest interest throughout the colony, and as the day drew near, Boston was thronged with visitors. Not only all the members of the Boston church, but many others were there assembled; for the whole little community was agitated to its depths. The utter sameness of that provincial life — in which no new excitements followed one upon another, dividing attention and driving each other into forgetfulness — was for once broken. The church was the common family, and from that common family the elders were now to cast out the most prominent, —

"17. That Abraham was not in a saving estate till the 22 chap. of Gen. when hee offered Isaac, and saveing the firmenesse of Gods election, he might have perished, notwithstanding any work of grace that was wrought in him till then."

"21. That an hypocrite may have Adams righteousnesse and perish, and by that righteousnes he is bound to the Law, but in union with Christ, Christ comes into the man, and he retaines the seed and dieth, and then all manner of grace in himselfe, but all in Christ."

"28. That so farre as a man is in union with Christ, he can doe no duties perfectly, and without the communion of the unregenerate part with the regenerate."

the best known of all the sisters. It is necessary to think of the domestic circle to enable men or women of to-day to bring home to themselves the intensity of interest then aroused. An excommunication in church or state, or even socially, is now a small matter comparatively. It causes scarcely a ripple in the great sea of life. The event of to-day, it is barely remembered to-morrow. It was not so then. It was as if with us a daughter, arraigned before brothers and sisters, were solemnly admonished by the venerated father and driven from the hearth at which her childhood had been passed. In that family the event would be the one subject of thought; from the minds and memories of those present no incident of the scene would ever fade. So it was in the Boston church. The members of that church felt and thought as the members of a modern family would think and feel of a similar episode in their home. It would be the event not of a day, but of a life, — the family tragedy.

When, therefore, "one Thirsday Lectuer day after Sermon," the hour fixed for the proceedings to begin was come, the Boston meeting-house was crowded with a devout and expectant audience. The General Court was sitting still at Cambridge, and the time of the church meeting — ten o'clock in the morning — interfered with its sessions; leave nevertheless was specially granted to the governor and treasurer of the province, both members of the Boston church, to absent themselves. They were present with the rest of the church when, two hours earlier than usual, the services began; but she who would have been the observed of all was not there. The seat reserved for her was vacant. Sermon and prayer at length ended, she came in, "pretending," as Winthrop expressed it, "bodily infirmity." When at last she had taken her place, one of the elders arose and broke the silence which prevailed. Calling the sister Anne Hutchinson forth by name, he stated the purpose for which she had been summoned, and read the indictment prepared against her. A copy of it, to which those who were to bear witness to the several counts had subscribed their names, had some days before been put in her hands.

The scene that ensued, though sufficiently interesting, was, from the religious point of view, far from edifying.[1] At first the woman at bay most pertinently asked by what precept of holy writ the elders of the church had come to her in her place of confinement, pretending that they sought light, when in reality they came to entrap and betray her. Then, presently, Wilson, her pastor, — the man she disliked of all men, and for whom even her dislike was probably exceeded by her contempt, — Wilson either took some part in the procèedings or was alluded to; and at once her anger flashed out in stinging words. She denounced him for what he had uttered against her before the Court at the time of her sentence. "For what am I banished?" — she demanded; declaring the heretical speeches, now attributed to her, the results of confinement. Presently the discussion of the articles was begun, and she was called upon to answer to the first; which was to the effect that "the souls of all men (in regard of generation) are mortall like the beasts." The debate then drifted into that region of barren

[1] A comparatively full report of the church proceedings in Mrs. Hutchinson's case was found in 1888 among the papers of President Stiles in the Yale library, and is printed in *Proc. Mass. Hist. Soc.* Series II. iv. 159–91.

theological abstractions in which those composing the
assembly believed themselves entirely at home.   The
accused cited texts and endeavored to draw distinctions; but in reply the elders — as was natural, she
being one and they many — cited several texts, and
drew an infinite variety of distinctions to each one of
hers.   " She could not give any answer to them, yet
she stood to her opinion, till at length a stranger," the
Rev. John Davenport, " being desired to speak to the
point, and he opening to her the difference between
the Soul and the Life, — the first being a spiritual
substance, and the other the union of that with the
body, — she then confessed she saw more light than
before, and so with some difficulty was brought to
confess her error in that point.   Wherein," as Winthrop goes on to remark, not it would appear without
considerable insight as to Mrs. Hutchinson's foibles,
" it was to be observed that, though this stranger
spake to very good purpose, and so clearly convinced
her as she could not gainsay, yet it was evident she
was convinced before, but she could not give the
honour of it to her own pastor or teacher, nor to any
of the other elders, whom she had so much slighted."

It is not necessary to follow the discussion further.
Three more of the articles were propounded; and
still, in spite of the storm of texts pelted upon her,
Mistress Hutchinson persisted in her errors.   She
even returned " forward speeches to some that spake
to her."   By this time the day was grown old, and
the patience of the elders was exhausted.   The single
woman, quick of tongue though weak of body, seemed
not only disposed to out-talk them all, but to out-
endure them as well; for it was not without reason
she had delayed coming into the assembly until ser-

mon and prayer were over. At length, as it grew towards evening and the fourth of the twenty-nine articles was not yet disposed of, the elders bethought themselves to hasten matters by administering to their erring and obstinate sister a formal admonition, the real purport of which apparently was that she should suffer herself to be convinced more readily. In the course of the proceedings one of her sons had ventured a natural inquiry as to the rule which should guide him in expressing his assent or dissent; and later on Thomas Savage, the husband of her daughter, Faith, did himself honor by rising in his place and saying, — " My mother not being accused of any heinous act, but only for opinion, and that wherein she desires information and light, rather than peremptorily to hold [to it], I cannot consent that the church should proceed yet to admonish her for this." Thereupon Thomas Oliver, one of the ruling elders, after declaring that it was grief to his " spirit to see these two brethren to speak so much and to scruple the proceedings of the church," propounded the following as a solution of the dilemma : —

" Seeing that all the proceedings of the churches of Jesus Christ now should be according to the pattern of the primitive churches ; and the primitive pattern was that all things in the church should be done with one heart and one soul and one consent, that any act and every act done by the church may be as the act of one man ; — Therefore, whether it be not meet to lay these two brethren under an admonition with their mother, that so the church may proceed on without any further opposition."

This novel though drastic parliamentary expedient for securing unanimity evidently commended itself strongly to the judgment of the Rev. John Wilson,

for he at once cried out from his place among the
elders, — "I think you speak very well! It is very
meet!" The motion was then put "and the whole
church by their silence consented." The admonition
was pronounced by Cotton, with whom also it was
left "to do as God should incline his heart" in the
matter of including Mrs. Hutchinson's "two sons or
no with herself." As, in the course of his subsequent
deliverance, the eloquent teacher took occasion to address the "two sons," saying among other things that
"instead of loving and natural children, you have
proved vipers, to eat through the very bowells of your
mother, to her ruin, if God do not graciously prevent," the inference would seem to be inevitable that
when the moment came John Cotton found his heart
inclined from above to include offspring as well as
mother in his admonitory remarks. Winthrop says,
and it may well be believed, that on this occasion
the teacher spoke with great solemnity and "much
zeal and detestation of her errors and pride of spirit."
He spake in this wise; and

"First to her son, laying it sadly upon him, that he would
give such way to his natural affection, as for preserving her
honor he should make a breach upon the honor of Christ,
and upon his covenant with the church, and withal tear the
very bowells of his soul, by hardening her in sin. Then to
her, first, he remembered her of the good way she was in at
her first coming, in helping to discover to divers the false
bottom they stood upon in trusting to legal works without
Christ; then he showed her how, by falling into these gross
and fundamental errors, she had lost the honor of her former
service, and done more wrong to Christ and his church than
formerly she had done good, and so laid her sin to her conscience. He admonished her also of the height of spirit,

and charged her solemnly before the Lord, and his Angels, and Churches there assembled to return from the error of her way. Then he spake to the sisters of the church, and advised them to take heed of her opinions, and to withhold all countenance and respect from her, lest they should harden her in sin." [1]

"So she was dismissed, and appointed to appear again that day seven-night."

It was eight o'clock of the March evening when the hungry and wearied congregation at last broke up. Through ten consecutive hours those composing it had sat on the hard and crowded benches. Mrs. Hutchinson had been ordered to return at the close of the

---

[1] It may not be uninteresting to quote from the report of these proceedings and the admonitory remarks of Mr. Cotton so much as relates to one point at issue, if only to illustrate the singular logical intricacies into which the discussion wandered, as well as the character of the treatment to which the accused sister was subjected : —

"MRS. HUTCHINSON : — I desire you to speak to that place in I. Corinthians xv. 37, 44. For I do question whether the same body that dies shall rise again. . . .

"MR. BUCKLE : — I desire to know of Mrs. Hutchinson, whether you hold any other resurrection than that of . . . Union to Christ Jesus ? — And whether you hold that foul, filthy and abominable opinion held by Familists of the community of women.

"MRS. HUTCHINSON : — I hold it not. . . .

"MR. DAVENPORT : — Avoid . . . Mr. Buckles question ; for it is a right principle. For, if the resurrection be past, then marriage is past : for it is a weighty reason : after the resurrection is past, marriage is past. Then, if there be any union between man and woman, it is not by marriage, but in a way of community.

"MRS. HUTCHINSON : — If any such practice or conclusion be drawn from it, then I must leave it, for I abhor that practice." . . .

MR. COTTON in his admonition : — . . . "If the resurrection be past, then you cannot evade the argument that was pressed upon you by our brother Buckle and others, that filthy sin of the community of women ; and all promiscuous and filthy coming together of men and women, without distinction or relation of marriage, will necessarily follow ; and, though I have not heard, neither do I think, you have been unfaithful to your husband in his marriage covenant, yet that will follow upon it." . . .

meeting to her place of confinement at Roxbury; but some intimation had been received from those supposed to know, that her courage was giving way under the tremendous pressure to which she had been subjected, and that, if properly labored with now, she might be made to yield. Accordingly, she was permitted to remain at Cotton's house. He probably had managed it, wishing to make one last effort to save, from what he looked upon as perdition, the most gifted of his parishioners. The Rev. John Davenport, that "stranger" to whose authority Mrs. Hutchinson had shown herself not indisposed to succumb in the congregation, was also Cotton's guest; and, during the intervening week, the two divines did not, it would seem, strive with her in vain. Indeed, they so far prevailed that she acknowledged she had been wrong, and even brought herself to the point of agreeing publicly to recant. So, —

"When the day came, and she was called forth and the articles read again to her, she delivered in her answers in writing, which were also read; and, being then willing to speak to the congregation for their further satisfaction, she did acknowledge that she had greatly erred, and that God had now withdrawn his countenance from her, because she had so much misprised his ordinances, both in slighting the magistrates at the Court, and also the elders of the Church. And she confessed that during her trial by the Court, she looked only at such failings as she apprehended in the magistrates' proceedings, without having regard to their position of authority;[1] and that the language she then used

[1] "2. For these scriptures that I used at the Court in censuring the country, I confess I did it rashly and out of heat of spirit, and unadvisedly, and have cause to be sorry for my unreverent carriage to them; and I am heartily sorry that any things I have said have drawn any from hearing any of the elders of the Bay."

about her revelations was rash and without ground ; and she asked the church to pray for her."

"Thus far," says Winthrop, "she went on well, and the assembly conceived hope of her repentance." Indeed, it is not easy to see what more could have been asked of any one. A woman, — full of pride of intellect, and of insatiable ambition, — she had confessed herself in error, and, in the presence of her adherents and the face of the world, humbled herself in the dust before the enemies she despised. With all her feminine instinct in that way, she had herself never devised so bitter a humiliation even for John Wilson. But this was not enough. She was not so to elude the lord-brethren. It is apparent they meant to rid themselves wholly of her ; nor was it any longer difficult for them to do so. Having at last found out her weak points they were more than a match for her, for they knew exactly how to go to work to convict her. They had but to provoke her to voluble speech, and she was sure to deliver herself into their hands ; nor, indeed, could it well have been otherwise, seeing they were engaged discussing the unknowable, many against one, and that one a loquacious woman.

She read her recantation from a paper, speaking evidently with a subdued voice and bowed head. As soon as she finished Thomas Leverett, the ruling elder, rose, saying it was meet somebody should re-state what she had said to the congregation, which had been unable to hear her ; whereupon Cotton reit-erated the heads of her "groce and fundamentall Errors," and her humiliating admission that "the Roote of all was the hight and Pride of her Spirit." Then presently Wilson, her pastor, stood up before the silent and spell-bound audience. His hour of

triumph and revenge had come; and, apparently, he
proposed thoroughly to enjoy the first, and to make
complete the last. At the meeting of the previous
week Mrs. Hutchinson had made an issue with Shepard and Eliot. The former of these two divines,
almost alone among his brethren, had in the November trial before the Court shown some degree of Christian spirit towards the accused, and afterwards he and
Eliot had labored long and earnestly with her at the
house of Joseph Weld in Roxbury. In the midst of
Cotton's admonition of the week before, Mrs. Hutchinson had broken in upon him with an assertion that
it was only since her imprisonment at Roxbury that
she held any of the erroneous opinions attributed to
her. No sooner had Cotton finished than Shepard
rose to declare his "astonishment" at "what Mrs.
Hutchinson did last speak, . . . that she should thus
impudently affirm so horrible an untruth and false-
hood in the midst of such a solemn ordinance of Jesus
Christ and before such an assembly." And now, a
week afterwards, the recantation being over, Wilson
called attention to the fact of its incompleteness in
that it left this question of veracity between the accused and the two ministers undisposed of. Speaking with great restraint and humility Mrs. Hutchinson
replied that what she had said when she interrupted
Cotton had been spoken "rashly and unadvisedly,"
adding, — "I do not allow the slighting of ministers,
nor of the scriptures, nor anything that is set up by
God: if Mr. Shepard doth conceive that I had any
of these things in my mind then he is deceived."
This response sounds to a modern reader sufficiently
humble and subdued. It did not so sound to the
Rev. Thomas Shepard when it was uttered in the

Boston meeting-house on what is now the 1st of April,
1638 ; on the contrary, that " sweet affecting and
soul-ravishing " divine made haste to declare himself
" unsatisfied," saying, — " If this day, when Mrs.
Hutchinson should take shame and confusion to herself for her gross and damnable errors, she shall cast
shame upon others, and say they are mistaken, and
to turn off many of those gross errors with so slight
an answer as ' your mistake,' I fear it doth not stand
with true repentance."

The following colloquy then took place : —

" MR. COTTON : — Sister, was there not a time when once
you did hold that there were no distinct graces inherent in
us, but all was in Christ Jesus ?

" MRS. HUTCHINSON : — I did mistake the word ' inherent ; ' as Mr. Davenport can tell, who did cause me first to
see my mistake in the word ' inherent.'

" MR. ELIOT : — We are not satisfied with what she
saith, that she should say now that she did never deny in-
herence of Grace in us, as in a subject ; for she being by us
pressed so with it, she denied that there was no Graces inherent in Christ himself.

" MR. SHEPARD : — She did not only deny the word ' inherent,' but denied the very thing itself ; then I asked her
if she did believe the spirit of God was in believers.

" MRS. HUTCHINSON : — I confess my expressions were
that way, but it was never my judgment."

The theological issue involved was unintelligible,
and the jargon in which the discussion was carried
on completed the confusion. The nominal point in
dispute was whether the sister on trial was not, or
had not at some time previous been, " of that judgment that there is no inherent righteousness in the

saints, but those gifts and graces which are ascribed
to them that are only in Christ as the subject." But,
while this was the apparent issue, the efforts of the
ministers were really directed towards extorting from
Mrs. Hutchinson a full and unconditioned confession
of error, — a recantation absolute and unequivocal.
Her submission was to be complete. The audience
composed of the members of the Boston church, —
her former admirers and still in their hearts her adherents — were in mind. Before their wondering
eyes and to their listening ears, the woman towards
whom their hearts yet went out was to be broken
down, discredited and humiliated ; and she was to
confess herself so without one syllable of reservation.

That Mrs. Hutchinson now found herself beyond
her depth, is obvious. It is stating the case none too
strongly to say that all the disputants, — ministers,
magistrates, elders and female transcendentalist —
were hopelessly lost in a thick fog of indefinable ideas
and meaningless phrases ; but, while all groped their
way angrily, numbers and the clatter of tongues were
wholly on one side. Apparently, feeling herself hard
pressed by men hateful to her, Mrs. Hutchinson could
not bring herself to yield to them as she had yielded
in public to Davenport, and in private to Cotton. So
she adhered to her statement, — " My judgment is not
altered though my expression alters."

Then at once Wilson gave the signal and the on-
slaught began. In referring to the proceedings during Mrs. Hutchinson's trial by the General Court at
Cambridge in November, 1637, and the treatment
the accused then received, a high authority on matters
of New England history has remarked that the reports of what took place " contain evidence that her

judges did not escape the contagion of her ill-temper." [1] This criticism of those composing the Court in question certainly does not err on the side of harshness ; and not impossibly the same sense of pious devotion to the fathers which manifestly inspired it might now see in the course of those controlling the action of the Boston church only another example of the contagious character of the victim's perverse disposition : but to one endeavoring to look upon a scene of ecclesiastical persecution which occurred in Boston in 1638 with the same eyes with which he looks upon other scenes of the same general character which occurred at about that time in England, in France and in Spain, a wholly different impression is conveyed. In dealing with vexed questions of an historical character it is best always to speak with studied moderation, avoiding metaphor scarcely less than invective ; yet it is difficult to read the report of the closing church proceedings in the case of Anne Hutchinson without the simile suggesting itself of some pack of savage hounds surrounding and mercilessly hunting down a frightened fox, driven from cover and crouching.

It was John Wilson's voice which now seemed to raise the familiar view-hallo, and at once the kennel opened in full cry. Magistrates and ministers vied with each other in passionate terms of hatred, opprobrium and contempt. Dudley, the Deputy Governor, though neither a member of the Boston church nor an elder, — simply a stranger present from curiosity, — Dudley cried out, — " Her repentance is in a paper, . . . but sure her repentance is not in her countenance. None can see it there, I think." Then Peters, the minister of the Salem church, exclaimed, —

[1] Palfrey, i. 486.

" I believe that she has vile thoughts of us, and
thinks us to be nothing but a company of Jews; "
and again, — " You have stept out of your place.
You have rather been a husband than a wife ; and a
preacher than a hearer ; and a magistrate than a subject ; and so you have thought to carry all things in
church and commonwealth as you would." After
Peters, Shepard took up the refrain, saying to the
congregation, — " You have not only to deal with a
woman this day that holds divers erroneous opinions,
but with one that never had any true grace in her
heart, and that by her own tenet.   Yea! this day she
hath shown herself to be a notorious impostor."   Wilson repeatedly broke in, — " One cause was . . . to
set yourself in the room of God, above others, that
you might be extolled and admired and followed after,
that you might be a great prophetess ; . . . therefore
I believe your iniquity hath found you out ; . . . it
grieves me that you should so evince your dangerous,
foul and damnable heresies."   Then, after taking
breath, he presently began again, — " I cannot but
acknowledge the Lord is just in leaving our sister to
pride and lying. . . . I look at her as a dangerous
instrument of the Devil raised up by Satan amongst
us. . . . Consider how we can, or whether we may
longer suffer her to go on still in seducing to seduce,
and in deceiving to deceive, and in lying to lie, and
in condemning authority and magistrates, still to condemn.   Therefore, we should sin against God if we
should not put away from us so evil a woman, guilty
of such foul evils."   Then Eliot, " the Apostle," —
" It is a wonderful wisdom of God . . . to let her
fall into such lies as she hath done this day ; for she
hath carried on all her errors by lies."   Finally Cot-

ton, turning at last fairly against his former disciple, announced that "God hath let her fall into a manifest lie, yea! to make a lie," and Shepard, eagerly catching up the phrase, exclaimed, — "But now for one not to drop a lie, but to make a lie, and to maintain a lie! . . . I would have this church consider, whether it will be for the honor of God and the honor of this church to bear with patience so gross an offender."

And so at last the pitiless chase drew to a close. Throughout all its latter stages, while it was exhausting itself by its own heat, the voice of the accused had not been heard, — evidently she sat there, mute, motionless, aghast. Once, after listening to a furious diatribe from Wilson, the hard-hunted creature seems to have tried to take refuge under Cotton's gown, exclaiming, — "Our teacher knows my judgment, for I never kept my judgment from him!" — but already Cotton, recognizing the inevitable and bowing to it, had abandoned her to her fate. Then she ceased to struggle, and the yelling pack rushed in upon her.

Long afterwards, in reply to the charge that he had contrived to transfer the odious duty of excommunicating his disciple from himself to Wilson, John Cotton asserted [1] that he stood ready to be the mouthpiece of the church in this matter, — no less than he had already been in the matter of admonishment, — had the task been put upon him; and there can be no doubt that, at the time, he gave his open assent before the whole congregation to the course which was pursued, and even silenced the scruples of the few who yet clung to their prophetess, by calling

[1] *Way Cleared*, 85.

to mind the precedents of " Ananias and Sapphira, and the incestuous Corinthian." The offence now charged against Mrs. Hutchinson was not heresy, but false-hood persistently adhered to. An impenitent liar was to be cast out. The matter was one touching morals, not doctrine; and accordingly, as Cotton claimed, lay rather within the province of the pastor than the teacher. It was for Mr. Wilson, therefore, to pro-nounce the sentence of excommunication; nor was there any reason for delay. A few voices were, indeed, heard timidly suggesting that the accused might be once more admonished, and time for repent-ance yet given her; but she herself sat silent, asking no respite. Then Wilson rose, and, in the hush of the crowded assembly, solemnly put the question whether all were of one mind that their sister should be cast out. The silence was broken by no reply; and, after the custom of that church, this betokened consent. Then the sentence of excommunication was pronounced; and Anne Hutchinson, no longer a sister, listened to these words rolled out in triumph from the mouth of John Wilson, the pastor, — " Therefore in the name of the Lord Jesus Christ and in the name of the church I do not only pronounce you worthy to be cast out, but I do cast you out; and in the name of Christ I do deliver you up to Satan, that you may learn no more to blaspheme, to seduce and to lie; and I do account you from this time forth to be a Heathen and a Publican, and so to be held of all the Brethren and Sisters of this congregation and of others: therefore I command you in the name of Christ Jesus and of this church as a Leper to with-draw yourself out of the congregation."

When, in obedience to this mandate, Anne Hutchinson, the outcast, moved through the awe-stricken throng, her disciple and devoted friend, Mary Dyer,[1] rose up and walked by her side, and the two passed out together. As they went forth, one standing at the meeting-house door said to Mrs. Hutchinson, — "The Lord sanctify this unto you;" to whom she made answer, — "The Lord judgeth not as man judgeth. Better to be cast out of the church than to deny Christ." At the same time another, a stranger in Boston, pointing with his finger at Mary Dyer, asked, — "Who is that young woman?" and he of whom he asked made answer, — "It is the woman which had the monster."[2]

The records of the First Church of Boston contain the following entry: —

"The 22d of the 1st Month 1638. Anne, the wife of our brother, William Hutchinson, having on the 15th of this month been openly, in the public congregation, admonished of sundry errors held by her, was on the same 22d day cast out of the church for impenitently persisting in a manifest lie, then expressed by her in open congregation."

[1] *Supra*, 408, n.   [2] Winthrop, i. *263; *supra*, 386.